Ethnicity, Identity and Culture

Ethnicity, Identity and Culture

Scheduled Tribes of Andhra Pradesh and Telangana

Malli Gandhi

RAWAT PUBLICATIONS
Jaipur • New Delhi • Bangalore • Guwahati • Kolkata

ISBN 978-81-316-1153-1

Published by
Prem Rawat for **Rawat Publications**
Satyam Apts., Sector 3, Jawahar Nagar, Jaipur 302 004 (India)
Phone: 0141 265 1748 / 265 7006
E-mail: info@rawatbooks.com
Website: www.rawatbooks.com

New Delhi Office
4858/24, Ansari Road, Daryaganj, New Delhi 110 002
Phone: 011-23263290

Also at *Bangalore, Guwahati* and *Kolkata*

Typeset by Rawat Computers, Jaipur
Printed and bound in India

To

Dr B.D. Sharma, IAS, (Rtd)

Former Member, Second Scheduled Areas and Scheduled Tribes Commission, Government of India

Contents

Preface

Equality of status and opportunity to all citizens of the country is enshrined in the Indian Constitution, which provides that no individual shall be discriminated on the grounds of religion, caste, sex or occupation. Indian democracy has been rooted on the twin pillars of distributive justice and inclusive growth. Recognizing this, the State has been empowered to take affirmative action in favour of certain historically disadvantaged social groups such as the Scheduled Tribes (STs) through reservation in educational institutions and employment. Tribal communities live in about 15 per cent of the country's areas in various ecological and eco-climatic conditions as diverse as remote snowbound hills of Arunachal Pradesh to remote islands of Andaman and Nicobar and Lakshadweep. The term Scheduled Tribes is defined in Article 366(25) of the Constitution and Article 342 prescribes the procedure to be followed for specifying STs. Although the Constitution does not spell out any criteria, the well-established criteria for specification of a community as ST include (a) indications of primitive traits, (b) distinctive culture, (c) shyness of contact with community at large, (d) geographical isolation and (e) backwardness.

So far, 705 Scheduled Tribes have been notified under Article 342 of the Constitution spread over different States and Union Territories. Many tribes are present in more than one state. Tribal groups are heterogeneous, and their differences are a function of the environment they live in, the degree of exposure to other communities, their economic status and past history. Total population of STs, as per 2001 census, is 8.43 crore constituting 8.2 per cent of total population. They are mostly concentrated in populous states of Madhya Pradesh (14.51%); Maharashtra (10.17%); Odisha (9.66%); Gujarat (8.87%); Rajasthan (8.42%); Jharkhand (8.40%); Chhattisgarh (7.85%); and Arunachal Pradesh (5.96%). In the States/Union Territories of Lakshadweep,

Mizoram, Nagaland, Meghalaya, Arunachal Pradesh along with Dadra and Nagar Haveli, tribals form a majority of population.

The decadal growth in percentage of tribal population is 24.45 per cent which is higher than the total population growth of 22.66 per cent. It is encouraging to note that STs have a much higher sex ratio as well as child sex ratio. Sex ratio among STs was favourable at 977 as compared to national average of 933 and child sex ratio was also higher at 972 as against the national average of 927. The Census informs that 81.6 per cent of main workers from these communities were engaged in primary sector activities. Of course, proportion of STs below poverty line is markedly higher than the national average. As per Planning Commission estimates for the year 2004–05, the percentage of ST population below poverty line was 47.3 per cent in rural areas and 39.9 per cent in urban areas. Workforce participation rate of scheduled tribes stands at 20 per cent for urban areas and 40 per cent for rural areas. There has been a conflict of interest between development issues and the need to protect socio-cultural and historical rights of tribal population. Exploiting the tribal areas for rich natural resources without adequately protecting the tribes is not only violating their constitutional rights but may also be counterproductive in the long run. The need to achieve ecological balance and environmental issues arising out of development plans in tribal belts, thus, requires serious discussion.

The Tribal Sub-Plan (TSP) strategy is being implemented since 1972 for achieving rapid socio-economic development of tribal people. The object of the strategy is to provide for a budget component (8% for Central Ministries/Departments and in proportion to tribal population of States/UTs in State Budget) to be spent on programmes and schemes for tribal welfare. The TSP concept is not applicable to states with 80 per cent or more tribal population. Government of India also formulated a Draft National Tribal Policy in 2006 mainly relating to alienation of tribal land, tribal-forest interface; conservation and development of particularly vulnerable tribal groups or the Primitive Tribal Groups and other important issues concerning tribals like enhancement of Human Development Index, Gender Equity, etc.

The goal of holistic empowerment of scheduled tribes whether social, economic or political, cannot, however, be achieved in isolation and would require proactive participation of other stakeholders such as state governments, civil society groups and grassroots level organizations. It also necessitates reform of existing legislations, wherever required, as well as sensitization of law enforcement agencies and judicial system. It would also entail a radical transformation in the mindset and societal perceptions within family, community and nation as a whole. An integrated approach which focuses on the holistic empowerment and development of STs is, therefore, necessary to ensure that the constitutional vision of equality is fully realized. This is based on the following:

- Social Empowerment, including education and health and nutrition.

- Economic Empowerment, including in agriculture, land alienation and acquisition, displacement, livelihood opportunities, forests and environment, etc.
- Protection from Atrocities.
- Political Empowerment, including implementation of PESA.

The present work is the outcome of extensive fieldwork conducted by the author in the present-day Andhra Pradesh and Telangana. It has 13 chapters. Chapter I deals with significance of tribal development in the present Andhra Pradesh and Telangana States. Chapter II focuses on the tribal revolts. The chapter highlights Adivasi revolts in colonial and post colonial era. Chapter III highlights how anthropological work started in Hyderabad with the study of Chenchus in Hyderabad and Farhabad hills by the anthropological team and also focuses on the encouragement given by the then Nizam's government for the study of human culture and civilization. Chapter IV deals with Kolams, their cultural life and development in Telangana. Chapter V deals with the cultural life and development of Thotis. Chapter VI deals with the society of Koyas and their cultural antiquity. Chapter VII deals with the life of Savaras and their transformation. Chapter VIII deals with Yanadis. Chapter IX deals with Yerukula a denotified community in Andhra Pradesh and Telangana States. Chapter X highlights empowerment of nomadic and denotified communities; the challenges faced by these sections of people and also focus on certain recommendations for their overall development. Chapter XI deals with the problems of rehabilitation programmes initiated by the government and how far these programmes are reaching them. Chapter XII deals with the education of Scheduled Tribe children and Chapter XIII focuses on the issue of violation of human rights among Adivasis in the contemporary society.

I sincerely thank Prof. V. Ramakrishna (University of Hyderabad) and Dr V. Lalitha for their support and advice during the course of my field work. I am thankful to the staff members of National Archives, New Delhi, Tamil Nadu State Archives, Chennai and Andhra Pradesh State Archives, Telangana State Archives, Hyderabad for providing me necessary records. I am equally thankful to the staff members of various libraries – Saraswata Niketanam Library, Vetapalem; Gowthami Grandhalayam, Rajahmundry; Jawaharlal Nehru University Library, New Delhi; University of Hyderabad Library; Bharatiya Adimjati Sevak Sangh, New Delhi; Nehru Memorial Museum and Library, New Delhi and Anthropological Survey of India, Mysore for providing me necessary records and books. I am indebted to all the village elders and school staff of various DNT schools with whom I had detailed interactions in tribal areas of Andhra Pradesh and Telangana, and whose valuable information has been utilized for the study. I am equally indebted to all the tribal parents, community leaders, and children in the selected schools without whose help the present work might have not been completed. I am equally thankful to District Education Officers, Mandal Education Officers, Mandal Resource Persons and the Project Officers in ITDA centres for their cooperation, information and timely help. I particularly thank Dr Vadrevu China

Veerabhadrudu, Joint Commissioner Planning Telugu Samkshema Bhavan, Hyderabad, Prof. P. Venkata Rao, Professor, Department of Anthropology, University of Hyderabad, Prof. M.L.K. Murthy, Retired Professor, Department of Regional Studies, University of Hyderabad, Prof. R. Siva Prasad, Department of Anthropology, University of Hyderabad, Shri P.S. Krishnan, Former Secretary, Ministry of Social Welfare, Government of India, New Delhi, Dr K.H.S.S. Sunder, Director, Samskar, Vijayawada, Andhra Pradesh, Dr. Meshram Manohar, Principal, B.Ed. College, Utnoor, Adilabad, Telangana and Dr Sasidhar Rao, Retired Professor, IASE, Hyderabad and Sri Harpal Singh, Correspondent, *The Hindu*, Adilabad, Telangana for providing their valuable insights and Shri Pranit Rawat, Rawat Publications, Jaipur for accepting the present work for publication. I am grateful to Shri Ravindra Kumar, Editor, Rawat Publications for his meticulous and competent copyediting of the book.

Malli Gandhi

Abbreviations

CPC	Criminal Procedure Code
CPI (ML)	Communist Party of India (Marxist-Leninist)
CTA	Criminal Tribes Act
CTs	Criminal Tribes
DNTs	Denotified Tribes
Edn	Education
G.O.	Government Order
G.O.M.	Government of Madras
GCS	Girijan Co-operative Societies
ITDA	Integrated Tribal Development Agency
KM	Kilometre
NACOD	National Advocacy Council for Development
OBC	Other Backward Classes
SCs	Scheduled Castes
SSLC	Secondary School Leaving Certificate
STs	Scheduled Tribes
TCR&TI	Tribal Cultural Research and Training Institute

Glossary

addakulu	Leaves
akshintalu	Grains made out of yellow rice with saffron colours
amma talli	Goddess of smallpox
bandi	Cart
bhoomi amma	Earth goddess
bisoye	Local officials in agency tracts
chedipe	Sorceress
cheyyi pattu kovatam	Capturing by holding the hand
chigurupannu	A rate varying from one third to a half
chochhuku povatam	To dash into the in-laws house
cholam/zonna	Maize crop
chorabadatam	Forceful entry of a girl into her in-laws house
deshmukh/ deshpande	Local Revenue Collector
dorala sattam	A group belongs to lords
dorlasattam	A section of Koyas living in the Gond tribal hamlets
gaddalu	Roots, herbs
gampa	Basket
gudem	Village
gurutappu	Money paid for committing an offence to the tribal head
ippa	A flower used to extract intoxicating drink in the forest

ippa sara	Local toddy
kalapapannu	Wood cutting tax
kotta	New
kudi devara	Idol worshipped by the Koyas
kula panchayat	A council organised by caste elders
kula tappu	Money paid to the community elders for committing an offence among the tribals
laggnam	Engagement
langoti	A lion cloth adorned by tribals
modalupannu	A tax decided by the Mansabdar on his own
maddikallu	Locally made liquor
mangalasutra/ tali	A sacred yellow thread tied round the neck of girls in the marriage
mantrasani	Local nurse
marumanuvu	Remarriage
medaram jatra	A biannual festival celebrated by the koyas in Medaram village
muttadari	Estate owner
panduga	Festival
penta	Huts/houses of chenchus
podu	Shifting cultivation
podu cultivation	Primitive cultivation
pujari	Local priest
rajatappu	Money paid to the tribal elders for committing an offence
samuto	A village committee among the Koyas consisting of 10 to 12 members
saptamatrica	Seven mother goddesses
sastangam	Prostrate adoration to god/goddess
shahukars	Rich money lenders
tadaka	Bamboo mats prepared by the tribals
talambralu	Yellow grains poured on the head of bride or bridegroom
talayari	A village servant
tappu	Penalty imposed for committing an offence or mistake
velpu	A tree coloured red cloth symbolysing a number of figures of ancestors family
veta	Hunting festival celebrated by the Koyas
voli/oli	Money paid by the bride groom to the bride at the time of marriage
yejjodu	Tribal doctor or local faith healer

1

Tribal Development in Andhra Pradesh and Telangana

Policies and Programmes

After attainment of independence, India is very keen on the upliftment of weaker sections, especially tribal people. The main task before the planners, administrators and politicians is the removal of social and economic inequalities and establishment of an egalitarian society. Their main concentration is on the accelerated development of tribals to enable them to catch-up with more advanced sections of society. The programme implementation process is expected to improve their levels of living, besides enhancing their aspirations. It is not only imperative to study the prevailing development situations of scheduled tribes in India but also to find out priorities for their overall development. This will help in planning future programmes better for their overall development. Unless the condition of tribal people is improved their status will remain poor as those who have been crippled and marginalized in history. There is a need to understand the historical process of development of tribal groups in India in general, and Andhra Pradesh and Telangana states in particular. While dealing with issues of tribal development, the main focus is to look into the issues related to administrative and political mechanisms such as: stagnation and changing situation in tribal agency *Mandals* (Tehsils), poverty in tribal areas, impact of government policies in the pre and post-Independent India, problems relating to tribal land alienation, tribal economy through credit and marketing systems, unrest in the tribal regions, their history, culture, tradition and demands of Adivasis. A few measures need serious consideration for the eradication of poverty in tribal areas as a strategy for development of Scheduled Tribes in Andhra Pradesh and Telangana.

I

Tribal Development in the Erstwhile Andhra Pradesh: Historical Perspective

India has been the home for many heterogenous ethnic groups. These groups generally lived in solitiude, having no communication with the outside world. As a result, they had no civilizational impact. This was mainly responsible for their poverty and social alienation. In the modern period, when the East India Company established its political, economic and cultural hegemony, they wanted to exploit forest produce too. For this purpose, they enacted forest laws. During the early 20th century, communication facilities such as railways and roads were developed in the hill areas and forests. Thus, an opportunity was provided to people from plains to infiltrate into tribal areas and satisfy their selfish ends. This resulted in loss of land and economic independence. Throughout the long history of undivided Andhra Pradesh, covering the periods of Satavahanas, Chalukyas, Rashtrakutas, Kakatiyas, Qutbshahis and *Asifjahis* Adivasis were pushed back into their homelands, woods and hilly regions. Adivasis continued to be the easy prey of Hindu and Mohammadan feudal lords almost up to twentieth century. In the prolonged process of exploitation tribals lost much of their ancestral land and were often robbed of the fruits of their hard labour.

The British colonial rule in India marks an important watershed in the ecological history of India. There was a drastic change in ecological and social policies under the colonial rule. It was commercial in its nature. In the early decades of colonial rule, the state was markedly indifferent to forest conservancy. A comprehensive piece of legislation was attempted to exclude customary use of the forest, which was prevalent over centuries, by the rural population all over India. Some officials within the colonial administration were sharply critical of the legislation.

The forest tribes who were hunters and collectors of jungle produce led a nomadic life. They were less attached to the soil. They were unable to evade the domination of superior people. They escaped to the hills and jungles. In these regions, they remained unquestioned masters of the wilds for many centuries. These tribes were small in numbers because they were relics of large communities. They got separated in the forests and hills of South India and in course of time they developed into different tribal societies. Their hunting and food-collecting mode of life forced them to live in small groups.

The British colonizers united India, extending their administration over the whole land. They also included jungle tribes in it. The British first became aware of the great riches that lay hidden in jungles and they began to exploit them. Timber was cut and exported. Forest products were collected and sold. Tea, coffee and rubber plantations were started on a big scale. Railway lines and motor roads were built into jungles. The invaders who began to exploit them, disturbed forest tribes. The government took control of jungles and leased plots to forest contractors. In some places, jungle produce had to be sold to the specific price fixed by contractors.

The tribes in Andhra Pradesh and Telangana were engaged in barter trade with the surrounding agricultural communities, exchanging forest produce such as herbs and honey for metal implements, salt, clothes and grain. They supplied their forest produce to neighbouring places. Gradually, population in the plains increased and more and more jungles were cut down by cultivators who converted them into farmland. The jungle tribes turned into shifting cultivators since their collecting forest produce could no more provide them sufficient food.

With the expansion of the Muttadari system, tribals became cultivators and depended upon agriculture for their subsistence. Their diet was supplemented by collecting fruits, nuts, roots, honey and by liquor tapped from palmyra and sago palms. Their principle source of food was millets, pulses and root crops in the jungle. The British concentrated on the development of backward tribals to bring them into the mainstream of life. The most visible sign of transformation of hill tribes was due the construction of roads. The road construction in the hills stimulated growth of markets. In its ceaseless search for more revenue, the British Government promoted the sale of alcohol and narcotics.

Apart from visible impact on the cultivating classes, state forest management also contributed to the decline of artisan industry. Chief among these was bamboo. Traders advanced money to illiterate tribals and exploited them. Sometimes, they were asked to go to courts. Tribes treated the court as a tiger's den. This was an advantage for traders who easily obtained *ex parte* decrees for confiscation of tribals' property. For a debt of 5 rupees, a trader would carry off produce worth a hundred.

The families of tribal population lived in small spaces. They were indebted to moneylenders. They had hardly any hope of even acquiring independent means of livelihood. They were often spending the little money they got from cooli work for drinks, instead of saving it for acquiring food, clothes, shelter and education for their children. Wage they got was so less that they could not afford the simplest necessities of life, proper food and clothes to cover their bodies, not to speak of ordinary amenities of life which every human being has a right to enjoy.

The construction of roads in forest areas made accessible for the military and plain traders to interface with tribal inhabitants. The British Government also built schools and dispensaries but staffed them with plainsmen, which also gave an opportunity to them to exploit tribals. A change occurred in the views of Forest Department with regard to the treatment of jungle tribes. Their traditional method of living was coined as a destructive practice of felling forests and burning them and growing a crop fertilized by the resultant ashes. The tendency was to regard them as natural enemies of forest protection.

The Forest Department felt the real solution to the problem was to stop crude methods of cultivation and convert natural forest into a valuable timber forest and provide tribes an alternative means of living. There were good guards and watchers of the forest under sympathetic forest officers who understood the necessity of adopting rigid departmental rules to the desultory habits of primitive tribes. The jungle tribes were an indispensable asset in forest protection. Some tribes were idle and turbulent in their habits. For example, the Chenchus. The preserving efforts made by officers of Forest Department provided Chenchus regular work. This had brought a change in their habits. Jobs such as line clearing, tree felling and making bamboo splits were provided. They were collecting minor forest produce and were given small plots of land in the reserve for cultivation and were taught how to till it. The Khonds were taught road making and to establish minor industries like bamboo work and brick making. The Lambadas were taught to weave bags out of Sunn hemp.

In the years of poor harvest, there was little for the tribals to eat. Sahukars in the harvest season sucked the tribals like a plague of locusts, taking the grain from the threshing floor and tamarind from trees. However, for the tribals there was no distinction between good and bad years. The British Government used to squeeze tribals through taxes like *Modalupannu* (a tax decided by the Mansabdar on his own), *Chigurupannu* (a rate varying from one third to a half), *Kalapapannu* (the wood cutting tax) and other taxes like Forest Tax, Grazing Tax, etc. from tribal people.

From the early 1860s with the establishment of a provincial constabulary, the government began to set up police stations in forest areas. The police became openly corrupt and rapacious. Before the mid-nineteenth century, there was no rival agricultural economic system to challenge *Podu* Cultivation. Animal husbandry was considered secondary in its importance. The practice of Podu cultivation was destructive in its nature. Adivasis who discontinued this narrated their woes: 'we daily starved having no food in our possession... we have no clothes to cover our body.' They expressed their feeling that the government should bestow attention on the betterment of their life. One hillsman succinctly put it: 'the forests have belonged to us from the times immemorial, our ancestors planted them and protected them, now they have become of value, government steps in and robs us of them'.

In some places the colonial government forced Adivasis to move into large settlements. They have lost their autonomy. They were forced into agrestic serfdom under more powerful cultivating castes. In South, some tribes like Chenchus, Konda Doras in desperation turned into bandits. Many tribal communities were affected by colonial forest policies. Lambadas, Yerukulas exchanged salt, grain and metal goods for bee wax, tamarind and honey collected by tribals. They were severely oppressed and exploited by colonial administrators.

The development and growth of private property also was responsible for the enactment of stringent laws under the colonial regime. In course of time, forests and mines came to be treated as the exclusive concern and property of the colonial state. The notion of reserved forests and the new abkari laws were only a few examples to attest this fact. Forest tribes were seen as a potential threat to the natural resources under colonial rule.

The Imperialist interest in other areas too, had their own bearing on the forest policy of the British. In the early stages of expansion in India, during the 19th century, establishment of military camps and introduction of railway lines meant a control over uncultivated forest regions. Added to this, depletion and shortage of optimal wood in England for ship building activity also motivated colonial officials to embark upon a forest-control policy in India. Colonial economic considerations led to the first step for control of the use of forests. In the later half of 19th century, the colonial government came to a conclusion that complete control of forests by the government was both desirable and necessary. Though there was a debate over government's attitude towards forests, involving both protagonists and antagonists from within the colonial bureaucracy, the final outcome was necessarily towards a regime of control over forests. In this process, forest tribes practised unproductive agricultural methods. They were considered as troublesome. Attempts were made through enactments of the forest acts such as Forest Act of 1865, 1878, etc. The government tried to settle tribals in the specified areas so as to control their activities, which were looked upon as inimical to forest regions. Whenever forest tribes were found flouting the law they would be dubbed as 'criminals'. Above all, these people in turn had been deployed by colonial state as manual labourers, the employment of which would have, otherwise, taxed the state heavily.

II

In some areas tribal revolts took a violent form. Several of the many *fituris* were directly or indirectly related to forest grievances. Ramboopathi near Rampachodavaram led Rampa Rebellion of 1802–03, in the Godavari agency area. Another revolt broke out around 1879 led by Chandraiah, Sambaiah and Thamman Dora. The revolt spread over 5,000 square miles. Another rebellion took place in Bastar in 1910. Another recorded fituri occurred in 1922–23 led by Alluri Sitarama Raju, fought against the British. Another revolt took place in the district of Srikakulam in 1967–70. In 1940, similar revolts took place in Adilabad district where Gonds and Kolams followed *podu cultivation*. But the state control over forests was endemic during the colonial rule. All the tribal movements have been short lived and unsuccessful. Tribal revolts were due to disputes relating to the *Muttadari* estates. *Muttadars* were the petty chiefs who were appointed by the British for keeping peace and collecting land revenue from tribal population. Taking ample advantage of their authority, *Muttadars* used violent methods to terrorize tribals and affect severe illegal exactions from the helpless and hapless tribal farmers.

The erstwhile Andhra Pradesh has the largest area of tribal concentration. Tribal communities are found in the hilly, forest and plain regions. The tribal communities can be classified into four broad regions: Adilabad region (Gonds, Kolams), Karim Nagar, Khammam, East and West Godavari region (Koyas and Konda Reddis), Srikakulam, Vijaya Nagaram region (Savara, Jatapu, Khond, Bhagata, Valmiki, Konda Dhora, Gadabas), Mahabubnagar, Prakasam, Kurnool, Nalgonda region (Chenchus). Banjara, Yanadi, Yerukulas are found in the plain areas. The State has 52 lakh tribal population. The largest concentration of the Scheduled Tribes are found in Khammam district.

The combined state of Andhra Pradesh has 21.3 per cent of its total area covered under the forests. The Tribal Sub-Plan area constitutes 63.43 per cent. The tribal economy is based on agro-forest economy. The tribal population are shifting cultivators (Konda Reddis), pastoralists (Sugalis), settled cultivators (Bagatas and Valmikis), and artisanal groups (Yerukulas). Tribal communities pursue a number of traditional economic activities such as hunting, cattle rearing, cultivation, minor forest produce, fishing, basket-making, carpentry, blacksmithy, pig rearing, etc. Indebtedness is a common feature in most of the tribal communities. From the beginning, tribal areas have attracted non-tribal population due to opportunities for trade, commerce and business. Hence, Non-tribes settled deliberately in tribal regions. There was a significant change in tribal areas due to the entry of non-tribal population into the lives of the tribal people.

III

Poverty in the Tribal Agency Mandals

Tribal people offer prayers to gods and goddesses to prevent them from evil powers and poverty. They pray for good health and longevity. However, their prayers were never conceded. In recent years, hundreds of tribals lost their lives in the forests. The National and State Human Rights Commissions took serious note of the deaths of tribal people in the State. Tribal people are always the victims of governments' apathy. Tribal habitations suffer due to difficult terrains, vocational disadvantages and primary health care services. Specialized services in the tribal agency mandals are not available. Lack of transportation further adds the miseries of tribal people. Tribal habitations are scattered in the hills. The health centres are not well equipped to tackle their emergency situations. Primitive tribes live in the top hill areas. They are completely neglected with regard to health care facilities. Health is not a priority in tribal areas. What bothers the tribal people much is their livelihood. They continue to work and earn even if they fall sick. Amoebiasis, Scabies, Jaundice, Malaria, Gastroenteritis, Fractures due to fall from trees and hill slopes are the most common ailments in the agency mandals. Malaria is widely prevalent. Health care system in tribal areas is functioning without infra-structure and medical staff. In the agency areas each tribal mandal covers 20 to 30 villages. Each health care centre caters to the medical needs of five hundred people everyday. Health assistants visit tribal areas only once in a week. In the absence of doctors, tribals swallow poisonous material, which cause death or other serious health problems.

Health cards have been introduced in the tribal areas in recent years. Tribal people were asked to maintain the health cards. Health assistants treat tribal people only when they show their health cards. They visit tribal areas rarely and spend much of their time by reading reports of tribal people. To the tribal people, health card is like a ration card. Health workers collect blood samples, distribute tablets, chlorinate drinking water sources and teach them the basics of hygiene. The over prolonged malaria impaired many of tribal people in forest regions. They are affected with neurological deficiencies. In desperation, tribals go to *Yejjodu* (tribal doctor or local faith healer). He is readily accessible to them. He encourages superstitious beliefs, black magic (*Chillangi*) and provides them with his own treatment. *Yejjodu* gives them medicine made out of leaves and roots. Tribal people stopped taking treatment in private hospitals because they cannot afford hospitalization charges. Government hospitals are closed due to no availability of doctors in the tribal agency. Though, on papers the medical infrastructure in tribal areas is very impressive. The Forest Department banned hunting in forest areas. Tribal people are asked to switch over to cash crops. There is acute shortage of food in tribal habitations. Rice, turmeric and ginger are grown for sale rather than consumption. Tribal people grow vegetable in small-holdings. They sell vegetables in *shandies* (local markets) and buy outside materials for their daily use. Most of the money they have earned from agriculture will be paid to moneylenders or banks as repayment of loans. There is no supervisory mechanism to control trading activities in tribal areas. The wholesale traders use different kinds of weighing machines (spring balances are often used to cheat tribal people). Tribal people are afraid of keeping their products for a long time. Markets are making the life of tribal people more vulnerable along with conniving traders and government officials. Tribal people collect leaves *(Addakulu)* for making leaf plates. They sell them in the Girijan Cooperative Corporation (GCC). Tribals get meager income for the collection of leaves and selling in GCC, which are very weak in functioning. The government opened a number of GCC depots in tribal areas. Of late, it is observed that GCC is also involved in malpractices. Cooperative credit societies are not serving tribal people well in collecting, buying and selling products of tribal people. Drinking alcohol is a big problem in tribal areas. Tribal people spend considerable amount of their hardwork in drinking arrack, toddy, *maddikallu* (locally made brew) without caring about their health. They do not bother for basic amenities such as kerosene, onions and chilies to last even for a week. They spend all their earnings in drinking. In the tribal villages women are the only breadwinners.

IV

Migration of Non-Tribal Population into Tribal Areas

After Independence, tribal areas have become congenial for the plain people to settle down in tribal areas. Traditional barter system was replaced with money transactions. The national Malaria eradication programme yielded fruitful results. This helped the traders, contractors and moneylenders to enter forest areas. Zamindars, Jagirdars and Inamdars became the defacto rulers in tribal areas. Tribal chiefs used to meet the obligations of rich moneylenders. The policy of populating tribal areas was started by government. *Deshmukhs* and *Desh Pandes* collected revenues and maintained village accounts. They were assisted by village *patwaris* and *patels*. They became administrative authorities to enable non-tribal people to encroach tribal lands. Tribal regions experienced a rapid growth of population due to migration, immigration of people from other regions. Richness in black cotton soil, availability of resources for cultivation, rich forest produce, good scope for trade, removal of migration barriers along with forest wealth have attracted non-tribals to enter tribal areas. The influx of non-tribals led to deforestation and land alienation. This resulted in the growth of proletarianization of tribal women, wage exploitation, bonded labour, flesh trade, etc. Tribal people faced negative consequences due to deforestation, concubinage, adultery and prostitution. Non-tribal contacts led to changes in various social customs in the tribal communities. Marriage by negotiations entered tribal culture. Bride price was replaced by dowry. The notions of purity and pollution became part and parcel of tribal life. Tribal communities exhibited their cultural connections with tribal traditions of upper Hindu caste groups.

Land Alienation in the Tribal Regions

Scheduled tribes are located in the remote, hilly and forest regions. Weekly *shandies* (local markets) are held at the centrally located tribal villages. Non-tribals penetrated into hills and jungles for various reasons. They developed contacts with tribal areas. Tribals depend on moneylenders. Money is needed for their socio-economic, cultural and religious life (bride price, performing rituals, ceremonies, etc). Money is also needed for purchase of several essential requirements. Non-tribal traders make use of this situation. The gullible tribals were ruthlessly exploited. In Visakhapatnam district, traders from Srungavarapu Kota, Madugula, Chodavaram and Narsipatnam established agency trade. The agency centres turned into commercial markets. In tribal regions demand for land increased due to cultivation, agriculture and mining activities. Business people entered tribal areas on large scale. Non-tribal contact developed monitization of tribal economy. There was a shift from exchange-based transactions to cash-based transactions. Tribal people imitated non-tribal practices. The process of land alienation began. Recognition of rights of individuals over land was granted with the issue of pattas. Land became a saleable and transferable commodity. Payment of land revenue in cash forced tribals into the hands of traders from plains, in times of shortage of money. Land revenue was permanently fixed. This lead to feudalism. Feudal lords encouraged plains people into the agencies. These people in course of time grabbed the best lands of tribals through various methods.

V

Government Policies and Programmes

After the Constitution of India came into force, agency tracts in the erstwhile Andhra Pradesh were designated as Scheduled Areas under Fifth Schedule of the Constitution. The national policy envisaged protection and integration of tribal people. Protective laws were passed for the elimination of exploitation of tribal people. After the state of Andhra Pradesh was formed in 1956, government responded to the disturbing situations developed in tribal areas. Government enacted comprehensive legislations, and stringent laws in the form of regulations since 1970. The regulations enabled tribal people to sell land and products at fair price to the government itself. The State government approved cooperatives and credit institutions to function in an effective manner. Government also appointed and gave powers to the district collectors, project officers, Integrated Tribal Development Agency officials and revenue divisional officers to safeguard interests of tribal people. However, the effective implementation of laws is not taking place in tribal regions. Officers appointed to serve tribal people have no interest, time or efficiency to solve the basic problems of tribal people in the agency mandals. After decades of tribal development, tribal people in the agency tracts still continue to lag behind with regard to various issues of tribal development. The constitutional spirit of tribal development is very much ignored by administrators and planners of development. Several bureaucratic procedures, local problems and hurdles stand in the way of tribal development. The implementation processes of tribal development schemes are not properly reaching tribal people. There are no protective measures. Tribal development is in the hands of politicians and industrialists. The benefits of tribal development schemes are not reaching them properly. The economic development of tribal people is neglected. Agriculture, animal husbandry, small-scale industries, cottage industries, provisions for credit facilities are not benefiting them. There are several drawbacks in the tribal development programmes and schemes. The irrigated lands in tribal agency mandals are very less. Tribal people are benefited very less through their agricultural practices. Tribal lands still remain under the control of non-tribals. Problems with regard to forest land, exploitation and growing aspirations of tribals lead to various movements in tribal regions. Forest legislations have seriously affected tribal people. Tribal development programmes drifted away from development activities. By and large tribal people remained producers of raw materials for the processing and manufacturing industries in the non-tribal areas. Private ownership of land has increased in tribal regions. Development programmes for tribal people focused on private property resources. Development of tribal people has been ignored in the process of modernization. Community-centred activities are replaced with individual and family-centred development activities.

People's participation and collective action of tribal people is very much essential for the sustainable development of tribal people. Participatory schemes will focus on common property resources. Globalization and privatization have affected tribal life, their collective action and community assets. Tribal women are harassed and exploited. They are living in poor working conditions. Their contact with outsiders, modernization, commercialization of tribal economic activities, introduction of government policies and development programmes have reduced the importance of tribal women and tribal youth. They are not integrated into the development process. Government policies, schemes and institutions should aim for the equalization of opportunities through various programmes and policies. Tribal women should have adequate control over resources and fruits of their hard work. International funding agencies should focus on participatory approach. Tribal people are affected due to deprivation and accessibility to natural resources. Participation in development process will help them to protect their natural resources and environment. Tribal communities today are able to freely express their desires and needs. Significant changes are also taking place in the situations of tribal communities. Officials working in the tribal regions should listen to needs of tribal people. Tribal people should gain greater control and autonomy over information and communication technology. Grama Sabhas should function affectively in tribal regions. The problems that are affecting tribal development such as illiteracy, adult education, health care facilities, rampant child labour, bonded labour, safe drinking water and education facilities should be given priority.

Cooperatives, Credit and Marketing in the Tribal Areas

Cooperation and mutual help are the cherished ideals in tribal society. It is a custom and practice for tribals. Cooperatives in tribal areas were established as a result of recommendations of the experts of tribal development. The Aiyappan Committee suggested cooperatives to eliminate exploitation of *Shahukars*. The Malayappan Committee in 1950 laid special emphasis for relieving tribals from the clutches of moneylenders. Taccavi loans were sanctioned to tribals in five easy instalments. Grain banks were established in tribal areas. Cooperatives and other credit institutions started functioning very affectively in the beginning. Government started Girijan Cooperative Corporation (GCC) for the development of tribal people. But the developed tribes started using institutional credit more than the non-developed tribes. Cooperatives in the tribal areas started after independence. But in course of time, the government realized the lack of sufficient financial base and operational inefficiency of cooperatives. The Andhra Pradesh Scheduled Tribes Finance and Development Cooperation was first of its kind in Asia. Gradually, Madhya Pradesh and Odisha states had established similar corporations in their states based on the experiences of Andhra Pradesh. The main objectives of Girijan Cooperative Corporation are to provide reasonable prices to tribals for their produce, sell domestic requirements to tribals, and offer credit services. Government also established Agricultural Development Banks, Forest Labour Cooperatives, Milk Sellers Cooperatives, Arak Sales Cooperatives for the development of tribal people. There are several problems with the functioning of these institutions and cooperative credit system in tribal regions. The cooperatives issue loans to tribals only for developmental purpose and agricultural inputs. Tribal people need money for consumption, marriage, fairs and festivals and to ward off evil spirits and other purposes. Moneylenders immediately respond to such needs. Cooperative Credit societies do not give due credit for the genuine needs of tribal people. The functions of credit cooperative societies are stereotype in nature. Further, to take loans from these credit societies tribal people have to produce many documents issued by revenue officials. For ordinary tribals it is an uphill task. The customary practice of taking loans from moneylenders and paying back the debt with interest and in kind is deep-rooted in tribal psyche. It is very difficult for tribals to pay back debts in cash due to their poverty-stricken conditions.

VI

Displaced Development

In tribal areas, human rights violations are being perpetuated on a large scale. Human rights violations are growing enormously in tribal habitations. Cases of violation of human rights are higher in agency tracts. Many tribals were forcefully evicted from their traditional habitations in the name of projects for their development. The rehabilitation packages are not properly designed. Tribal people are evacuated from their regions. Many of the tribal people ended up as bonded labourers. Forest officials and other government officers harass tribal people. Poor tribal people have no other choice but to vacate their habitations and houses. Tribal people have been denied access to minor forest produce, which is the basis of their daily subsistence. Tribal people are also prevented from cultivating lands they have occupied since times immemorial. Many of human rights violations in tribal regions are due to the decision of governments to implement the World Bank-funded economic development projects. These projects totally denied traditional rights of forest dwellers in their habitations. Discrimination against tribal people had steadily increased. It was stated that: 'every day we are being beaten up, tortured and forced to run away from our communities where we are living'. The impact of globalization had increased the burden of tribal people, rural and poorer sections. In tribal regions, child rights violations have been increasing. A large number of tribal children are working as wage labourers. Stories of torture and sexual abuse of tribal girl children have become common phenomena. Yet the law enforcing authorities turn a blind eye and a deaf ear to the violation of human rights' cases due to pressure lobbies. Tribal farmers committed suicides due to their inability to free themselves from the traps. Government machinery is least concerned about the situations of tribal people.

Unrest in the Tribal Areas

Land is a primary source for the development of tribal people. Tribal people want their lands restored and every tribal family should be provided at least two acres of land. The forest conservation act should amend its law. Allocation of land for tribal people according to the forest conservation is very difficult. The forest conservation act curbed the basic rights of tribal people. Tribal people are living under severe restrictions in forests. They were not provided with alternative land. Much of the land identified for distribution for tribals is forest land. This stopped the distribution process in several states. Governments should quickly settle the issues and problems concerning tribal people in forests. In recent years, a large number of reports reveal that tribals have taken oath not to vacate their lands and give space for setting up commercial industries. This led in some places to police firing. Many tribals are fighting against their displacement and livelihood. It was stated that the police have killed tribal people for setting up of commercial industries in the agencies. Adivasis are not ready to surrender their land for industrialists. This is the common reaction everywhere in tribal areas. Government treated a vast majority of tribal people as the encroachers of government lands. Tribal people did not possess pattas for their lands. Indigenous people fear from displacement, loss of livelihood and repression by the police, threats of irrigation and revenue officials. Tribal people protested against Polavaram project in West Godavari district of Andhra Pradesh. Koya tribal people are badly affected due to projects. Many tribal families have lost their villages and habitations in Khammam district. Their villages have been submerged in water. Government resettled Koyas on the fringes of reserve forest. Godavari floods seriously affected tribal economy. They grow cashew, cotton, paddy and other crops. It was stated that they slogged for 20 years to come to the stage that they were able to send their boys and girls to schools. Now the government was forcing them to resettle in other places where they have to restart their life, which is very difficult and unimaginable for them. Polavaram project affected nearly 2 lakh tribal population and a total number of 280 tribal villages in Khammam, East and West Godavari districts. Government is adamant. Government wanted to harness river water and to build project on Godavri river in Polavaram village in West Godavari district. Government did not bother about the issue of displacement of tribal people. Several times, officials have promised tribal people the best 'resettlement and rehabilitation package'. Medha Patkar visited the ill-effected tribal villages and stated that 'the polavaram project perpetuate the cultural genocide of the tribal people of Andhra Pradesh. The government's offer of land for resettlement is a sham. Tribals are left to fend for themselves. It is unimaginable how the government of Andhra Pradesh is going ahead with a project involving a large number of tribal peoples' displacement. What is the worth of a project that submerges two lakh areas of fertile land and uprooting thousands of Adivasis?'. Tribal people spearheaded their struggle against the government and the project. They made a long march of 600 km protesting against the attitude of government towards their development.

VII

Demands of Adivasis

In the recent times members of Adivasi communities began demanding the implementation of Scheduled Tribes and Traditional Forest Dwellers Recognition of Forest Rights Act without any delay. The State and Central governments have to take active measures to implement the Act. There is unrest among tribals due to bureaucratic procedures and delay in the process of implementation of government schemes in the state. Various tribal organizations had submitted memoranda to government officials to implement the Act. They expressed their concern that the government should not yield to the pressure groups. Pressure groups opposed the implementation of the Act in some states. The Wildlife Protection Act of 1972 enacted by government resulted in lakhs of tribal people losing their homes. Tribal people were evicted from forests. It was stated that: 'We are surviving as a distinct people and leading a miserable life every day. We want to live a life with quality and dignity'. Government had already declared forests and wildlife sanctuaries as National Parks. There are acts and provisions to protect forests and wildlife.

But there are no stringent provisions with regard to the protection of Adivasis and traditional forest dwellers. What is required is a democratic and transparent policy to empower tribal people. Government should empower Grama Sabhas at the village level, subsequently at the taluk, district and state levels. Government should compulsorily involve experts on tribal welfare and forest dwelling communities in the process of tribal development. It was noted that: 'We are the Government in our villages. We rule the forests and the agencies. Forest is our homeland. Forest is our mother and father. We are the friends of the wildlife'. The National Advocacy Council for Development of the Indigenous People urged central and state governments to implement the Panchayati Raj Extension to the Scheduled Areas Act (PESA) 1996, with full spirit in the scheduled and non-scheduled areas. All the state governments should pass orders and take active measures on Adivasi ownership of forest resources, including their rights over access and use of minor forest produce. Their languages should be provided equal status and should be quickly revived. They should be provided with quality education in their mother tongue. Their culture, traditional knowledge and identity must be recognized. Their system of life must be appreciated as a symbolic relationship with nature. Their rights to self-rule and forest resource management must be recognized for the development of indigenous people. They should be involved in the decision-making process. The state government should make all efforts to bring them into mainstream social structure.

Summing Up

The Integrated Tribal Development Agencies should be treated as special zones. Tribal people should be made to participate in decision-making bodies. Tribal people should be empowered through participatory process. This brings social change in tribal regions. They gain greater autonomy and control over their environment and resources. Relevant knowledge should be disseminated in tribal regions. The 73rd Amendment of the Indian Constitution made significant recommendations towards this direction. Government should act seriously to realize the Constitutional obligations. No amount of tribal development will be appreciated when issues like ill-health, underdevelopment, backwardness, illiteracy, child labour, Naxal menace, atrocities, discrimination and land alienation are not resolved to the benefit of indigenous forest dwellers. These problems surrounding tribal development should be immediately tackled by government taking into the consideration of the present experiences in tribal agencies. Structural adjustment policies of government in terms of liberalization, globalization, deregularization, privatization, are posing threats to tribal development. Tribal people are already affected by the problems of land alienation, deforestation, restriction of the utilization of forest resources, and the new market values. Tribal people are unable to bear the competition of skill development and investment. There is an urgent need that tribal people should be provided full employment opportunities. Tribal people should gain power of purchasing. Public distribution system should be streamlined. Food shortage in tribal regions should be eliminated. Government should raise production capacity of the tribal people. They should use the resources optimally and improve their indigenous technology. Government should improve environmental conditions in tribal agencies. Tribal people should be kept far away from market forces. Human resource management and development should be treated on priority. Tribal people should be encouraged to participate in development process.

References

Arnold, David, 'Rebellious Hillman: The Gudem-Rampa Risings: 1839–1924', in Ranajit Guha (ed.), *Subaltern Studies 1*, OUP, New Delhi, 1982.

Bhowmick, P.K., 'Tribes in the Changing Circumstances of India', *Man in India*, Vol. 71, No. 1, 1991.

Fuchs, Stephen, *The Aboriginal Tribes of India*, Macmillan, New Delhi, 1972.

Government of Madras, Board of Revenue (Land Revenue Forests) Proceedings, Forest No. 48, dated 25 April 1917.

——, Development Department, G.O. No. 1634, dated 6 December1922.

——, Proceedings of Chief Conservator of Forests, Proceedings No. 321 (Press), dated 15 July 1932.

——, Revenue (Special Department), G.O. No. 2293, dated 11 December 1919.

Guha, Ramachandra and Madhav Gadgil, 'State Forestry and Social Conflict in British India', *Past and Present*, Vol. 123, No. (1), 1989.

Mishra, Kamal K., 'National Forest Policy and Tribal Development', in R.N. Pati and B. Jena (eds), *Tribal Development in India*, Ashish Publishing House, New Delhi, 1989.

Mouli, Chandra, 'Socio-Economic Changes in the Tribes of Andhra Pradesh', in M.K. Chaudhri (ed.), *Trends of Socio-economic Change in India, 1871–1961*, Indian Institute of Advanced Study, Simla, 1969.

Pathy, Jagannath, 'Social Basis of Banditry and the Criminal Tribes Act', *Social Science Probings*, Vol. 1, No. 4, 1989.

Prasad Rao, D.L. and P. Venkata Rao, 'Cooperatives in Tribal Areas', *Tamil Nadu Journal of Cooperation*, Vol. 75, No. 3, 1983.

Prasad Rao, D.L., 'Shahukar and Tribal Society', *Tribe*, Vol. 8, No. 3–4, 1971–72.

Raghavaiah, V., *Tribal Revolts*, Andhra Rastra Adimjati Sevak Sangh, Nellore, 1971.

Rangarajan, Mahesh, 'Imperial Agendas and India's Forests: The Early History of Indian Forestry, 1800–1878', *Indian Economic and Social History Review*, Vol. 31, No. 2, 1994.

Reddy, V.R.K., 'A Critique on Tribal Life in Hyderabad State 1901–1954', *Itihas*, Vol. 15, No. 1, 1989.

The Hindu, Andhra Pradesh Edition, 'Globalisation has Hit Tribal People', 11 December 2007.

The Hindu, Magazine, 'Displaced Development', Saturday, 8 June 2000.

Venkata Rao, P., *Dimensions of Transformation in Tribal Societies with Reference to Andhra Pradesh*, Sarup & Sons, New Delhi, 2004.

——, *Tribal Development: Policy and Practice*, Sarup & Sons, New Delhi, 2001.

Verma, R.C., *Indian Tribes through the Ages*, Publication Division, New Delhi, 1990.

2

Tribal Revolts in Andhra Pradesh and Telangana

Barrington Moore declared that Indian peasant revolts were relatively rare and completely ineffective and, related this apparent passivity to the peculiarities of Indian social system, particularly to the caste system. However, recent historiography has disproved this hypothesis. The history of rebellious peasants and tribals is now being thoroughly studied. Though interest in tribal struggles is of fairly recent origin, yet, it has shown that there, indeed, has been a long tradition of revolt and protest among tribals and peasants. The presence of tribal revolts (1879–80) in the agency tracts of Rampa is an attempt to enhance our understanding of such revolts and protests of Adivasis. Rampa and its adjacent hills have assumed historical significance for being the hotbed of a major revolt that occurred during 1922–24 under the leadership of Alluri Sitarama Raju. The present chapter is concerned with earlier major revolts that occurred in the same place and on which considerable research has focused on the problems of Adivasis. The Rampa tracts, with thick forests, witnessed a series of disturbances in the 19th century, which culminated into a major revolt in 1879–80 and subsequently till today.

I

Reasons for these revolts are not far to seek. Encroachments on their traditional way of life, threat to their subsistent economy, restriction on shifting cultivation, imposition of new taxes and civil rule, harassment at the hands of police, indiscriminate exploitation by non-tribals and British authorities, all in turn strengthened the resolve of tribals to rise in revolt. By 1879, forest rights were curtailed to such an extent that they were left only with a shadow of what they formerly enjoyed. Rampa became the seat and centre of the melting pot of 1879 tribal revolt which soon spread over 5,000 sq miles. It took the British army 20 months to suppress it. This chapter deals with the nature of the revolt, social origins of the principal participants and the long-term impact of the final settlement.

The militancy of the peasant and tribal has been the subject of an active debate for a long time now. Marx took for granted the idiocy of rural life and described peasants as sack of potatoes. Lenin believed that peasant was to serve as a surrogate in a revolution. Quite contrary to this, Eric Stokes opined that while cities may go up in revolt, it is the countryside that makes or breaks revolution. The urban elite would remain intellectual without peasant support argued Sunil Sen. Peasant participation, whether it be in China, Mexico, Algeria, Cuba or Vietnam, has laid to rest any question or doubts about their militancy or ability to effectively fight for their cause. Coming to the Indian peasantry, as mentioned above, Barrington Moore's hypothesis of the passivity of the Indian peasant has been seriously challenged.

The fact remains that not only during the colonial period but even earlier, the countryside voiced its grievances through revolt, whenever it felt the oppression of the feudal chiefs, landlords, moneylenders and the State became intolerable. Had Moore's argument been correct, then writing the history of peasant movements in India or for that matter, Rampa revolt would have been a futile exercise. The countryside was and is always a fertile ground for uprisings and the history of the Indian peasant and tribal is the history of resistance, rebellion and uprisings. The periodic outburst of peasants and tribal action raise the question of why does the peasant or tribal revolt? What impels the individual towards an action? No doubt, in such analysis a study of the changes in the material conditions of the tribal or peasant is imperative; however, one needs also to have an understanding of the mentalities or world-view of the tribal and peasant.

James C. Scott in his study of the Vietnamese peasantry and revolutionary action posited a hypothesis of the moral economy of the peasant, which when threatened would impel the peasant towards revolutionary action. He argued that this moral economy was based on two principles of norms of reciprocity and the right to subsistence. No doubt, Scott's hypothesis was formulated within the framework of a peasant economy. It may be argued that the concept of a moral economy could be applied in the study of the tribals of Rampa region. For the Rampa tribals the forest ecosystem was a world in itself, with its own moral economy. When this was disturbed, they revolted.

To avoid any semantics and ambiguities, it is essential that the terminology used should be clear. K. Venkatramulu has provided a list of definitions which gives a overall picture of tribal characterization. The term 'tribe' is used to denote a stage in the evolution of social and political structure. Marx described that early stage of socio-economic development as primitive community in which property was tribal property with a very elementary stage of division of labour, and simple social structure. A tribe is a group of people speaking a common language, with uniform rules of social organization, and working together for common purposes such as trade, agriculture and warfare. Other typical characteristics being a common name, a contiguous territory, a relatively uniform culture or way of life, and a tradition of common descent. The term is not to be applied to societies that have achieved a strictly territorial organization within a large state but is usually confined to groups whose unity is based primarily upon a sense of extended kinship ties.

Anthropo-historical studies have shown that tribal isolation has been relative and never absolute. Peasants and tribes interacted with each other, albeit, on a minimal level. Though tribes took to agriculture, they did not settle as the non-tribal peasants. Moreover, peasants colonizing tribal areas and tribals having contacts with peasants is not a modern phenomenon, and too much should not be made of this distinction between tribals and sections of the rural poor, for apart from some isolation and really primitive food-gathering, the Adivasis were and are very much a part of Indian society as the lowest stratum of peasantry also subsisting through shifting cultivation. D.D. Kosambi tells us that 'the Brahmins acted as pioneers in introducing plough agriculture that replaced the slash-and-burn cultivation in certain tribal areas'. However, it was through the peddlers, moneylenders and mendicants that interaction of tribal and non-tribal was established.

The chief characteristic of the tribal economy was its subsistence nature where agriculture played a dominant role. Agriculture is the kingpin of the tribal economy, though we may not find settlement agriculture. However, agriculture being seasonal in character, implemented with primitive technology, and the landholding capacity of the tribal being small, the income thus derived was very low and inevitably led him to depend upon other sources of income, i.e. forest produce. The forest gave him minor produce like gum, tamarind, mohwa flower, seeds, roots, honey, etc. Besides supporting them economically, the forest was central to their world-view and culture.

Except for climatic disturbances, the tribal faced no material insecurity like unemployment and depression. The gradual opening up of tribal economy under the aegis of the colonial state caused them immense difficulties. The twin problems that faced the tribals, in general, were credit and marketing. Traditionally, shy in plains, they depended upon the peddlers for marketing their forest produce, who in turn acted as moneylenders for the tribals whose income fell below the subsistence in times of famines and festivals and when they indulged in costly religious and social practices. This facilitated control over tribals and tribal economy. The debt servitude was deepest and often socially most explosive where the moneylenders appeared as alien intruders. Slowly the master of forests started becoming servant. The growing tensions often expressed themselves in the frequent incidence of crimes like grain theft, lootings, murders, etc. which took serious proportions in the wake of naked exploitation facilitated by the intrusion of colonial administration and economic policies.

The incorporation of Asian societies into a western dominated global economy and the development of centralized bureaucratic states, often under the aegis of colonial domination, led to a radical transformation of the world of most Asian peasants. Tribal society, too, could not escape from the clutches of colonial domination. While it paved way for the institution of peasant mode of production in the tribal economy and brought tribes under the established administration, it caused unforeseen hardships for the tribal. Shocked with the frequent tribal uprisings, the English sought to keep a close watch on the tribal regions. The agency system, established in early 19th century with the objective of quelling revolts, was the earliest administrative measure adopted. Working within a colonial framework they had no perception of larger issues of social change or economic development and they even thought that continuance of primitive condition was advantageous for their exploitation.

The British strengthened the feudal rule of rajas, chiefs and zamindars in the tribal society and created conditions in which tribal economy and political system were undermined by the rampaging market forces. Tribal areas were brought under the permanent settlement by which tribals became occupancy tenants or sub-tenants, thus leaving them at the mercy of zamindars and their subordinates. The communal mode of production started breaking down with the recognition of private rights in land. The survey and settlement operations in the hitherto unsurveyed tribal regions coupled with the introduction of a legal system facilitated the alienation of tribal land. Forest acts, abkari regulations and other such regulations denied the tribals their traditional right to forest produce. Police stations became symbols of corruption and state terrorism. Famines which visited tribal areas frequently, thanks to the imperial policies of British, also denied them their traditional dependance on forest produce, a produce that acted as a cushion in times of distress. Construction of railways hastened their miseries, as more people came from outside to stake a claim on forests. The more the tribals were exposed the more they felt insecure. Anthropologists of British imperialism may argue that British policies were a mixed blessing for breaking down the isolation of tribal people and bringing them into the mainstream of life. For the tribals it meant loss of autonomy and becoming a victim of more and more rapacious outsiders.

Tribal movements in colonial era have been characterized as primary and secondary forms of resistance. In the initial phase traditional chiefs and zamindars fought for their lost privileges. This type of primary resistance started declining by 1860s when the colonial phase itself was changing with deeper penetration of colonial capitalism. Now the movements entered into the secondary form of resistance in which the initiative for revolt shifted from traditional chiefs to the tribes themselves. In 20th century, with the emergence of Gandhi and intensification of Indian national movement, tribal movements were brought under umbrella of the national movement. The Indian National Congress and other national leaders led the tribals in the struggle for independence on local grievances and mobilized them for national objectives. Tribals by themselves had not much to do with the political movement. Their life was disrupted and this gave them enough cause for rebellion. These movements highlight the capability of effective mobilization through their traditional institution of chiefs and clans based on bonds of kinship.

The tribal movements differed from the peasant movements, both in terms of strategy as well as demands. Tribals and peasants revolted in the face of increasing pressures as a result of the expansion of colonial economy. The peasant, however, fought on the plains for primarily agrarian grievances. The tribals, fighting in the forests, adopted guerilla tactics to resist. The tribal fought for more than economic grievances. The tribals fought to preserve their autonomous identity and their entire way of life.

II

Tribal Chiefs in Andhra Pradesh and Telangana

The Circars of Srikakulam, Rajahmundry and Ellore (later Godavari District) were called Northern Circars during the British rule, because of their relative situation to the Fort St. George, the headquarters of the Madras Presidency. The zamindaries of plains along with the tribal estates of that region were transferred to the East India Company after the treaty of 1768 concluded between the English Company and the Nizam. An attempt has been made to bring to light the activities of the tribal chiefs who involved in a general revolt in the aftermath of the Padmanabha War of 1794, which resulted in the disintegration of the Vizianagaram zamindari, and consolidation of the Company rule in Coastal Andhra region. Evidence is mostly based on the material collected from the District Records (Factory Records) preserved in the State Archives, Hyderabad, besides some other secondary sources.

The Circumstances which led to the Battle of Padmanabha – 1794

The Battle of Padmanabha took place between the Vizianagaram Zamindari and the English troops at Padmanabha near Bheemilipatam of Visakhapatnam district on 10 July, 1794. Vizianagaram was the earliest and the most powerful zamindari of the region. Pedda Vijaya Rama Raju (1734–57) was the most powerful of all the zamindars. He had the title of Manne Sulthan (Lord of the Tribal Estates), conferred by Jaffar Ali Khan (1752), the *fouzdar* of Chicacole under Salabat Jung in order to utilize his services in controlling the tribal chiefs of this region. After the death of Pedda Vijaya Rama Raju, Ananda Raju came to power (1757–60). He invited the English into the Circars to eliminate the French. The combined forces defeated the French in the war of Chandurti in 1759. Thus, the French were eliminated paving the way for the foundation of Company's power in the Circars. He died in 1760 and was succeeded by Chinna Vijaya Rama Raju (1760–94). The Company also obtained 'Mughal Farman' (1765) for the transfer of Circars to the Company. The Nizam also obliged it with treaties in 1766 and 1768. Thereafter, Vizianagaram had to depend on the Company for its power in the Circars. Vijaya Rama Raju made settlement with the English at an annual *peshcush* (present) of three lakh rupees. He wrote to Madras Government in 1768 referring the grant of Jeypore by Salabat Jung in 1752 and requested the Company for its renewal. The Company renewed it in 1769.

Diwan Sita Rama Raju exercised full powers and waged wars against the tribal estates to collect tribute and bring them under control. The hill chiefs revolted and caused disturbances by joining together under Vikramadeo of Jeypore. Sita Rama Raju took the support of the English troops and exercised unlimited authority over the hill estates. The Carnatic affairs in 1768 and the tribal disturbances in the Circars forced the Company to depend on Vizianagaram. Meanwhile his expeditions caused disturbances in the hill estates and resulted in the fall of revenue collection. He could not pay his *peshcush* punctually and his arrears accumulated to ₹ 3 lakhs by the year 1773. His despotic nature and differences with Vijaya Rama Raju led to financial crisis and the administration became weak. So, in 1775 Sitarama Raju was sacked from Diwanship. The Circuit committee (appointed by the English Company in 1777 to enquire into the political and financial conditions of the Circars) recommended the reduction of the military forces of the zamindari which was then 12,000 men. The savings thus effected, amounting to nearly 5 lakhs should be added to the *peshcush*. Jeypore should be made a separate zamindari completely independent of Vizianagaram and the rebel hill chiefs confined in the fort of Vizianagaram should be immediately released. Vijaya Rama Raju was prepared to accept most of the conditions but was unable to pay higher *peshcush*. He represented to the Chief in 1793 regarding the hill troubles and substantial financial loss and requested him to send four companies of sepoys to restore order. The Chief in turn decided to conduct an enquiry into the causes of the hill troubles. He also wanted the Raja to inform him 'what was the amount of his claims upon the hill people and how long they had been due'.

When the arrears became heavy, the Madras Government ordered the sequestration of his whole zamindari by granting him a pension. On 2nd August 1793, the fort of Vizianagaram was occupied by the Company troops. The zamindari was divided into three divisions and collectors were appointed. When the Company tried to lease the taluks to others, people sympathized with the Raja and none came forward to rent the villages. To keep Raja away, the Company later ordered him to leave Vizianagaram and go to Masulipatam with a pension of ₹ 1,200 per month. But Vijaya Rama Raju felt it unworthy to his dignity (his ex-Diwan Sitarama Raju was granted ₹ 5,000 per month by the company). On 11 May, 1794, the Raja proceeded few miles but soon returned expressing his unwillingness and reached Padmanabham, a sacred place near Bheemilipatam. The Company officials tried to negotiate with him but failed. Later, the company sent its troops against him on 10 July, 1794. A fierce battle with a duration of 45 minutes took place and the Raja was killed in it. Nearly 300 men sacrificed their lives along with the Raja.

III

The Rampa Outbreak and the Method of Dealing with Savaras of Hill Tracts in Madras Presidency (1860–1900)

Hill Tracts and Savaras

Misunderstanding arose in consequence of certain Savaras who inhabited the Parlakimedi hill tracts/villages in Ganjam district were declared to lie within the Parlakimedi boundary and refused to pay rent to the Bisoye of Gumma who was the Kimedi representative. The civil officers of the Ganjam district advised the Bisoye of Gumma to file suits against the reluctant Savaras. The Bisoye of Gumma lodged complaints against the Savaras and filed cases against them. These complaints were transferred to the Principal Assistant at

Chicacole by the government agent. The Principal Assistant passed *ex parte* decrees against all the defendant Savaras. Ultimately, the court had passed the writs, and orders were issued to execute the property of Savaras. The officers who were dispatched to execute the writs were attacked by armed Savaras in villages and forced the officers to withdraw the writs. Horsley, the then agent in Ganjam attributed the attitude of the reluctant Savaras to the intrigues of the Maharaja of Jeypore. The Maharaja of Jeypore was a zamindar in the neighbouring district of Vizianagaram. The agent of Ganjam suggested to the Government to handover the administrative charges in the hands of the Maharaja of Jeypore. Thus, there were differences between the Maharaja of Jaypore and the government Agents.

The Government of Madras had explained the position of matters with regard to the Maharaja of Jeypore. The government had expressed its extreme surprise and regret at the hasty and imprudent course taken by the agent officer. The Governor in Council of Madras province had directed the Agents that until the District officers were able to visit the locality of Savara hill Ganjam districts, attempts should be made to settle the differences in an amicable manner. The Governor General in the council considered the orders issued by the Madras Government as appropriate. The Governor in the council of the Madras Province considered the proceedings of the officers of the Ganjam district as 'hasty and imprudent'.

In the past, Savaras had given serious trouble to the government. The government considered the matter with very serious repercussions. The district officers due to their hasty nature invited trouble for the government due to the ill-feelings developed by the district officers. The government had sensed that the ill-feelings produce serious complications. The proceedings of Horsley had transformed the plaints of the Bisoye to his subordinate officials for disposal without attempting to effect an amicable settlement. This appeared to the Governor General in Council to have been most injudicious. He was constrained to suggest for the Madras Government to consider in the public interest that more serious officers should be placed in Ganjam district. The government wanted a person whose judgement was more reliable should be entrusted the responsibilities of Ganjam district.

Ganjam district was an important district to the Madras Government. It had witnessed several local insurrections. During this time, Horsley was appointed as an officer to control Ganjam district. As a local zamindar, Horsley showed his ignorance in over controlling the Savara lands. Parlakimedi was one of the largest Zamindaris in Ganjam district. Parlikimedi appeared extraordinary zamindari to the government. It felt that the hasty conclusions of Horsley brought serious friction between British Government and the Maharaja of Jeypore. The Maharaja of Jaypore wanted to betray the British local authorities.

During the year 1876, the Gumma Bisoye filed civil suits in the Parlakimedi District Munsif Court against the Savaras of Pedda Kollakote. They did not pay their share to Bisoye. Under the civil procedure code, the Bisoye asked for an injunction order. He complained that Savaras were leaving to the Vizagapatnam Hills with all their movable property. Bisoye also provided the evidence to the local Munsif. He issued orders of arrest of the Savaras. The Savaras opposed the orders of execution. The Munsif referred the matter to the Principal Assistant Agent, Grahame. He lodged criminal complaints against the Savaras for disobedience of orders. Grahame stopped further proceedings and spoke to the Bisoye very seriously about his arbitrary proceedings. He had submitted the papers to the Agent Master, for further orders. Grahame proceeded to the Hills but found that the dispute could be settled on the plains.

The then Agent Master had pointed out that the District Munsif did not have the power to issue orders under Civil Procedure Code. The CPC was not in force in the Hill regions. The Agent also did not have the power to try a civil case, which Bisoye had lodged against the Savaras. The Agent had powers only in jurisdiction in such cases under Clause 2, Rule IX of the Agency rules. The proceedings were not taken on criminal side. The District Munsif suggested that the parties should be summoned to the plains. An endeavour should be made to settle the matter amicably. Bisoye should file regular suits in the Agent's court. The case must be referred to the Principal Assistant Agent for settlement. Bisoye was also warned that he would be removed from his post if he continued his arbitrary proceedings causing injury to the Savaras. The Principal Assistant Agent should report his proceedings showing the result, the nature of the dispute and his opinion about the dispute, etc.

Grahame sent word to Savaras several times to appear before him for peaceful settlement of the dispute. But the Savaras refused to meet Grahame. He, therefore, formed an opinion that the Savaras were at fault and Bisoye had not committed any mistake. He wrote to the Government that Bisoye should not be blamed for his acts towards Savaras. The Gumma Bisoye filed civil suits against Savaras (Suit Nos. 3 to 24). Horsfall was then an acting Agent. He transferred the civil suits to the Principal Assistant Agent, Grahame for necessary inquiry and speedy disposal of the civil suits. Suit No. 27 was transferred to Leman. The Principal Assistant Agent, Grahame tried the cases and passed *ex parte* decrees, as the Savaras (defendants) failed to appear before him despite repeated requests. Bisoye made applications and submitted to the Acting Principal Assistant Agent, Happell. He executed the decrees and warrants of arrest which were issued on the Savara tribal population. These agents gave detailed particulars of the government efforts made by the officers in the district to personally inquire into the dispute. They also made efforts to amicably settle the dispute between Bisoye and the Savaras. The Savaras had completely resisted the efforts made by the officers. The officers complained that Savaras were apparent offenders. The Government officers secretly informed that the Savaras should not be blamed as they had acted under the orders of the Zamindar of Jeypore.

Horsley was not responsible for the instruction. He joined the district which was far. The government had opined that 'from the first, every effort has been made by the officers of the district to personally inquire into the dispute and make amicable arrangements between the Bisoye and the Savaras'. Bisoye was incautiously instructed by an agent to file regular suits. *Ex parte* judgements were given. Thereupon, execution of Savaras were granted. The Bisoye was an incumbent service tenement. The quit-rent assessed was payable to the Parlakimedi zamindar. The Inamdar continued to depend on the will of the government. Obviously, he was bound by the instructions of the Governor's agent when any particular course he was pursuing was censured as likely to lead to disaffection or breach of peace. Government protected the Bisoye in the enforcement of his ancient and prescriptive legal rights. It had also observed that there were plausible grounds for popular clamour and contention – any rights of Bisoye arising on a very recent determination of a long standing boundary dispute during the continued existence of which his claims have been so constantly questioned as to deprive them hitherto of pecuniary value and his arbitrary proceedings having called for full version by both the agent and the Principal Assistant on more than one occasion. The agent's influence should be exerted to promote an amicable solution.

Kollakotta Decrees

Agent to the Governor in Ganjam reported that there were 20 decrees in the court that were stayed by an order of the Government. The same was committed to the High Court. The High Court had the powers to work as Superintendence and as the Agency Court. The twenty decrees were known as 'Kollakotta decrees'. Government did not ask for the execution of 20 decrees on the Savaras but the Bisoye applied for the execution of the decrees on the Savaras. The Principal Assistant Agent sought direction from the government. The government asked explanation for the delay in the execution of the decrees. The Principal Assistant Agent replied that under the orders of the government applications for the execution would be removed from the first quarterly return of 1881.

The Hostile Feeling of Savaras in the Agency Tracts

The Savaras of agency tracts were under the Gumma Bissoi. The Savara areas were enforced with rent payment to Gumma Bisoye. He used to press the poor Savaras to pay highest rates of rent to him. Savaras did not pay rents to the Bisoye. Government asked to pay rents directly to government if they find that payment of rents was not liked by Savaras to Gumma Bisoye. Government was ready to pay tax amount to Gumma Bisoye. In Jeypore, Savaras were paying rent to the government directly. The same was followed by Bustar. In Jeypore and Bustar, rents were paid to the government with the help of the Chief Commissioner, Central Provinces. The Chief Commissioner used to credit the money to Gumma Bisoye under *Peshcush* or *Nuzzur*. The Savara villages were awarded to the Gumma Bisoye. The award was ratified by the government on 7 October 1876.

Colonel Robertson in Kimedi sub-division stated about the difficulties faced by Savaras in their villages. He had stated that: 'It is a pity now that these villages were given over to the Gumma Bisoye who never had anything to do with them before, and they will not acknowledge his authority or pay rent to him ... they are willing to pay it to the Government or to Jeypore'. The government was asked to open new reserves at Kimedi, Poota Singhy, Godavari, Vizagapatnam and Jeypore divisions/stations.

Hill Tracts

In the hill tracts the most important issue was the state of affairs of Gumma Bisoye. Pootasinghy was occupied by the Gumma Bisoye in 1869. Savaras looked upon the police and Gumma Bisoye with great distrust. They did not like to meet or communicate with them. If they were approached, they immediately used to rush into the jungles. Every movement of the police was suspected by Savaras. They were afraid of the warrants brought by the police. They were afraid of the police suspecting that they were the agents of Bisoye. Affairs in the Savara inhabited stations were very much tensed. It was as much the same when the first disturbances broke out in Rampa 20 years ago in 1860. There was the same hostility of the ryots (peasants) to their local chiefs. The local chiefs were unable to obtain rents. They demanded the Savaras to pay old and current rents. The accumulated arrears amounted to a large sum in the hill tracts which the Savara people were unwilling and unable to pay.

Savaras were afraid of the police entering their villages. They felt that the government was using the police. The police were only representing the government orders. The government was supporting the Bisoye's claims of high rent from Savaras. Every act of the police and Bisoye was viewed by Savaras with extra caution. They expected that it was the intention of the government to enforce Bisoye's claim by force and the police were employed for the purpose of collecting revenue. Under these circumstances, collision may occur at any time and the consequences could be very serious.

The Kollakotta Savaras were intimately connected with their neighbours. The Poota Singhy Savaras took to arms again and again. The force in Kimedi Maliahs was very strong and divided into three 'dalas' or parts. Savara force in Poota Singhy was very strong. The entire station and Savara inhabited lines were stockaded. Their strong protest could not be stopped for any length of time. These matters were officially communicated to the court.

Government wanted to quickly settle the matter. It had appointed Carmichael to negotiate the matter with Savaras. Carmichael suggested Bisoye to make amicable solutions and withdraw his decrees. In upper India, the issue of grants was withdrawn by paying grant to the government called as 'Malikanah' allowance. According to this allowance 10 per cent of the revenue will go to the government. The government used to collect revenue directly from the occupiers of land. Government made it very clear that the Bisoye has very less rights. He was subordinate officer and under the charge of the court of wards. It was very clear that Savaras never admitted the decrees and title holder's position of the Bisoye. Government felt that it was of recent origin due to which problem arose in hill tracts. The Bisoye had no right to collect more than the revenue specified by the government. He has only power to collect a small fee as rent. Government found fault with Bisoye for executing 20 decrees with the court agent of Ganjam in the High Court. It asked Gumma Bisoye to withdraw cases and execution of the 20 suits against Kollakotta Savaras in hill tracts. With this, the Gumma Bisoye had withdrawn his applications for the execution of decrees in the 20 suits against Kollakotta Savaras.

IV

Method of Controlling the Inhabitants of the Hill Tracts in Madras Presidency

Government of India did not desire to examine too closely the administrative errors which had tended to produce and prolong the Rampa outbreak. More especially, as the Government of Madras was fully alive to them. In order to prevent such outbreaks in the future course, or to deal with them effectively if such instances occur again, the first essential thing that appeared to the Government of India was to be more active and sympathetic in these hilly regions. Also, in these respects it was feared that there were undoubtedly some shortcomings during the progress of the Rampa outbreak. The Governor General in Council was glad to believe that such apathy was rare amongst members of the Madras Administrative Service officials. Nevertheless, it was hoped that the wide-spreading and the prolonged ill-consequences which had been brought about in this instance by supine and inefficient administration will be prominently borne in mind by all public officers who would in future be employed in administering these wild tracts.

The government after end of the Rampa Rebellion in the wild tracts found Carmichael the popular government official of that time and he was posted to the Hill Tracts. His appointment and posting to the Rampa region was fully approved by the Government of India. The Governor-General in Council was glad to observe that: 'In deputing to the Rampa country an officer Carmichael with experience and ability, and in vesting him while so employed with the fullest authority to act on his own direction, the Government of Madras has taken the surest means of going to the root of the administrative difficulties with which it has to deal, and of developing the feeling of local responsibility without which control over distant operations must often be found ineffective, if not positively injurious'. It was hoped that Carmichael will enact more positively and find permanent solutions to all the disturbances, problems and pending questions. Government hoped that he will set right, promote and strike positive relations between Savara inhabitants in the hill tracts and officers of the government on more satisfactory lines than that hitherto existed in the hilly tracts.

V

Dom Uprisings

Doms were called Pariahs. They lived in Jeypore. They were considered as bad characters by the government and local people. They were identified as regular dacoits. Scott, the then Superintendent of Police stated that 'they have been in the habit of robbing and plundering and carrying off women. The villagers have taken the matter into their own hands, and seizing several of the Doms have handled them very roughly and it is reported, killed many of them'. There were two leading village heads in Vizagapatam hill tracts. They were arrested for their homicides. They were kept in the prison at Koraput. They awaited the trial. The villagers had in consequence had gone out on future.

Scott, the then Superintendent of Police was a strict official. He used to frighten poor people. The matters with such kind of officials used to take very serious turn. The officer commanding at Vizianagaram had requested the Government to deploy several parties of Sepoys to control the disturbances in hill tracts. Government deployed police force at Koraput, Potinghi, Arakuhill, and in Pachipenta. Each party in the police constabulary consisted of 50 men. The 17th Native Infantry was stationed at Potinghi (Koraput). The 29th Native Infantry was stationed at Aruku. The 28th Native Infantry was located at Luchmipuram at the head of Narainapatnam Ghat.

Government had appointed Moore, as the New Acting Special Assistant. Mounsey was the then Collector in Aruku and Fawcett was the senior Acting Assistant placed at Luchmipuram. Prendergast was the police officer at Parvatipur. He was ordered to go to Luchmipuram with his police battalion and spread police constabulary in Parvatipur, Bobbili and other places. Fawcett, Mounsey, Travers, Moore were stationed at Vizianagaram. Scott was stationed at Koraput.

The hill tracts were pregnant with rebellions. The worst feature of the cases of hill men was that there was almost the certainty of an outbreak. Naidus were the powerful local community people convicted for their killing of several Doms in the hill tracts. They were arrested and punished. The worst hit area in the hill tracts was Pachipenta Mandal. Opium was grown abundantly here. They used to supply in large quantities to Indore from this place.

Lindsay Arbuthnott gave full evidence to the Court Martial in Madras. Government relied on his report. A map was drafted locating the places in order to give an idea about rebellions in the hill tracts. In Mulkangiri provinces there were several cases registered of killings of Doms by Mulkangiri Naidus. Dead bodies of Doms were recovered by local police at Nundigram and Mulkangiri. They were killed by cubs. Naidus used Tungees, Tulwars for killing them. Actually, Naidus and their followers did not intend to kill the Doms. They intended to threaten them. Doms were taken from their houses and given severe blows on their heads. The Maharaja of Jeypore sent his people to try and persuade Naidus. But they returned quietly to the villages and the Naidus knowing about Raja of Jeypore deploying people did not injure any Dom. The Inspector reported the matter in his report. The local Naidus demanded the police to arrest Doms on charges of theft.

In Dusmutpore, Haynes, the then police officer stated that the village of Dondabedda, three miles from Gerlugooma, was attacked and seven houses belonging to Ghasis were sacked under the direction of Naidus by the neighbouring villagers. The same situation continued even in Araku, Paderu and Wondragedda. There were rumours of rebellion at Araku. These disturbances in the hill tracts were due to the Doms and Naidus. People at Mulkangiri rose with arms. The Doms waited at Madeoputti to see the Maharaja to narrate their grievances to him. If the Maharaja did not come, they intended and determined to attack Naidus at Koraput. After hearing the plan, nearly 400 Naidus stationed at Pachipenta Ghat were ready to take revenge on the Doms. This had become a universal topic for conversation with the people of Mulkangiri, Pullabeda,

Nundigam and the neighbouring places. Many small parties ranging about fifty each formed as *dalas* (groups) to take revenge on Doms.

VI

Anti-British Struggles of Golkonda Chiefs

Golkonda zamindari was also surrounded by thick forests and mountains. On account of its location and climate it was very difficult to enter into the agency tracts. The zamindars of Golkonda hailed from the family of Jeypore Rajas. They possessed the title of 'Bhupathi' (landlord). Nelakanta Bhupathi was granted this zamindari by Jeypore Raja. At the time of transfer of Circars to the Company, Virabupathi was the zamindar of Golkonda. He was paying a rent of ₹ 5,000 per annum. His payments fell in arrears and later he had undertaken depredations. The inaccessibility of the region did not allow the Company to take any severe action against him. In the year 1774, Golkonda was transferred to Vizianagaram by the Company in order to avoid the depredations by the zamindar of Golkonda. Vijaya Rama Raju expelled Virabhupathi with the assistance of the British troops. He surrendered later and restored with settlement of ₹ 19,000 as tribute. In 1776, Golkonda was put under Vizianagaram as it again fell in arrears. Virabhupathi was again expelled. The differences between Vijaya Rama Raju and his brother Sitarama Raju provided an opportunity to Virabhupathi. He reoccupied it in 1777, without informing either Vizianagaram or the British.

Sitarama Raju with the military assistance of the English re-established his supremacy over Golkonda in 1779, but he failed in restoring peace and order. Disturbances continued even in the presence of the Company troops and tribute could not be collected regularly. Later on, Golkonda was granted to Bhirava Bhupathi by the Company as it totally failed in curtailing the disturbances. The Circuit Committee also proposed in 1784 to let him continue under Vizianagaram zamindari. In 1785, Bhirava Bhupathi was assassinated by Malla Bhupathi. Disturbances continued even during this period and Malla Bhupathi and his followers were arrested to restore peace. Chinna Bhupathi who became the zamindar, also failed to pay tribute regularly. Sitarama Raju sent Ramchandra Raju to collect revenue. He treacherously killed Chinna Bhupathi and his followers. The relatives of Chinna Bhupathi killed Ramchandra Raju and his party as a revenge. Then Malla Bhupathi was released and restored to Golkonda. Malla Bhupathi again did not pay regularly; but as he was loyal, the Company allowed him to continue as the zamindar. The Company also observed the poor collections and conditions of the zamindari, and fixed the rent at ₹ 11,000 in 1796. As per the permanent settlement, it was fixed at ₹ 10,000 in 1804. Malla Bhupathi did not pay regularly and the Company also could not take any harsh measures because of the inaccessibility of the region. In 1805, Malla Bhupathi passed away and Krishna Bhupathi succeeded. Though the zamindars changed, there was no improvement in the payments and the disturbances continued. Thus, from 1769 onwards the zamindars of the Golkonda created disturbances against Vizianagaram zamindars, provoked by the petty hill chiefs. Though

Vizianagaram and the British troops marched several times, they could not restore tranquillity even after 1803. During the pre-British period the Vizianagaram zamindari, though was powerful, did not interfere in the internal liberty of tribal chiefs. They maintained friendly relations on the basis of mutual trust and cooperation. The dependence of tribal estates on Vizianagaram zamindari was also nominal. But when the British Company took over the Circars in 1768, they made Vizianagaram zamindari as an agent of the English and forced it for more revenue. In turn, the Vizianagaram zamindari, particularly during the Diwanship of Sitarama Raju had to wage wars against the tribal estates for the recovery of the arrears, to cater to the needs of Colonial masters. Tribal chiefs of the region, in the beginning, resisted the Vizianagaram zamindari's forces when it acted as an agent of the British Company. But after the Padmanabha War the same tribal chiefs gave shelter to the minor son of the Raja in the hills and formed a combination of hill chiefs to fight against the British. In fact, the disturbances caused by them were responsible for the restoration of the Vizianagaram zamindari to the Raja. Gradually, all other tribal estates were also restored to their earlier chiefs. Even after the restoration of their estates, tribal chiefs continued their struggle throughout the British Rule. The strategy with which the British could control the plain zamindars did not yield expected results in the case of tribal estates. The hills and thick forest helped as natural shelter to the tribals and they easily defied outside powers. The underlying spirit of the tribal tradition is to live in peace, with dignity and independent of any external control. Freedom is dearer to them than any other interest. The heroic struggles of Golconda chiefs and their followers against the foreign domination unfolds the above truth.

VII

Tribal Unrest: Unrest among Gonds

Gonds are one of the numerically largest tribes in Telangana. The traditional habitat of Gond tribe is the forest tracts of Adilabad district. They speak Gondi language. According to 1971 census, Gonds constitute 69 per cent of the tribal population in Adilabad district. It is generally mentioned that tribal areas are rich, whereas tribals are poor. Though the forests of Adilabad contribute more than one-third state revenue from forests, and most of the new material required by the Sirpur Paper Mills, tribals form negligible percentage of the labour force, most of whom are imported from outside by the forest contractors. A study conducted by Tribal Cultural Research and Training Institute in Utnoor Tribal Development Block reveals that more than 60 per cent of these indebted families borrowed money from private moneylenders, indicating the continued stronghold of moneylenders on tribal economy and life. While the scheduled tribes population registered an increase of 57 per cent during 1971–81, the population, other than scheduled tribes and scheduled castes, registered an increase of 75 per cent during the same period in the Utnoor taluk. This exemplifies the magnitude of large-scale immigration. This was confounded further by granting the status of Scheduled

Tribes to Lambadies (Sugalis) in Andhra Pradesh through *G.O.Ms. No. 798 (Edn.)* dated 23.6.1976, although they do not enjoy this status in the neighbouring Maharashtra. The Lambada (Sugali) community was declared as Scheduled Tribe in Telangana area since 1977. This inclusion of Lambadas (Sugalis) of Telangana area in the list of scheduled tribes attracted large-scale immigration of Banjaras from Maharashtra into the state. This accelerated migration from Maharashtra led to large-scale encroachment of land in tribal areas of Adilabad. The increased growth in population through migration increased the pressure on bamboo forests for local requirements and no rest was given to the bamboo forests. As a result bamboo potentials started dwindling and the forest area in Adilabad district has been reduced by 25 per cent. Due to non-scientific exploitation, most of the trees of Gum have dwindled due to illicit felling for encroachments. The minor forest produce trees too have dwindled and as a result the production of minor forest produce decreased rapidly in the district which adversely affected the Gond economy. In spite of the implementation of the Land Transfer Regulation by the government, exploitation of tribals by outsiders could not be fully controlled due to large scale migration of non-tribals into the tribal areas. Further, the hitherto non-tribal community of Lambada (Sugali) was declared as a Scheduled Tribe, which enabled this former non-tribal community to get protection under law at par with other Scheduled Tribes. This caused resentment among the other local Scheduled Tribe groups like Gonds, Kolams, etc. This situation was further aggravated by the issue of *G.O.Ms. No. 129* in 1979, which enabled the small landholders belonging to non-tribal communities to legalize their previous illegal possessions. According to the *G.O.Ms. No. 129* dated 13.8.1979, all non-tribal landless poor in occupation of lands in the Scheduled Areas up to 5 acres of wetland or 10 acres of dry land should not be evicted for the present under the provisions of the Andhra Pradesh Scheduled Areas and Transfer Regulation, 1959. Utilizing the order as handy, most of the rich immigrant non-tribal peasantry had shown an artificial fragmentation of their landholdings to bring them under the preview of the *G.O.Ms. No. 129* and got exemption from the proceedings of the eviction. The operation of the restorative agencies came to a halt. As a result, the native tribals did not get any benefit of the restoration activity. The issue of this G.O. and subsequent inaction of the enforcement machinery made the tribals lose faith in the welfare intentions of the government. Thus disillusioned, the tribals fell an easy prey to the preaching of extremists. This paved the way for unrest in tribal areas, especially Adilabad district.

Indravelly Gond Uprising – 1981

This situation of crisis has been fully exploited by the extremists. Many of the Gond youth were drawn into the fold of extremists, the ultimate result being confrontation between the police and the tribal masses in 1981. The Gond Darbar held on 6 February 1981, at Keslapur declared that the problems of tribals had come to a boiling point. On April 20, 1981 a conference was planned by CPI (ML) at Indravelly. The meet was banned. Section 144 was imposed. Gonds from numerous villages started pouring in, as they were quite unaware of the situation prevailing in Indravelly. Gonds took out a procession, which came into conflict with police, resulting in loss of many a precious life. In the police firing, sixty persons were reported to have been killed on the spot. Observers have compared the massacre at Indravelly to the British suppression of demonstration at Jalianwala Bagh. Some of the steps taken by the government to mitigate the critical situation after Indravelly incident do not seem to win the confidence of the tribals. The Gond Development Council constituted with non-official Gond leaders appeared to be an eyewash to the tribals who viewed it with suspicion.

Forest Related Grievances

The strict enforcement of Forest Conservancy Laws restricted the movement of tribals into the forest, which was necessitated in the wake of their increase in population and pressure from non-tribal encroachers. Further, forest boundaries and revenue boundaries very often overlap each other. A patta given by the government in Revenue Department is objected to by the government Forest Department as the patta land boundaries overlap forest boundaries. One of the reasons for tension between tribal population and forest officials is the uncertainty about the status of considerable amount of such disputed land. Pattas issued by the Utnoor Tehasildar have not been recognized by the Forest Department. For years, cultivation on much of this disputed land was tolerated provided the tribal occupant bribed the forest guards. But in 1978, forest authorities started a campaign to evict tribals from such land and collected fines of ₹ 200 per acre on land on which cash crops had been sown. These fines were collected irrespective of whether there was any yield and economic position of the tribals fined. As this campaign coincided with the almost complete failure of crops, the inevitable result was that Gonds had to take loans from moneylenders. Even some lands held on patta long before 1940 have been included in the reserved forest during recent adjustments of forest lines. Gonds of Jamuldhara village in Utnoor taluk have been cultivating lands since 1942 and they have not been given permanent rights to the land. Forest Department is disputing the legality of their possession. In an appeal to the Magistrate's court, the Gonds won their case, but the Forest Department appealed to the High Court, and there too the decision went in favour of Gonds. However, no action was taken to legalize the possession of Gonds by granting of patta. Forest officials continued to threaten the Gonds with eviction. Another cause of tribal unrest is the continuous irritation of illegal fees collected by forest guards from the tribals. In Hyderabad State, there was a tax on ploughs. This tax was collected by Forest Department on the grounds that wood had been taken from the forest for making of ploughs. Though this tax was abolished as part of the liberalization of the government's policy, forest guards continued to extract annual fees from tribal cultivators. For each plough ₹ 40 was demanded from each household in addition to twenty-five kilograms of sorghum, twelve kilograms of red gram and ten kilograms of paddy. Those who did not have these grains had to buy them in order to satisfy forest guards' demands. Anyone who refuses to pay the illegal fees is certain to be harassed by the forest guards, who can prevent tribals from collecting even legally permitted forest produce and may charge the defaulter with forest offences which had never been committed. Much of the Gond's hard won cash had to be used to pay such illegal fees to forest subordinates.

Extreme economic distressed conditions prevailed in 1988. The drought of 1987, heavy rains in July and August 1987 and severe drought of 1988 hit the Gond economy one after the other. Even the wives of Gond Patels (heads of villages) had to sell away their silver ornaments of sentimental value in distress to purchase jowar. Condition of the landless tribals was much worse as their landlords became paupers. In response to the distressed conditions, a series of famine raids were organized by the extremists in which hundreds of tribals participated to loot shops and houses of landlords. From the loot, each family was reported to have been distributed one quintal of jowar, one kilogram of chillies and ₹ 20 for purchase of spices. Some traders were also said to have been forced, at the point of gun, to bring jowar from the market and distribute it, free of cost, to tribals. The much publicized government scheme of distribution of jowar at ₹ 1.25 per kg did not materialize till August 1989, i.e. till two years after its announcement in August 1987 by the then Chief Minister. A quick decision on this would have saved tribals from the rigorous famine. The extremists have fully utilized this lapse on part of the government. Tribals also started differentiating between these two schemes of jowar distribution. In the extremist's scheme, jowar was distributed free of cost and it was done at the time of need. The Government jowar had to be purchased by tribals and it came very late, i.e. months after tribals suffered very badly during famine. Tribals also questioned 'where from do we get money for purchasing jowar after a series of draughts and floods?' Forced by circumstances, the famine raids made the tribals willing participants in extremist movement. The tribals who participated in famine raids were arrested by police under anti-terrorist act which further widened the gap between the government and tribals. Land and life are synonyms for tribals living in Tribal Sub-Plan areas of the state. The transfer of land from tribal owner to a non-tribal is the major problem in tribal areas. The Andhra Pradesh Scheduled Areas Land Transfer Regulation, 1959, provides comprehensive protection to tribal land. Land alienation in scheduled areas continued unabated inspite of restriction on land transfer to non-tribals. To remove the persisting lacunae in the Land Transfer Regulation, it was amended by Regulation I of 1970. This new regulation placed absolute prohibition on transfer of immovable properties in Scheduled Areas to any person who is not a member of Scheduled Tribe. A Full Bench of Andhra Pradesh High Court in writ petition No. 4204/77 held that the Regulation I of 1970 had no retrospective operation and did not affect transfers made prior to the said regulation. This decision of the Full Bench of High Court significantly affected the implementation of Land Transfer Regulation in Telangana Region. The influential non-tribals continued their occupation of tribal lands by means of predating of land records. Several distortions have crept in during the implementation of Land Transfer Regulation Act. The names of tribals have been replaced with those of non-tribals through manipulation of land records and several protected tenants were not even registered in the Protected Tenants

Register and were denied benefits. Manipulation of land records, benami transfers, fictitious adoption of tribal children by non-tribals, concubinage (large areas of fertile lands were purchased by non-tribals and registered in the name of tribal women by keeping them as their own mistresses) and predating were some of the means adopted by non-tribals to circumvent Land Transfer Regulation, to retain their control over tribal land on large scale. The above-mentioned facts have generated unrest in the tribal areas of Adilabad, which witnessed revival of serious extremist activity.

References

Arnold, David and Murali Atluri, 'Sitaramaraju's Rebellion: A Response and a Rejoinder', *Social Scientist*, Vol. 13, No. 4, April 1985.

Arnold, David, 'Rebellious Hillman: The Gudem-Rampa Risings: 1839–1924', in Ranajit Guha (ed.), *Subaltem Studies 1*, OUP, New Delhi, 1982.

Atluri, Murali, 'Alluri Sitaramaraju and the Manyam Rebellion of 1922–24', *Social Scientist*, Vol. XII, No. 131, April 1984.

Bhowmick, P.K., 'Tribes in the Changing Circumstances of India', *Man in India*, Vol. 71, No. 1, 1991.

Fuchs, Stephen, *The Aboriginal Tribes of India*, Macmillan, New Delhi, 1973.

Furer-Haimendorf, C. Von, *Tribes of India: The Struggle for Survival*, OUP, New Delhi, 1998.

Government of Andhra Pradesh, *Contingency Plan to Wean Away Tribals from Extremist Activities in Tribal Areas*, Tribal Welfare Department, Hyderabad, 1981.

——, *Government Orders and Instructions on Tribal Development of Andhra Pradesh*, Vol. II, Tribal Welfare Department, Hyderabad, 1983.

——, *Scheduled Tribes and Social Justice*, Andhra Pradesh Judicial Academy, Secunderabad, 1996.

——, *Tribal Welfare in Andhra Pradesh: An Appraisal*, Tribal Welfare Department, Hyderabad, 1986, p. 32.

Government of Madras, Board of Revenue (Land Revenue Forests), Proceedings, Forest No. 48, dated 25 April 1917.

——, Development Department, G.O. No. 1634, dated 6 December 1922.

——, Proceedings of Chief Conservator of Forests, Proceedings No. 321 (Press), dated 15 July 1932.

——, Revenue (Special Department), G.O. No. 2293, dated 11 December 1919.

Guha, Ramachandra and Madhav Gadgil, 'State Forestry and Conflict in British India', *Past and Present*, Vol. 123, No. (1), 1989.

Keyes, Charles F., 'Peasant Strategies in Asian Societies: Moral and Rational Economic Approaches - A Symposium', *Journal of Asian Studies*, Vol. XLII, No. 4, August 1983.

Kingston-Mann, Ester, *Lenin and the Problem of Marxist Peasant Revolution*, OUP, New York, 1983.

Kosambi, D.D., *The Culture and Civilization of Ancient India in Historical Outline*, Vikas Publishing House, New Delhi, 1976.

Lewis, John W. and Kathleen J. Harford, *Peasant Rebellion and Communist Revolution in Asia*, University Press, Stanford, 1974.

Mangamma, J., *Alluri Sitaramaraju*, A.P. State Archives, Hyderabad, 1983.

Mishra, Kamal K., 'National Forest Policy and Tribal Development', in R.N. Pati and B. Jena (eds), *Tribal Development in India*, Ashish Publishing House, New Delhi, 1989.

Mouli, Chandra, 'Socio-Economic Changes in the Tribes of Andhra Pradesh', in M.K. Chaudhri (eds), *Trends of Socio-economic Change in India, 1871–1961*, Indian Institute of Advanced Study, Simla, 1969.

Pathy, Jagannath, 'Social Basis of Banditry and the Criminal Tribes Act', *Social Science Probings*, Vol. 1, No. 4, 1989.

Prakash Reddy, G., *Politics of Tribal Exploitation*, Mittal Publications, Delhi, 1987, p. 59.

Prasad Rao, D.L. and P. Venkata Rao, 'Cooperatives in Tribal Areas', *Tamil Nadu Journal of Cooperation*, Vol. 75, No. 3, 1983.

Prasad Rao, D.L., 'Shahukars and Tribal Society', *Tribe*, Vol. 8, No. 3–4, 1971–72.

Rader, Melvin, *Marx's Interpretation of History*, OUP, New York, 1979.

Raghavaiah, V., 'Tribal Unrest in Andhra Pradesh', in A.R. Desai (ed.), *Peasant Struggles in India*, OUP, Bombay, 1979, pp. 174–78.

——, *Tribal Revolts*, Andhra Rashtra Adimjati Sevak Sangh, Nellore, 1971.

Ramaiah, P., *Tribal Economy of India: A Case Study of Koyas of A.P.*, Light and Life Publishers, New Delhi, 1981.

Rangaiah, M. Venkata, *The Freedom Struggle in Andhra Pradesh*, Vol. I, Government Central Press, Hyderabad, 1965.

Rangarajan, Mahesh, 'Imperial Agendas and India's Forests: The Early History of Indian Forestry, 1800–1878', *Indian Economic and Social History Review*, Vol. 31, No. 2, 1994.

Rao, P. Venkata, *Dimensions of Transformation in Tribal Societies with Reference to Andhra Pradesh*, Sarup & Sons, New Delhi, 2004.

——, *Tribal Development: Policy and Practice*, Sarup & Sons, New Delhi, 2001.

Rao, P.R., *History of Modern Andhra*, Sterling Publishers, New Delhi, 1983.

Reddy, M.P.R., *Peasant and State in Modern Andhra History*, Clio Book Club, Kavali, 1986.

Reddy, V.R.K., 'A Critique on Tribal Life in Hyderabad State 1901–1954', *Itihas*, Vol. 15, No. 1, 1989.

Sarkar, Sumit, *Popular Movements and Middle-Class Leadership in Late Colonial India: Perspectives and Problems of a History from Below*, K.P. Bagchi and Co., Calcutta, 1980.

Sastry, M.S.K., *Agency Laws in Andhra Pradesh*, Asia Law House, Hyderabad, 1994.

Singh, Sangeetha et al., 'Subaltern Studies II: A Review Article', *Social Scientist*, No. 137, October 1984.

Stokes, Eric, *Peasant and the Raj*, Vikas Publishing House, New Delhi, 1978.

The Hindu, Magazine, 'Displaced Development', Saturday, 8 June 2006.

Verma, R.C., *Indian Tribes through the Ages*, Publication Division, New Delhi, 1990.

3

Anthropological Work in Hyderabad and Farhabad Hills

A Study of Chenchus

Scope of the Study

Anthropological investigations in Hyderabad were started in 1931. It was carried out in Hyderabad on the basis of archaeological remains and aboriginal races found in the hilly regions within the state. Hyderabad State occupied an important position with regard to racial anthropology of India. Many key answers to the tangled questions of racial history of South India were sought here from the living population and the skeletal remains spread over the entire state. Anthropological work in the state began with the study of living aboriginal population of Chenchus, who originally inhabited the Farhabad Hills. The then Nizam, Usman Nawab Ali Khan provided all the support for conducting research in the state. Ghulam Ahmad Khan was appointed as the census commissioner who extended active cooperation to anthropologists. The chief objective of the chapter is to study how anthropological work had critical observations with regard to the tribal community (Chenchus), their indigenous knowledge practices, domestic life, housing patterns, social organisation, etc.

I

Chenchus of Hyderabad and Farhabad Hills

Chenchus of Hyderabad State are one of the aboriginal races in India. They lived in the Farhabad Hills of the state. They were undoubtedly the branch of the Chenchus of the neighbouring Nallamalai Hills. The Hyderabad State and Nallamalai Hills were linked by the Krishna River. Chenchus drifted away from the main stock at an early period due to the floods of Krishna River. There are no authentic records to state when the separation of Chenchus of Hyderabad State took place. However, there was sufficient evidence to prove that separation and isolation took place due to the Farhabad Hills. The hills undoubtedly helped in providing safe shelter for many of the primitive tribes. Chenchus lived in small *pentas*, where *pentas* are called cluster of huts. The 1931 census report stated that there were a total number of 33 *pentas* with a rough population of over 2,000 people. Male population used to move about in jungles in search of food and odd jobs. Each *penta* consisted of a few individuals. Anthropologists had their first survey in Farhabad and Vettul Palin *paraganas* and collected measurements of Chenchu population.

The number of individuals measured was very small. The mean measurement of Chenchus inhabiting Farhabad Hills was 1649±9.23. Head was long and face was generally narrow. The mean auricular height was 120.48±0.85. Chenchus possessed a rather rounded appearance to the face. Skin colour varied from dark chocolate brown to black (ranging from no. 23 to 33 in Von Lusehan's scale). Colour of hair was black and most often it was curly. Chenchus possessed plentiful of hair on their heads. Colour of eyes varied from black to dark brown (86.96%). Compared with the other aboriginal tribes of Southern and Central India (for example the Kadars, the Nace Malayans of the Cochin Hills and the Bhils of Central India), Chenchus had close relationship with South India. There was a definite Negrito strain among the Kadars which had entered into other aboriginal tribes, now found in the hills of Central and Southern India. To what extent this type forms the general substratum of the aboriginal population of India is very difficult to say. Chenchus were considered as the lowest category among the aboriginals of Madras province along with Waddars. They formed into a group comprising 10 to 40 families. They wandered about the tracts for a few square miles forming the beat, gathering honey and berries and digging roots in the hills.

II

Biological Parameters

The anthropological team, while studying primitive characteristic features of Chenchus classified them under that group which was then called in the language of racial anthropology, *Astrologic*, the name given to the aborigines of Australia, in whom the characteristic traits were found in a specially marked form. They had a short stature, dark complexion and long head with prominent eyebrows and broad nose with a depressed root. The hair varies from wavy to curly but was never frizzy or woolly as was so often mistaken. Among the Australians the vault of the skull was often raised into a keel form, but among the aborigines of Ceylon (now Sri Lanka) and India this was usually absent. The racial element was dominant among these people. They linked their racial elements with the aboriginals of Australia, Sri Lanka and the Island chains of Indonesia and Melanesia. Their hair, their colour, the abundance of sweat glands in their skins showed their adaptation to tropical conditions.

Chenchus on the banks of river Krishna, the Gonds in the region of Bastar and the central provinces and Santhals of Chotanagpur were all found on the east of 76° longitudes. Lower western coast of India was occupied by comparatively poorer people of the Mediterranean race, and that Central and South Eastern India contain a good mixture of aboriginal blood, hinting at a series of persuasions the aborigines had to make along the line of safety and seclusion. The Mediterraneans, perhaps, in their first advent mixed with the aborigines probably on equal terms and thus we find sporadic sprinkling of regular features amongst the aborigines here and there. Later on the same people who developed higher forms of culture began to press the older people (aboriginals) making them flee to the South, to the lands which had equable climatic conditions. Seligman thought that the presence of skulls of Australians in Java was a strong proof of the link between India and Australia.

Physique of persons living in higher altitudes was distinctly superior to that of their fraternity in the lower regions, who were comparatively short in stature and emaciated. Handsomeness, as we understand it was known and men grew their hair and dressed it in a knot either at the back or on the upper left head. They did not comb their hair but pruned it with fingers and the falling hair was scrupulously collected, plaited and wound round the knot. The barber's razor of Sheffield make had found its way into the huts and was liberally used for mowing down beards. Baldness among men or women was unknown among the primitive people. Women grew their hair which was neither cut nor combed. Women's hair was generally short and curly. Men's garment was a strip of cloth about three to six inches wide and 30 inches long. It was an abbreviated *langoti*, passed between thighs and the ends thereof were held to the waist covering nakedness by a plant fibre. If the piece was longer, the extra length was left to flap about behind. It was the ceremonial dress and was certainly a distinct advance on the teak leaves. Occasional visitors to the hills distributed country *dhotis* but men did not use them. *Dhotis* were slung over the shoulder when standing and put under the buttocks when sitting. The top over edge of the left ear was bored and a few wore a brass ring with a bead in the centre. Men used to wear a waistband of a double piece of hide, crudely cut from goat's skin and sewn together. They often carry in this flint stones and also stick knives into it. Chenchu women's original dress was a two-piece costume of broad teak leaves held round the waist by means of fibre. A *choli* for the upper part of the body completed their dress. Chenchu women did not know the use of thread and needle. They were often scantily clad like the other poor women of the depressed classes. Several strings of beads adorn necks: one worn in childhood, another at the time of puberty and a third of two or three rows at marriage. They were taken off only when a woman became a widow. Before the advent of beads they collected half-dried *polka* seeds and pierced them with a thorn and when dry, stung them into two or three rows and wore them round the neck. Glass bracelets were worn by women. Absence of them was a sign of widowhood.

Nature, Behaviour and Domestic Routines

Chenchus were noted for their truthfulness and honesty. They speak truth and show their honesty with people whosoever they come across. If they commit a crime they always plead guilty. They were very kind and hospitable to their visitors. In every Chenchu village a guest house was built by the Forest Department officers. Chenchus compromise in their attitude towards wrong-doers. They bow their head to their chief. Chenchus have no idea of indigenous medicines. They were amenable to the treatment of others. They had a strong efficacy of drugs to be administered for various ailments. Chenchus were fleet footed. Though they were poorly fed, they had extraordinary physical endurance. They carried heavy head loads on their head. They also negotiate steep and narrow gradients with greater care and facility. Chenchus cannot bear cold weather. They were always half clad and sat by the fire side to warm themselves. They imagine that rest of the world was much colder than their surroundings. Chenchu women were dutiful wives. They always aspire to do something for civilization. In the absence of their males, Chenchu women would not go beyond the limits of their surrounding villages. When urgently required, they take an elderly woman for company or her husband's relative to accompany her. Polygamy or pluralities of wives were prevalent among them. They easily accepted such a practice. Bickering and quarrels take place during this occasion. Chenchu woman who was not tolerant to the prevalence of the other wife was at liberty to quit home with her children. Children were well looked after by Chenchus. They chastise their siblings for naughtiness.

Dwellings and Details

Site of the Chenchu *Pentas* was usually on a plateau. They did not call their *Penta* as village. *Pentas* were a mere cluster of huts bearing none of the features of Indian villages. *Pentas* evolved after a series of incursions of different races. The names of *Pentas* were not given by them. Some of the names of their villages were like Vitteval Palli Penta, Mallapuram Penta, Tapsi Penta, etc. These were the names assigned by them to the forest clearings for settlements. For example, Tapsi Penta was a spot well noted for *topsi-toe* (Chenchu hamlet). Puli Chalma Penta was the name of a *Penta* given by the Chenchus. Puli means tiger and Chalma means a pond. Communication between the *Pentas* was occasionally by the names of paths across the jungle where they were spotted. Chenchus were deprived by rains, grass and vegetation during winter season. The connectivity of houses of the Chenchus is normally a furlong away from the *Penta*. Their graves were named by earth mounds overlaid with stones. Normally, Chenchu villages were surrounded by rubbish heap and often remained unhygienic.

Normally, there was only one type of hut found in a *Penta*. A well seasoned piece of wood, six cubits long and twelve inches of circumference at the bottom would be planted. With a split bamboo or some plant fibre, three cubits in length, a circle would be drawn round the pole from its base and sufficiently long to go round the circle would be fixed and secured to the ground by means of plugs. From the top of the central post, bamboo rafters would be laid to rest on the mat wall, and with similar material the framework of the conical roof would be completed and covered with thatch. Entrance to the hut would be obtained by the rectangular opening, about two cubits high and three feet wide. Doorway of the hut may not open towards the west. A smaller hut was exactly half the size in all respects. The mat wall was mud-plastered. Within the hut, a hearth of stones would be made and household utensils such as cooking and waste pots, baskets, winnowers were kept on the left, the right half of the hut space being reserved for sitting and sleeping. Bows and arrows and muzzle-loading guns were struck into the roof from inside the hut. Halfway up the roof they had a shelf of bamboo mat.

Weapons, Fire and Manufacturing

Weapons of the warfare among Chenchus were bows and arrows. Chenchus only used them for their self-defence. The stave was of a single piece of wood. It was cut, trimmed and shaped with notches at both ends. The string was made of the fibre of a plant. Fibre was cleaned, dried and twisted into a cord and greased. Centre of the cord, where the arrow was placed, was bound with leather. The arrow was of bamboo. The butt-end of arrow was plain. When not in use, the string of the bow was released from the top notch. Iron-tipped arrows were also used for shooting wild animals, but no poison would be applied to the tip. Anthropological teams had stated that safety matches had not yet gone into the villages of Chenchus. However, it was observed by anthropologists that it was convenient for Chenchus to make fire in the old, time-honoured method with flints.

The best art or industry known to Chenchus was basket making. They split bamboo into slats and weaved in hill pattern and made into square and round boxes with lids. Winnowers were also made by them. Chenchus had no musical instruments of their own. They used a three-stringed instrument which was copied from one used by a wandering mendicant. Three well ripened fruits, round in size were scooped out and the shells were dried. Two of them were of smaller size than the third one. They were fixed to a hollow bamboo, three feet in length and the larger one between the smaller ones. Three key-holes were cut at the other end of the bamboo and keys inserted. Brass strings were supported on a bridge as in a violin. The instrument was held in the left hand and with the middle finger of the right hand strings were jerked to vibrate.

III

Agriculture, Livestock and Food Habits

Chenchus rarely till land. They were devoid of the human instinct to grow their food on the soil. They were timid to approach bullocks and did not know how to handle the plough. They rent their agricultural implements to other labourers. The soil they select for agricultural purpose naturally would be virgin and good for raising crops. They do not have the desire for owning much land and privation had grown very much among the Chenchus. Cattle of Chenchus consist of buffaloes, not their own but belonging to graziers, left in their charge for some time. They rear goats and chickens. Dogs are their pet animals. Names they used to give to their dogs are *Laddu* and *Pappy*. They borrowed these two names from Banjaras. One is distinguished from the other through its colour. *Nalla Pappy* means black dog and *Tella Pappy* means white dog. They cut and eat cats. Therefore, the existence of cats in their village is rather scarce.

Food of the Chenchus consists of roots (*gaddalu*). Herbs and fungi were also eaten by them. These roots are: *Noola gadda, Chenchu gadda, Vellaru gadda, Pedda dajira, boda-gadda, ajavla gadda and orra gadda*. The berries included in their food are *Chinta pandu* (tamarind), *Nimmi pandu* (neem fruit), *Ippa pandu* (Mohwa), *Tumki pandu, Tui pandu, Medi pandu* and *Mirli pandu*. Tamarind fruit is eaten mixed with ashes obtained from burning the bark of the same tree. Mohwa flower was boiled and eaten. No salt would be added to the cooked food, whether of roots, fruits or Jawar. Pumpkins were cut into large pieces and boiled and eaten without salt. Chenchus appreciate salt but they find it difficult to purchase it. They eat animal flesh whenever available to them. They also eat animal skin after the hair had been removed from the skin. Small birds, squirrels, rats and mice are roasted and eaten by them. Chenchus collect Mohwa flower. They drink *Ippa Sara,* a processed drink. The only narcotics generally used by Chenchus is tobacco. It would be obtained by bartering honey or other minor forest produce. They retain it for a long time, chew the juice of it and spit it out after keeping it in their mouth for a long time.

Dance

Generally, Chenchus are in an intoxicated state during the festive occasions and marriage ceremonies. Men and women dance to the beating of a circular drum. A satisfactory description of the dance was a difficult process. Their dance tunes were very suggestive of the Savara tunes and one or two approached a jig or reel in time, as by Savaras and Khonds, a hide-gong was used. The dance of women suggests more that of the Porajas, but they had another dance in which they sing and clap their hands in time, clapping their palms against the palm of each neighbour. Women take the upper part of their sari and hold the wide ends in the hand and dance. The nature of their song was to adore and worship their ancestors and natural things.

IV

Lifestyle of Chenchus

The daily life of Chenchus was a very uncertain one. They used to get up early in morning and go off to the jungle in search of roots and berries for the family. Women sweep the floor and cook food and bring water. Young children cling to their mothers at home while the grown-ups were busy doing odd jobs. Before noon, men return home and were served with food. After them, women and children eat. Thereafter, elders collect together and discuss matters of common interest. Chenchus rise in the morning and do their work. They were comfortable with whatever they get. Bathing and washing of clothes was very rare phenomena among Chenchus. If they went out to any place in the afternoon they came back before sunset for fear of wild animals. They sit around the hearth, eat, drink and sleep. Chenchus could said to be an organized body, so far as compatible with their primitive culture. If the *penta* was the unit of organization it was interesting to note that it was not inhabited by one particular sect or 'Kulam' to the exclusion of all others. Except in matter of choosing a wife, there was no occasion for accentuating clan feelings.

Exogamy

Chenchus were divided into: *Nimalus, Thokalu, Erravulu, Sigilu* and *Maindlu.* The origin of Kulam was a matter of conjecture. Various accounts were heard but one was not without interest. *Thokalu* in Telugu means tail. A person who was fond of eating tail in preference to another piece of flesh and whenever an animal was slaughtered they cut the tail and reserved it for that man, saying this was for *thokaluvadu* (tail man). His offsprings were called *thokaluvandlu.* Another version was that the name had been taken from the squirrel, which in these regions was reddish-brown in colour and as large as a rabbit in size with a big bushy tail. This variety was called the Malabar squirrel. *Nimalu* was the name given to the class of Chenchus who happen to live in a lime grove. The man who relished some red roots more than any other variety came to be called *Erravulu* or perhaps it may have a remote reference to the Mediterranean man, as all fair people were generally called red by the primitives. *Siggilu* was presumably a corruption of *Sigiri,* tender edible leaves of the tamarind tree. *Maindlu's* origin was obscure and worth investigating. One assumption was that, this sect was regarded as the most respected one and it had remained pure from contact with other people. '*Munda*' means head. However, their origin was uncertain. It has been assumed that there was some form of totemism since most of them trace their clan formation to animals and trees. The five groups of Chenchus were exogamous. *Thokalus* and *Erravalus* were regarded to be relatives. Similarly, *Nimalus, Siggilus* and *Maindlus* relate with each other as brothers and sisters. These two groups, therefore, intermarry. A Chenchu, whichever sect he/she may belong to may not marry any but the daughter of his maternal uncle or that of his paternal aunt. If internally a man married a woman of his own totem he was charged with incest, outcasted and banished from the limits of the colony. Relationship through female line was seldom recognized as Chenchu society was patriarchal in nature. Strictly speaking, Chenchus were not monogamists. The chief or those who had the means, marries two wives. On the ground of barrenness or sterility on the part of a wife, or even on the excuse of incompatibility of temperament, a Chenchu takes a second woman. A brother's widow, if she was willing, was taken over by the younger or elder brother.

Property Relations

Property of Chenchus consists of a hut, earthen utensils, crude implements, mats and baskets. To this list, chickens may also be added. They also possessed goats. On the death of a man, his first son inherits property. If the widow was childless, property of the deceased goes to the first brother of the deceased, if the deceased had no brother, his sister claims it. If none at all, the nearest relatives and people of the *Penta* distribute the belongings among themselves. No case of adoption was known to Chenchus in the olden days. A settlement of disputes was made by the headmen after they had heard the case in a

Panchayat of elders. Oath was generally taken on heaven (*Akasa Amma*) and earth (*Bhoomi Amma*). More reliance was placed on the evidence tendered on oath taken on trees such as Mohwa and Tamarind, which provide witness with food. It may be interesting to mention that the most sacred oath with the Gond was on the tiger-skin and Bhils took oath on the dog. He who commits a breach of the settlement will be fined and the money and material collected in the name of fine would be eaten by the 'panch'. The fine was realized by way of Mohwa flower and liquor.

Position of Women

Chenchu girl lived in the house of her parents until her marriage. Chenchu woman before puberty enjoy as much freedom of movement as boys of that age, but after that she was looked after and protected. Seduction of an unmarried girl against her wishes for immoral purposes was an offence punishable with a fine and a compulsion to marry the girl. There was no betrothal ceremony, but the girls' consent was first obtained. Divorced women may marry again. A woman was also at liberty to give up her husband, whose affection or attention, she had reason to believe, had been diverted to another woman.

V

Religious and Social Customs

Chenchus are known as animists. They also have beliefs in deities. Their deities have definite names, characteristics and functions. The principal deities of Chenchus were: *Akasa Amma* (sky goddess), *Bhoomi Amma* (earth goddess) and *Amma Talli* (smallpox goddess). They usually worship the sky goddess which they believe as supreme goddess. They also worship *'Lingam'* which was represented by a piece of stone or wood. They worship the sun. Appearance of the soul of a deceased person in any form was incredible to the Chenchus. They wash the dead body in sitting posture so that the water may wet both sides. Otherwise the spirit would return home.

Puberty

In the case of a boy, the change of voice was the first indication. He was seen flirting with the girl of his age. Appearance of moustache was a sure evidence of his attaining manhood. In the case of a girl, she was secluded in a hut specially erected for her. An old woman attends upon her. Both were unclean for 3 or 4 days. The girl then will be bathed and her soiled linen will be buried. Otherwise, it would be washed and dried for further use. The girl after bath will be given a piece of clean cloth and a bodice and her forehead will be marked with yellow powder which was supplied by graziers. No ceremony will be performed on that occasion. Such grown-up girls sleep in their own hut but away from their parents. Boys either sleep in a corner of the same hut or with friends of their age elsewhere. But no separate dormitories or halls exist for them.

Marriage

If a girl has attained womanhood, it will not be published in any manner but through her parents and relatives the news goes from one mouth to another. A lad, who was in the know of things, approaches his mother with a desire to marry the girl. The mother informs the father, both the father and the mother then set out to the girl's home. Preliminary enquiries would be made – first through an old woman who acts as an intermediary. Then the mother of boy speaks to the mother of girl and the father to the father. The consent of girl will also be obtained. If everything goes well, a date will be fixed for the marriage. Chenchus were extraordinarily ignorant of time and distance. The fixing of a day was, therefore, not significant. It means the lapse of a few days and nights. If the bride belongs to another *penta*, a messenger will be sent there in advance to inform them of the bridegroom's arrival. Parents of the boy with their relatives and friends, headed by drummer, set out carrying a load of Mohwa flower and liquor. On sighting the *penta* the drummer beats the drum and the bride's party from that *penta* comes forth to meet the guests and the bridegroom. They exchange greetings, eat, drink and dance. They next proceed to the *penta* and spend their night. Soon after the sunrise all collect together and the bride's parents provide a feast of Mohwa flower, roots and liquor. The girl would be given, by the lad, a piece of cloth, a bodice and also some strings of beads which she wears. The guests eat, drink and dance. Father of the girl then turns to the bridegroom and tells him to look after his daughter kindly and well. This would all be the marriage ceremony and no priest would be employed to perform any rite. As a matter of fact, the priest does not exist in the Chenchu society. The party then sets out on the return journey at noon. The girl resides with her mother-in-law, till a separate hut was created for the new couple. Until then the bridegroom sleeps elsewhere. In the day time, however, the young man takes his wife to the jungle where they may cohabit.

Childbirth

As soon as pain begins the Chenchu males move out of the hut and the old women of *penta* were called in to assist the labouring women. Utensils and other articles were collected in one part of the hut allowing the other half of the space for lying in. The expectant mother was made to squat with her legs propped up. A large stone will be placed to support her back. She was held by the shoulders by another woman. An experienced woman sits in front of the pregnant woman and renders her timely assistance. The baby would be washed and laid beside mother. Should the mother die in the childbirth, she would be taken out quickly and buried and the child, if alive, will be given to another woman for feeding milk. The period of confinement would be six to seven days. Both the midwife and other women were considered to be unclean. Their meal was served at the doorway. Their vessels were not touched by others. On the seventh day, the woman was given a bath and the stained clothes would be washed and dried. The midwife in the meantime sweeps the floor and plasters it with mud, and then takes her to bathe. She would be cleaned later and goes out to call the husband to come inside the house. Naming of the child will take place after 10–12 days. Parents choose the name themselves for the child. No ceremony would be held for the naming ceremony. The common names among Chenchus were Lingadu, Biyadu, and Guravadu. These are all the principal names kept for the males. Lingamma, Guruvamma and Idamma were the names given to females. Most of these names were derived from their goddesses. The mother feeds the child for one or two years or till another child is born.

VI

Anthropological Work at Farhabad Hills

Anthropological work among Chenchus was started first with a marriage that the Chenchus followed in Farhabad hills in Deccan. The team of anthropologists had visited their abode by foot. Chenchus family made all arrangements for the wedding. The age of the male for the marriage among them was counted with the summers; say 18 summers mean 18 years. The marriage of the Pedda Guravadu, who was working as a *chowkidar* informed about the marriage of the primitive Chenchus near Farhabad hills and took the anthropological team for the study. There was a touch of animism, superstition in the whole marriage. Guravadu was the chief of Puli Chalma Penta. He was appointed as the caretaker of the forest bungalow at Farhabad. By sect all the Chenchus were Tokalu. The bridegroom was his son named Cinna Guravadu. Peda Guravadu in the capacity of a chowkidar of the bungalow had come in contact with the officials of the anthropological department and had learnt some tactics generally employed by subordinates.

Anthropologists had observed and stated that it was customary for the Chenchu host to invite not only the relatives of the uniting but also the headman of the adjoining *pentas*. All of them came to the marriage. The chief of the Mannanur *penta* found his way up the hill. He came along with 500 Chenchus along with his drums and graced the occasion. Starting around 10 o'clock in the night, the procession reached Farhabad in the morning around 6 o'clock. The drum sounded in the stillness of the forest. The quaint signal of the drum was heard by the anthropological team many miles away. Guests began to pour into the *penta* and assembled under the shady *Mohwa* trees. They had brought liquor in large pots along with them.

Chenchus celebrate marriages according to ritualistic practices. The bride and the bridegroom will be given a bath and were liberally adorned with vermilion paste on their foreheads and the ends of their clothes with turmeric. Mothers of both the parties stood by the side of their respective children and the other elderly women and children formed into a procession. By common consent the marriage knot will be tied by Guravadu taking the ends of the sari and dhoti. A long and wide piece of cloth canopy was made and the procession started from the hut to the Mohwa tree, by the band and a party of dancers. Under the tree was seated Bayyadu, the grand old man of the Chenchus, much revered for his age and experience. Guravadu and Lingadu came up and touched his feet, retracted their steps and danced.

While the couple was being bathed and dressed a few men prepared food for the feast. Coarse rice together with a quantity of dal, chillies and salt was barely adequate for thirty adults and as many children. With the process of cooking rice they were not acquainted, but it had gone to their entire satisfaction. They had arranged to kill a sheep for the feast. The sheep had been conveyed from a distance of 14 miles. Bayyadu was the first person to get his share. But he did not appear to be pleased. He seemed to say, 'liquor first, and food next'. The first glass was handed to him and he got spirited. He broke silence and cracked jokes and uttered a series of popular sayings that amused the people. The first spark of wisdom which escaped his mouth was '*mamidi chakalu iste mata ragaladu*' meaning that if you give mango bark, speech will come. Apparently, he meant that anything sweet, even if it be the rind of a mango, will unmuzzle wit. This was his subtle reference to liquor. He repeatedly referred to *Dilli* (Delhi), the present seat of the government of India, wherefrom he said, *Pedda Sarkar* came. Of the geographical situation of the city he had, of course, no idea, but he constantly affirmed his faith in its existence somewhere within the reach. 'Is not all the earth one'? he questioned. Evidently, he had recalled the stories handed down to him by his forefathers of the incessant wars and skirmishes, as a result of which the Chenchu tribe had been driven into the impenetrable forests and hilly regions. On being asked what festivals they usually celebrated, the old man promptly answered *'Udu Chettu Puste Ugadi Vachinte'* which means if udu plant blossoms with flowers, Ugadi festival had arrived. Chenchus had no idea of time but their contact with people in the plains, the Telugu New Year day has come to be known as a festival and the advent of it is determined by the flowering of the Udu tree. It was a day of rejoicing, not for the beauty of the nature but for the prospect of a good supply of flowers and fruits on which they subsist. Another significant saying of theirs was *'Chitapuli Vaste Sivaratri'* meaning that if a leopard comes, it is Siva's night. Siva is a god of destruction and it was to propitiate him that Lingam was being worshipped by Chenchus. So then, if by chance one night a leopard prowled about the *penta*, that night was said to be Siva's night.

If a man was fatally ill, they gather a bamboo post, some dry grass and plant fibre. After he had breathed his last, the body was brought out, propped up and washed by a group of men. The upper garment which he had, was taken away by the brother or a near relative and the body was laid down on the grass. A bamboo post was placed on the body and wrapped and tied up. Two men carried the body on their shoulders to the graveyard. Then they dug the grave, about three feet deep and about the length of the body, running east to west, untie the bundle, draw off the bamboo post and the body was lowered. It was laid on the stomach, head towards the West, face turned to the right and the palms of the hands turned upwards. The position of the body in the grave as laid on the stomach was unique and the anthropologists' team remarked that 'we have never found any other people burying their dead in that manner'. The *langoti* was then drawn off and kept near the feet. The grave was then filled with earth, and stones were then heaped over it. When leaving the grave, Chenchus walked round the grave once and departed from the foot end of the grave. In case of women, Chenchus observed mourning for 3 to 7 days.

Later, the anthropological team observed their language. They reported that Chenchus speak Telugu with a peculiar intonation. They also mix Urdu words with their language. Almost all Chenchus speak their language. They do not know other languages. Females speak Chenchu language more perfectly than the males. The city of Hyderabad reserved to itself all the Spanish, French and the German speaking people. Gulbarga had furnished sufficient attraction to the Turks and Raichur and Linsugur to the Italians. The Portuguese in Hyderabad, Aurangabad, Warangal and Gulbarga do not show any influence on Chenchu population. The English speaking population inhabited all the districts of Hyderabad state except among the Chenchus in Sirpur-Tandur where the majority of Chenchus survived. The anthropological team also mentioned about the gipsy and Bhil dialects. Some primitive people in Farhabad hills used to speak the Gipsy dialects. These dialects were the vehicle of the thought of tribes of the vagrants inhabited in Farhabad hills and the surrounding hilly regions. The linguistic survey had associated their studies and research work with the anthropologists of Anthropological Survey. The Linguistic Survey of India had obtained and corelated their studies and findings with regard to the gypsy tribal categories. They had opined that the Bhili dialects were a corrupt form of Gujarati. They were uncertain about the Gypsies, whether they were original Aryan race or the Dravidian linguistic group. The Gipsy languages, a majority of dialects were of Dravidian origin and appear to be a corrupt form of some of the vernacular, northern and southern languages. These languages returned as Hindi-Gipsy languages.

VII

Current Developments

Acculturation is a key process which can encompass all other processes with regard to change among the Chenchus. Their territorial categorization depends not only on ecological setting or geographical location, but equally on the extent of culture contact. The phenomenon of their change could be explained through several aspects: migration, displacement and rehabilitation, crystallization of religion, administration and administrative agencies, Naxalite movement, merchants, etc. These variables have a common thread, that is, acculturation. However, it can be said that acculturation is a gradual process among the Chenchus. This may be due to the value orientation of the present-day Chenchu society. In this context, it is apt to understand Redfield, who said that in the absence of money economy, isolated, homogeneous societies tend to have well-organized cultures and to be sacred and collectivistic. The idea of *well-organized* seems to be relative but *to be sacred and collectivistic* seems to be apt in the context of Chenchu community also.

Belief in the idea of *superiority of culture* and its *sacredness* might be hurdles in the process of acculturation and its protection is the *collective responsibility* of the people. This can be understood from their stories of origin. However, continuous and intensive contacts are paving the way for acculturation of the Chenchus. It happens in several phases. For instance, the acculturation of elite happens in the first phase followed by the acculturation of commoners close to multiethnic setting. It proceeds further into other territories either because of occasional contacts with the people of other cultures or with the people of their own community who are carrying elements of other cultures. As a whole, the transition of Chenchus has been influenced by two major factors: contact with other ethnic groups and change in the ecological setting. The process has given rise to diversity and creating ethnic subidentities or categorical identities within the community but not significantly altered the ethnic identity as a whole. But, it is difficult to forecast the consequences of an intensive acculturation if the entire community comes into contact with other ethnic groups. The categorical identities may crystallize; consequently, ethnic group may stratify or the entire group may reorient itself for an alternate identity. It is difficult to assume development of caste-like hierarchy in the case of Chenchus as observed among a few other tribal communities in India as well.

References

Avadhani, P.S.R. et al., *A Monograph on Chenchu, Census of India, A.P., Part V, Ethnographic Notes*, Manager of Publications, New Delhi, 1961.

Bhowmick, P.K., *Chenchus of the Forests and Plateau: A Hunting-Gathering Tribe in Transition*, Institute of Social Research and Applied Anthropology, Calcutta, 1989.

Blake, N.M., A. Ramesh, M. Vijayakumar and J.S. Murty, 'Genetic Studies on Chenchu Tribes of Andhra Pradesh', *Human Heredity*, Vol. 30, 1980, pp. 291–98.

Furer-Haimendorf, C. Von, *The Chenchus: Jungle Folk of the Deccan*, Macmillan and Co., London, 1943.

Government of India, *Census of India, Monograph Series, Part V, No. 4, The Chenchus, Ethnographic Study*, Manager of Publications, New Delhi, 1961.

——, *Special Tables for Scheduled Castes and Scheduled Tribes, Andhra Pradesh Series, Series 2, Part IX (1)*, Controller of Publications, New Delhi, 1981.

Gupta, P. and A. Basu, 'A Note on Somatology of the Chenchu', *Man in India*, Vol. 41, No. 2, 1961, pp. 129–38.

Jaya Rao, S.S., *Special Tables for Scheduled Tribes, Census of India, 1981, Andhra Pradesh, Part IX (III), Series 2*, Controller of Publications, New Delhi, 1988.

Khan, G.A., 'The Chenchus', in J.P. Mills et al. (eds), *Essays in Anthropology Presented to Roy Bahadur S.C. Roy*, Maxwell and Company, Lucknow, 1942, pp. 261–64.

Kumar, Vijaya S. and V. Reddy Narayana, 'Towards Tribal Development: A Case Study of the Chenchus in Andhra Pradesh', *Man and Life*, Vol. 14, No. 3–4, 1988, pp. 179–85.

Mohan Rao, K., *Socio-cultural Profile of Tribes of Andhra Pradesh: Hyderabad*, TCR&TI, Tribal Welfare Department, Government of Andhra Pradesh, 1993.

——, *Tribal Profile of Andhra Pradesh*, Tribal Cultural Research and Training Institute, Hyderabad, 1969.

Mukhopadhyay, Rajatsubhara, 'Dilemma of Tribal Transformation: The Case of Chenchus', *Vanyajati*, Vol. 1–2, 1984, pp. 81–92.

Pratap, D.R., *Tribes of Andhra Pradesh*, World Telugu Conference, Hyderabad, 1975.

Pratap, D.R., V.V. Ramana Rao and T. Aruna, *Fertility of Chenchu Women*, Tribal Cultural Research and Training Institute, Hyderabad, 1976.

Ramesh, A., N.M. Blake, M. Vijaya Kumar and J.S. Murthy, 'Genetic Studies on Chenchu Tribes of Andhra Pradesh, India', *Human Heredity*, Vol. 30, 1980, pp. 291–98.

Rao, P. Venkata, 'Aging in the Tribal Context: A Study of the Chenchu', in D.K. Behera and George Pfeffer (eds), *Contemporary Society: Tribal Studies*, Concept, New Delhi, 1999.

Reddy, A.P., M. Vinaya Kumar, K.C. Malhotra and B.N. Mukherjee, 'Genetic Relationship between the Chenchu, Irula and Yanadi: A Reassessment', *Journal of Indian Anthropological Society*, Vol. 18, No. 1, 1983, pp. 31–34.

Reddy, G.P., 'Introducing Agriculture in a Tribal Community: The Case of Chenchus', *Man and Life*, Vol. 1–2, No. 5, 1979, pp. 81–92.

——, 'The Role of Liquor in the Culture of the Tribes of Andhra Pradesh: Its Economic Implications', *Vanyajati*, Vol. 17, No. 2, 1961, pp. 37–45.

——, *The Chenchus: Ethnographical Note*, Office of the Registrar General of India, New Delhi, 1960.

Sastry, V.N.V.K., 'Chenchu Mallanna: Then and Now', in K. Timma Reddy (ed.), *Saivism*, Telugu University, Hyderabad, 1994.

Sirajuddin, S.M. and A. Basu, 'Population Structure, Consanguinity and Its Effect on Fertility and Mortality among Chenchus of Andhra Pradesh', *Human Science*, Vol. 33, 1984, pp. 179–200.

Sirajuddin, S.M., 'Blood Groups A1, A2, BO, MN, Rh (D), PTC and Colour Blindness Studies among Chenchus of Andhra Pradesh', *The Anthropologist*, Vol. 24, No. 1–2, 1977, pp. 14–20.

——, 'Reproduction and Consanguinity among Chenchus of Andhra Pradesh', *Man in India*, Vol. 64, No. 2, 1984, pp. 81–92.

——, *Human Biology of the Chenchus of Andhra Pradesh: A Demographic Study*, Ph.D. Thesis, Karnataka University, Dharwad, Karnataka, 1985.

Subbarama Raju, P., C. Sudhakar and C.H. Uma Mohan, 'Chenchus and Social Transformation: A Primitive Tribe in Kurnool District of Andhra Pradesh', *The Anthropologist*, Vol. 11, No. 3, 2009, pp. 167–72.

Subbarama Raju, P., R. Suguna Kumari and C. Sudhakar, 'Chenchus of Kurnool District: A Study in Social Organisation and Socio-economic Conditions', *Man and Life*, Vol. 32, No. 1–2, 2006, pp. 1–10.

Suryanarayan, M. and Gangadharam, *Chenchus and Development in India: Problems and Prospects*, Inter-India Publications, New Delhi, 1982, pp. 247–94.

Trivedi, G.M., *Linguistic Study of the Chenchus of Andhra Pradesh*, Anthropological Survey of India, Calcutta, 1978.

Varaprasad, G. and Gangadharam, 'Ethno-medicine and Herbal Treatment among the Chenchus: A Primitive Tribe of Andhra Pradesh', *Man and Life*, Vol. 32, No. 1–2, 2006, pp. 35–42.

Venkataramulu, K., *Tribal Development Policy: A Case Study of the Chenchus of Mahabubnagar District* (unpublished M.Phil. Dissertation), Department of Political Science, University of Hyderabad, Telangana, 1983.

Vittal, C.P., 'Socio-economic Transformation of a Primitive Tribal Group: A Study of Chenchus in Andhra Pradesh', *Man in India*, Vol. 72, No. 2, 1992, pp. 189–206.

4

Kolams and their Culture

I

Kolams are found in the tribal areas of Telangana and Maharashtra. In Telangana, they live in Adilabad district. Kolams' traditional habitat can be divided into three areas on the basis of geo-ethnic conditions. The first zone comprises Kolam settlements in Yetmal, Nanded and Chandrapur districts of Maharashtra and the second zone comprises taluks of Adilabad, Utnoor, Wankidi and Asifabad of Adilabad district. In these places Kolams retained much of their distinct way of life. The third zone comprises settlements which are established in the Telugu speaking areas where Kolams are called *manne* who are found in Sirpur, Chennur taluks of Adilabad district. Adilabad district is the traditional home of various tribal communities. As this is a border district, Telugu, Marathi, Hindi and Urdu speaking castes and communities and in addition to this, several tribal groups are found. Among them, Gonds usually considered Kolams as their *Pujaris.* They claim that they are the original inhabitants of these areas and their ancestors are priests to the Gonds. Gonds call them as *nayakars* as they manufacture baskets, and winnowing fans, etc. Kolams live in exclusive villages or hamlets of their own, leading a distinct way of life. There is a peculiar way of selecting a house-site for their habitation. On an auspicious day, the village priest places a small heap of jawar grain in the evening. Next morning, they go to the particular place and carefully examine the jawar grains. If this heap is found undisturbed, Kolams consider the place as auspicious and erect a stone in memory of the village deity called Nadiamma or Burriavva. Kolams' settlement is called Guda. Kolams always prefer their settlements to be very near to their paddy fields. Since they are very brave they do not fear to reside in the interior places. Another notable point which the Kolams observe is they do not have a fence, or hedge around their houses. The construction of a fence is a taboo for them. They draw a line on the four sides of a village by chanting mantras. This line is called Polakamma Geeta. They establish their settlements in the places convenient to podu cultivation. Once Kolams used to abandon their settlements after the death of a person as it was considered inauspicious and settled down in a new place. But this is now restricted due to the forest conservatory laws. The Kolams speak a dialect which is classified as a Dravidian language. It has no script. It has some forms of Telugu and Kannada languages and Kolamies stimulate Gondi dialect. Bhau Mandaokar opines that in Kolami roots of many words from Tamil, Telugu, Malayalam and Kannada languages were found and as such he hints that Kolami could be the aboriginal dialect which contains the original roots of these four languages. Col. Mackenzie is of the view that 'all their songs and ballads are borrowed from Marathas, even their workmen when grinding corn, sing Marathi songs'. The numerals and other words of Kolamis are:

English	***Kolami***
Numerals	
One	Okkon, Okkan
Two	Indig
Three	Muyyal
Four	Naling
Five	Pach, Ayda
Six	Saha
Seven	Sat
Eight	Aatha
Nine	Nav
Ten	Dah
Eleven	Akra
Fifteen	Pendara
Nineteen	Eakunis
Twenty One	Eakvis
Eighty	Ansi
Words denoting animals	
Rat	Elka
Camel	Lotti
Dog	Aate
Jackal	Kolyak
Crab	Ende

English	*Kolami*
Words denoting animals	
Deer	Gorya/Pot Gorya
Ass	Gaddi
Monkey	Mutha
Bandicoot	Ghusi
Cow	Kute
Musk-Rat	Shisudrak
Pig	Turre
He-Goat	Bokodyak
She-Goat	Meke
Heron	Beglyak
Panther	Bibtyak
He-Cat	Potpilli
Crocodile	Mosali
Horse	Gurram
Words denoting plants	
Cotton	Karve
Chironjee	Shire Mak
Tamarind	Sitta
Jamun	Jamre
Toddy Palm	Shindibonda, Tadamak
Papaya	Popoyi
Palas	Modgumak
Pipal	Ravi
Mahua	Hirip
Lemon	Nimbu
Words denoting colour	
Black	Dondak
Red	Lal
White	Telmi/Yerodi
Yellow	Pisudi
Blue	Tevvak
Pale Green	Hirvat

English	***Kolami***
Words denoting parts of body	
Head	Tal Tye Kan
Nose	Mungad/Sudi Bogga
Ear	Kev
Lip	Pedawe
Cheeks	Pukli
Throat	Dodar
Hand	Kiya
Leg	Getta/Kal
Finger	Vende
Stomach	Potta
Thumb	Angthe
Small Finger	Sir-Vende
Forehead	Kapar
Waist	Tikane
Hair	Tir
Mouth	Moti
Palm	Tara
Shoulder	Buiam/Satta
Knee	Tonge
Tongue	Nalka
Words denoting relationship	
Mother	Amma/Takama
Step Mother	Napa Amma
Father	Tak
Brother	Ban
Sister	Tondari
Father's elder brother	Don Ban
Mother's elder sister	Debek
Grandfather	Donban/Dhoba
Grandmother	Budyaban/Murtalbek
Grandson/daughter	Marage/Marge

English	Kolami
Words denoting relationship	
Father's sister	Appa
Daughter-in-Law	Koral
Mother's brother	Mamak
Mother's younger sister	Sanma
Mother's sister's husband	Kakok
Father's brother	Kakok
Boy	Kike
Daughter's husband	Eltam-Sangin
Words denoing birds	
Bird	Zaware
Crow	Kaka
Pigeon	Dori/Kebutar
Tortoise	Kanwwe
Indian Cuckoo	Kokilak
Cock Eagle-fight	Gadda/Morghar
Lapwing	Tewwak/Parvyak
Parrot	Mituk
Butterfly	Guge
Jungle Cock	Adavipot

II

Social Life

Kolams are divided into the following four parties (*Khers*) identical with social aspects of the Gonds, Pardhans and Thotis. They are as follows:

1. *Eedu Dayal Kher* (seven spirits or shaktis group)
2. *Aaru Dayal Kher* (six spirits or shaktis group)
3. *Idu Dayal Kher* (five spirits or shaktis group)
4. *Nali Dayal Kher* (four spirits or shaktis group)

In Kolam dialect, dayal means divine power. Stephen Fuchs described the term Kher to denote site of the ancient village. He also described it as 'the chabutra in the village, a mud platform under a tree where the stone figures of the village gods are put up'. Eedu Dayal Kher is the name of the divine figures or spirits: Muthyalamma, Kainjalamma, Nadidiamma, Kunthiamma, Gardiamma, Galiamma. The surnames of Kolams of these Khers are Khanda

Dar, Madavi, Daboli, Jharia Shiela, Paper, Kalagamma, etc. In six Dayal Kher, Akkas Kanni, Dhatir Kanni, Thom Khanni, Jal Kanni, Pathard Kanni, Kanni Minni, are the names of divine spirits. The surnames of these families are Kirkad, Magva, Chikati Devane, Boram, Kodipa, Mathveli, Peddala, Manjula, Kammani, Janmi, Potharaju, Mekela, Thalla, Bogarapu, Pipplai, Arkilla, Bhimer, etc. In Nali Dayal Kher, Potharaju, Thumkad Raju, Ded Nadu Raju, are the names of the spirits or Shaktis of Nali Dayal Kher. The surnames are Jambada, Darigam, Indapuram, Borgama, Kurma, Reddy, Chintapuri, Pasala, Madugam, Sappa, Thumgeda, Bhimidi, Edla, Bandi, Burusa, Eagam, Ushepalli, Jampam, etc. Kolams also have limited clans. Kolam's clan structure is similar to Gond's clan structure. Manne group of Kolams are living, and their clan names resembled those of neighbouring castes. Generally, these surnames are based on the original place of residence, their occupations or the animals which they domesticate in the day-to-day life. The party system is influenced by geo-cultural regions in which they are living.

Kolams observe certain taboos with regard to their totemic clan's species. For example, Madavi clan's people do not kill or eat the flesh of pig. Tiger is the totem of kurma clan people. They do not eat fish. Tortoise is the totem species of Tekkam. Almost all the clans of Kolams except people of Kurma clan people can eat the flesh of Kondenga. Family is the basic unit of Kolams social structure. Monogamy is the general rule of family-structure but polygamous families' are rarely found. Joint family system is not widely prevalent. Among the Kolams, child marriages were once prevalent but now they are not in vogue. They practice five types of acquiring mates, namely marriage by negotiations, marriage by service, marriage by elopement, marriage by capture, marriage by intrusion, and cross-cousin marriages are encouraged. But one cannot marry one's own sister's daughter. They have preference to the geographical proximity and social affiliation with regard to the selection of mates. During the marriage ceremony, bride's party and groom's party cut jokes with each other. For example, the following song among Kolams depicts the situation during a marriage ceremony:

> 'Amme Pilla Kandakad, Amme Pilla Kandakad,
> Mograknet Puvvakisha, Puvvabarabar Kandakad
> Imme Bala Kandkhan, Imme Bala Kandkhan
> Shikuknet Khutekisha, Khut barabar-Kandkhan
> Amme Pilla Kandakad, Amme Pilla Kandakan.'

The kinship system of Kolams is interesting. Saga is the general group of people who belong to the same clan. This system is borrowed from Gonds. Kolam families are patriarchal in their social structure. Their women enjoy equal status with men in their day-to-day activities. It can be assessed by the general attitude and their role during important social ceremonies. If anybody insults or molests any Kolam woman, the accused is made to pass through between her two legs. This is the great insult among the Adivasi communities. Kolam women are industrious. They collect forest produce and bring firewood from jungles and maintain household activities. Kolam women help their husbands in agricultural operations. The initiative for marriage comes from groom's party but initiative for divorce or desertion comes from women. Bride price system is prevalent among tribal families and Kolams are not an exception to it. There are certain taboos and ratifications which are imposed on Kolam women. Whenever she is in menstruation she cannot come out of the house from the front door. But these are not observed by the Telugu speaking Mannewar.

Among Kolams, various phases of life are associated with different ritualistic performances with a number of duties and obligations. Precautions are observed carefully at every stage of life to avoid evil influences of spirits. For example, Kolams believe that if a pregnant woman witnesses the full eclipse then she gives birth to a blind or a physically handicapped child. It is inauspicious to have a delivery in the same house or hut where they are living. For that purpose *maila gudise* (pollution hut) is temporarily erected. During the first menstruation period the girl is considered as unclean and impure. Even in that case a temporary hut is constructed. The initiation ceremony is unique. All the Kolams of the settlement meet and decide the day for celebration of ritual in consultation with the village priest. The boy is dressed like a woman and he visits the shrine of village deity, Ooramma with the accompaniment of his brother-in-law and the village priest. The bridegroom presents anklets and bracelets to the bride at time of the marriage. That is the reason why marriage is called Kadaim Pendli. On the eve of marriage, boy's parents, the groom accompanied by relatives go to bride's village and are accommodated in a house called Dhanasi Illu and this is called *vididi* in Telugu. After the marriage, bride and bridegroom are taken to shrine of Pochamma, a village deity. Marriage ritual among Mannewars is similar to that of Telugu people. But some similarities are also found like that of Kolams. Kolams believe in Punarjanma or rebirth. While carrying corpse to the graveyard, legs of corpse would be towards front side of the procession. They offer food like jawar gruel for eight days and on the eighth day, the jawar food is offered at the place of the burial ground with a feeling that the departed soul will come in the form of a crow and take the food. This food is known as *mutidadina pusekad*. Community feast is arranged on the occasion. No musical instrument is used in any of the death rituals, but Mannewars take dead body to burial ground with beating of drums and blowing of trumpets.

III

Economic Life

Kolams have subsisted by shifting cultivation. Generally, Kolams used to shift their residences to the site of cultivation where they construct houses and then start felling trees. They follow ceremonial methods in constructing their houses. They sacrifice a pig and a hen to the village deity. They used Kanka, a small instrument to disturb the top soil. Kanka is a bamboo stick which is called *sasire* in Kolami dialect. In the first year, they cultivate jawar which is generally the staple food of the Kolams. In the second year, they cultivate minor millets. During the third year, they start producing some crops and then they shift to another area. If they are fortunate enough to get fertile land, they settle down permanently or for a longer period. Permanent cultivation of Kolams began upon the introduction of Conservancy Act. The traditional occupation of Kolams is basket making. They produce varieties of baskets, grain bins and wattles. To get raw material from the forest area they used to live close to forest. The names of baskets which they prepare are *sakepurgu* (small basket), *katwale* Purgu (medium size basket), Chitri (round shaped basket), *palle* and Dala (big size basket), Khettu (winnowing fan), Gummi (medium size grain bin), Gade (big size bin), *kadaka* (bamboo net), Thadva (wattles), *parya*, Sopile (winnowing fan), Gummenti Thadaka, Gadaka Thadva (for using in the cart), Pona (a cover made of bamboo for shade), *petle* (box type basket), etc.

Kolams used three types of tools namely axe, sickle and small knife. At present basket making is not the main profession of Kolams. Cultivation is the main profession and basket making is a subsidiary profession. In the absence of agricultural land, Kolams survive mainly on agricultural labour. Both males and females follow the same occupation for their livelihood. Generally, basket making is the profession of Yerukulas and Mahendras. There is no relation between these tribal groups. In addition to the agricultural labour, minor forest produce is the subsidiary source of income for these people. Percentage of female workers engaged is more in minor forest produce when compared to male members, that too when their houses are near the forest and only when there is a possibility for their engagement in these occupations. In olden days the Kolams were considered as experts in magical formulae and describing medicinal herbs. They used to render traditional services to the patients who require their help. This expertise is inherited from their forefathers. That is the reason why they are called Pujaris by Gonds. But the magical services of these people are not used by the Gonds in the modern times in view of the availability of modern medicines. Kolams depended upon various edible roots, fruits and leaves available in the forest area during lean season. They depend upon forests for their house construction; agricultural implements and minor forest produce collection. As the forests are gradually vanishing, edible tubers, roots, leaves and fruits are not available to the people. Fence is a taboo for Kolams so they are not accustomed to grow vegetables or fruits in their backyard. The main occupation of Kolams is agriculture. They attach much importance to possession of land. The economic status of Kolams depends upon possession of extent of land. If one has more land he is considered to be an influential person and wields much social and political power. Some of the landless Kolams become nomads and wander from place to place. Dry land cultivation is the only type of agriculture being practised by Kolams. Due to lack of irrigation facilities, Kolams are unable to cultivate land and to adopt scientific techniques of cultivation for high yield. The assets and liabilities of Kolams include land, livestocks, carts, wells and oil engines. Kolams have thatched houses. That is an indicator of their poverty-stricken conditions. The main source of income is farm and agriculture labour. Sometimes, they get income from forests and other labour work like road construction. Expenditure on rituals and ceremonies and their alcoholic habits are considered to be unproductive expenditure. They take loans from private persons and other financing institutions. Bamboo used to occupy an important place in their day-to-day life, but now, because of reservation of forests they have discontinued bamboo work. Until the early 1940s, many Kolams led a happy life in the wooded hills of Adilabad district. But the Kolam settlements were haphazardly included in reserve forests. Kolams were expelled from their territory and their life was disturbed. This sudden expulsion of Kolams had the effect that many families lost touch with their kinsmen also. The expulsion occurred wrongly at the time when the Gonds were given pattas. Nizam government did not provide any justice to their economic life. Consequently, Kolams entered into a new phase of life as landless labourers. This had transformed the life of Kolams and in turn they became poor. Catastrophe caused by thoughtless expulsion of the majority of Kolams brought a change in their day-to-day life.

IV

Religious Life

Lord Bhima is a pre-eminent God of the tribe and he is described as greater than other gods. He is like *Bhagwan* of Bigas, Bhils and Murias and Shri Shambu Mahadev of Rajgonds. The only difference between these gods and Bhimanna is Bhimanna lacks some of the features of creator and sky gods. For these gods, animal sacrifice is not there. But Bhimanna has animal sacrifice. Kolams call him as Ayyak. The main features of Bhimanna are summarized by Haimendorf as: (i) all Kolams worship Bhimanna as their pre-eminent god; (ii) He is worshipped under different names; (iii) Bhimanna is considered a benevolent god accessible for the prayers and offerings of men. His help is taken to cure all the diseases or to face misfortunes such as crop failures and also control over wild produce of forest. His help is there in food gathering and honey collection; (iv) Bhimanna maintains direct control with Kolams. At the time of sacrificial rites or on many occasions his pronouncements by speaking through the mouths of his devotees denote the coming events. That means Kolams believe that Bhimanna can foresee future; (v) While Bhimanna's power is great but it is not absolute; (vi) All diseased Kolams are believed to join him who thus appears as the lord of the dead as well as the living; (vii) Bhimanna is worshipped with animal sacrifice. They do not accept meat of oxen or pig; (viii) The rites performed in the worship of Bhimanna resemble numerous features of the clan deity *persapen* of the Raj Gonds; (xi) Kolams believe that Bhimanna is accessible to the prayers, members of other tribes through the Kolam priest. Lord Bhimanna (Persa Deyyam) is the chief deity to Kolams and the shrines of this deity are found in every settlement of Kolams. Pagidimadra, Dantanpally, Sirasagone, Sungapa and Golleti are the important shrines of Bhimanna in Adilabad district. In every shrine, wooden staves with mounted bunch of peacock feathers are found in the centre of thatched shrine. In Pagidimadra settlement there is a sacred part symbolizing the deity called Anna Rani. This is not found in any other Bhimanna temple. The priest of Golleti Ayyak reported that a Kolam farmer in the olden days was ploughing land, the blade of plough was made out of a small furrow over the stone covered under earth. Bhimanna asked the farmer to construct a shrine of

Bhimanna in that place. The priest said that there are two staves which represent Dharmaraju and Arjun. So three shrines were constructed. The shrine of Pothuraju in Indapur was constructed and people say that Pothuraju is another Bhimanna. Temples of lord Bhima at Chinnai (Maharashtra), Dantanpalli (Asifabad) were constructed and Kolams go and worship there. Lord Bhima's idol is prepared out of wood of four sacred trees, which present the four phratries. The colour of flag varies from phratry to phratry.

Name of the Phratry	*Wood Used for the Idol*	*Colour of the Flag*
Nali Dayal Kher	Jalli tree (*Arachis fruiticose*)	Red
Idu Dayal Kher	Andugu tree (*Stryuchnos Potatorum*)	Yellow
Aru Dayal Kher	Ippa tree (*Bassia Latifaia*)	White
Yedu Dayal Kher	Maredu tree (*Aegle marmeios*)	Green

Irrespective of the colour of flag, every flag should have an emblem of sun and crescent like that of Gonds. Kolams differentiate between benevolent and malevolent deities. Bhimdev, Sitadevi, Laxmi, Hidimbi (Idumala Devi) are benevolent deities. Idumala Devi, consort of Bhima is worshipped along with Lord Bhima. Nadidiamma or Pochavva, Kusuba are considered as malevolent deities. It is believed that Kusuba brings property to the keeper of idol. This idol is prepared by Pujaris. Kolams believe in spirits and rebirth. Spirit of the dead takes birth in the form of a child. Grandchildren will be named after the names of their grandparents. It is the duty of every Kolam to conduct the final death ceremony called *mootidadina pusecad* on the 8th day after death. They attain much importance to ancestral worship. They consider availability of food in the forest, good rainfall and the outbreak of epidemics as the acts of gods and goddesses. The festivals and rituals they celebrate are a source of recreation and psychological satisfaction to Kolams. They perform these festivals to appease gods and goddesses. They request these gods to forgive their mistakes. The song is in praise of clan gods like Ghettala, Pikkalal. They reveal their physical ailments to gods and goddesses.

'Rena Rena re Rena Re,
Annete Marge Ghettalal Pejite,
Ghettalal Pejite,
Annete Marge Pikkalal Pejte,
Pikkalal Pejite.'

Polakamma Panduga is celebrated by Kolams in the month of March. It is celebrated at the time of blossoming of Mohwa flowers. Like other tribals, Kolams do not eat new foodgrains or flowers, seeds without offering to their gods and goddesses. Mohwa tree is sacred to the tribals and it occupies important place in their socio-economic-religious life. The articles they prepare like bows, arrows, flute and other things are placed in the shrine when they worship Lord Bhimanna. Mondos is the New Year festival of Kolams and it is performed in the month of Saita (March). They propitiate Bhoodevi, their bulls and ploughs with turmeric and kumkum. They offer good food and nine varieties of grains to bulls. Polakamma Panduga is celebrated on the full-Monday. On the festive day they prepare jawar gruel. The village headman and priest assemble at the shrine of Polakamma or Nadidiamma. After decorating the goddess and surrounding areas, the Pujari distributes gruel to all the villagers. They have to sacrifice a goat or chicken. Goat will be given and it has to shiver then only it is suitable for sacrificial purpose. In case of chicken some grains are offered to eat. If it does not eat then it is considered that it is not suitable for sacrifice. After sacrificing the goat, jawar gruel is mixed with the blood and it is placed in four corners of the village. During these celebrations, shaman falls into trance and while dancing forecast about the future prosperity of the village. Shaman is beaten with a hunter or he beats himself. Then he takes out the pandal and throws it away beyond the village boundary.

Bhimanna panduga is performed on the full moon day of Bhavai (April–May) months. In the evening, they prepare sweets with wheat and jawar flour mixed with jaggery. The village priest along with his wife goes to Ooramma shrine accompanied by villagers. They offer Kudumulu to the deity. Five unmarried girls smear turmeric paste to these idols brought by the village priest. Then all the villagers, especially ladies sing songs of Bhimadevara. Men-folk collect various seeds from all houses and keep them in front of Bhimanna's idol. Then they sacrifice fowls, goats or any other animals. The village priest distributes the churned seeds to all villagers and sows a few seeds in front of lord Bhimanna. These churned seeds are carefully preserved by the villagers. These are preserved and sown in their fields later. Except for oxen and pig other animal sacrifices take place. Mamidipanduga takes place in the month of April or May. The person who plants a mango tree arranges community festival. After one year, the owner uses the mangoes for himself or sells them to others. Mogataram is celebrated in the month of May. The village headman and priest go to their fields and propitiate Bhoodevi to have good yields. Akkadi is a festival celebrated in the month of June and July for the well-being of their cattle. They wash bulls and take them to Akkadi Raju shrine along with the priest. Each family sacrifices one chicken to the deity. The priest prepares idols of tiger, snake and other wild animals. These images are called *sisalu* in Kolami. They pray to god to protect their cattle from these wild animals. They keep the idols made of flour in a branch cut from a thorny bush called Gonti tree. One person would be dragging these thorny branches and 5 others will follow him with sticks in their hands. Community feast will take place and the priest draws a long line across the path with turmeric powder in the name of the deity, Akkadi Raju and all the cattle are made to cross the line. Jamremasa festival is celebrated in the month of June. They sacrifice a goat or chicken and eat on the festive day. The head of family celebrates the festival individually. After this festival, fasting is observed by the whole family and they offer coconuts to Lord Hanuman. Kolams celebrate Kotha and pola festival in Pora month (July and August). Kotha is eating of new grains. They go into the forest and bring teak plant leaves and prepare them into leaf cups. They keep materials collected in the forest in these cups and offer them to their goddess Pooramma or Pochamma shrines. One leaf will be hidden in roof of the priest's house and then another leaf cup in the house of village elder. People then propitiate Pochamma and sacrifice two chickens. The village priest brings new grains from the field and it is cooked along with jawar flour at the shrine. After giving offerings to deity the priest distributes food to all people. Then they return home and worship Bhimadeva. Kolams do not touch a teak tree and do not eat their new produce without celebrating festivals. Pala and Badaga festivals are performed in the month of July. One day before the festival, bullocks are washed in a stream and a mixture of turmeric powder and oil is made on necks and horns. All these bullocks are taken to Bhimadevara or the Hanuman temple. Womenfolk bring cooked rice from their houses. In the evening, they place a bamboo stick at the door of each house. This is known as Badagas. They keep cooked rice and boorelu in the name of this Badaga. The man of house carries bamboo stick along with cooked rice and other food to the village boundary and throws away Badaga there. Then all of them distribute rice and return home. Especially in Dantan Palli village, the Badaga festival is called Shivabodi and they propitiate the deity of Shiva.

In the month of Deevala (September–October) Kolams celebrate Diwali festival. They propitiate Bheema Devara. They offer coconuts to local Bheema and prepare sweets and keep earthen lights in their houses. During these times they perform Dandari and Gusadi dances. There is a change between the headgear of Kolams and that of Gonds. It is flat in its design, whereas Gonds' is straight. Kolams celebrate Bhimannas festival in the month of November and December. His idol is given a bath in a stream and installed in the temple. New flags are installed. Village priest officiates the proceedings. Villagers worship Bhima and other deities. In the month of November and December Duradi festival is celebrated. In the month of February, they celebrate Thick Thali festival. During that period they do not touch non-vegetarian food. In all these rituals, priests or the medicinal men observe fast and take bath and perform magical tests. These religious rituals are observed very strictly by Kolams. Kolams maintain their own Kula Panchayat where they have Nayakan (village headman), Dayyalak (village priest), Mahajan (in charge of village community house), Tharmaka (who prepares sacred food for the deities), Gatier (who distributes the sacred food to the villagers), Karobari (assistant to the village man), Havaldar (who invites the villagers for meetings) – all these posts are hereditary in their nature. Violation of traditional norms is known as tappu and those are decided by Kulapanchayat. It maintains community ethos, morals and values, and regulates behaviour of villagers. It also maintains social order and it is the duty of this council to maintain harmonious relations with supernatural world. They believe in sacred things and judge the sense of right or wrong which springs from unconscious roots of social feeling, though it is unreasoned, compulsive and wrong. They have a strong feeling about the happenings of their life. They are not concerned with outside world. They live in their own world.

V

Cultural Life

Kolams are known for their dance and music. Men play a major role when it comes to dance. They perform dance in all the festivals celebrated by them. Men dance not only for marriages but also for all the festivals. They dance from the festival of Akkadi during the month of June–July up to Diwali festival. They perform Dandari dance which is colourful. These are known as Gusadis. They are believed to be possessed with supernatural powers while they perform dance. The dance pandal is decorated with Mohwa flowers and branches of leaves. They prepare various designs of rangoli with rice powder. There are two sets of Gusadis. One of the set of dancers wear a dhoti in the traditional type and hold small towels. Others wear gusadis wrap, a cloth around their waist which falls down to their knee level and these people do not wear anything on the top and dance with bare body. They have Gusadi Rokali in their hand. Rokali is made of solid wood and is carved. Kolams store these things sacredly in the upper portion of house and do not touch them thinking that these possess supernatural powers. Gusadis wear headgear which is made of long peacock feathers. They look beautiful with headgear. Their belief is that lord Bhima resides in this headgear and it is considered very sacred. Another interesting thing is that they wear jingling brass bells on their ankles, waist and hands. All these create a melodious sound when they dance. Basically, they have seven steps which are elaborated upon. Among the seven steps five steps, are very important. They are: Ayyak Ni Gudum, Onti Gudum, Udul Gudum, Kinkiri Gudum and Jllar. These steps usually are set to Tishra and Mishra gati. Gudum means step in Kolami dialect. Their dance is accompanied by drums and flute. Drums are known as Dappu. Flutes are made of bamboo. They regulate the whole show. According to the tune of the director, and according to the beats of drums, dancers change steps. Their movements are vigorous and robust. All the important food crops like jawar, bajra are harvested before Diwali and that is the reason why Diwali is called the festival of plenty. Dance troupes of one village visits the other as a part of traditional gesture of reciprocity. They are expected to host guests and give them hospitality. Foot movements are more and hand movements are less. They sway their hands up and down according to music. Gusadi is the vanguard for the procession and provides protection. Another dance which is performed as an interlude is called Ghorpad dance. They represent the age-old tribal nature of imitating nature. Dancers who are always in pairs, imitate Ghorpad and dance lying prostrate to the tunes of music. This is a difficult dance and is performed by a few persons only. Usually costumes, dancers include bark of trees, feathers of peacock, animal skins, and towels or handkerchiefs. As dancing and singing are very common, various musical instruments are used. These include Daf, Panl, Dholok, Chonak, etc. Turbudi is prepared from the skin of a goat. Like many other tribal communities, Kolams have traditional folk songs which are sung on occasions. These are ritual songs, relating to husband and wife, songs indicating social change, agricultural songs and hunting songs, etc. These songs indicate they are according to the style of Gond songs and have many Gond words. Traditional themes include ritual songs or pooja songs which are in praise of their traditional gods and goddesses. Marriage ceremony itself is an occasion on which small sonnets are often composed. Another traditional song is related to the occupation of farming, grass-cutting, fuel-wood collection, etc. Women working as labourers take guidance from men and exchange funny words and carry on conversation so as to ease the tension of work. Hunting songs include references to animals and birds and there are chorus songs. These are meant to keep up the morale of hunters. Modern songs are educative in their nature and useful in the development of Kolam children. Kolam tribe is ethnically akin to Gonds, so they do not have separate tales or mythology excepting the mythological account of Bhimanna and his consort Idumala Devi. Their folk literature is not very rich as that of Gonds, Pardhans and other tribes in vicinity. One or two examples of the songs of the Kolams are mentioned below:

'Which kingdom our father-in-law is ruling
Whose hospitality is going to enjoy
Our father-in-law rule Telangana area
They are coming to take our sister to their home
Mother-in-law and father-in-law both are coming
They are coming in bullock cart
These bulls are white in colour
They rule on the eastern side
Those who are coming in the eastern side
Are coming in red bullock carts
They are creating musical sounds'

Marriage Song of Kolams

'The marriage bond is a permanent bond
It is related to days and years
Stars in the sky, moon and Ganges is flowering in a speedy manner
These bonds belong to days and years
Forest is decreasing day by day
People are facing difficulties
Difficulties because there is no rain
The writer calls it as a land of misery
When are we going to see good days in future?'

Song relating to Kolami culture in General

'Kolamies are dancing with musical instruments
They are playing Tudum and flute
People joined at one place and worshipping Shambu Maharshi for blessing the people
They wear peacock headgear carrying a bag in their shoulders gusadam rocked their hand
They are dancing accompanied by musical instruments'.

VI

Summing Up

Kolams are leading a primitive way of life among several tribes of Adilabad district. During Babjihar revolt of 1940, Kolams worked under the leadership of Komaram Bhim. This was a revolt against land problems of Adivasis. Komaram Somu, a Kolam leader assisted Komaram Bhim in the revolt against exploitation and extension of forest reserve boundaries over their cultivated lands. The first step was to form special forest co-operative societies to provide Kolams and Naikpods with decent plough lands and means of cultivating them. Most of the Kolams who were living near the forest areas were benefitted. But all schemes did not reach Kolams who were living in the interior places due to the lack of proper communication facilities.

The introduction of Integrated Tribal Development Agencies (ITDAs) at the beginning of the Fifth Five-Year Plan was a beneficial development. Unfortunately, these agencies benefitted more advanced groups. Lack of literacy among Kolams was the prime reason why they were not brought under the gamut of Integrated Plans. There was disparity between tribals and non-tribals and this disparity was seen even among other tribal population groups. At that time Government of India recognized Kolams as a Primitive Tribal Group during the years 1979–80. Tribal welfare department organized training camps at Panapattor, a major Kolam settlement in Utnoor Samiti area. This was meant to study the socio-economic conditions that prevailed among Kolams of the entire Adilabad district. Hundir, a Kolam leader was trained in this camp. There was a real necessity to improve the conditions of Kolams. The actual scheme was launched by the government for the development of the Kolams during the year 1981–82. Anti-poverty programmes were implemented from that year. Irrigation facilities and horticultural programmes were introduced to generate extra income for Kolam families. Primitive tribal groups were in the subsistence economy. During the year 1985–86, an amount of rupees 11.6 lakhs was spent for the benefit of 1,281 Kolam families. The beneficiaries were supplied plough bullocks and schemes of calf rearing were also provided. Later, a separate Kolam development officer was appointed exclusively to look after implementation of schemes in Kolam settlements. Land was the main source of livelihood and land was granted to the extent of minimum three acres to landless Kolami families. Ashram schools were provided for Kolam children in Asifabad and Utnoor Mandals in spite of its lopsided development among Kolams because of lack of education among them. There was not even a single graduate from Kolams in the Adilabad district but we find some graduates in Medak district (due to false certificates).

Social structure of Kolams is largely influenced by social structure of Gonds. Their social norms are identical with Gonds. These Kolams are called Kolawar by the virtue of their profession of making baskets, wattles and winnowing bamboo fans. After the introduction of forest conservancy laws and land assignment policy, Kolams became subsidiary cultivators and are avoiding podu cultivation. Their traditional occupation of basket making is lost due to the fact that bamboo is not available in the surrounding forest.

Kolams' chief occupation is agriculture. Even now some of them are depending on Podu cultivation. Some cultivate the land and some assist others by rendering services to land owners. In spite of varied schemes of rehabilitation methods launched by the government, they are below the poverty line. In the Kolam settlements, traditional Kula Panchayats were introduced to promote social justice and regulate the behaviour of individuals. In spite of the government efforts, Kolams of interior places are not much benefitted. Still they are considered primitive tribal groups. Kolams were totally swamped by the dominant culture of Gonds and others. Dominant caste groups are making strenuous efforts for creation of identity of their tribe. Their living conditions will be improved in due course of time with the developmental activities of the government. Family is not only a basic link in tribal community but is also a vital transmission unit of cultural heritage. Generally, Kolams follow monogamy. They believe in the levirate system. Women are an asset in their economic sphere. Joint family system is not widely prevalent among Kolams. They believe in nuclear family system. Of course, tribal women enjoy more freedom in the family than ordinary Hindu women. The average size of family is 4 to 5 members. The sex ratio is not in favour of females. Among Kolams marriage by negotiation is very popular. The elders arrange marriages through negotiation. In this type of marriage, bride price also exists. They also follow marriage by service which means that bridegroom is expected to serve would-be-in-laws family before marriage takes place. It is a probation time in his life with regard to marriage. If he satisfies the elders of family they will perform the marriage. The other type of marriage that exists among them is marriage by love and elopement. If satisfied, boy and girl meet at some place without the knowledge of the parents, and elope to some other place. Parents will come to know of it and later they perform marriage. In the marriage both girl and boy act together. In marriage by capture, boy forcibly takes the girl and marries her. Marriage by intrusion means that if a Kolam girl wants to marry a boy and if boy refuses, the girl then intrudes into the boy and refuses to leave. She is very stubborn in this matter.

The Kinship system of Kolams is classificatory with interesting special features. Among Kolams, various phases of life are associated with ritual performances. Kolam women generally work and attend to normal domestic duties till delivery time. No specific rites or rituals are being observed at the time of menstruation. In marriage, the boy presents anklets and bracelets to the bride. Kolams trace their origin to Hidimbi. She is being worshipped by Kolams ardently. Kolam women are like other women. They are very industrious. She collects tuber, roots, edible fruits, minor forest products from the jungle. She cooks food, maintains her family, and attends to all domestic chores, in addition to rearing children. She also assists her husband in all kinds of agricultural operations. In spite of such hard work, tribal society is still a patriarchal society in which man is the manager of house. Kolams believe in rebirth or *punarjanma*. Kolams generally burn the dead but in few cases cremation is followed. Kolams have a rich socio-cultural life.

References

Basham, A.L., *The Wonder That Was India*, Asia Publishing House, Bombay, 1965.

Deogaonkar, S.E., *The Media Damaged*, Inter-India Publications, New Delhi, 1982.

Furer-Haimendorf, C. Von, *The Gonds of Andhra Pradesh*, George Allen and Unwin, London, 1979.

Government of Andhra Pradesh, *Babijhari Incident*, Government of HEH the Nizam, Hyderabad, 1945.

——, *District Gazetteers*, Adilabad, 1976.

Government of India, Revenue Department, *Census of India*, Vol. XXIII, HEH the Nizam's Dominions, Hyderabad, 1933.

Government of Maharashtra, *Monographic Survey of Kolams of Maharashtra*, Tribal Research and Training Institute, Pune, 1979.

Grigson, W.W., *The Challenge of Backwardness*, Government Press, Hyderabad, 1947.

Hassan, Syed Sirajul, *Castes and Tribes of HEH the Nizam's Dominions*, The Times Press, Bombay, 1920.

Hazra, D., *The Kolam of Yeotmal*, Anthropological Survey of India, Mysore, 1983.

Karve, Iravathi, *Kinship Organisation in India*, Asia Publishing House, Bombay, 1965.

Lowie, Robert H., *Primitive Society,* Routledge and Kegan Paul Ltd., London, 1960.

Mohan Rao, K., *The Kolams: A Primitive Tribe in Transition*, Book Links Corporation, Hyderabad, 1990.

Rao, P. Sethu Madhava, *Among the Gonds of Adilabad*, Popular Book Department, Bombay, 1949.

Redfield, Robert, *Peasant Society and Culture*, The University of Chicago Press, Chicago, 1956.

Singh, K.S., *Our Tribal Heritage, Special Issue on National Tribal Festival*, Ranchi, 1989.

Thurston, E. and K. Rangachari, *Castes and Tribes of Southern India*, Vol. IV and VI, Cosmo Publications, New Delhi, 1975.

Venkata Rao, P., *Dimensions of Transformation in Tribal Societies with Reference to Andhra Pradesh*, Sarup & Sons, New Delhi, 2004.

——, *Tribal Development: Policy and Practice*, Sarup & Sons, New Delhi, 2001.

5

Thotis of Telangana

I

Andhra Pradesh and Telangana are the home to 35 tribal groups apart from various nomadic, semi-nomadic and denotified communities. They are found mostly in the thick forests and the bordering areas of the two states. Some tribal groups are living in the border areas of Maharashtra in the north, Madhya Pradesh and Odisha in the north-east. Out of the 35 recognized scheduled tribes, 30 tribal groups are found in 3,030 sq km of the scheduled areas and contiguous non-scheduled, sub-plan areas of Srikakulam, Vizianagaram, Visakhapatnam, East Godavari, West Godavari, Khammam, Warangal, Adilabad, and Mahabubnagar districts. The scheduled areas are the primary habitat of tribal groups of both the states which constitute 11 per cent of the total geographical area.

On the basis of geo-ethnic characteristic features, the tribal areas in these two states can be subdivided into the following geographic regions:

Tribal Region	*District*
Gond-Kolam Region	Tribal areas of Adilabad district
Koya-Konda Reddy Region	Tribal areas of Karimnagar, Warangal, Khammam, West Godavari, and East Godavari districts
Khond-Savara Region	Tribal areas of Visakhapatnam, Vizianagaram and Srikakulam districts
Chenchu Region	Tribal areas of Mahabubnagar, Nalgonda, Kurnool, Prakasam, Guntur districts.
Plain Areas	Tribal area inhabitations of Yanadis, Yerukulas, Banjaras or Sugalis.

Adilabad district is situated in the extreme northern part of Telangana. It is a part of, Gondwana region and identical tribal groups are found in the adjoining districts of Maharashtra and Madhya Pradesh. The district has natural boundaries of important rivers like Penaganga in the north, Wardha in the north-east, Pranahita in the east and Godavari in the south. Most of the rivers in and around Adilabad district are the tributaries of river Godavari. Godavari River has the greatest influence on the socio-religious life of tribal's in the region. Predominant soils in the region are black cotton and sandy looms. Important commercial crops are grown in this region. Important materials available in this region are coal, limestone, manganese and clay. The district has the richest forest area covering 42.43 per cent of the total geographical area of Telangana. Several tribal communities have their own names for self-identification (ethnonym). They believe that these popular names were given to them by outsiders (ex-ethnonym). For example, Gonds call themselves as Biru Gonds or Thotis. Pradhans call themselves the Patadis. Gondi, Koya, Kubi, Kui, Kolami, and Yerukula languages belong to Dravidian linguistic family. Mundari linguistic family members are Savaras and a section of Gadabas. The Indo-Aryan language speakers are Lambadas, or Banjaras.

II

Thotis are numerically one of the smallest tribes of Telangana. Thotis are predominantly found in the Adilabad district. According the to 1981 census, their population was 1,785. Like Pradhans they were also the traditional bards to Gonds. Syed Siraj-Ul-Hassan considered Thotis as the subtribe of the Gonds. R.V. Russell had classified Thotis as the subdivision of Pradhans (Thotis and Pradhans are the descendants of Gonds). Thotis are a distinct tribal group having a different lifestyle. Their social structure and clan organization are identical with that of Gonds. Unlike Pradhans, the mother tongue of Thotis is Gondi. Gonds call Thotis as Birdal (receiver) and Thotis call Gonds as Dhani (doner). Womenfolk also sing songs along with their husbands during rituals and functions at their patron's houses. Womenfolk exclusively attend to tattooing. Most of the tattooing designs and marks on the bodies of womenfolk belonging to Gonds, Kolams, Pradhans are the works of Thotis. Thurston regarded Thotis as village servants. In the Rayalaseema region of Andhra Pradesh, scavengers and other village menial servants are called Thotis and most of them belong to Scheduled Castes. Even Muslims scavengers are also called Thotis. Some of the nomadic mendicants who are known as Rama Jogulas in Karimnagar district are also styling themselves as Thotis in order to grab concessions extended to Scheduled Tribes. Thotis are numerically the smallest tribe living in 40 villages, in and around Adilabad district. Even though their mother tongue is Gondi, they speak Telugu language quite comfortably, due to the impact of Telugu speaking areas around their regions. Their main occupation is the narration of mythological stories like Pandavas, Annora (about the goddess of Lakshmi), the birth of sky and earth, about their clan deity, Jellidevara, etc. All these stories are narrated to Gonds in their language, and for that, they receive some financial benefits. In some places like Malkapur, Rajaram Palli, Utnoor, and Medipalli of Adilabad district, they narrate stories in the Telugu language. Thotis are normally found in Utnoor, Malkapalli, Nishani, Toshur, Danora, Duparpet, Vagapur, and other places in Adilabad district. Nearly 776 people living in Yadulapahad village near Tiryani Mandal. The total population of Thotis was 11,872 during the year 1998. Thotis have their own caste organization. Thotis are called Birdu Gonds. Their surnames are plenty. They consist of four groups and 61 subsections. Each section consists of different Velups, different patrons and goddesses (4 Velupu goddess, 5 Velupu goddess, 6 Velupu goddess, and 7 Velupu goddesses). Educationally Thotis are very backward. There are no graduates among them. Very few people have passed SSLC examination. They are appointed as primary teachers in schools. Besides storytelling in different places, they are also working as agricultural workers and wage labourers. They are leading a subsistence life in a modest manner. Thotis are recognized as Scheduled Tribes during the year 1976. Despite their rich socio-cultural heritage, they are economically very poor and leading a very backward life in the State of Telangana.

III

Culture is a creative and regulative physical power. Culture is conceived as the phenomena of the the material world. Nature gave essential qualities and quantities of things for tribal people. It taught them the way of life. Tribal people are true sons of the soil and dependent on nature. They consider nature as their god and goddess because nature fulfils their needs, desires, and wants. They enjoy pleasure and endure sorrows in nature. Nature is their father, mother, teacher and, everything for the tribal population in the country. Nature consists of trees, plants, rivers, mountains, animals, forests, etc. They are the beneficiaries of nature because of the valuable natural resources which satisfy their basic needs. Nature helps them to survive. The predominant feature of the tribal population in India is that they are worshippers of nature. In the history of religion and cultures, nature worship is the definite and complex system of belief. The concept of nature worship is total among the tribal population. Tribals worship stars, rain, animals, plants, water, fire, and so on. They are comprehended as natural objects or forces that influence them and are thus in some way or the other being venerated or placated. In religion and culture, the spiritual environment of man and woman is functionally structured by means of personified natural power and natural spirits.

India has the largest tribal population in the world. The States of Andhra Pradesh and Telangana have 50 lakh Scheduled Tribes; have the largest tribal concentration in South India. The tribes present a fascinating diversity with their variegated socio-cultural traditions, plurality of occupations and diverse linguistic heritage. Tribal heritage constitutes a colourful component of cultural heritage. The total population of Scheduled Tribes in the country is 683.81 lakhs, and they constitute 8.08 per cent of the total population. The tribal population of Andhra Pradesh and Telangana is 6.14 per cent of the total population. The concept of tribe varies from state to state or area to area. It depends upon local socio-economic conditions of a particular community and the consequent inclusion of a particular group in the list of scheduled castes. A community may be a scheduled tribe in one state, and it may be a scheduled caste in another state, and the same may be a backward class in another state. For example, Lambads or Banjaras or Sugalis are scheduled tribes in Andhra Pradesh and Telangana. But they are classified as scheduled castes in Karnataka state and, Delhi and they are considered as the backward class in Maharashtra State.

IV

Traditional human societies maintain social order through various systems of horizontal as well as vertical stratification in their social relations. The vertical stratification is found where various endogamous groups live together, whether they are tribal or rural caste groups. Further, horizontal strata are found within the endogamous group in order to regulate conjugal relations. These systemic social structures serve as foundations for the growth of caste or tribe. These groups maintain very close symbolic relationships, not only with the environment that is forests and hills but also with other tribal groups. There is a tendency of borrowing or imitating partially or completely the significant social principles from a dominant group which is living in the same habitat. Several tribal and other service communities borrowed and adopted prestigious and other status traits and grafted them into their social system.

With regard to the origin of Thotis there were many mythological stories. According to one mythological story, it was stated that Lord Shiva appointed one servant to guard Amrutham (nectar) placed in a garden (tota). The process was going on. One day suddenly, an ant fell into that nectar and the servant had taken that ant with his hand. This was noticed by Lord Shiva. With much anger his hands were chopped off by Shiva. In general, Thotis were appointed to guard gardens. As time passed, the word Thota was changed to Thotis.

According to another legend, Umara Devi and Ohm Guru were wife and husband. They had got two daughters, namely Heera Devi and Etma Bhai. Heera Devi got married and gave birth to a child named as Birdu Phang (considered as the main guru of Thotis). Later, he was married to Yadhobhai, and he was blessed with four children, namely, Anna Sural, Dhanna Sural, Koti Sural, and Kalpa Sural. It was believed that from these people, the Velpus of Thotis (gods and goddesses), their clan system, and their surnames came into existence. Thotis were subdivided into four sections. Each section contains different surnames. Total surnames among Thotis are 61 in number. Sarpa Saga consists of eight surnames.

Genealogy Table

Ohom Guru (husband)	Umaradevi (wife)
Heera Devi (daughter)	Etmabhai (daughter)
Birdu Pank Mahabhag (son-Main Guru)	Yadhobhai (wife)
Anna Sural (son)	Dhanna Sural (son)
Koti Sural (son)	Kalpa Sural (son)

Velpus (Gods/Goddesses)	*Total Surnames in the Subsection of the Tribe*
4	12 (Chakati, Sedamati, Naitaam, Teekam, Sidaam, Kooval, Parchaki, Madapach., Talanda)
5	8 (Adal, Valkal, Arka, Chikram etc.)
6	25 (Atram, Todasam, Geedam, Pendram, Urvetta)
7	8 (Madavi, Vedamal, Marusukolal, Purkal etc.)
Sarpa Sage	8
Total	61

In Telangana, Thotis are found in 46 villages. In the Adilabad district, they inhabit Utnoor, Malkapalli, Yadula Pahad, Nishani, Tosham, Daunora, Duparpet, Vaagapur, Chincholi-B, etc. They are also found in Karimnagar and Warnagal districts. Originally their mother tongue is Gondi. However, nowadays, they are speaking Telugu language due to the impact of surrounding Telugu speaking people. They are living in forests. Their chief resources are coming from forests. They satisfy their basic needs through forest products such as fresh vegetables, fruits, and the roots which are available in the forests. They also hunt animals for their food. They live in huts. Their walls are covered with bamboo sticks. They live in rectangular houses. Males wear dhoti. They tie a cloth on their heads. Women wear sarees and blouses. Due to the impact of surrounding areas, they are now wearing modern dresses which the civilized people are wearing.

Thotis wake up early in the morning and start their work. They pray to Lord Eswara. Some of them go to houses of Gonds and collect things from them. They take whatever Gonds give to them. Some Thotis go out for work. Rest of the Thotis go to the forest and hunt animals and get back to their houses by evening. If any strange person comes to meet them, they utter 'Ram-Ram' and keep the palms closed and touch the other person's palm with the tips of fingers. It is a sort of respect. They offer a seat and things that are available at their disposal.

Males play a predominant role and lead as head of the family. Nuclear families and monogamy families are also found among them. However, in some places, polygamy families also exist. Men play an important role in the family. They go out for work. Final decisions will be taken by males only. They work as agricultural labourers for daily wages. Some work for daily wages and lead their families. Women also play a significant role among them. Family is not only a social unit but an economic unit in Thoti society. Women help their families by doing tattooing work. They also sing in the streets and earn money. Thoti women do excellent tattoos. The main occupation of Thotis is narrating stories about Pandavas and some stories about Lakshmi, Parvathi, and other gods and goddesses. Women are experts in tattooing work for Gonds and their families.

After delivery, child is taken to the bath with the help of a woman called Mantrasani, or the midwife (Mantrasani is an expert in delivery cases).

Thotis worship water, one among the five primary elements. Their clan deity is Jellidevara. They also practise giving sacrifices to their gods and goddesses. They worship gods and goddesses and celebrate the feast. They offer broken rice (Nuvvalu) to their gods and goddesses. They mix raw sugar in rice and offer Prasad to their dead people. For the new baby, naval is cut after showing to father. Parents offer two and half kg of maize, one saree, and blouse and an amount of rupees 10 to midwife.

Child marriages are more among Thotis. They marry girls at the age of 13, 14, and 15 years soon after puberty. Girls are made to sit on mats when they get menstruation. Saree and blouse will be offered by a maternal uncle. Maternal uncle's blessings are a necessary custom among Thotis. During the menstruation period, she is not allowed to do any work for three days. Parents keep her utensils and nobody will be allowed to touch it. After taking a head bath on the fourth day, she is allowed to do her routine work in the house. They marry boys after getting of 21 years of age. The marriage ceremony takes place for three days. The head of the family will make a decision when he is financially self-dependent. Marriage will be celebrated in the house of the bridegroom. The sisters-in-law will play an important role in the marriage. The maternal uncle plays a key role. He has the right to ask sister's children as daughter-in-law if he has a son. White colour dhoti will be kept in turmeric water for some time, and the same will be given to the bridegroom. Before they take the bride and bridegroom for marriage, five pots (gurugulu) will be placed. One is kept in front and remaining at four corners of the stage. In the middle, rangoli will be made, after which two poles will be vertically placed. For Naivedya (offerings to the god), they put turmeric powder, Kumkum powder, food items, and five broomsticks. These five sticks will be placed in pots, and five rounds of the thread will be tied to poles, which are vertically placed. Pots are filled with turmeric and Kumkum powder water. The procession will be led by musical instruments. Everyone will take an active role in the procession. Clothes will be given to the new couple. After the procession, the whole atmosphere will be of delight. The bride will salute the west pole with folded hands and the bridegroom will salute the east pole. After that, the bride will be asked to press the leg of bridegroom and vice versa. Talambralu (grain is poured on the head by the bride and bridegroom for luck), and Akshintalu (grains made out of yellow rice with saffron colour) will be placed on the deity. The couple will take a bath and wear new clothes. Marriage songs will be sung and, dances will be performed to entertain the new couple.

Thotis carry their dead bodies to burial ground. Four bullock carts of wood also will be taken for the cremation. Each cart contains fifty wood pieces. Dead body will be placed on the wood and at the bottom of its legs, they put some goat dung, which indicates that the placement of legs. In the process of cremation, they also place an axe. Generally, cremation starts at the midnight and ends by the early morning. Meanwhile, at the time of cremation, males will dance. They take rounds around the funeral pyre. This process will be conducted for hours. During early morning females come and join the males. No lady will be allowed to take part in cremation. After cremation, females get the ash together with the help of bundle of tree twigs and do some nadakalu (9 movements or steps). Five women do this dance. This is performed to make the soul of the dead person rest in peace. When everything is over, they arrange for a get-together, including children for feast at the place of burial and get back to their houses and take a bath. The most important factor that we can find among tribals is that they take pains and pleasure in the same manner. We also can observe that on certain occasions like puberty, delivery, and funeral ceremonies, all the community members will definitely take part in it. They celebrate this as a community function. They also arrange for a community feast. They dance and sing. Kinship bonds among Thotis are very strong. They share lives with kins, both in pleasure and pain. They are simple-minded, straightforward and know only to share and enjoy life. They are people without inhibitions, restrictions and are selfless. Arrogance and power factors do not trouble them.

Thotis worship celestial bodies. They mainly worship the sun and the moon. They also worship earth elements. Jalli Devara is their clan deity. They worship Shiva and other Hindu gods. Thotis' clan deity will be lifted and carried by one of them in a procession. While in the procession of goddess, some chant mantras and take the goddess to the public. Everyone will join this occasion, and offer a heap of rice to the deity, according to their velpus. If they are four in number, they keep four rice piles and if it is five velpus, they put five rice piles and if six or seven they do in the same manner. They offer some Dhupam (to burn/offer incense) to the goddess as Naivedya and take it to the public; everyone will receive and do the sastangam (prostrate adoration to the goddess). Each category of Velpus will take his part of rice as prasadam (food offered to god), which is cooked and eaten by the particular family members. In the procession, everyone wears traditional costumes, dhotis and towels tied to the head. Nowadays, the Thotis are wearing pants, shirts and other costumes because of the impact of modernization.

Thotis observe certain omens. For good and auspicious occasions, they strictly follow their omens. These beliefs are continuously followed right from their forefathers. Some of the beliefs which are considered as good omens are: They consider it a good omen if blue jay or Indian roller bird appears or flies from the right to the left side. If a blackbird flies from left to right, it is considered as a good omen. If any lady coming with full of water in a pot on her head is seen, they consider it as a good omen. If they find a pair of animals coming from the front a it is a sign of good luck for them. Thotis consider some omens as sign of a bad luck for them. For example, the cat, a single Brahman with the shaved head, a barber are considered as bad omens by Thotis.

V

India is a country where we can find a lot of cultures mixed with social milieu. Festivals are very common. Festivals vary from place to place and region to region according to their historical background. However, important festivals have remained the same in any region. In the case of Thotis, there is some little variation. Thotis celebrate their festivals seasonally and according to their traditions and culture. Their main festivals are Akidi festival, Kottesudu or

Novang festival, Polalu festival, Siva Sandhi, Satti festival, Devali, Dasara festivals, Jangobhai Kolupu, Siva Ratri, Sankranti, Holi, Jellidevara festivals. Thotis celebrate the Akidi festival during June/July. They celebrate this festival when rains begin. Every Thoti member gets together for the first time to visit their donors (Gonds) and start praising them. They do all the necessary needs in order to obtain land for cultivation. Thotis celebrate Kottesudu or Novang festival during the month of August. During this time, seeds that were sprinkled on earth will be rooted in the land. Polala festival will be celebrated by them when the crop is ready for harvesting. They take fresh grains and offer them to their gods and goddesses. Then only do they take their share. During the Sivasandi festival, Thotis take water in pots to sacrifice animals (goat) and pray to gods. They celebrate the festival during Pinkham Amavasya in September. Sati festival will be celebrated for growing fresh vegetables. Vegetables will be offered to the god, Bhimmanna and they worship him. During Devali festival, Thotis clean and decorate their houses with Ganga water and put lamps in their houses and sacrifice a hen to gods and goddesses. During the Dasara festival, Thotis clean and decorate their cattle and prepare feast. They celebrate the festival only within the family. The Jangobhai Kolupulu festival will be celebrated before Sankranti. Thotis observe fasting till the Kolupus are done to the goddess. The Sivaratri festival will be celebrated with fasting for half a day. They do not sleep on that particular day. They narrate stories about Lord Siva. During the Sankranti festival, they wear new clothes. They clean their houses, and decorate them with rangoli. During the Holi, all of them will enjoy the festival. They play with colours mixed with water on this occasion and they do not follow gender difference. All the Thoti members – men, women, children will participate and enjoy. During the Jallidevara festival, they worship their clan deity. They take their god in a long procession lifting him towards the sky. Males, females including children, get together and play an active role in the festival. Thotis also celebrate other festivals like Naga Panchami, Kartikamasa Poojalu (during October–November), and Krishnastami with great bhakti and devotion. After the worship is over, they have a feast, including palm wine, palmyra toddy and date tree toddy.

VI

At Yadula Pahad village in the Adilabad district, there are forty families. The percentage of elementary education is very poor among them. The dropout rate is very high among them, particularly among girl children. They are still leading a primitive life. Poverty, ignorance, lack of exposure to the outside world are making them less educated. In addition to that, land alienation is the crux of the problem among tribals today. Tribal communities are living in the scheduled areas. Their lands get slowly and gradually impoverished. Their lands are alienated. They are steeped in poverty and exposed to various forms of exploitation. Women face many difficulties at the hands of contractors and rich people. They do agricultural labour work. For the sake of land, non-tribals marry tribal girls and leave them in the lurch after some time. The number of children enrolled in higher education is very poor. They do not send their children to schools due to long distances. The government have to provide quality school education in order to attract them towards schooling. They should be empowered, socially and economically. About 5 per cent of children have completed their primary education. Around 25 per cent of children have passed class X. Around 10 per cent of children have enrolled in higher education. There are no graduates among Thotis.

Due to the lack of education and exposure to societal knowledge, Thotis are not good enough in political matters. Nowadays, some of them are educated (passed SSLC and Intermediate level). The Thotis have village Panchayat and village Sarpanch posts. One of them is elected as their Sarpanch who takes care of the village and people. In Yadula Pahad village in Tiryani Mandal in the Adilabad district, the socio-economic condition of Thotis is very poor. They are spread over 318 kilometres. Thotis are living in 39 villages. According to the 1991 census, their population is 18,899 (9,598 males and 9,301 females). The literacy rate is 20.48 per cent (males 29.73% and females is 10.81%). Percentage of decadal growth is 14.01 per cent. The sex ratio during the years 1981–1991 is 969 and 965 respectively.

Dancing in India was exalted from the highest realms of external values. The immeasurable qualities of god's omniscience are depicted through dance. Dance is meant to improve, excite and teach man the way of life. It cannot continue to do that with old forms. Today, dancers have changed and yet their artistic integrity and comprehensive knowledge and reverence to tradition remain intact. Art and science are the creation of the human conception. Knowledge is the product of human mind. Man is a rational being, distinct from all other animals and is bestowed with the power of thinking and imagination. He thinks and brings into existence the knowledge of animate and abstract objects and in his way and conceives of several arts and sciences by formulating, amassing, adding and systematizing his immense store of experience. Even the conception of gods and goddesses is the outcome of human imagination. Imagination does nothing but leads to the science of philosophy and a major part of philosophy gives birth to religion. The conception of religion is the fountain spring of all art and this form of thinking has been the way of living a harmonious social life since times immemorial.

Dance is an integral part of life for scheduled tribes in India. They dance at their fairs and festivals and even when they feel happy, they begin to dance and sing. Always, they identify with nature. Some of their dances may be categorized as hunt dances/animal imitation, dances of fertility rites, rituals, magic, purification of spirits, shifting cultivation, agricultural dances, seasonal cycle dances and devotional dances. Thoti tribes perform dances during their cultural occasions. They perform varieties of dance on different occasions. Technical aspects in dance are visualized and analysed during field study. Thotis perform Dandari dance, Juvari dance with different hand and leg movements. They also perform Dimsa dance, Gera dance, Burri dance, Satti dance, Chanti dance, Sattik dance Penu Yahaval dance, Phendol dance, Bhoula Surasuval dance, Lagede dance, etc. Further, Thotis have their musical instruments. With the help of different musical instruments, the Thotis perform their dances with rhyme and rhythm.

In Dandari dance, females take part. There is no age disparity or difference in participation. All the members of the group club their hands. They put their hands on their waists and dance according to tunes. They keep 45 degrees angle while dancing. They take rectangular, and semi rectangular circular rounds with clapping. They beat their right palms with left palms. They make more of torso movements. They also make leg movements, front and back and make head movements with a downcast face. After that, they raise themselves on their toes. In this dance, we can observe more of their footwork. They perform Juvari dance on marriage occasions, particularly at the time of engagement (Laggnam). The Juvari dance is basically performed by females. A very interesting factor is that Thoti females are formed into two separate groups. Each group consists of 7 to 10 members. They face each other. They interlock their hands with partners. In this dance, women standing in corners will play a crucial role. While dancing, they take out one foot to the front. One foot will be accompanied by another foot. They bend their head, and come back and raise their heads and hands. In Dimsa dance, both men and women take part actively. They shake their hands. They make more torso movements in this type of dance. They set eight rhythmic beats. They also clap according to tunes. They use drums (Dolu), Sannai (Pepri) as musical instruments. Thoti men, women and children take part in Gera dance. They have eight beats in this dance. They move their legs forward and backward. They move to side directions. They move their hands in front and back. Satti dance is performed by Thotis in order to worship their god, Bhima. They raise their right hand upwards and get it back immediately. They do very little footwork in this dance. However, they perform more hand movements in this dance. Pochamma dance is offered to their goddesses. They set eight matras for their dance. They perform rigorous movements in this dance. They move their hands and head rapidly and rigorously to and fro in this dance. In Chanti dance, both men and women take part. They set eight beats in this dance. They clap their hands together. They move their feet to the right and left side. They make semicircles in this dance. In Penu Yahaval dance, Thotis lift their god and goddesses to the sky. Everyone takes part in this dance. Normally they do not allow their children for this type of dance. They dance without any set pattern. They dance according to their way. They do not follow any specific pattern in this dance. They worship Jalli Devara, their clan deity with Phendol dance. They do fast movements in this dance. They set five matras in this dance. Bhoula Surasuval dance is a marriage dance. When a bridegroom ties the *tali*, they perform this dance. They make small movements according to their moods. There is no rhythmic pattern in this dance. Lagede dance is performed when the marriage celebration comes to an end. While blessing the couple, talambralu (rice poured upon the head of bride and bridegroom) the dance is performed for the good luck of the bride and bridegroom. They make slow movements. They exhibit deep ecstasy while doing their movements in this dance.

Thotis perform their dances not only on happy occasions but also on sorrowful incidents. They dance in a funeral processions when the dead bodies are being cremated. They perform their movements according to musical instruments. A group of people will be identified to perform this dance. They dance in front of the dead body. They also dance with sorrow during a cremation. They dance very slowly with simple movements. They stretch their hands gently to and fro along with their leg movements. They dance for three rounds, clockwise and anticlockwise. They dance for four hours in order to show respect for their departed ones. While performing the dance, some take rest, and others join in their place.

VII

Thotis use musical instruments such as Kalikom, Dakkhi, Kikri, Pepre and Kujja musical instruments. Kalikom is made of copper metal. This is a very big instrument for the purpose of trumpeting. Dakkhi is a percussion instrument. Kikiri is an instrument made of horsetail strings. Pepare is a Sannai. This is a clarinet instrument. Kujja is made of buffalo and horsehair which is tied to that instrument. This is also a string instrument used by Thotis. They have traditional costumes such as dhoti, a towel for males and a saree for females. Nowadays, they have completely changed their dress patterns due to the influences of urban people. It is a clear indication that the rich cultural life of tribals is changing. They do not go for makeup while dancing. They apply little talcum powder to their faces in order to present themselves in a sophisticated manner. However, this is not a special makeup for tribals. Thotis do not wear costly ornaments. They do not have money to purchase gold and silver ornaments. Ornaments made of copper, bronze are used by them. There is no specific rule to wear ornaments while they are danceing. They always wear very normal and simple ornaments. There are no specific settings and decorative items. Their dances are normally performed at the marriage ceremonies. Flowers and rangoli are favourite items used by them. Dance is an integral part of tribal life. Though they are not financially well off, they have a genuine urge to protect their culture and customs. Nowadays, changes are taking place very fast in their materialistic and cultural world. They are slowly forgetting their dance patterns. No doubt, they will still have to preserve their art and culture.

Nowadays, there is a change in the materialistic culture and non-materialistic culture among Thotis. Materialistic culture consists of changing living conditions such as household utensils and articles, dress and clothes (men, women and children) including attitude towards modern dress, personal decoration and ornaments. And the non-materialistic culture consists of education, knowledge, social customs, traditions, beliefs and religion. Previously, there was a high percentage of illiteracy among Thotis, but gradually it has declined to some extent. There is a clear development in the fields of education and other aspects. All these developments are due to the impact of modernization. There is a change in social order, but their culture and traditions have remained unchanged to some extent.

References

Abbasayulu, Y.B., *Tribal Programmes and Their Beneficiaries: A Comparative Analysis of Tribal's and Non-Tribal's in Utnoor Block of Adilabad District in Andhra Pradesh*, Centre for Harijan Studies, Hyderabad, 1981.

Ahmad, S.H., 'Anthropometry of the Pardhans of Mandla District', *Man in India*, Vol. 52, No. 3, 1972, pp. 253–57.

Blake, N.M., A. Ramesh, M. Vijayakumar, J.S. Murthy and K.K. Bhatia, 'Genetic Studies on Some Tribes of the Telangana Region, Andhra Pradesh, India', *Acta Anthropogenetica*, Vol. 5, No. 1, 1981, pp. 41–56.

Bose, N.K., 'Integration of Tribes of Andhra Pradesh', *Man in India*, Vol. XLIV, No. 2, 1964, pp. 92–104.

Furer-Haimendorf, C. Von, 'The Pardhans: The Bards of the Raj Gonds', *The Eastern Anthropologist*, Vol. 4, No. 1, 1950–51, pp. 172–84.

——, *The Gonds of Adilabad*, Vikas Publishing House, New Delhi, 1949a.

——, *The Gonds of Andhra Pradesh*, George Allen and Unwin, London, 1949b.

——, *The Raj Gonds of Adilabad: A Peasant Culture of the Deccan, Book 1: Myth and Ritual*, Macmillan and Co., London, 1948.

Gafoor, Syed Khaja Abdul, *Social Service among the Tribes and Backward Classes in Hyderabad*, Government Printing Press, Hyderabad, 1952a.

——, *Tribes and Tribal Welfare in Hyderabad*, Government Printing Press, Hyderabad, 1952b.

Ghosh, G.C., 'Dermatoglyphtic Assessment of the Raj Gonds, Pardhans and Kolams', *Man in India*, Vol. 58, No. 7, 1978, pp. 53–64.

Government of India, *Census of India, 1961, Andhra Pradesh, Vol. 11, Part V-B, Ethnographic Notes No. 1, A Monograph on Gonds*, Manager of Publications, New Delhi, 1970.

——, *Census of India, 1981, Special Tables for Scheduled Castes and Scheduled Tribes, Andhra Pradesh, Series No. 2, Part IX, No. 1*, Controller of Publications, New Delhi, 1988.

Mohan Rao, K., *Tribal Profile of Andhra Pradesh*, Tribal Cultural Research and Training Institute, Hyderabad, 1969.

Murthy, J.S. and A. Ramesh, 'Selection Intensities among the Tribal Populations of Adilabad District, Andhra Pradesh, India', *Social Biology*, Vol. 25, 1978, pp. 302–05.

Sastry, V.N.V.K., *Girijana Samskruti, Parivartana (Telugu), Tribal Culture and Transformation*, Tribal Cultural Research and Training Institute, Hyderabad, 2005.

Singh, K.S., *People of India, Andhra Pradesh, Vol. XIII, Part 1, 2, and 3*, Anthropological Survey of India, New Delhi, 2003.

6

Koyas' Society

Cultural Antiquity

The primitive tribes persisted in forests and hills for many centuries without even having casual contacts with people in plain areas. They did not have proper communications with the centres of civilization. There are only certain instances where individual and small tribal groups of tribal people were being absorbed within the Hindu caste system in India. But, such cases of assimilation attracted very little attention of masses. On the part of Hindu society, there was no conscious drive to assimilate and reform tribal groups. Therefore, the tribal groups are showing their little eagerness to exchange their own lifestyle with neighbouring civilized society in the country.

I

Northern part of India dominated the early history of the subcontinent. The Deccan part, for a long time, was not focused much. But, Deccan consists of vast forest lands with poor communication facilities and the little known tribes. No doubt, centres of higher culture arose in the fertile lands of India. Before the third century AD, Andhra kings influenced their culture across the Deccan. A large part of wooded tracts and the hilly country remained home for the aboriginal, nomadic food gatherers and primitive tillers of the soil. They were predominantly ignorant of ploughing and higher forms of agriculture. They raised crops in forest clearings and cultivated lands. First, the Chalukyas and then the Rashtrakutas established themselves in the Deccan. Hindu culture flourished in numerous important towns in the areas where tribal folks persisted. In the beginning, they lived with their primitive style of life. With the expansive force of progressive population, tribals got separated and stretched themselves to the civilized country. Muhammadan invasions of 13th, 14th centuries, the subsequent growth of Bahmani Kingdom and Mughal conquests threatened the aboriginal culture. The sparsely occupied jungle tracts, on the whole, remained outside the political scene.

The end of 19th century witnessed a lot of improvement in the communication technology. Government extended its effective administration over the whole parts of the Nizams dominions. The Nizam dominions remained as the last refuge for aboriginal tribes. Aboriginal tribes had their civilizational impact in the Nizam dominions with their material culture. Hindu settlers had infiltrated into the Nizam dominions. Aboriginal tribes maintained their age-old trading activities with the plains' people. The hill folk for many centuries maintained their casual relationship with the plains' people through their trade and barter system. Some land grabbers penetrated into forest tracts. They were supported by the machinery of government. Aboriginal tribes were forced into the refugee areas. The poor tribals could not get any help. This had endangered their economic and cultural existence. There was no specific defence mechanism for the hill tribes. There was too much constabulary maintained in the hills by government. Tribal population could not maintain themselves in the hilly areas. They were driven to forests. Assimilation or extension was the only alternatives for tribes. The outcome of struggles of the tribes was one of very imbalance. The tribals have to face odds. They were no longer able to defend their rights. The newcomers waged their powerful battles. Tribals lost much of their ancestral land. They were often destined to the ranks of the landless depressed classes. After independence, India awoke to the problems of aboriginals. Government recognized that the tribal folk were exploited by the pressures of advanced population and tribal population in the country needed protection, safeguards and guidance to safeguard themselves from the cultural, social and economic ruination and disintegration.

In India, aboriginal tribes are facing the problem of physical isolation. During the 20th century, the problem of this physical isolation has come down to some extent. The enormous growth of Indian population caused the greedy peasants to invade the sparsely populated tribal regions. Rights of the tenants were specified. Most of the tribal lands were alienated. Wherever tribal areas are very backward, ignorant and illiterate tribal population are more, in such areas, despite constitutional safeguards the danger of encroachment of tribal areas are rampant. Tribal masses are unaware of the concept of individual ownership of land. They are accustomed to free use of their communal land. Aboriginals are often slow to avail themselves the facilities available to them. Therefore, special efforts are required to assist tribes in obtaining their ancestral land.

Hindu society is tolerant about the culture of many groups. Higher castes specified certain standards to lower sections of people. These groups were denied equal status. Higher castes did not make any efforts to deflect them from their harmful ways of life. In the recent years, there is a change in the attitudes of higher classes. In the past, higher sections were never allowing tribes into their villages. Tribal populations were ridiculed due to their food habits, dressing pattern, marriage customs and their ways of worship. Modern society is critical about some tribal ordeals, customs and traditions. They feel that polyandry, animal sacrifices, brewing liquor, omens and tribal panchayat judgements are still needed in modern society. Many tribal people in India share certain basic social attitudes. In the Indian urban society, there are many primitive tribes. Even in the tribal custom we can observe caste distinctions, equality of sexes, preferences for adult marriage, liberty of divorce and independence of nuclear family. Aboriginal tribes are exposed to the influence of upper-caste Hindus. The features of Hindu society such as child marriage, untouchability, dietary taboos, restrictions on the freedom of women are clearly seen.

The anthropological term tribe is applied to people who are considered primitive and who live in backward areas. Sometimes, the term is synonymous with the term 'race'. A tribe is an ideal state. It is a self-contained unit. It constitutes a society in itself. The tribe is a collection of individuals who generally share a common culture. A tribe is a society having a clear linguistic boundary. Theirs is a well defined political boundary. Their linguistic, cultural traits are imposed on members of the tribe. Every tribal group has a cultural boundary of their own. They live in the framework of their folk art, and have formal and informal interactions within their groups of people. Origin of races in India can be dated back to Mohenjodaro civilization, 3250 to 2750 BC. Indian megalithic cult bears similarity to that of the Mediterranean culture. South Indians are very much familiar with the Mediterranean culture. Evidences of irrigation, construction of dams for agricultural purposes, pottery, copper objects, terracotta figurines establish the fact that the Mediterranean culture entered into South India through the North–West. H.H. Risely recognized three principal races in India – the Dravidian, the Indo-Aryan and the Mongolian. J.H. Hutton felt that the earliest occupants of India were the Nigrito race, followed by the Proto-australoids. B.S. Guha stated that aboriginal population could be categorized into four types according to their physical features. Some aboriginal tribes possess short, long and moderate height of heads with small flat noses. Some tribes are pigmy type with spiral curved, coiled hair. Some are Mongolian type. They constitute a component of Assam and North Burma. Some other tribal groups are like the mongoloid type. They were characterized by a medium structure with high heads and medium nose. Some aboriginals in Central and South India possess short, long and moderate height of heads with a small flat nose. G.S. Venkatachar affiliated Gonds of the Central provinces with the pre-Dravidians of South India. They are a dark, negroid race. Their physical features are of very short structures. They have low foreheads, flat face and nose. In southern India, we can find some of the most primitive tribes. The plains' people increased their penetration into the forests. Thus, a good number of tribes got employment as farm workers and forest labourers. Until recent times, the poor tribals led a miserable life even without possessing a hut. The Madras and Andhra Pradesh governments have made many efforts to settle some of their tribes in the colonies. But the efforts of the government did not succeeded fully due to poor planning. Administrators did not properly assess the real needs of tribal population in the forest region. Tribal people in India were the spirited freedom fighters and opposed colonialism during the freedom movement. The Khonds of southern Orissa (Odisha) and north coastal Andhra, Konda Doras of Andhra Pradesh actively participated in the freedom movement. The Konda

Doras under the leadership of Alluri Sriramaraju waged war against the British. Kurichiyas of Wynad under the leadership of Payyachi Raja of Kottyam fought against the East India Company. In the agency tracts of Andhra Pradesh, the tribal riots and fituris invited the attention of the government to the existence of severe oppression on the Adivasi people. The British Government answered tribal revolts by killing and shooting down the troublesome, brave tribal leaders. The last revolt of tribal people in the agency areas of Andhra Pradesh was led by Alluri Sitaramaraju. This fituri took place during 1920s. In this fituri, the great tribal leader Alluri Sitaramaraju was shot dead. Hundreds of tribesmen were arrested and kept in the jails. They have lost not only their leader but also their future.

Anthropologists, sociologists, social reformers and government officials have employed a different criteria to distinguish tribal people from non-tribal population. They showed factors such as racial features, occupation, language, religion, culture, etc. to distinguish the people as a tribal population. They showed some important features such as that tribal people live away from the civilized world. They predominantly live in the inaccessible parts of forests and hills. They belong to Negrito, Austroloid or Mongoloid racial features. They speak the same tribal dialect. They profess primitive religion known as animism. Worshipping ghost and spirits is an important element of their worship. They follow primitive occupations such as gathering, hunting. They are characterized as cultivators, flesh or meat-eaters. They are naked or semi-naked. They love nomadism, drinking and hunting. Sociologists, anthropologists and colonial writers have developed certain myths regarding the tribal population in the country.

Andhra Pradesh and Telangana states occupy an important position with regard to the tribal population. There are 35 tribal groups of people with different traditions and economic status. They are living in different habitations in the state. They are found in the hilly regions, plains and forests. The scheduled area of the state comprises of 11,595 square miles. The aboriginal tribes live in the forests of Salur, Parvathipuram, Palakonda and Patapatnam taluks of Srikakulam district; Paderu, Chintapalli, Narasipatnam, Srungavarapukota taluks of Visakhapatnam district; Gumma Lakshmipuram, Salur, Pachipenta, taluks of Vijayanagaram district; Ellavaram, Ramachandrapuram taluks of East Godavari district and Polavaram taluk of West Godavari district. In the state of Telangana, they are seen in Acchammapeta taluk of Mahaboobnagar district, Utnoor, Asifabad, Adilabad, Sirpur, Laxettipeta taluks of Adilabad district, Mulugu and Narasampet taluks of Warangal district, Ellandu, Burgampadu, Bhadrachalam, Nagur, Kothagudem taluks of Khammam district, etc.

Agriculture is the main occupation of scheduled tribes. Twenty-nine per cent of tribals are cultivators, and 21 per cent of them are agricultural labourers. Naikpods and Koyas in the districts of Adilabad, Warangal, Khammam and Karimnagar are largely the settled plough cultivators, Bhagatas, Savaras, Gadabas and Khonds are Podu cultivators. They too are settled cultivators. Chenchus of Nallamala forest and Umnabad plateau are food gatherers and hunters. Pradhans and Thotis are musicians and bards.

Gonds and Sugalis are pastoral people. Now they have taken up agriculture. Savaras, Jatapus in Srikakulam district have constructed bunds on hill streams to water their terrace fields. They grow jawar, maize, cholam, ragi, redgram, blackgram, horsegram, beans and peas. They are growing banana in Palakonda and Srungavarapu Kota areas of Srikakulam and Visakhapatnam districts. Tribals of Araku valley grow oranges. Almost all the tribals collect the minor forest produce like tamarind, myrobalan, shikakai, hill brooms, soap-nuts, marking nuts, adda-leaves, honey and chirongi. Tribals in Srikakulam, Visakhapatnam, East and West Godavari districts collect Pathalagaridi (Rauwolfia, Serpentina) which has a foreign market. Chenchus are experts in bamboo cutting and honey collection. Tribal population supplements their diet by hunting, fishing and food-gathering. Now they are engaged in non-agricultural operations like household industries, mining, construction works, trade and commerce, transport and communications, and a few of them are in government services.

II

Koyas in Andhra Pradesh constitute a large section of Scheduled Tribe population. They are predominantly concentrated in the southern part of Andhra Pradesh. They are the decedents of Gond race. In the southern borders they are merged with bison horn Marias. Some of them are living in Bastar, lower Godavari regions. They possess bison-horn headdress. Koyas speak the Gondi dialect. Majority of Koyas have lost their own language. They are now speaking Telugu. In Khammam, Warangal and Godavari districts, Koyas form the majority of tribal population. The present habitat of the Koyas lies within 80 degrees and 15–82 degrees east longitude and 17 degrees 15 minutes and 18 degrees 45 minutes north latitude. They are concentrated in Polavaram, Mulug, Eturu Nagaram taluks of West Godavari and Warangal districts, Rampachodavaram and Yellavaram mandals of East Godavari district, Bhadrachalam and Nagur provinces of Khammam district. The land of Koyas is in Godavari valley. They spread in approximately 3,676 sq miles. They are living in 1,050 big and small villages. They are spread over Bhadrachalam, Nagur, Chodavaram and Yellavaram taluks.

There are many mythological stories with regard to the origin of Koyas. According to a myth, Koyas originated when the Pandava brothers were in exile. One day Bhima went for hunting in the jungle. He met a tribal woman. He loved her and got married. Children of them were called Koyas. The Pandava brothers occupied a very significant place in Koya folklore. Koyas possess outstanding physical features. Godavari River has a great influence on the economic, social and cultural activities of Koyas. They are generally restricted to foothills and the adjoining plains. Generally, Koyas are very sturdy. They have a short flat nose with spreading nostrils. Their lips are thick and projecting. Their complexion varies from light copper brown to dark colour. Their hair is straight. They are noted for their truthfulness and simplicity.

Koyas are engaged in the economic occupations such as agriculture, agricultural labour, forest labour, collection of minor forest produce, fishing, hunting and other occupations such as basket making, manufacturing of bamboo products, etc. Some Koyas living in the forest still follow Podu agricultural practices. But majority of them had taken to permanent cultivation. Government allotted them a large number of cultivable lands. After the establishment of the Singareni Colleries at Yallandu in Khammam district, Koyas in the surrounding villages began to work in the coal mines as unskilled labourers. Koyas are divided into several functional subdivisions such as (1) Gutta Koyas (hill Koi), (2) Gumpa Koyas (basket), (3) Oddi Koyas, Adi Koya (original), Commara Koya (Smith), (4) Doli Koyas, (5) Musara Koyas, (spill), (6) Gommu Koyas (basket), (7) Kapu Koyas, Matwa Koyas, (8) Pattadi Koyas, and (9) Linga Koyas. The Gutta or Racha Koyas are living in the hills. Gommu Koyas are living on river banks. They are speakers of their native language. They speak in their own dialect.

The objectives of the present chapter are: (a) to analyse various aspects of Koyas. Their social, economic and cultural life has been analysed. Like any other caste and community, Koyas are also engaged in agricultural and other allied occupations. They have a separate identity and a distinct culture of their own. They are extremely poor and illiterate. Under these conditions, they are easily subjected to exploitation by others. Most of the Koyas embraced Christianity to raise their social status. The lifestyle of Koyas is very simple and very close to the nature. An attempt is made to study the demographical aspects, economic conditions, family organizations, religious beliefs, rites and rituals, acculturization, art forms, welfare programmes initiated for the development of Koyas by the government and non-governmental organizations. (b) The effort also focuses on the recent changes brought about in the cultural life of Koyas. However, the main objective is to draw proper conclusions based on the data collected and analysed. In the end, a few suggestions are made for their upliftment. It also covers the recent cultural contacts and the reactions of the non-tribals towards Koyas. An attempt is made to draw an ethnographic map of Koyas and provide useful insights of acculturization process of Koyas in India.

Fieldwork method, interview schedules, oral testimony, case study method, observation method and primary and secondary sources have been used. A total number of ten Koya villages have been randomly selected in Nagur, Bhadrachalam taluks of Khammam district. Several Koyas and non-tribal people were interviewed, and their observations were recorded, analysed, and results were recorded. The information provided by them is a useful source of data concerning the lifestyle of Koyas.

Ethnographic Profile

Koyas are one of the predominant autochthonous people of India. The present habitation of Koyas lies between 80° 15' to 82° East longitude and 17° 15' to 18° 45' North latitude. Their habitations are known as 'Koyalanadu'. They are predominantly living in the Godavari valley. They are generally restricted to the foothills and the adjoining plains. Koyas are known as 'Dorala Sattam' (Lords Group). It is believed that a section of the 'Gondi' speaking people became Koyas. Koyas are strongly influenced by the neighbouring Telugu speaking people. A good number of Telugu people recognised the typical cultural traits of Koyas. According to 1961 census, the Koya population in Andhra Pradesh was 2,20,246 (consisting of 1,10,185 males and 1,09,961 females). Koyas are chiefly inhabited in the agency and plain villages of East Godavari, West Godavari, Khammam, Warangal and Adilabad districts. In the district of Khammam, they constitute 68.2 per cent of the total population. Only 2.9 per cent of Koyas are literate people. Aiyappan in his report on the 'Socio-Economic Conditions of the Aboriginal Tribes of the Madras Province' stated that the Koya tradition originated in the Bastar state of Madhya Pradesh and that the Godavari and Sabari valleys make the Koya land as a whole. Their lands are divided into five separate administrative units. Gonds are considered as their kin. In the first half of the 19th century, Koyas of Bhadrachalam lived a miserable life. Bhadrachalam taluk was under the control of the Nizams. The Nizam's government strictly controlled the movements of Koyas. Until 1816, the local zamindars maintained troops of Rohillas. The Rohillas were not paid salaries by the government. Therefore, they looted and plundered Koya lands in order to eke out their livelihood. Cain stated that clothes of the poor Koya women were stripped, and their women regarded as objects of ridicule. They could never lie down to rest at night. Before the sunset their slumbers are rudely disturbed. Their houses were burnt. Their property was carried off. As a rule, they had hidden their grains in caves and the barks of the large trees. In 1859, Koyas were brutally plundered for the last time in Parnasala. During the year 1930, the Madras Gazetteer reported that a tradition says that famine and internal disputes drove the Koyas from the highlands of Bastar and Berar to the regions extending from Bhadrachalam on the banks of Godavari down to the neighbourhood of Khammam district. Koyas have a dialect of their own. Their dialect is mixed with Telugu. Koyas were divided into five classes. They are Gutta Koyas (hill Koi), Addili Koyas, Perumboyadu Koyas, Koikammara and Dollolu Koyas. Gutta Koyas holds the highest rank among Koyas. Koikammaras are the blacksmiths. Dollolu Koyas act as religious counsellors. They took charge of the Koyas deities. Koyas regard themselves as five important clans: Perumboyadu, Modugutta, Peregatta, Matamuppayo and Vidogatta. Cain further stated that the lowland Koyas say that they originated from five tribes. They do not know the first of the five tribes. The only names Koyas give are Paredugatta, Mandegatta, Perumboyina and Wikaloru. These tribes are further subdivided into many families.

In the district manuals, Koyas are described as 'simple minded people'. They look poor and untidy. The jungles in which they are living are unhealthy. They suffer from chronic fever. They lead an unsophisticated savage life. Their knowledge is very limited. They do not have any knowledge beyond the daily events of their villages. However, this withdrawal of Koyas from the busy civilized life is favourable for their growth of certain virtues which are lacking in the civilised people. Like the Khonds, Koyas are noted for their truthfulness. When interviewed, Koyas stated that they have come from Madhya Pradesh and settled on the hills in the province of Bhadrachalam and Godavari. They had some internal conflicts with Gutti Koyas. They frequently attacked Koyas and troubled them by looting their grain, forest produce and livestock.

Etymology

Koyas are hill dwellers. They are tillers, artisans and weavers. The subdivisions of the Koyas are Kammara Koya, Linga Koya, Are Koya, Musara Koya, Kaka Koya, Matwa or Matta Koya. In most of the cases, the names of Koyas indicate their occupation. For example, Gampa Koyas are basket markers. Neta Koyas are weavers. Kammara Koyas are blacksmiths. Musara Koyas work on brass metal. They speak the Koya language with some dialectical differences.

Appearance and Personality of the Koyas

Generally, Koyas are of medium colour. They are sturdy. They possess a short flat nose spreading up to nostrils. They possess thick lips. Their lower lips are slightly projected. Their complexion varies from copper brown to dark chocolate colour. They possess wavy hairs. Their hair is straight. It is observed that the appearance of Koyas strongly resembles the African and Austroloid tribes. Aiyappan also supported the same view. He found the negrito element among Koyas. They are distinguishable to the local people. They also resemble the South Indian Proto-Austroloids.

Dress Pattern

Generally, the dress of Koya woman consists of a saree, and a small lion cloth. Women wrap the saree several times round their waist. They tie the saree slightly above to the ankle, throwing one end over the left shoulder. They wear saree girded well above the knees with one end drawn between the legs when they go to agricultural work. Gutta Koya women wear bright red coloured sarees. They wear full-length sarees at the time of weddings and other ceremonial occasions. Various colour combinations are also used to create a festive atmosphere. Women generally cover their breasts. The menfolk of older generations are semi-naked. They cover their waists with a small cloth. Young people wear shirts and dhotis. They dress similar to those of people in the plains.

Ornaments

Women wear necklace, bangles, anklets, bracelets, etc. Their ornaments are made of precious metals like silver. They wear necklaces made in different sizes and varieties of beeds. Usually, they wear septum. They pierce their nostrils and lobes during childhood. Married women wear 'pustetiltadu' or 'Tali'. Some Koya women under the influence of the Christian missionaries do not wear 'tali' or 'mangalasutra'.

Tattooing

Koya tribes are exogamous sects. They are called as Gattas. The Koyas are divided into Phratries. They are known as five Gods, four Gods, seven Gods, six Gods in Maharashtra and Aido Ghatta, Aro Ghatta, Mudo Ghatta, Nutomuppayo, Peramboya and Rayibande. In Andhra Pradesh, they are known as Arava Gatta, Idava Gatta or Raayibanda, Mudava Gatta, Naluva Gatta or Paredigatta, Yedava Gatta, Nutomuppayo (one hundred thirty) and Peramboya. In some places, members of the Mudo Gatta, Naluva Gatta and

Idava Gatta are recognized by various tattoo marks they occasionally wear on their foreheads. These tattoo marks are horizontal or perpendicular lines used by them.

Language

Ethnologically and linguistically, Koyas are divided into two main groups. The first group speaks Gondi dialect. The second group speaks Telugu language with a rural accent. Koyas have a typical language of their own. They speak the Koya dialect. They speak Telugu with the hill accent or characteristics. There are dialectical variations of the language of Koyas in different areas where they are living. Koyas living in the Godavari region speak their ancient language which is very close to Gondi or Kui. The dialects of Gonds, Khonds and Jatapus, are essentially Dravidian. The Gutta Koyas, Adi Koyas and Gommu Koyas are the original inhabitants. They speak in a dialect of their own. In the Godavari district, Koyas use Telugu words. They are not well versed in Koi language of the Bastar region. There are variations and slight difference in the phraseology of the inhabitants of two villages located within a mile or two. The words are borrowed from the Telugu language into Koi language. Its connection with Gond language is quite clear. Koi language has a great influence of Telugu language. An introduction to the grammar of Kuvi or Kondh language was produced by Schulze, Rev. F.V.P. (1911) and Lingam Letchmaju and Steaphen Tyler. Tyler in his work, referred to the context and variations in the Koya kinship terminology. There are variations in the use of terms among Koyas. These variations occur at the phonological, morphological and lexical levels. For example, among the Gommu Koyas the term aane (siso) is pronounced by the same Koyas in another place with a changed dialect as 'aande'. Still in other areas they use an isogloss in the pronominal endings. Gutta Koyas speak eelaari whereas Gommu Koyas speak eeladi. There are other variants in morphology, particularly in the case of the distribution of the plurals. There is variation within the communication network. Their dialect differs from place to place.

Koya Kinship Terminology

	English	*Telugu Reference*	*Koya Reference*
I	Father	Ayya, Nana, Tandri	Eyya
	Father's brother	Pedananna	Tappe
	Mother's sister's husband	Pedananna	Tappe
II	Mother	Amma	Evva
	Mother's sister	Anti	Talluru
	Father's brother's wife	Aunti	Talluru
III	Father's father	Tata	Daadal
	Mother's father	Tata	Taataal
	Mother's mother	Avva	Kaako

Cont'd...

...Cont'd

	English	*Telugu Reference*	*Koya Reference*
	Father's mother	Avva	Emma
IV	Father's sister	Atta	Pooye
	Mother's brother's wife		
	Wife's mother		
	Husband's mother		
V	Mother's brother	Mama	Maamaal
	Wife's father		
	Husband's father		
VI	Elder brother	Anna	Enna
	Eldest male		
	Parallel cousin		
VII	Younger brother	Tammudu	Tammundu
	Youngest male		
	Parallel cousin		
VIII	Eldest sister	Akka	Ekka
	Eldest female		
	Parallel cousin		
IX	Youngest sister	Chellelu	Eelladi
	Youngest female		
	Parallel cousin		
X	Elder brother's wife	Vodina	Enge
	Cross cousin		
	Eldest female		
XI	Younger brother's wife	Maradalu	Eendaadi
	Cross cousin		
	Youngest female		
XII	Elder sister's husband	Bava	Baataal
	Eldest male		
	Cross cousin		
XIII	Younger sister's husband	Baamardi	Erundu
	Youngest male		
	Cross cousin		
XIV	Sister's son	Koduku	Marri
	Brother's son	Abbaye	Peeka
XV	Daughter	Kuturu	Mayyaadi
	Brother's daughter		Piikidi
	Sister's daughter		
XVI	Sister's son	Alludu	Aane
	Daughter's husband		
	Brother's son		

Cont'd...

...Cont'd

	English	*Telugu Reference*	*Koya Reference*
XVII	Sister's daughter	Kodalu	Kodyiaadi
	Son's wife		
	Brother's daughter		
XVIIII	Son's son	Manamadu	Tammudu
	Daughter's son	Manamadu	Erundu
	Son's daughter	Manamaralu	Eelaadi
	Daughter's daughter	Manamaralu	Eendaadi

III

Community and Social Organization among Koyas

Koya villages comprise 20 to 25 families. These families are closely knitted as a unit. The heads of individual families of Koyas are born in the locality. They are members of their community. They acquire rights on land automatically. Some Koyas were immigrants from different places with a common consent of the rest of Koya tribal families. Koya village is a rigid unit and exclusive in its composition.

Koya villages are very small. But they are very beautiful and picturesque. Koyas clear jungle in forest. They make a few acres of cultivable land. They make some acres of vacant land around their house for cultivation of crops. While clearing the land, Koyas do not touch Ippa flower plant and tamarind trees. They treat these plants/trees as of greatest service to them due to their yield and shade. Edgar Thurston stated that 'the Kois do not remain long in the same place. They are a restless race. Four years suffice for them to exhaust the soil in one particular locality, and they do not take the trouble to plough deeper. They migrate to another place where they make a fresh clearing and erect a new village'. Recently, government had provided settlements for Koyas. It was observed that Koyas maintain a close tie between the families living in settlements. There are mutual cooperation and harmony among them. The atmosphere in the community of Koyas is intensely democratic. There are no special privileges for the village head. He does not exercise his authority over his fellow-villagers. He presides over the Panchayat, but all his decisions must be endorsed by community members. Aiyappan stated 'The society of the Koyas is controlled by an extremely democratic organization – their Kulapanchayat'. Koya village is a unit of administration. Pinna Pedda is the head of such a unit. Office of the Pinna Pedda is hereditary. Democratic principles are applied to it. If a Pinna Pedda dies, his heir usually will be elected as the head of village assembly. If the heir is a minor or incapable person, village elders elect a person to officiate on behalf of the minor/incapable person. Above Pinna Pedda there was 'Kula Pedda' or Patel. The office is hereditary. They correspond with village Munsifs. Government had appointed 'Talayaris'. They were appointed in a very small number. There was one Talayari for seven to eight villages. Each village appoints their own Vetti.

In the Koya country, a group of ten to twelve villages form a Samutu. The Samutu was headed by the Samutu Dora or Kula Dora or Pedda Kapu. He has to be guided by the opinion of members of the council. The Samutu appeals against Pinna Pedda or Patel. All are liable for any punishment for their mistakes like any other ordinary citizen. Government-appointed Patel created a big confusion in their functions. The democratic will among Koyas are very strong. Even Patel is a mere president over the debates. How the village elders are represented in the Samutu is not very clear. Fines are levied as three parts in the Kulapanchayats as Kula Tappu. They are called as Kula Tappu, Guru Tappu and Raja Tappu. Koyas pay these fines to community members or to their religious head. They use money for drinks. Money is equally divided among village heads. All disputes in the village are settled by the Kulapedda. Normally, his decisions are final. The whole community uses the money received as a fine for drinking. Sometimes the amount of fine is very heavy. In case of violation of social restriction, the fine amounts to 100 to 1,000 rupees. Koya society has to give sanction for the social boycott of its members. Heavy fine will be imposed if a person refuses to pay the fine. Panchayats conduct enquiries in an orderly and dignified manner.

The Tribal Cultural Research and Training Institute, Hyderabad, described the traditional panchayats of Koyas. They have called the Koya Panchayat as an extremely democratic organization. The office of Koya Panchayat is hereditary. If any member/head of the Kulapanchayat is not acceptable or leading an immoral life, the entire village will choose another leader. Koya leader must be familiar with all the cultural patterns of their own community. He must evince enthusiasm in social and religious festivals. Kulapedda or Patel was recognized by the government. The traditional panchayats have not lost its influence in tribal villages. Even after the inception of statutory panchayats, their social control is very strong. But the Gram Panchayats and Samitis are dominated by plains' people in the tribal areas.

Housing

In the natural habitats of Koyas, they construct houses with bamboo. They construct houses with thatched roofs, grass and palm leaves. They live in the thatched houses. They build their houses in a circular and rectangular fashion. Walls are generally constructed with mud. Doors are made out of bamboo mats. It is called 'Tadakas'. Their huts are generally covered with melons and gourds. Their surroundings and houses give a graceful appearance. Government constructed some 'pucca' houses for Koyas in their colonies. At present, concrete houses have replaced thatched houses. These houses are built with bricks and cement. In the Lakshminagaram settlement in Bhadrachalam, it was observed that Koyas had built the annexing huts as concrete structures. Many Koyas complained to the government that concrete structures are not conducive for their dwellings. They preferred natural habitats than the cement and concrete houses. In Akkannagudem, near Venkatapuram, government authorities constructed a colony for the rehabilitation of the Koyas. Some are living in Doli and Jella regions. Their colonies are situated in the hilly region. Government constructed houses with bricks and cement but Koyas refused to live in such houses. At Pathrapuram colony, government also allotted house plots to Koyas. They were also provided with building materials such as bamboo, tiles, etc. Koyas constructed their own houses under the supervision of the government authorities. Many of Koya colonies are still not electrified while their neighbouring colonies are enjoying the benefit of electricity. Government made all possible efforts to bring back Koyas from hilly regions. Government constructed nine dwelling units for Koyas. In Pathrapuram, government had constructed two colonies, in Lakshminagaram government constructed one Koya colony. Similarly, government-sanctioned one Koya colony in Paragallipalli, two Koya colonies in Wazeedu, one Koya colony in Educharlapalli, one Koya colony in Alubaka and one Koya colony in Ankannagudem.

Food Habits

Rice and jowar are the staple foods of Koyas. They also consume maize in considerable quantity. They dig out edible roots and tubers from the soil. They use them in the preparation of food items. Koya women living in the hill settlements go out often for digging of roots. They continue the digging of roots for many months. Some poor families mainly depend on tubers and feed their entire family with them. Koya women revealed that they go for digging 'Yelleru Gadda' a kind of a tuber used as a substitute for food. Other tubers are Sheenda Gadda, Nalla Sheenda Gadda, Vaimu Gadda, Nara Dumpa, Jena Dumpa, Kasaki Dumpa and Kasya Dumpa. Yelleru Gadda and Sheendra Gadda resemble small turnips. They slice them and soak them in running water for twenty-four hours. They boil the tubers with frequent change of water before they make them ready for eating. The tubers are important for their sustenance due to their prolific growth in the forest. They collect them very easily and all-round the year. Vaimu Gadda and Nara Dumpa were collected only during winter season and at the time of monsoon. Koyas prepare Ganji, Java (porridge) by grinding or with the flour of jowar, maize and millets, etc. They use a kind of stone for making flour out of jowar, maize and millets. They also use flour for cooking food. Fishing and hunting are two important activities of Koyas. They supplement their diet with them. Koyas use bow and arrow, and other weapons to hunt animals. Koyas eat beef. Aiyappan reported that Koyas eat wild lizards, flesh of rabbits, deer, wild boar and buffalo. During obsequies they kill cows. They kill only the old cows. Koyas eat beef during the festivals and ceremonies. On all occasions of death, a buffalo is killed and feasted by them. Koyas never eat the flesh of a bird. Some families do not eat the meat of goats. Honeycomb is used as a side dish. They drink heavily. Koyas praise Ippa plant very much. They eat flowers of Ippa plant. These flowers are fleshy and round. They eat dried flowers. They dry the flowers, roast them a little bit in the oil and eat them. Koyas extract oil from Ippa nuts for cooking and lighting of lamp. They make an intoxicating drink from these flowers. The extraction of intoxicating drink from the Ippa flower is very interesting. Liquor is an integral part of life of the Koyas. Drinking habit of Koyas is largely due to Ippa flower. From the flower a strong spirit is distilled. This is noticed when the flower is fully blossoming. The other type of common beverage for Koyas is the juice from Palmyra plants. Aiyappan says that Koyas consume toddy with very low alcohol content. They do not get intoxicated. They consume sweet toddy. It is a part of their food habits. They do not intoxicate themselves. It is interesting to note that some of the Koyas with the influence of Christian fathers abandoned drinking Ippa drink. This is due to the impact of Christian church and Bible Gospel in the Koya settlements.

IV

The Economy of Koyas

For many centuries Koyas lived a secluded life. Therefore, they could not earn much. There was no opportunity for them to earn wealth. Land was a common property for all Koyas and was considered as a joint property. Villagers jointly tilled land and cultivated some forest land. Koyas still follow primitive agricultural methods. They did not save grain or wealth. They increased food supply by increasing their agricultural production. There was no medium of exchange. They did not hire labour on wage. Landlords contacted Koyas and penetrated their villages. They showed, taste for rare and unknown commodities. Koyas were often exploited by plains people in bartering their goods, baskets, forest produce, etc. Majority of Koyas are living under extreme poor economic conditions. Only 1.5 per cent of the people are above poverty line. They are employed in civil and excise contracts, trade, business and government services. The main occupation of Koyas is agriculture and other allied occupations. Poor sections of Koya community are working as agricultural labourers in the fields of non-tribal population. Their main economic activity includes collection of minor forest produce. Koyas of Yallandu region is working as industrial labourers to the coal mines of Singareni collieries. All the members in Koya family contribute in economic activity. Women work in fields along with men as agricultural coolies. They are also going for construction works. Child labour is very much prevalent among Koyas. Majority of Koyas are engaged in making of bamboo products such as mats, baskets and tadakas, etc.

Agriculture

Podu cultivation is an extensively practised agricultural operation. This is known as 'shifting' cultivation. Members of Koya community who enjoy common ownership of land were not living in one settlement. Koyas were free to cultivate any part of forest land by clearing jungle and burning trees. Nowadays, Podu cultivation was banned in the forest due to large scale destruction of forest wealth. According to Aiyappan, the 'Koyas do extensive Podu cultivation'. They also do a bit of wet cultivation. Koyas plough the Podu land to facilitate easy tilling of surface soil. He does not cultivate Podu more than his requirement. The acreage under Podu in Koya land is about 4,000 acres. It remains the same more or less year after year. The cultivation practices of Koyas were very simple. Koyas select a piece of land and cut all the bushes and trees except the fruit yielding plants. They burn trees and use the ashes as manure. They do not remove the burnt stumps. They do not clear land further. They throw seeds on the land for cropping. For three or four years, natural fertility of soil yields them a crop. When undergrowth begins to appear, and the soil gets impoverished, Koyas abandon the land which again turns into a scrub jungle. In his note on the cultivation in agency tracts of Godavari district F.R. Hemingway wrote that – the majority of the Koyas and the hill Reddis in the agency carry on shifting cultivation. They call it Podu. They practice this form of cultivation by burning forest and clearing land. There are two methods of agricultural practices among Koyas: Chalaka Podu and the hill (Konda) Podu. The former consists of cultivating certain recognized clearings for a year or two at a time. Koyas allow the forest to grow for a few years then again burn and cultivate them. The latter practice of Podu is because Koyas do not return to Podu land for a longer period and sometimes they abandon agriculture on such a land forever. Konda Podu agricultural practice is in operation more in hilly regions. This agricultural practice is widely in use in Koya settlements. Chalaka or ordinary Podu cultivation is a step towards their progressive agricultural practice.

Local tribal populations have suffered from the alienation of their land by members of the migrant families. They are economically and politically powerful. Haimendorf observed that within the past forty years or so, Koyas had been reduced to the position of landless agricultural labourers. Koyas only succeeded in retaining lands in remote villages. Only in such places Koyas preserved a relatively high economic status. Rice, jawar and maize are the main crops cultivated by Koyas. Nowadays, Koyas are also cultivating commercial crops such as cotton, chillies, tobacco, etc. But their level of agriculture is very low due to lack of irrigational facilities and primitive techniques of cultivation. In Khammam and Warangal districts in order to wean them away from Podu cultivation government has introduced land colonization scheme. Each Koya family was provided with some cultivable land. They were also provided with financial assistance for the redemption of their land. Bullocks and agricultural implements were given to them. Some members of Koya families (Pathrapuram and Lakshminagaram settlements) stated that though the government has allotted agricultural lands to them, irrigational facilities are not there. They are solely depended on rain water. Hence, most of them were unable to cultivate their lands assigned to them. Loan facilities were not arranged. Gathering forest produce, such as tamarind, saarapappu, tuniki fruits, chilla seeds, shikakai, ritha, ippa flowers, etc. are other avocations of Koyas. Koyas sell forest produce in the nearby shandies and Girijan cooperative societies. Koyas earn their subsistence income from agriculture, agricultural labour, industrial labour, bamboo based products and collection of minor forest products. They spend money on food, house-keeping, education, medicine and entertainment.

Animal Husbandry

Koyas own a considerable number of cattle with them. They do not have bulls for the purpose of cultivation and carting. Koyas hire them at the time of cultivation. The risk of damage of the bulls will be borne by owners. They are unable to feed their cows. Green pasture is available only for six months that too in the rainy season. The demarcations of forest are very close to their villages. They do not have ample grazing grounds. The Koyas realized the value of livestock. This is from economic and nutritional point of view. Animal sacrifice is common in all religious rituals performed by Koyas. Koyas are also engaged in bee-keeping and sericulture activities. Fishing is an important avocation of Koyas.

Industrial Labour

In Khammam district, Singareni collieries were established. Koya villages were surrounded by the company. It began to work in mines. Koyas were appointed in the company as unskilled workers. During the last five to six decades, many of Koyas settled around Yallandu and Kotha Gudem mines. Haimendorf had mentioned that many Koya labourers were employed in the company. Out of 8,000 working labour force, majority of them were Koyas during the year 1943. At present more than five thousand Koyas are employed in the colleries. Officials in the Singareni colleries feel that Koyas are very effective work-force. They effectively move heavy machines in the company. Koyas have abandoned their traditional occupations and are permanently settled in the colleries. Another company where a large number of Koyas were employed is the Bhadrachalam Paper Board Limited located in Sarapaka, Bhadrachalam. At present, Koyas have vastly extended their economic activities.

V

Family and the Role of Women

The family of Koyas are patriarchal. However, women play a significant role in the family. Attending to all the household duties such as cooking, cleaning, washing clothes, child-rearing are the important activities of women. Koya women also work as agricultural labour. They work in agricultural farms as daily wage labourers. They earn money for the survival of their family members. Earnings of their males were spent on liquor. They do not meet domestic chores. Koya males do not allow their women for domestic work when their women get menstruation. Koya males do not hesitate to do household work during the pollution days of women. Koya woman plays a very important and influential role in the tribal family. In almost all the major issues concerning family members, Koyas give a lot of weightage on the opinion of their womenfolk. In the matrimonial matters also, bridegroom's mother calls upon the parents of the girl to participate in discussions of marriage proposal. Koya woman plays a key role in selecting bride and bride-groom for their children. Further, Koya women greatly influence her children in imparting social and cultural knowledge regarding their customs and habits of their tribal society. Koya woman helps her husband in all agricultural operations. She also participates in religious functions. As in the case of the other tribal women, a Koya woman also enjoys complete freedom to choose her life partner, to seek divorce and to opt for remarriage. Koyas have nuclear families also. Nowadays, the joint family system is completely disappearing among tribals. This can be observed among Koyas. Male children desire to set up separate families soon after their marriage and wish to lead an independent life. Generally, Koya women are very healthy and do not bother too much about their health.

VI

Religion, Customs, Ceremonies and Festivals of Koyas

The religion of Koyas is influenced by various religious groups of Hindus. Their rituals, beliefs and customs were influenced by the neighbouring Hindu population. Koyas believe in various supernatural powers. They depend on the power of supernatural things. Their emotions and reactions accompany the worship of various deities. They do not know the form of god. From their ancestors, they got the belief of worshipping gods and goddesses for good crops and protection from diseases and other misfortunes. Koyas are also influenced by Vedic, Upanishadic and Puranic ways of worship. They had a deep influence of Saiva, Vaishnava sects. This is clearly visible in the ritualistic lore throughout their life. Koyas of Andhra Pradesh worship the mother goddess in different forms. They call her by different names. They worship Adisakti and Vindhyavasini and Saptamatrikas. They believe Saptamedemulu was their homeland. Koyas also worship Mamili Devata, Kommalamma, Katurudu, Adamarazu, Korra Raju, Mutyalamma, Kudidevara, Maridi Mahalakshmi, Poturaju, etc. Till the 19th century, Koyas worshipped Mamili Devata in order to ensure good crops in their fields. They used to sacrifice animals. This practice is in vogue in Koya villages even now. J. Cain writes: 'The Goddess Mamili Devata or Poleramma must be propitiated by the tribals early in the year, or else their crops will undoubtedly fail, and she is said to be very partial to human victims. There is a strong reason to believe that two men were murdered during the year 1976 near a village not far from Dummagudem as offerings to this goddess. There is no reason to doubt that every year strangers are quietly put out of the way in Bastar, to ensure favours from the thirsty goddess'.

Muthyalamma is the goddess who was supposed to preside over smallpox and cholera. Chicken is sacrificed in order to appease the goddess. Haimendorf stated that: The sanctuary of Muthyalamma is very close to their village and receives care and attention throughout the year. Prayers and gifts of food are offered to the deity at regular intervals, usually on Saturdays or before the rites of first fruit crops. Village women clean and decorate the stone, a tree representing the goddess. Muthyalamma is considered very important for good health and environment of tribal villages. The goddess helps or harms according to the seriousness of the worship of tribals. It is a custom among Koyas to keep the idol of 'Kudi Devara' in their houses. Kudi Devara ensures prosperous life for Koyas. They perform Puja (worship) every day with devotion to the goddess.

Among Koyas, 'ancestor' worship is also prevalent. They worship their ancestors during the occasions of Velupu. They carry this occasion during the auspicious period. They take family around the village. The Velpu is a large tree covered with red cloth. They cover a large number of ancestral figures with different coloured cloths – white, green, blue, yellow. They stitch red cloth with the main cloth. Hummingway stated: The Velpus consist of small pieces of metal, generally iron. It will be less than a foot in its length. They keep the Velpu in a hollow bamboo. They deposit the Velpu in the wild and unfrequented spot.

Further, J. Cain wrote: Koyas believe in supreme Velpu which is recognized with much supernatural power. Koyas have hidden this Velpu in Bastar. They also contain Velpus for each family (Gatta) and each village. The idols of gods and goddesses are guarded with great secrecy by Pujaris. The Velpus were shown by Koyas on certain rare occasions. It can be easily noted that the conception of village deities was entirely foreign to Koyas. Their main habit is to live in scattered groups or houses. They frequently shift from one side of the village to the other. They believe that gods and goddess will live on different sides of villages. They are very much concerned about their welfare. Koyas also worship hill-gods and mother-earth. Their gods and goddesses are represented by tangible objects such as sacred stones, pots, trees, kept in a special sacred place. Their deities are specially linked with the organized village life. In the bigger and larger settlements their cults and cult objects had got particular prominence. Aiyappan had also described the character of Poturajau. Backward Hindu castes in the Telugu country worship a godly figure by name Poturaju. The name Poturaju is itself significant. Literally 'Poturaju' means 'the beast king'. Poturaju was the younger brother of the mother goddess of the Telugu folk Pantheon. In front of the mother goddess, we can see some wooden poles as horn polls. Poturaju stands in between the villagers and the mother goddess. His function was to protect people. The mother goddess was mainly malevolent. Cain wrote: All the Koyas, hail the Pandava brothers, especially Bhima and Arjuna with great reverence. They consider that the wild dogs are the messengers of the Pandava Brothers. Koyas were influenced by Christianity. Missionaries converted Koyas into Christianity. Some of them however, remained unchanged owing to their conservativism or strong belief in Hinduism. However, in recent times this situation has changed enormously. Almost all the Koyas are being converted to Christianity. Activities of Christian missionaries have gained a great momentum in the tribal areas today. Many of Koyas had opted to observe Christianity in villages. Christian brothers and sisters visit tribal areas and pray for curing of their ailments. Koyas believe that they are hale and hearty with the prayers of Christian missionary. Many of Koyas have taken to Christianity and observe the Christian way of life. Women today do not even wear the turmeric, ornaments, flowers and other symbols of Hinduism. Under the influence of Christianity, Koya men and women gave up drinking and the ways of Hindu life.

Festivals and Rituals

Most of the festivals and ceremonies celebrated by Koyas are communal in character. They celebrate these ceremonies annually. They perform them during a particular season. At present, Koyas celebrate very few festivals. In the earlier times, the Koyas used to celebrate festivals for every grain crop. They used to celebrate their festival when 'Ippa flower' were ready to be gathered. They used to celebrate their festivals when pumpkins were ripe or while tapping toddy from trees, etc. At the time when they get zonna (maize) crop and paddy, they used to celebrate festivals. Cain wrote 'they used to take the fowl into the field, used to kill it and sprinkle its blood on the ordinary stone, put up for the occasion. After completing they take part in the new crop. If any member in the Koya family neglects to participate in the ceremony the community members boycott them. They name the ceremony, as Kottalu'. The word is derived from the Telugu word 'Kotta' or new. Paddy (rice) straw cords will be hanged on the trees in order to show proof for celebrating the festival. It was stated that first fruits would be offered to the local gods and goddesses.

Soon after receiving Cholam Zonna crop, Koyas celebrate another festival. They call the festival as Bhumi Panduga or Earth festival. It is also called 'Bhudevipanduga'. On the morning of the festival day, all men of every Koya village turn to forest side to hunt animals. The person who fails to bring any hunted animal will be chased by the womenfolk of the village. They throw mud and send him out of the village. He should not enter the village till next day. The successful man will parade into the village with his hunted animals and receive presents from every house member. They call this as 'Vetapanduga'. Another important festival cerebrated by Koyas is Bhudevi or Bhumi Panduga. They worship the earth goddess. When there is a full moon in the sky they celebrate this festival. Before the monsoon sets they will celebrate the occasion. They burn all the Podu lands and clear it for sowing. Men, women and children will gather in one place outside the village and offer sacrifices to their gods and goddesses. Koyas cook millets and dal in large pots for the meal. The village priest prepare special food to offer to the god. They prepare the place for offering sacrifices. They keep food on leaves. Pujari invokes the earth goddess. They also pray to all the main gods. They kill buffalo. The blood will be tapped in a cup. They sprinkle the blood on the grains of different crops. Members in the Koya village bring some amount of grains in order to get the blood stains and blessings. They keep separate leaves for separate varieties of grains. Later they mix all the grains and take it home. The priest places the grain in front of the god for about an hour. They chop the buffalo. They prepare food and cook meat in several pots. They serve the meal to all Koyas who were present there with the grain. They complete the festival before sunset. After taking food, men and women dance with the rhythm of drums. They return home safely soon after they perform the dance.

Another important festival the Koyas celebrate is called Mutyalamma Panduga or festival for Mutyalamma Devata. She is the goddess of smallpox or cholera. When the disease is rampant in 'Koya Gudems' Koyas propitiate the goddess by performing certain special ceremonies to the deities. Stephen A. Taylor observed that 'the Podu is not just an alternative form of land use or a set of agricultural practice; it implies the whole nexus of the Koya's religious beliefs, attitudes, self-image and tribal identity'. Among the Koyas, there are three important rituals. One is associated with their disease, another is associated with the clan and the third one is associated with their Podu cultivation. Koyas are still following Podu cultivation in some places. They participate in Podu cultivation which is an essential component of their life.

Medaram Sammaka and Sarakka Jatara are the main celebrations for the Koyas. The Jatara will take place in Mulugu Taluk, Warangal district. Koyas worship the goddesses namely Saralamma and Sadalamma once in every two years in the month of Magha on the full moon day (usually in February). Thousands of Koyas from different villages assemble there and offer fowl and animal sacrifices to their mother deity. Koyas are celebrating the Jatara since 1260 AD. Some Koyas who are very poor, do not celebrate any festivals as their economic status is very backward. Koyas also celebrate Hindu festivals such as Ugadi, Dusshera, Deepavali, Sankranti, etc. They also visit Bhadrachalam in order to worship Lord Ram during certain important festive occasions.

The festivals and ceremonies observed by Koyas have two important features in common. They perform festivals and ceremonies with yearly intervals. Their festivals and ceremonies are all associated with definite phases of seasonal cycles and economic activities. Their ceremonies are connected with social and economic activities. They constitute the ritualistic underlining. They are intended to influence the course of nature for the advantage of people. They involve the gods. Their rituals, ceremonies are magical as well as religious. The sprinkling of seed grains with the blood of sacrificial animal will no doubt have the fertilizing effect. They believe that with the intervention of the Mother Earth, the yield will be good.

Their attitude towards the unseen powers is great. They deem it as the weapon for their success and failures. Their life is reflected by the rites and ceremonies they perform. Koyas depend entirely on the powers of gods. Each and every activity they perform in their life is closely connected with rituals. The rituals accompany various religious and community activities. Koyas do not believe in any philosophy prevalent among the primitive races. They do not think about the nature of god and how to propitiate gods and goddesses.

Birth Ceremonies

When the child is born, Koyas place the child on a cot. The mother resumes normal work quickly. The woman fetches water, firewood, leaves and minor forest products. She also attends to the domestic work, cooking and taking care of family members. On the seventh day, the newborn baby will be given a bath. The family members will invite all the neighbours and their nearest relatives. They all assemble together and name the child. Parents soon after keeping the child on the cot, keep a flower of the Mohwa tree (Bassia) in the hand of child. They pronounce a name which they think is apt or suitable for the child. If the child closes the hand over the ippa flower it is generally regarded as a sign that the child should acquire fame. If a child rejects it or cries they take this as a sign that they must choose another name. The elders throw away the leaf and select another name. They follow the same process of keeping another flower or a leaf in the child's hand. This process will continue until the child shows approbation. Sometimes, names will be selected among the friends. In such circumstances, the owner of that name gives his appreciation. He/She will place a coin in the hands of the child. If they do not have money, the father of the child will fulfil this. This ceremony is commonly followed with a feast accompanied by dancing and singing. Parents give a feast to all the members. Liquor will be served. Nowadays, this practice of naming the child with elaborate procedures is not taking place any more. Many of the Koyas got converted to Christianity, and those who attend the church will take small children and ask the Church priest to give them a suitable name.

Among Koyas, the practice was that if a child dies within a month of the birth, parents bury the child very near to their house. The belief of parents was that raindrops would fall on the graveyard of the child and plants will grow on it. They believe that god will bless them with another child in due course of time. Koyas bury bodies of young people, males and females very nearby. They stay a cow or a bullock and cut it and put a piece in the hand of a dead person. Koyas carry the corpse of dead person on a cot and place the body on the funeral pyre. Pujari or the Koya priest offers two pieces of cloth to the dead person. They remove the cot and bury the body. After burying of the dead body, they organize a small feast. After three days, people who attended the funeral slowly return to their places. They contribute cholam to the dead. Again they perform a feast. If a married woman dies, her tali will be put into her mouth. The pyre of a man will be lighted by his nephew, and the woman corpse will be lighted by her son. The people who attend the funeral will not observe pollution.

Superstitions and Ordeals

Koyas believe that death or diseases are not due to natural, specific causes. They believe that demons are their enemies and are solely responsible for death or diseases. The common practice during olden days was taking ordeals or leaving the entire place. Nowadays, this kind of practice is not taking place. If Koyas are pretty sure that a person is going to die, friends, family members will be assembled. They place the corpse of the dead person on a cot. They keep the body of dying person straight. If they suspect any person was indulged in witch-craft, the accused will be tried in front of a panchayat. They take a pot, partly filled with some water. They pour ghee and milk on the top of the pot and place it on fire. As soon as water boils, they throw stones into it and the accused will be asked to take the stone from hot water. If the accused takes the stone without causing injury Koya elders declare the accused as innocent. But if the accused develops some injury to the hand then they declare that the person is involved in a malicious act. They punish the guilty with suitable fine. Koyas believe that a sorceress named '*Chidipe*' rides over the boundaries of seven villages in the night and returns to its home in the morning. When the Chidipe does not like a man, she goes to him bare-bodied during the midnight. The Chidipe closes the door of the house in which she was dwelling and enters the house of the person. The Chidipe sucks blood of the person by putting her legs on the person. She will make him motionless and senseless like a dead wood. In such kind of time, they consult horoscope of the person, to find out whether their fortune is good or bad during that day. They take answers from hatching of the clutches of an egg. They also keep four grains or four seeds to elicit an answer. These seeds/grains will be named as male cattle (potu), sheep, etc. Or they put grain or a heap of ash under their cot to throw away evil spirits. They believe that night journey is inauspicious for them.

VII

Music and Dance

Music and dance have evolved as an expression of emotions of joy, pain, grief or terror or wonder in the face of the incomprehensible and sublime. Cave paintings during the ancient times suggest many ritual practices of hunter-gatherers such as hunting, collecting, distribution, and so on. The most primitive tribes expressed their feeling and emotions in the form of dance. The African tribe, Bantus used to reveal their feelings more precisely than anybody else. In the Bantu community, a person met another person and used to ask him how and what do you dance for? In the eastern countries different classes of people during their social gatherings prefer to dance. They are aware of what they are dancing for. Music and dance are an essential part of tribal life. Dance and music reflect the life of the aboriginal, indigenous groups of people. They represent their feelings, emotions, seasonal patterns of life throughout the year.

In all primitive communities, the functional nature of their primitive dance forms is aesthetic in nature. It had served many purposes. In religious rituals the aesthetic purpose of dance is very much seen. Primitive tribal communities have maintained their religious identities through their dances. Different racial groups of tribal, sub-tribal, regional groups of people have been practising different dance forms almost in every moment of their life. From birth to death, tribes follow their dances. Their spiritual aspiration, fear and joy are being expressed in their dances. They celebrate their birth ceremonies, puberty, initiation, fertility, courtship, marriage and death ceremonies and burials through dance. Different dance rhythms, steps are used by them to project reason for the dance, to alleviate the tediousness of hard work.

Adivasis prepare their physique to perform various dance movements. They decorate themselves ritually, tribally, mutilate their bodies with colours and costumes. Their dances have survived through generations. They preserve their art as a mark of respect and identity. Sometimes, their rich cultural heritage is ignored. Their dance, music and art forms are a part of national heritage. Tribal dances of the primitive, urban, settled, nomadic tribes have profound significance. Their art forms have acted as central points for their existence. The social structure of tribal communities gained much of their social cohesion from the group activities of dance. At every point of the life of aboriginals dance prevails. This illustrates their entire life cycle attaches importance to dance. Their very existence and feelings of emotions are intertwined with dance. Dance has become an important form for tribal communities to adore gods and goddesses, spirits and nature worship to understand the moods of deities, to please them, appease them, or entering into the communication with their gods and goddesses. The very understanding of the tribal world and their cosmos are expressed through their dance. Their celebration of different cult's objects and recounting of mysteries of their deities are traditionally organized in their dance forms. The incredible dance movements of tribals reflect their basic physical response to their world.

Like the dance of bees indicates to the rest of the hive the presence of pollen, Adivasis reveal much more through their dance movements about the highest points in their life.

Dance is one of the creative expressions of people closely associated with land and living religion that had different environment and background. There is a close link between tradition and trends of thought. Nature is always the strong inspiration for dance. Dance is coupled with customs and religious heritage that has a lot of common elements in it. Tribal dances in India are fully spontaneous. They are free to perform their dances in their surroundings. Natural grace is filled in tribal dances. Their dances are seasonal and religious. Their dances are very popular in rural India. They live more closely with their natural surroundings. They are vivid, temperamental, strong, and often primeval and filled with the zest of living. Tribal dances are costumed in beautiful colours. Tribal's being the earliest inhabitants have poured and brought life to their dance, song and music. Their dance is as old as civilization. Dance and music originated along with them.

Dance among the Koyas

The dance pattern of Koyas is thrilling and exciting. The original dance is very rich, forceful and tenderly expressive. The characteristic feature of Koya dance is its vigour. It has a rich quality and purpose. Koyas perform their dance on important ceremonial occasions. Their dances range from lactic life to funeral life. Their dance form is not abstract and mimic.

The Circle dance is very popular among Koyas. In this form of dance, Koyas gather into a circle, hold their hands and perform the dance rhythmically. They form into 'S' shape and dance beautifully. They form into inner and outer circles. Often, women and children will be gathered in the inner circles and men will be formed in the outer circles. Koyas perform another dance which is called ceremonial mourning dance. This dance is being performed during the time of the funeral ceremony in order to show their grief for the departed soul. They perform this dance in an abstract form. This pattern is very much there in the tribes of South Africa. They express their grief, sorrow, misery by action, rhythm and movement. Both men and women express their sympathy and sorrow. It is a common belief that such kind of expression will make the departed soul happy. Soon after completing the funeral ceremony, they start their dance movements during the time of lifting the corpse. They take anti-clockwise steps in a circle and move around the corpse holding each other's hands. Movements are always in a particular line. They hit their feet to the ground and jump slightly. Koya women hold their hands above their head. They show their despair on their face. Koya dance is simply derived from their social expressive urges. Their collective desire is to move, to exercise in a rhythmic fashion and to entertain one and all through their performance. A large number of Koya women in their hamlets enjoy their festivals by singing and dancing in circles in their *Gudems* (hamlets). The steps and movements of body and arms, legs and limbs are a fine gesture if one looks at their dance performance. They perform the dance in eight rounds. In each circle, Koy girls face each other, make themselves into circles and dance in eight counts. They turn to the right side, left side in the inner and outer circles repeating the same and different movements. They put fire candles and lights while dancing. Drummers beat drums rhythmically. Stepping simultaneously, they jump from place to place. They eventually encircle the camp to join in their dance joyfully. The campfire, lights provide them sufficient background to participate enthusiastically in the dance performance. The whole atmosphere is filled with joy and happiness. Such dances portray the happy and sorrowful events of their life. They show their abstract ideas with their dancing.

In the dance performance of Koyas, there is an implicit expression of some sort of need, desire to offer to their gods and goddesses. Perhaps they dance for the sake of fertility, their success in hunting activities, for rains, for a good crop, harvest and so on. Their dance consists of mimic patterns. Symbolic theme of their dance matches their need, in their performance. Their cultural temperament determines their dance to a greater extent. Their dancing style is unique to them as developed by their ancestors. Koyas perform bull fight dance. The dancers wear a headgear. Their headgear consists of horns and feathers. They also attach a veil to their headgear. Dancers hold drums and move in a circle. They form themselves into an 'S' form shape and form into a circle. Two persons come in between the circle and move in and out. He is considered as a bull and others try to hit and throw the bull from the circle hitting the horn of the dancer. School ground is being used nowadays by the Koyas to perform their art. Men adorn drums over their neck and place them on the thighs of the right foot. They play a hornpipe instrument to bring out musical sound.

Koyas perform their dance with the help of musical instruments. The rhythmic beats of drums will raise anybody's spirit to join the dance with Koyas. The audience, who see the performance of Koya dance, will immediately attract them and encourage them to join in their steps and movements in circles. Their dance performances are spectacular; show their cultural richness which they have created with sound, rhythmic movements of their life. A carefree mood in dance and performance will not be entertained by one and all among Koyas. They provide sufficient knowledge and background skill to perform their dance from their childhood days onwards.

Dance to Express their Happiness and Joy

Koyas exhibit happy movements through a simple dance. In this type of dance, they form into a circle. They hold the shoulders of each other. They go round in a circle. They move in the anticlockwise direction. They make simple movements in this form of dance. They make 1, 2, 3, 4 rhythmic steps. In count 1, they keep their right foot straight and step forward. They remain on the line or circle. Later they take the right foot back. On the third count they tap their feet on the floor and keep the left feet in the same position. In the fourth count they bend their body a bit forward. Finally, they come back to the first and second positions and gradually to the third and fourth positions. Men and women are placed closely to each other. They face each other in their inner side of the circle and perform their movements.

Music and dance ceremonies of tribal people explain the nature of their life. Their dance and music exist as a direct correspondence between tribals and their universe. Koyas are no exception to this. They dance for joy, for grief, for love, for prosperity and to avert any sort of calamity or danger. They use dance for religious purposes and for recreation. They are excited in their dance and music than in themselves. Like the tribes in Africa, Koyas are not so primitive. They express every emotion of their life with rhythmical body movements. However, there is a lot of change in their music and dance performances now. Due to the influence of modernization, globalization and Christianity, many old dance forms of the tribals have been disappearing fast. The ritualistic patterns of the dance and music of Koyas are severely affected due to these influences.

Ritualistic Dances

Koya men dance around the palm tree before they consume the *ippa sara* (toddy). In their dance performance, Koya men will be interlinked by holding each others hands. They hold their palms tightly and form into a circle. They move in an anticlockwise direction. They move into right and left side directions. They take four steps to each side and remain where they were in the original position. They repeat the same steps to the left side in an anticlockwise direction. They repeat their dance alternatively to the right and left sides in six counts in each side or direction. The belief of Koyas is that they had learnt their dance from their ancestral god Bhima. G.F. Paddison had described the dance of Koyas as a merry business. Koyas begin their dance with a simple song in their own language. Then they break into different groups and say some words in Telugu. Later, they burst into a delightful action and sing their song. During the Bhudevi festival (while adorning the earth) Koyas first come in a group, say half dozen young persons. They adorn colourful dresses, wear big size metal rings, basket caps, buffalo horns and pendants made out of peacock feathers. They bring tom-toms and musical instruments. Some adult women also followed Koyas in two batches. They joined the group by clapping their hands. They hold their waists with each other's hands. Young men performed dance following rhythmic steps to the drum beats. They showed their actions as if they are cutting an animal to offer to the earth mother, cutting the animal into pieces with devotion. Women started chanting words. They came slowly taking one step forward and backwards. Older women in villages started giving advice to young women and children and started narrating how they used to perform during their younger days. Women started moving round in steps in circles showing various incidents that happen in their life. Women surrounded various motifs and figures situated in a nearby place. Older women stood in a circle with their arms, and the younger Koya women took arms from the hands of older women and lifted them. They moved half round, half front and half backside directions. Smaller girls enthusiastically joined the performance clapping their hands. Edgar Thurston has mentioned that Koyas prophitiate the goddesses of earth called *Paiditalli*. They propitiate the mother goddess during winter months (December). All men, women and children get together in a village and collect cholam from each house. They call a Pujari from a nearby village and ask him to prepare bread with the collected cholam. They bring pots of water, pour it on each other and perform the dance for some time.

Among Koyas, ancestral worship is very strong. They follow their ancestral people at the time of Velpu. Every family member worships their ancestors. What is a Velpu? Velpu means a tree. Koyas select a large tree and tie different coloured cloths with a number of figures. These figures are considered as their ancestors. They collect different varieties of cloth and stitch pieces of cloth with main cloth. In Bhadrachalam, Koyas perform velpu. In order to commemorate the work of a dead person, they prepare a figure like Velpu. They tie ornaments, hair, bells to the figures. They march in a procession through the houses of Koyas in the village. If there is a relative or the head of a village Koyas stop there for a while. They give attention to the arrival of Velpu to their village/house. Members in the group sing, dance, march and make certain activities. This brings a religious symbol, unity, common feelings, shared experiences and respect for work by a particular person, matter of faith and spiritual respect. Thus, Koyas guide themselves to shape their world physically and spiritually. Young people within the tribe express their world through their knowledge. Every person accepts the knowledge, the world prevailing in the society of Koyas.

VIII

Welfare Measures

Successive governments had introduced various schemes for the economic development of Koyas. These schemes are based on a free allotment of land with necessary agricultural requirements, better housing facilities, health and veterinary schemes, education and cooperative stores, etc. In Nagur, Venkatapuram Mandals in Khammam district, many of Koyas had been evicted from the hill slopes, forest dwellings. Separate colonies were built as a part of rehabilitation programmes of Koyas. Agricultural lands were assigned. However, a number of Koya families have not got land pattas for their forest land till date. In the case of people who got land they were not provided with funds even on loan basis for the development of their land and cultivation. Irrigation facilities are seldom provided. The fate of agricultural operations was completely left to the mercy of rain gods. Under these pitiable conditions and with the denial of access to forests and forest produce, these unfortunate tribes have been reduced to a status of mere labourers working for contractors of roads and buildings, landlords, government officials, etc. The poor, economically backward Koyas earn only 80 rupees in a day.

Education

Under the Koya education scheme, arrangements were made for the supply of free textbooks, slates, uniforms and mid-day meals. Teacher training centres have been opened at Sudimalla in Yallandu taluk and at other places in

Khammam and Warangal districts. Koya tribal teachers are trained in these teacher training institutes. Some of the trained teachers are posted in tribal schools as teachers. Several village schools have been opened in tribal areas. Stipends are provided to the Koya boys and girls as incentives. Their schools and school buildings are very impressive. They look like modern towers. However, activities in these schools are not very encouraging. Koya tribal schools require adequate attention when compared to the schools in plain areas.

Cooperative Societies

In order to save and safeguard Koya tribals, cooperative societies were introduced in the tribal areas. These societies cater to the daily needs of Koyas at reasonable prices.

Medical and Health Facilities

Government had set up special medical units in the tribal villages in order to provide medical and health services to Koyas. The first full-fledged medical unit with a medical officer was started in Yallandu taluk. However, medical units started in the Koya villages are inadequate. Koyas are very much dependent on their traditional methods of medical treatment.

Political Developments

Koyas are fully aware of their political rights. They are conscious of their vote. When interviewed, some of them have informed that they are aware of activities of the political leaders. Koyas said that they pretty well know whom to vote and whom not to vote. They are asserting themselves nowadays. They cannot be wooed by political leaders. Koyas cannot be taken for granted by political leaders to achieve their political gains. By the performance of Koyas it is evident that they are in favour of those who stand by them. They support political leaders who have interest to fight for their legitimate cause. The Bhadrachalam Parliamentary constituency is reserved for tribal representatives.

Keeping in view the needs of tribals and their development as a whole, government should give top priority for the development of communication, networking facilities. The tribal blocks must be connected with inter-village and intra-village roads in their respective jurisdiction. Transport, communication facilities such as post offices, telegraphs, railways, roadways must be developed very fairly. There is also an urgent need to connect the remotest Koya villages with the progressing townships.

The Role of the Voluntary Organizations

In India there are several organizations which are working for the welfare, development and upliftment of tribal people. Adimjati Sevak Sangh is one of the pioneering institutions for the promotion of the welfare of tribes of India. The Sangh had established many ashram schools, hostels for tribal children of Koya community. Mahila mandalis, anganvadis and some Christian missionaries are actively working for the welfare of Koyas. Today, a large number of the Koyas have converted to Christianity and lost their rich cultural heritage due to the civilizational effects and the role of the NGOs.

IX

Conclusion

Jawaharlal Nehru said that people should develop along the lines of their own genius and imposition of alien values should be avoided. There are two factors which are closely related to the tribal development in India. (1) The integration of the tribals into the wider context of Indian society. This is accomplished by general public opinion and policies and the programmes initiated by governments. (2) The absence of the spirit of appreciation of the culture and values of tribal people in our society by promoting infiltration of non-tribals into tribal areas. There is no hesitation in saying that so-called legislations and welfare measures adopted by the state and central governments did not benefit the tribals nor showed any positive results and desirable changes in their lives. The aboriginal Adivasis are always self-sufficient, independent and do not expect any kind of help or reform from the plains' people or mainstream society. Tribal communities are forcefully displaced and dislodged from their traditional homeland, their natural resources and habitations. Adivasis are innocent and free children of the motherland. They have been subjected to unholy purification. Tribal people will progress only when the vested interests do not affect their environment and political pressure groups and corrupt officials do not enter their villages. These pressures should be kept away from tribal people. The entry of non-tribal people in the tribal areas should be completely curbed. Tribals should be provided with land and their problems should be addressed through a redressal mechanism. The Indian government had introduced many new policies. These policies and programmes do not auger well for the development process of scheduled tribes in the country. Further, future and development of Adivasis are severely affected due to these policies of the government. The living standards of scheduled tribes are going down every year. The population pressures from outside the tribal societies have resulted in scarcity of land, water and natural resources in the regions of scheduled tribes throughout the country. Their resettlement and displacement policies are severely affecting the poor Adivasis. They are undergoing a difficult phase due to displacement. Tribal people have no political background or support. Due to their poverty and non-political backgrounds they continuously remained backward for centuries. They should wage a freedom struggle to achieve the basic aims and goals of the tribal policy in the country which includes a piece of land to cultivate, a 'pucca' house for living, source of water for survival and agricultural purposes, a primary healthcare centre to solve health hazards, schools to educate their children, banks and financial institutions for their economic needs, a sympathetic and justified approach by government and civil society organizations towards betterment of their conditions, and a conducive environment to promote their culture and to guard tribal people from the destruction of forests, and encouraging their skills, techniques in the larger interests of Indian constitution and the general public.

References

Aiyappan, A., *Report on the Socio-economic Conditions of the Aboriginal Tribes of the Province of Madras*, Madras Government Press, Madras, 1948.

Clarke, Mary, *The History of Dance*, Orbis Publishing, UK, 1981.

Furer-Haimendorf, C. Von, *The Aboriginal Problem in Mulug and Narasarao Pet Taluqs: A Tour Diary*, 1947.

——, *The Aboriginal Tribes of Hyderabad, Vol. II: The Reddies of the Bison Hills*, Macmillan, London, 1945.

——, *Tribes of India*, OUP, New Delhi, 1982.

Government of Andhra Pradesh, *The Koyas of Andhra Pradesh*, Tribal Cultural Research and Training Institute, Andhra Pradesh, 1966.

Government of Madras, *Madras District Gazetteers: Cuddapah*, Government Press, Madras, 1930.

Majumdar, D.N., *Races and Cultures of India*, Asia Publishing House, New Delhi, 1974.

Mehta, Usha, *Tribal Dances in India*, Cyber Tech Publications, New Delhi, 2011.

Mohan, *The Koyas a Video Film*, EMRC, Hyderabad, 2009.

Ramaraju, B., *Glimpses into Telugu Folklore*, Janapada Vijnana Prachuranalu, Hyderabad, 1985.

Thapar, Romesh, *Tribe, Caste and Religion*, Macmillan, Delhi, 1977.

Thurston, Edgar and K. Rangachari, *Castes and Tribes of Southern India*, Cosmo Publications, New Delhi, 1909.

Tyler, Stephen A., 'Fields are for Planting: Swidden Agriculture among the Koyas of South India', *Journal of the Indian Anthropological Society*, Vol. IX, No. 1, 1974.

——, *Cognitive Anthropology*, Holt, Rinehart and Winston, New York, 1969.

Vidya Sagar, *Badhrachalam*, Visalandhra Book House, Vijayawada, 2010.

7

Savaras

Social and Cultural Life

Savaras are one of the ancient tribes of India. The name of Savaras has been mentioned in epic literature. It tells us that Savaras are in touch with the greatest Indian traditions from ancient times. They feel proud about their mention in the greatest epics. Habitations of the Savaras in Andhra Pradesh are mainly confined to the hill ranges and thick forests. They are living in the Eastern Ghats of Andhra Pradesh. They are predominantly found in Srikakulam district. Their habitations are located at the heights of 1,000 to 5,000 ft above mean sea level (MSL). Savaras are concentrated in Palakonda Taluk. They are living on fertile wetlands. Savara villages are fed by river Nagavali and its tributaries – Vottigedda, Suvarnamukhi and Vegavathi. The tropical climate of Savara habitations varies from region to region. They are living in humid atmosphere. They are living predominantly in the coastal taluks. They are living in the extreme seasonal variations. They are living in the temperature zone ranging between 43°C and 13°C. Summer is too hot and winter is too cold in their forest regions. The north-east monsoon waters Eastern Ghats of the region. They are living near the fast-flowing hill streams, rivers and rivulets. Savaras are familiar with the rivers of Nagavalli, Vamsadhara, Suvarnamukhi, Vegavathi, Mahendratanaya, Gomukhi, Champavathi, Bahuda and Kumbikotagadda.

I

Out of 35 Scheduled Tribes in Andhra Pradesh and Telangana, Savaras are one. Majority of Savaras are found in the districts of Srikakulam, Vizayanagaram and Visakhapatnam. A large majority of them are concentrated in Srikakulam district. Their habitations are largely found in Salur, Parvathipuram and Palakonda taluks of Srikakulam district. They are found in the villages of Mandara, Tekkali and Srikurmam. Their habitation covers

6,000 sq miles of mountainous territory in East Godavari and Visakhapatnam districts. Roughly, two-thirds of the Savara population is concentrated in Palakonda taluk. According to the Census 1961, their population was 68,185 people in Srikakulam district.

Savaras are the children of forests. Their habitations are located within the forests. Forest is their natural source of food and shelter since times immemorial. Forests where Savaras live are located in the Central Indian geographical region. Savara habitations exhibit variety of local changes in their quality, composition and density of their population. The linear settlement pattern is the distinctive character of Savaras. They follow traditional forest economy. They are following improved agricultural practices today. Agriculture is their main occupation. Savaras work hard in their 'Podu' agricultural lands and earn their living. They work very hard throughout the day in the forest. They spend their evenings by singing, dancing and on other forms of folk arts. They have a rich culture of music and dance. Savara tribals are being cheated by moneylenders who are ravaging their cultural life in many ways. Savaras strictly follow their marriage rules and prohibitions. The role and position of women in their society is very significant. Their rites and rituals connect them with their life cycle, marriage, birth and death ceremonies. The socio-cultural life of Savaras is exhaustive and suggestive.

Savaras are found in Madhya Pradesh, Orissa (Odisha), Bihar and Andhra Pradesh. The present population of Savaras in Odisha state is 3,11,614. Savaras are more than half of the total population of the state of Odisha. They are found in various districts in Odisha namely Ganjam, Sambalpur, Koraput, Bolangir, Puri, Cuttak and Damoh districts. In the state of Madhya Pradesh, Savaras are found in nine districts. In the state of Andhra Pradesh, 98 per cent of Savaras are living in Srikakulam district. The rest of Savaras are found in West Godavari, Visakhapatnam and East Godavari districts. Very few Savaras are living in Guntur, Chittoor and Nellore districts.

According to 2001 Census, Savara population in Andhra Pradesh is 1,22,979 (61,410 males, 61,569 females; 1,21,427 rural, 1,552 urban; 60,597 males are living in urban areas and 60,830 females are living in urban areas).

The literacy rate among Savaras, according to 2001 reports is 34.50 per cent. Savaras usually live in exclusive settlements of their own. They build their settlements on hill slopes. They live near hill streams to facilitate easy access to Podu and terrace fields and for fetching water.

Savaras are one of the autochthonous tribes of India. They are also referred to as Soura, Sowrah, Saurah, Sawara, Sawra, Sabara, Sabour, etc. In Sanskrit 'Savara' or Sabara means 'mountaineer'. Puranas described Savaras as Vindhya maulikas. Savaras are the aboriginals of Vindhya mountains. There are many references to them in the ancient and medieval Indian literature. In Ramayana, Rama is said to have met a Savara women, Sabari. Rama received fruits from her. According to Sitapati (1938–1943), linguistic evidence supports the theory that Savara had been in Malwa before they migrated southward. On the linguistic and ethnological grounds, Sitapati further stated that they are pre-Aryans and pre-Dravidians.

Savara area is described as the basin of Vamshadara-Jamboo river of which Gunpur taluk holds the upper reaches. Parlakimidi Taluk holds the lower reach. Between Gunpur and Parlakimidi two-thirds of Savaras are living. They are also found in Palakonda, Parlakimidi, Tekkali and Sompet Taluks. According to 1981 census, the total population of Savaras in Andhra Pradesh is 81,121. There is a slight increase in their population. According to 1971 census, only 6.6 per cent of Savaras are literate. They are predominantly found in Vizianagaram, Srikakulam and Visakhapatnam districts. Two-thirds of Savara population are living in the districts of Koraput and Ganjam in Odisha State.

Savara village is called as 'gorjan'. Savaras live in homogeneous settlements. Savaras are one of the ancient tribal groups living in the districts of Srikakulam and Vizianagaram. Savaras were spread over the Indian subcontinent long before the advent of the Aryans. Archaeological and historical evidence reveal that Savaras had lost their eminence in political, social and religious spheres. They have created a civilization of their own. Savaras have passed through various stages of life. They had passed their life from a nomadic tribe to the people who ruled large territories. Savara rulers and their army chiefs fought with Aryans and Dravidian kings. They invaded their territories. Hindu epics, Ramayana and Mahabharata have mentioned about Savaras. In the Vedic hymns, they were called 'Nishadas'. In Ramayana, there is a story about Savaras. When Rama was wandering in search of Sita, he comes across an Aryanized Savara woman named Sabari. Rama met her near the Panchavana lake. Rama eats fruits offered by her. This place is presently identified as Chhattisgarh. This is in the neighbourhood of the upper streams of Mahanadi. In Mahabharata, Savaras are mentioned as Sakas and Kambojas. Krishna's charioteer conquered Savaras. During Mahabharata period, Sahitya Darpana mentions that Savaras were leaf gatherers and woodcutters. They spoke Sabari and Ahiri dialects. Savaras are considered as the descendants of Vishwamitra who lived around 800 BC.

Savaras are one of the indigenous tribes of prehistoric times. They were experts in manufacturing of painted pottery, copper tools and weapons. Indian archaeologists are of the opinion that the bearers of Navada-Navadatoli culture as well as copper hoards belong to indigenous tribes such as Nishadas, Pulindas and Sabaras.

In the Skanda Purana (Kasi Khand), Savaras were referred as a nomadic tribe. They were the woodcutters of jungles. They were described as Vindhya Maulikas. They were the aborigines of Vindhya mountains. They lived in hills and forests. Savara country was very extensive in the olden days. It was spread on either side of Vindhyas (hills and forests of the present Madhya Pradesh state). Their territories spread up to Ganges in the North and Godavari in the South. They inhabited up to the Pennar river and along valleys of the Krishna river. They had settled down along the Basin of Vamsadhara river. They had permanent settlements in the plains of Srikakulam district.

Savaras faced invasions from the East. Upper caste Hindus of the plains of Srikakulam district invaded their settlements. They had driven them to the hills and forests. Savaras inhabited plains of Srikakulam district. They have got certain village names of that area. They had drawn their names on the walls of Siva temple. Their settlements were located near Tiraluru railway station on the Madras (now Chennai)-Howrah railway line. The word 'Savara' is derived from the word 'al-dub' literally meaning 'splitting of broom stick'. There were border disputes between Savaras and Telugus. On certain occasions it was a custom among the Savaras to hold a broomstick in their hands and break it. Near the entrance gate, on the interior wall of the Siva temple at Mukhalingam a figure was carved. The figure depicts a Savara person cutting a Mahuva tree and an idol is springing out from Mahuva tree.

Archaeological evidences indicate that Savaras have inhabited areas in South India. They inhabited Palakonda taluk in Srikakulam district. In a temple in Srikakulam district an inscription indicated that Savaras once raided Palakonda. According to Korai copper plate inscription, the founder of Kalinga dynasty 'Kamarnava' was defeated and killed at Dantavur near Srikakulam. Sabaraditya was the predecessor of Kamarnava and was a local ruler. Sabaraditya killed Kamarnava in 720 AD. Several ancient monuments depict that Savaras had several movements in Shahabad district. Savaras claimed Shahabad as their habitation in that local area. Rajput kings under the Bhojpur chief had driven them southwards. Thus, Savaras made inroads to the South. The rule of Savaras ended during 720 AD in Shahabad. According to Herbert Risely 'the local tradition describes the Savaras as being conquered. They were expelled from the Shahabad plateau around 500 AD by the Chedi rulers'. An inscription in Bhelsa (Vaidisha) of 1000 AD recorded that minister of the King, Raja Krishna was defeated by Kaundinya Vachaspati. He defeated Chedis. He was a Savara community person. Hall considered him as the Commander-in-Chief of the Chedi army. In one of the Chedi grants it was mentioned that Pallava king, Nandivarma claimed that he had released Sabara Chief Udayana at Nelvedi. He captured his peacock feather banner. Foulkes identified Sabaras with the Savaras of Eastern Ghats. The findings of D.N. Majumdar in the Sonar plates, confirm the contention of Foulkes as true and correct.

Savaras were mentioned in the historical accounts as early as the first century AD. Plini had mentioned the 'Surai', an indigenous people were inhabiting the interior places in Palibotri. Ptolemy also recorded 'Sabaras' as a nomadic people occupying the hilly regions of Ganga river. Cunningham stated that Savaras extended their country as far as South. They extended their rule up to Pennar river. Somatist Van Chest supported the inference drawn by Cunningham. They found some somatic characters among Savaras. The somatic characters found in some of Scheduled Castes were also found among Savaras. Cunningham stated that Savaras occupied the valleys of Krishna River. He had stated that Savaras of the eastern ghats are the single branch of the widely extended tribe. They were found in large numbers in the south-west of Gwalior and Marwar. Some of them were found in southern Rajputana. Savaras or Saharias of Gwalior territory occupied jungles of the Kota frontier. They spread up to the westward side of Marwar river. Tod mentioned them as the people of mixed race. It was believed that 'Kirata Survarna' was the original appellation of Savaras. Savaras of Sambalpur speak 'Bibhasa' (dialect). They are charcoal burners. Banabhatta in his '*Harshacharitra*' also mentioned about Savaras. He informed that Savaras acted as guides to Harshavardhana in his search of Rajyashree in the Vindhya mountains. Varahamihira had mentioned two types of Savaras. They are: 1. Parna Sabaras and 2. Naked Sabaras. Parna Sabaras learnt the art of weaving cloth with Vilva leaves. They adorned leaves around their waist. Naked Sabaras simply wandered naked without any cloth or leaves. The well-known poet Vakpati in his poem *Gaudavaho* also gave an account of Savaras. Similarly, Dandin and Banabhatta in 7th century AD vividly described Savaras. Amar Singh also mentioned about Savaras in '*Saluvabhyudayam*'.

II

Population

These accounts of the origin, development and historical background of Savaras make it clear that they are one of the ancient inhabitants of India. These evidences enable us to assert that once upon a time Savaras were spread and distributed in eastern part of India during 800 BC to AD 1200. Savaras are one of the dominant aboriginal tribes of India. But, fact remains that for centuries Savaras lived in isolation in the hilly regions and forests of the region. No proper attention was paid either during the British period or after Independence for the development of these people. Today, Savaras inhabit different states of Indian Union. They are exhibiting different social, cultural, political and linguistic patterns. They posses distinctly varied ethnic characteristics. The present Odisha State reports more Savaras. There are 3,11,614 Savara people in Odisha. They are distributed in 13 districts of the state. Ganjam district has most of Savara population of around 96,128. Ganjam is followed by Sambalpur with 82,595, Koraput 36,324, Bolangir 31,071 and Puri 26,188. Other districts had 1,000 population in each district. In Andhra Pradesh, according to 1961 Census, their population is 68,185 that was 5.14 per cent of the total tribal population of the state. Savaras are found predominantly in Srikakulam district which is bordering Odisha. More than 90 per cent of Savaras inhabited Srikakulam district alone. Savaras are also found in West Godavari, Visakhapatnam, East Godavari and Guntur districts. The distribution of Savaras is shown in the table given below.

Predominantly, Savaras are living in Srikakulam district (92,165), Vizianagaram (29,005), and West Godavari (210). In Srikakulam district Savaras constitute 35.43 per cent of the tribal population. The following table shows the distribution of Savaras in Srikakulam district.

Name of the Taluk	*Population of Savaras*	*ST Population of Malva*	*Total Population of the Taluk*	*Total % of STs of Taluk in %*	*Total Population of Saravas in the Taluk in %*
Srikakulam	259	501	2,17,993	57.70	0.23
Parvathipuram	12,857	62,131	2,18,471	20.68	28.44
Palakonda	11,088	26,316	3,44,646	42.13	8.11
Tekkali	5,279	5,541	1,89,984	95.27	2.92
Sompeta	6,040	6,613	1,40,941	91.32	4.69

From the above statistical figures it is evident that Savaras are inhabiting border areas of the district in the close neighbourhood of Odisha. The density of tribal population in Srikakulam district is highest in the state of Andhra Pradesh. There are 49 persons of tribal population per square mile. The state average of the persons of the Scheduled Tribes per sq mile is 12 persons.

Physical Features of Savaras

Fawcett has described the physical features of Savaras. Savaras are of middle height. They posses flat faces. They contain thick lips. They have broad and flat noses. Their cheekbones are very high. Their eyes are slightly oblique in shape. They are fair. They appear fairer than Odiya and Telugu people of plain areas. Savaras are shorter and fairer people. Their faces are distinctly Mongolian type. They go up and down the hills frequently. They carry heavy loads on their shoulders when they climb hills. They endure heavy loads of weight. They can climb 3,800 metres/feet hill without any break. Usually, Savaras wear dresses. Their dress consists of large bunches of feathers. They generally wear white coloured dresses. They make coloured turbans for their heads. Turbans act as protection for their head. They tie their hair on the top or one side of their head. They posses ornaments for their heads. They stick hair pins for their hair. They tie a knot for their head either at the top of the head or on the side of the head. Savaras use wooden piece ornaments for their head. Brass metal hairpins are also used by them for their head. They also adorn peacock feathers or jungle cock's feathers on their head. Savaras smoke pipes. Older people are very fond of smoking tobacco. Savaras wear brass necklaces around their neck. A Savara man wears as many as 30 necklaces at a time. They wear various lengths of necklaces. Sometimes their necklaces are rounded for thirty times. They wear white or coloured cloth around their waists. They wear the piece of white cloth as Gochi. Women wear saries. They wear necklaces like their men. Women tie their hair. They wear only one cloth. They tie their Sarees around their waist. During festivals or while performing their dance, Savara women wear white cloth up to their shoulders. Every male member among Savaras wears a small ring. Their rings are made up of silver. Men and women wear a silver ring for their noses. Females wear two silver rings for their two parts of their noses and in the septum. Men and women wear bangles. Women also wear anklets. The brass necklaces, anklets, ear rings, studs are all made in Savara hilly regions. They are also experts in making brass metal ornaments. The main weapon of Savaras is the bow. They also make ornaments with peacock feathers, swords, daggers, etc. Savaras use very small size bows. Bows used by Savaras are much smaller than the bows used by other hilly tribal people. Size of the bows used by Savaras is about 3½ feet long. The sizes of their arrows are 18 to 21 inches. The bow is made of bamboo. The needles of arrows are tipped with iron. To shoot birds, Savaras use some kind of blunt-headed arrows. Savaras train their children from their childhood in using bow and arrows. They can easily shoot anything up to the range of 25 to 30 yards. Kapu and Konda Savaras differ in their dressing pattern. Kapu Savaras dress like plains people. Konda Savaras wear their traditional dresses. Savara women wear 'Pacha bottu' either on their hands or foreheads. They believe that after their death, that was the only thing which remains with them. Savaras call the person who does this kind of marks on their bodies as 'Daya'.

III

Society of Savaras: Life Pattern

Savaras do not have a uniform pattern of social structure. They represent different patterns of society in their habitations. They have varied cultural, social, political and linguistic patterns of their own. In general, society among Savaras consists of twenty-six endogamous divisions. They do not have a clear cut exogamous subdivision among them. The following are some of the names of the Savaras: Arsid Savara, Bhima, Basedor, Besend, Bobbili, Dondiya, Goutara, Jadu, Jara, Jati, Jurai, Kampu, Kindal, Kimsed or Kisser, Kudumba, Kumba, Lambolanja, Luang or Luara, Malia, Mara, Kapu, etc. Edgar Thurston subdivided Savaras into two broad subcategories, viz. hill Savaras and plain Savaras. Savaras are further divided into eight groups which are as follows: (1) Among the hill Savaras, Jati Savara or Maliya Savaras consider themselves as superiors. They feel the other sections of Savaras as inferior. They are non-vegetarians. They eat meat of buffalo. They do not consume the meat of a cow. (2) The second section of the Savaras are called as Arsi, Arisi or Lombo Linjiya Savaras. In Savara language 'Arsi' means monkey. Lombo-Linjiya refers to the long tail of monkey. Some Savaras are identified with this name. They wear a long piece of cloth on their waist. They follow weaving as their main occupation. They weave coarse cloth worn by Savara tribes. They also do agricultural work. (3) Luara or Mirli Savaras do ironwork. They are experts in making arrowheads and other household articles. (4) Kindal Savaras are expert basket makers. They manufacture rough baskets for keeping and storing their grain. (5) Jadu Savaras live in hilly areas. They live in Kollakota and Puttasingi villages in Srikakulam district. (6) Kumbi Savaras are potters. They make different sizes of earthen pots. Fawcett writes 'these pots are made in few villages in the Saora hills. Earthen vessels are used for cooking, or hanging up in the houses. They are used as fetishes for their ancestral spirits or certain deities'. (7) Plain Savaras are also called as Kapu Savaras. They are cultivators. They are also called Pallapu Savaras. They are identified as Suddha or good Savaras. Among Savaras, the first generation people restricted themselves to hilly tracts, thick forests, jungles and valleys. Some Savaras took to plains life. Traces of amalgamation became apparent among them. They became a hybrid racial group. They differ in their original appearance and manners. Among Savaras, the Kapu Savaras retained many of their traditional customs and practices. However, Suddha Savaras have adopted language and customs of Odiya people. (8) A section among the Kapu Savaras called themselves as 'Kuduaga' or 'Basery'. Gidugu Ramamurthy stated that this word (Basery or Kuduaga) was derived from the Savara word 'base' which meant salt. This name was applied to Savaras who were living below the ghats. Savaras used to attend fairs and sell salt. Thus, the name is given to them. Gidugu Ramamurthy also referred to section of Kapu Savaras. They have adopted customs of upper-caste Hindus. Kapu Savaras are also known as Kudumba Savaras. A subdivision among Kapu Savaras are also called Kudumba Savaras. They have surnames like Bobbili and Bhima. Bobbili is a town in Vizianagaram district. Bhima was the second person among the five Pandava brothers.

Housing Pattern among the Savaras

In the Oriental manuscripts, it is recorded that Savaras build their houses along the mountain streams. They construct their houses in the middle of the forest. They live forty to fifty miles deep in forest areas. They extend up to fifty miles. The main reason stated by Savaras to live in the deep forest were (1) Podu agricultural work, (2) whenever Savaras face any threat or danger from rulers or neighbours they can easily escape to deep forests, and (3) to avoid hostility and friction from other sections of people.

Savaras mainly follow the linear type of housing structures. Savaras living in the agency tracts and adjoining plain areas of Srikakulam and Vizianagaram districts have exclusive settlements of their own. They never build their houses with other tribal population. They do not live with other non-tribal population. In Seetampeta agency, Devanapuraguda and Akkanaguda villages are exclusively inhabited by Savaras. Savaras generally establish their settlements on hill slopes. They live near hill-streams. This helps Savaras in the easy access to the Podu cultivation. They can bring firewood easily to their field and burn them before they begin their Podu cultivation. They also can collect roots, tubers, leaves and other minor forest products easily. They can also easily facilitate water to their fields.

Savaras follow a definite structural pattern while constructing their houses. A Savara settlement consists of two rows of parallel huts, facing each other's houses. Their settlements consist of two linear rows of huts. Their houses are divided into several compartments. Each compartment is occupied by a single family member. Some Savara settlements consist of only one linear row of houses, whereas most of Savara settlements consist more than two linear rows of houses. The parallel linear houses of Savaras always extend from east to west. Houses of Savaras face either north or south direction. The alignment of rows of Savara settlements, their entrance doors are typically made and designed by them. Their entrance doors face east or west. They cannot withstand heavy heat in their localities during summer season.

To keep their entrance doors either east facing or west facing they have got some sentiment for this. A story was prevalent among Savaras that a tiger faced east. Savaras consider north and south represent the front and back parts of the body of a tiger. That is the reason why they prefer their entrances either to east or to west.

Savaras generally construct their houses with wood. Their houses consist of wood logs with a height of 6–8 metres. They plaster their house walls with red mud sand. They invariably construct their houses a few feet above the ground. Their houses are above the normal level of ground. They construct their houses on uneven grounds. Their houses are normally five feet above ground level. Roofs of their houses are thatched with the grass. They usually prefer only one door for their houses. Their houses consist of few ventilators. They construct a big room in front of their main gate of the house. A total number of six to eight people can easily stand in this room. They also make arrangements with the cross-beams of four feet height from floor. They store grain in baskets. Women make arrangements for cooking. Savaras cut buffalo meat into small pieces and dry them under the sun. They store them in boxes. They take precautions to avoid bad smell from the stored meat. They do not store sweets. They keep their knives, axes, swords, bows, arrows on the lintels of their houses. Agricultural implements will be placed under a roof. They keep big implements on the walls. Gidugu Ramamurthy Pantulu wrote: Whenever a tiger enters into the cottage of Savaras and carries away one of Savara villagers, the villagers desert their settlements. They often give sacrifices to spirits. Even when they are affected by diseases like Cholera they abandon their small villages. When they face any calamity in their villages they change their dwelling places. Some of the males among Savaras have many wives. They construct separate houses for their women. They also frequently shift their places for the convenience of their wives. During the death of their cattle, and diseases, they desert their houses and villages.

One of the traditional customs that prevailed among Maliah Savaras is that if a Savara family selects a new place or site for dwelling purpose, they place grains of rice in pairs. The number of grain pairs equals to the number of married couples in their house. They cover grain pairs with a coconut shell. They examine the pairs of grains on the following day. If they find all the grains in the shell they consider the sign as auspicious. Among Kapu Savaras, grains of the rice will be folded up in leaflets of betel plants or placed in a split bamboo.

IV

Lifecycle and Ceremonies among the Savaras

Every Savara member will cope up with their new social environment. They pass through critical interaction period in their social set-up. They live a group life. They believe in super natural and superhuman powers. They cope with societal stress and strains. They pass through successfully every stage of their life: birth, infancy, adolescence, youth, married life and death. Savaras perform many ceremonies and rituals. They perform magical rites to protect their people at every stage of their life. They conduct various rites and rituals from their birth to death. Even after death they facilitate their departed souls. They wish that their departed souls should lead a happy life in the world of spirits. Savaras do not indulge in sexual intercourse generally during night times. They believe that human organs of females sleep during night time. They prefer forest to do sexual intercourse during day time. Young couple in a Savara family generally indulges in sexual intercourse in the forest. They tie wooden poles and make a small comfort for their activity. They keep branches of trees in their personal places. They put special marks ('X' shaped marks) at their places of intercourse. This gives an indication to others that nobody should disturb them by going through such places. Nowadays, Savaras are discontinuing this practice. This practice of Savaras is on the wane. Many of Savaras prefer night time for their sexual intercourse, particularly in their houses. A woman is not considered for sexual intercourse when she misses her menstrual cycles (Aganathi). There are no special food taboos and working taboos waived for a pregnant woman. They restrain pregnant women from doing heavy manual work or labour contract work. They prevent them from going to burial grounds. They fear that evil spirits will harm the pregnancy of women. They also conduct abortions if they get any suspicion. They prefer magico-medical treatment for abortions. They take their women to a person called *Kudan* or *Kudanboi*.

Savara women conduct delivery of woman outside the main house. They perform it in the varanda or in the cattle shed. The place where delivery is conducted will be closed from all sides to provide privacy for women. Soon after the woman gets delivery cramps she sits on a stone holding a rope which hangs from the roof of house. She stretches her legs wide apart. The *'Kudanboi'* conducts delivery of Savara women. During the time of delivery all the males will be requested to leave the house except two or three males for help in case of any emergency. In case women feel the difficulty of giving birth to the child, Kudanboi inserts a leaf in the hair of the women who suffer form delivery pains. Savaras are experts in psychotherapy. For making easy delivery, medicinal doctor stands outside the house and recites hymns loudly such that women will be able to hear them clearly. He chants hymns and breaks coconut. Soon after breaking the coconut, he expects the woman to give birth to the child. The persons who conducts delivery invariably delay the breaking of coconut. As and when the person senses delivery, they break the coconut. If delivery gets further complications, Kudan gives the root of 'Uttareni' plant. Kudan keeps the plant in the mouth of a woman thrice. Savaras believe that soon after keeping Uttareni plant in mouth delivery will be done very quickly by the woman. 'Kudanboi' cuts the umbilical cord with a knife. Kudanboi buries the placenta in a pit covering it with cow dung. Savara women are very strong. Pregnant women also work in the fields. Savara women may sometimes deliver in the Podu lands or in the forest. Savara woman herself cuts the umbilical cord with a broken piece of the pot and brings the baby home.

The mother and child will not be given bath after the delivery. On the day of delivery mother will be fed with hot rice. They will not provide any curry with hot food. Savaras believe that hot food will give pregnant women sufficient strength and stamina to give birth to child. Mother will be given a massage with castor oil. After the delivery Savara women observe birth pollution. It extends to nine days. The 'Desari' will fix up the date of bath or purification bath. Till then, Savara woman cannot enter the house. If the mother gives birth to a girl baby she is permitted to enter the house on the third day. If the mother gives birth to a male child she will be permitted to step in on the fifth day. Even though she is permitted to enter the house she will not be allowed to touch household articles. She will be permitted to sleep on a cot which is placed in the corner of room. The Desari fixes 9th day for purificatory bath for the woman and child. Kudanboi shaves the head of new born child.

Savara woman will be taken to the stream with a few relatives and she will be given bath in the stream. After the bath, she will be brought back. The mother places child before the 'Lingor'. Lingor is a figure drawn on the wall of the house by Savaras. The mother and other people sprinkle turmeric rice to Lingor and child. After taking the blessings of 'Lingor' the woman is allowed to move and attend to her regular work in the house freely.

The name-giving ceremony to a child among Savaras is an elaborate ritual. Usually, the child is named after the day on which it is born. The name of a child ends with the sound 'a' if the child is a male. If the child is a female the name ends with 'i' sound. Some of the names of Savaras are as follows:

Names of the Savaras

Day of Birth	*Name of the Male Child*	*Name of the Female Child*
Monday	Sombra	Sombari
Tuesday	Mangadu	Mangi
Wednesday	Buddha	Budi
Thursday	Lakkiya	Lakkior Gurbari
Friday	Sukru	Sukri
Saturday	Sanniyya	Sanni
Sunday	Addiyya	Addi

If the child cries loudly soon after the naming, Savaras believe that their ancestors disagreed with the name of the child. In such cases, Savaras name the child with one of their ancestors' name. Savaras approach 'Kudan' to verify whether their ancestors' were reborn. Savaras offer the Kudon with a 'Solla' of rice. He will also be given a small pot of liquor. The Kudon keeps rice on the winnowing fan. He recites hymns. He falls into a trance and utters loudly the name of the ancestor who was born as a child. During such occasions Savaras sacrifice a goat during the birth ceremony. They call birth ceremony as 'Ideesung' ceremony.

The name-giving ceremony in some of the Savara settlements is performed elaborately. It is also a costly affair for Savaras. Therefore all brothers in a house share the expenses of function. The auspicious day for the name-giving ceremony will be fixed by Jatapu 'Desari'. Savaras offer him rice, liquor and money. The Desari drinks and spinkles liquor on the floor. He informs the auspicious day to the parents of child. On the day of name giving ceremony the Desari will be brought to the village. Savaras wash the feet of the priest. Meanwhile 'Kundan' draws designs of 'lingor' on the wall. He sprinkles some liquor and turmeric on Kudan. They also sprinkle blood of sacrificed animals on 'Lingor'. Savara women cook ceremonial food called 'Bonam'. The child will be laid on cradle. Some turmeric mixed rice will be sprinkled on the child. Savaras serve ceremonial food (Bonam) to the 'Gamang', 'Buyya' and the Kudan. As the Desari is from the Jatapu tribe he hesitates to accept food from Savaras sometimes. Savaras offer him four seers of rice, liquor, dhal and new clothes.

Savara woman resumes her normal work, household activities, or economic activities within two months after delivery. She actively resumes her work and usually contributes to the economic status of her family. Parents of Savara women will take care of her postnatal health. During the lactation period Savara women mainly depend upon their grown-up children. In the same way, Savara woman also depends on grown-up children for 'Podu' cultivation work and food gathering activities. Savaras live in nuclear families. The assistance of the elderly woman will not be available always for a pregnant woman.

A Savara child will be given breast-feeding for a period of 1½ year to 2½ years. Savaras clean child's mouth daily. They prepare some kind of a paste with garlic and pepper powder to ward off the diseases of children. They give loin cloth to their children at the age of 4–5 years onwards. The small children usually accompany their parents or elder siblings to Podu fields and forests. Savara women train their young daughters to help them from the age of seven. The girl child helps her mother in the household work and boys help their parents intending cattle to the fields.

Girl children attain puberty by the age of 12–14 years. At the first sign of puberty the girl child will be asked to sit in the corner of house. Mother approaches the 'Desari'. She offers rice and turmeric to find out whether the attainment of puberty day is auspicious or inauspicious for her. If the Dasari returns the turmeric and keeps the rice for himself, Savaras find it auspicious. If the Dasari keeps the turmeric and returns the rice, Savaras find it inauspicious. They fear that in such cases some member in the girl's husband family will die. They disapprove such situational marriages.

The girl who attains puberty will be given a turmeric water bath. She will be asked to sit near the Varanda or front door, or cattle shed. She will not be permitted to enter the house. Savara people will not allow the girl to touch household articles. She is debarred from taking up any work. She is strictly considered to be polluted. Girls are kept in isolation until her menstrual flow ceases completely. As soon as menstrual period gets over, the girl will be taken to the nearest stream to take bath and wash her clothes. Savara woman dries her cloth in the sun and while returning she wears clothes and comes back to the house. The girl cleans the entire house by smearing cow dung. She returns back to her normal work and household activities.

During the monthly cycles, Savara women observe pollution strictly. Woman confines herself to a corner in the house. Savaras do not arrange any separate room or place for the girls at the time of their menstruation. Savara males allow their women to go to outside work when Savara woman is in the process of monthly cycles. Savaras believe that if women touch seeds or grains when they were in menstruation time, the seeds will not sprout or grow properly. Savara girls attain womanhood soon after attaining puberty. Savaras perform marriages for 15–16 years old children. Soon after attaining, 15–16 years of the age they approach the 'Desari' on an auspicious day with 'Mahuva' liquor and rice. Desari sprinkles liquor and recites hymns. Desari arranges a knot behind his head. In a year or two that person will get married. However, such ceremonial initiations are not being performed for girls. Savaras living near the plain areas have discontinued such practices.

The next important stage after puberty is marriage. Among Savaras, there are four types or methods of performing marriages. They acquire spouses according to their four methods, socially accepted by them. They are: (1) *'Penkui'* – a marriage by negotiation and mutual agreement. (2) 'Dingdengboi *or Dandaboi*' – a marriage by elopement with an unmarried woman or married person. (3) *'Kinarsung or Illarikam'* – a marriage by service and (4) *'Ulaiboi'* – a marriage by exchange.

'Penkui' or marriage by negotiation is a long drawn process. It is very time-consuming. Acquiring a spouse by Savaras through this type of a marriage is a costly affair for them. This kind of marriage involves series of formalities. This involves various reciprocal visits and exchange of pots of liquor and other ceremonial gifts among Savaras. The party from bridegroom initiates negotiations. The marriage party consists of relatives, village elders like Gamang, Buyya, Kudan and Desari. First the village elders and bridegroom's parents receive consent of marriage from the parents of bride. Elders of both the parties then sit together and decide the amount of bride price. Formally, they exchange gifts before the actual performance of marriage ceremony is initiated. The village elders, parents of the bride and bridegroom play a significant role in this. Among Kapu Savaras, marriage ceremony takes place in the following manner. The Desari fixes the auspicious day for marriage celebration among Kapu Savaras. Father of the bridegroom, the Gamang, Buyya and Kudan of their village along with a few relatives of the bridegroom visit the brides village. They also take a pot of liquor along with them. Kapu Savaras call it *'Jing-Jing-bridal-sal'*. Kapu Savaras also call *'Dangidiboidalsal'* that is the bride is mature and ready for marriage. They carry bangles (*'kaddu'*) and beads (*'buddu'*). Savara women accompany the wedding party. They keep a pot of liquor, bangles and beads. If the girl is inclined to marry the boy she will leave the house. If she dislikes the marriage she takes liquor pot, beads, bangles and throws them in the open space or in front of the house. If the brides' parents accept the proposal they invite the Gamang, all their relatives and village elders. All the members drink liquor brought by bridegroom's party. Generally, Savaras give 3 to 4 months to make arrangements to perform marriage. The bridegroom and his parents often take liquor to please bride's parents, village elders and their relatives. They strengthen their ties with their frequent visits. The marriage proposals, once accepted by the elders in the Savara community, will not break generally. If they want to break their marriages they approach *'Dangidiboi'*. They do not wait for a long period to perform marriage. The girl sleeps with her mother-in-law and helps her in all her household activities. The bride and bridegroom do not sleep together. After some days the bride's parents will be invited to the bridegroom's house. In their meeting, village elders decide the bride price or *Voli*. Generally, they fix two *gamangs*. Parents of the bridegroom will pay two *gamangs* to bride's parents. The '*Desari*' will inform the bride's parents the day on which the bridegroom's parents have to visit their house in return.

The bridegroom along with his parents, relatives and village officials proceed to a party arranged for them by the parents of bride. A golden or silver ring will be offered as a present/gift to the bride. They also take 20 seers of rice, 10 seers of dhal, one arrowhead, one or two pots of liquor and bride price. Generally, quantities of these items depend on the economic condition of bridegroom's family. The brother of the bride will be offered a pot of liquor separately. The '*Desari*' of the bride's side keeps some leaves, cups near the liquor pot. He invokes the deities sprinkling liquor on the leaves and cups. The Desari gives a small amount of liquor to all the people who were present there. Then they seat the bride and bridegroom in a yoke. The Desari smears turmeric on the faces of the couple. They will be taken to a nearest pond and they will be asked to bathe themselves. The couple will be offered new clothes to wear. They will be asked to sit side by side and hot food will be served to them. The bridegroom will be forced to eat one morsel of food from the plate of the bride. Later, the bride and the bridegroom exchange their plates. They exchange plates for three times. The Desari will take the bride and the bridegroom outside and will ask the bridegroom to give the right hand to the bride and vice versa to wash their hands by each other. Later, the Gamangs, Desaris, Buyyas and other villagers take their food. They spend the rest of the day in singing and dancing and their cultural activities.

The parents, relatives and the villagers of the bride's party proceed to the bridegroom's village. The parents of bridegroom cook 20 seers of rice and 5 seers of dhal. They also keep 5 to 6 pots of liquor. The Desari of the bridegroom's village serves food to the bride and bridegroom in two adda leaf plates. He smears turmeric water on the faces of bride and bridegroom. He exchanges their plates after both of them having eaten a morsel of food. The Desari repeats the process three times. After eating food, the Desari keeps the right hand of the bridegroom over the right hand of bride. He takes both of them outside of the house to wash their hands. The Desari serves food to all the relatives. Then, the parents and relatives leave the village of bridegroom the next day. The bride stays back with the bridegroom. However, nowadays Savaras are not following this system of elaborate procedure of marriage. Savaras feel that it is time consuming and a costly affair. Savaras generally arrange matrimonial alliances by negotiation and mutual consent. They erect marriage pandals, and Mangala Sutram is tied around the neck of the bride. They are following Hindu customs. But this was not done in the past.

Marriage by Elopement

Another type of marriage prevalent among Savaras is marriage by elopement. They call this 'Dum-Dum-Tup'. This will be preceded by courtship period. The boy and girl exchange their mutual love. They involve in sexual intercourse either in the forest, agricultural operations, during their Podu cultivation activities or during the shandy market visits. The girl first accepts proposal of the boy for elopement. The boy intimates his intentions to his parents. If the parents accept his intentions, on an auspicious day relatives of the boy and his friends intimates the girl about their waiting for her near a marked place either a stream, well or forest. They approach her and convince her to accompany them to the boy's house. Generally, the girl accompanies them. Sometimes, the girl pretends not to accompany them or unwilling to elope with the relatives or with the boy.

In such cases, girl will be forcefully carried away to the boy's house. Immediately they inform to the Gamang. Gamang, in turn informs the same to the parents of the girl. Gradually the elopement of the boy and girl will be informed to all Savaras in the village. After knowing the news of elopement, parents on both the sides send their mediators for negotiations. The main intention of such negotiations is whether both of them are really liking each other to live together as wife and husband. Parents of the two parties offer liquor to please each other and compromise to settle the marriage. They quarrel sometimes and with the help of the village elders and friends, they settle the matter. Both the parties secure money to pay 'Danda' or bride-price. They purchase liquor and distribute the same among community members.

'Desari' fixes a day for the payment of Danda in consultation with two parties. On that particular day the parents of girl accompany their village Gamang, Desari, Buyya and Kudan and with a few relatives to the boys village. The girl's parents do not go straight to the house of the boy. They select some mediators and try to settle the issue from their house. They select an influential house and inform of their arrival for the negotiators to village elders and parents of the boy. The boy's parents also invite their Gamang, Desari, Buyya, Kudan and other relatives for the negotiations. When all the members of both the parties assemble at the place the Gamangs of the villages ask the boy whether they are willing to live as wife and husband and get married to each other. After the consent of both the parties the girl's father will receive 'Danda' from the parents of boy. Gamangs of the two villages will act as mediators. They try to compromise the two parties. They fix the amount of Danda. The Gamang of the girl's village will take responsibility for returning the Danda money to the parents of the girl. The Desari of the boy's village sprinkles liquor and invokes deities and ancestral spirits. All of them take liquor. The parents of boy's side arrange a small feast in the village. After the feast, parents of the girl and their party return to their village. The parents of the girl will purchase a goat or buffalo with the 'Danda' money. Sometimes, among Savaras even married couples also resort to this kind of payment of Dandaboi to the village elders. They secure their second and subsequent spouses if they are not happy with their family life.

Marriage by Service

Another kind of marriage that Savaras generally follow is marriage by service. They call this marriage as '*Kinarsung*'. When the parents of the girl do not have males in their house, they adopt their son-in-law as sons for the protection of their family members. He will look after the interests of their family. Savaras prefer son or daughter of a sister or brother of wife as spouses for boys and girls. Some Savaras do not like to live in the houses of father-in-law. Very few

Savara families are adopting this method. Generally, father-in-law of a Savara will look after the boy well and gives a share.

According to this marriage, mutual consultation and agreement between the parents along with elders of the village including 'Gamang' is compulsory. The boy will proceed along with his parents and village elders to the house of the girl. They select an auspicious day for the occasion. They carry one saree (Sindri), some liquor along with them. The party from the boy's side will not directly go to the house of girl. They wait in front of the girl's house. Girl's parents naturally invite boy's parents and the village Gamang into their house. Gamangs from both sides will ask them what they have brought along with them. They, in turn, say that they could not bring anything with them as they could not get – clothes, food, oil, animals, etc. Then father of the bride says 'we have everything, you can live with us happily'. Desari sprinkles liquor and invokes deities and their ancestral spirits. All of them take liquor. After taking food, all of them return home. On an auspicious day, the parents of the girl invite all of them to come for marriage. Desari of the boy's side will decide the marriage day. All of them come to the village along with the Gamang, Desari and Buyya. Relatives do not carry anything with them. Soon after reaching the house of the bride, water will be given to wash their feet. They enter the house. The bride and bridegroom will take a bath. They dress themselves with new clothes. They sit for a feast. First, food is served to the bride and bridegroom. After taking a part of the meal they exchange their plates three times. The 'Desari' take the boy and the girl outside. He places the right hand of the bridegroom and keeps it on the bride's left hand. He washes the hands of the boy and girl. Food is served to all the members and relatives. Soon after having food they return to their village leaving the bridegroom in the girls' house.

Savaras call the marriage by exchange as 'Uliboi'. In a Savara family, when they have a daughter and a son for marriage they exchange the girl and boy for the marriage. Parents of the boy and girl make informal consultations in the beginning. Later, Gamang of the village conducts negotiations. Bridegroom goes to the other village along with the Gamang and other village elders. They carry liquor along with them. They ask each other to bestow their sisters for marriage. As the informal talks take place earlier, there will not be much difficulty for the settlement. Marriage will be celebrated in either of the two houses. They entertain guests with a dinner. They treat village elders with liquor.

Among Savaras, marriage is the institution on which the superstructure of a family is built. Divorce drives a wedge in the institution of marriage. Divorce causes the ultimate destruction of the superstructure of a family. Elopement of a married woman is not very frequent among Savaras. Divorce is socially sanctioned among them. Economic, social and psychological factors mainly contribute to the dissolution of family. Economic bankruptcy, poverty, friction in the internal family structure lead to dissatisfaction on the part of the woman. This leads to the consequent development of an erroneous relationship with another man. It is imperative on the part of the paramour to pay community fine (Kulatappu) or 'Maganali' (Danda) when a Savara woman deserts her husband and elopes with another person. Village elders have to recognize their disunity. The disunity of wife and husband has to be socially acceptable. Neither Savara women nor Savara men have the claim over children born due to the first marriage. The family plays a key role among Savaras. Unlike other tribal groups of the region, Savaras are not an exogamous class. The simple unit of the social structure of Savaras constitutes a nucleus family. Their families are patriarchal. Husband is the head of the family. He is mainly responsible for proper maintenance of the family. However, wife plays no less an important role. She looks after children, household chores, assists husband in family pursuits. She also performs social, religious ceremonies in the family. Most of the Savara families are monogamous. Polygamy is very rare among them. Polygamous families are very limited among Savaras. Majority of monogamous families are nuclear families. Their nuclear families consist of a husband, wife and their children. The size of a family varies from 4 to 5 members.

Death Ceremony

Savaras attribute death to evil spirits. Among them, if a male person dies in the evening after 5 pm the corpse will be placed on the Verandah. Two persons will be asked to keep a constant watch over the body. An oil lamp will be burnt constantly throughout the night. Savaras believe that Kulba (Atman) of the dead person will do harm if that dead person was not watched carefully. Those near the dead body do not sleep the whole night. They spend their night singing and dancing, honouring the dead person. They burn firewood next morning. Women bathe the dead body with water. Savaras apply turmeric or oil to the dead body. They wrap the body with a cloth around the waist. They put a turban or a new saree on the dead body depending upon the sex. They place the body on a cot. '*Chigmar*' (carriers of the corpse in Savara community) carry the dead body to cremation ground. There are four Chigmars who actually carry the body to burial ground. They are known as 'Madothambereta'. Savara men and a few women follow the dead body to the cremation ground. They cremate their dead bodies. Some of them who were converted to Christianity bury their dead bodies. Some women will be asked to stay back to clean the house and prepare food for the burial attendants. They arrange pyre in a particular manner in the burial ground. They place three wooden logs in the north-south direction. They form layers alternatively. In case of females, they keep the dead body keeping the face upward. They keep head of the dead body towards East and legs to the West. All the personal belongings such as knife, digging stick, cot, etc. will be burnt along with the dead person. One of the 'Chigmars' will go around the pyre three times and sets fire to the dead body. They wait till the body is burnt. After the body is burnt the 'Chigmar' and other relatives of Savaras go to a stream and take bath. They go to their houses in wet clothes. After going home they take bath again and change their clothes. Later, they take food. The next day, one of the family members of Savaras goes to the 'Desari'. They take rice and liquor along with them to Desari. He fixes an auspicious day for the performance of

'Chinarju'. All members of Savara family will be informed about the auspicious day. They celebrate the ceremony and arrange music on that day. On a fixed day, the 'Kudan' is approached with a 'Solla' of rice and a pot of liquor. The 'Kudan' fasts on that particular day. Along with Kudan all the relatives proceed to the forest. They take a branch of a tree. The Kudan places five grains of rice and arranges it in a set pattern on the ground and chants hymns. The Kudan cuts a small branch of the sapling and gives it to relatives of the dead person to take home. A small pit will be dug and ashes will be poured into the pit. The Kudan places the tree sapling in the pit and covers it with sand. Savara women plaster the tree with cow dung. Stones will be collected and arranged one over the other as walls to the small plant. The Kudan sacrifices a fowl to the sapling. Later all of them return home. Meanwhile, the 'Buyya' sacrifices a goat. They cook food 'bonam' and serve to all the people who attend ceremonial rituals. They fix 9th day for celebrating the ceremony for the dead person.

Status of Savara Women

Savaras give much importance to women in their society. Among the 35 tribal groups, this is a rare phenomena. They take an active role in social, economic and ritual life. But they do not offer share in their family property. Savara woman is permitted to play her due role in performing ritual practices. Savara woman plays an important role in social and religious ceremonies. They do not participate in these ceremonies at the time of their menstruation period. Savara woman carries the sacred pot containing food and other offerings to the spirits of the deceased ancestors. Some of memorial services are offered by women to their ancestors. They are allowed to present themselves at the time of sacrificing fowls. A woman is not permitted to see buffalo sacrifice. They are also not permitted while chanting hymns during ceremonial occasions. Both young and older women are not prohibited from sleeping on cots. They are free to do so. Even in the presence of their elderly males sitting or sleeping on cots by women is not objected. No food taboos are imposed on Savara women. Even drinking liquor is not prohibited. However, usually girls and young women do not drink liquor on festive occasions. Old women frequently take traditional liquor. Among Savaras there are women medical doctors or practitioners. They are called 'Kudanboi'. She diagnoses and treats certain ailments. She conducts deliveries. She also knows sooth-saying. She employs magical charms while treating diseases and ailments.

In the Indian society woman is treated as a perpetual slave to man. But in all-pervasive roles of Savara women, it can be definitely stated that Savara society highly respects their womenfolk. Savaras respect women as assets for family. Savara man treat women in their family as cherished possession. Any abuse or obscene act directed against Savara women invokes violent reactions from menfolk. Sometimes, Savara women themselves punish the culprit. They do not treat unmarried girls as a burden. They utilize their valuable services in Podu cultivation, agricultural and other economic activities in their houses and outside. There is no dowry or lavish spending of money in their marriages. Moreover, unmarried girls are potential brides. They fetch money through their hard work to her parents and guardians. Hence, an unmarried young girl is a welcome addition to any Savara family. Thus, position of women in Savara family is very respectful. Savara woman is in no way inferior to their male counter part.

V

Kinship Organization among Savaras

Kinship is a structural system of relationship among Savaras. Close relationship exists between members of the same family. Savaras maintain a close relationship among themselves. Individuals in a Savara family are bound to one another. They maintain the interlocking ties among themselves. They maintain an individual relationship by affinity. Their kinship ties are clearly seen at the time of birth, marriage and death ceremonies in their villages. They unite by their language. They have their own dialect. They also speak Hindi, Odiya and Telugu languages. History of their families (genealogies) is known to all age groups and both the sexes. Women feel shy to speak of their family history. But males often tell about their family history. Rivers held that there was a casual relationship between kinship terminology and social organization or that the characteristics of a kinship nomenclature are determined by social or sociological factors. Kinship relations of Savaras are primarily determined by their language and psychology. They use their kinship relations in social life. Spatial proximity or remoteness is an important factor in regulating the frequency and intensity of interpersonal relationships between various relatives of the village.

Savaras are not totemistic group of people. They are governed by their own social rules and regulations. They do not marry same persons in the village. Marriages among persons of the same village are prohibited. Those people who come as new persons into a Savara village and accept for a marriage relationship are generally accepted by Savaras. Ponyam Savaras call their extended families as '*Suda Birinda*'. It consists of the descendants of 5–6 generations of their common ancestors. They call the small, nuclear families as *Sanna Birinda* or lineage. This refers to small groups of Savaras who descended through the male line from a common ancestor. Savaras follow a classificatory system of terminology.

Kinship Terms Used by the Savaras

English usage	*Telugu usage*	*Savara usage*	*Term of address*
Grand Parental Generation (Father's side and Mother's side)			
Father's father	Tatayya Tandi Tandri	Joju	ya Joju
Mother's father	Tatayya Amma Tandri	Joju	ya Joju
Father's mother	Tandi Talli Nanamma	Yayu	ya Yayu
Mother's mother	Talli-Talli Grandmother	Yayu	ya Yayu

Cont'd...

...Cont'd

English usage	*Telugu usage*	*Savara usage*	*Term of address*
Parental Generation Patrilineal			
Father	Nanna	Bappa	ya Bappa
Father's eldest brother	Peddananna	Bada Bappa	ya Badappa
Father's younger brother	Chinnana	Dada	ya Dada
Father's eldest brother's wife	Peddamma	Antalai	ya Antaai
Father's younger brother's wife	Pinni	Yayan	ya Yayan
Father's eldest sister	Atta	Nanni	ya Nanni
Father's sister's eldest or youngest husband	Mama	Mamu	ya Mamu
Matrilineal Generation Patrililineal			
Mother	Amma	Nano	ya Nono
Mother's brother eldest or youngest	Mama	Mamu	ya Mamu
Mother's eldest or youngest brother's wife	Atta	Nani	ya Nanni
Mother's eldest sister	Peddamma	Antalai	ya Antalai
Mother's eldest sister's husband	Peddanamma	Bada Bappa	ya Bada Bappa
Mother's youngest sister's husband	Chinamma	Dada	ya Dada
Affinorl			
Eldest wife	Bharya	Dukri	ya Aa
Youngest wife	Bharya	Kunjar	ya kunyar
Wife's mother	Atta	Kunnar	ya Kunnar
Husband	Bhartha	Oiyatap	Ooli
Husband's father	Bhartha Tandri (Mama)	Kunyar	–
Husband's mother	Bhartha Talli (Atta)	Kunnar	ya Kunnar

English usage	*Telugu usage*	*Term of address*
Elder brother	Bada Bhainya	ya Bhavnya
Youngest brother	Chote Bhainya	By Name
Eldest brother's wife	Kake	ya Kake
Youngest brother's wife	Kaun	By Name
Sister	Munni or Tonan	ya Nunni or ya Tonan
Eldest sister's husband	Kaku	ya Kaku
Youngest sister's husband	Rayom	ya Name or ya Rayom
Father's brother's son	Bhanya	ya Bhanya
Father's brother's daughter	Munni or Tonan	ya Tonan
Father's sister's son	Marangertur	ya Marangertur
Father's sister's daughter	Marangeru	ya Marangeru

Cont'd...

...Cont'd

English usage	*Telugu usage*	*Term of address*
Mother's brother's son	Bhanya	ya Bhanya
Mother's sister's son	Toman or Nunni	ya Tonna or ya Numi
Mother's sister's daughter	Nunni	ya Numi
Wife's eldest brother	Kunyarban or Kaku	ya Kunyarban or Kaku
Wife's youngest brother	Rayom	ya Rayom
Wife's brother's wife	Tonan	ya Tonan
Wife's sister	Kinnarbi	ya Kinnarbi
Wife's sister's husband	Bhanya	By Name or ya Bhanya
Husband's sister	Kinnarbi	ya Kunyarban
Husband's sister's husband	Bhanya	ya Bhanya
Husband's brother's wife	Tonan	ya Tonan
Son's wife's father	Marangeru	ya Marangeru
Son's wife's mother	Tonan	ya Tonan
Son's wife	Bhanji	By Name
Daughter's husband's father	Marangeru	ya Marangeru
Daughter's husband's mother	Tonan	ya Tonan
Daughter's husband	Bhanja	By Name
Son	Gabruvan	By Name
Daughter	Dangriyo	By Name
Brother's son	Gabruvan	By Name
Brother's daughter	Danjriyo	By Name
Sister's son	Bhanja	By Name
Sister's daughter	Bhanji	By Name
Wife's sister's son	Kinnarbiyon	By Name
Wife's sister's daughter	Edirababaion	By Name
Husband's brother's son	Kinnarbiyon	By Name
Husband's brother's daughter	Edirabaion	By Name
Wife's brother's son	Bhania	By Name
Wife's brother's daughter	Bhani	By Name
Husband's sister's son	Bhania	By Name
Husband's sister's daughter	Bhanji	By Name
Son's son	Ja Ja	By Name
Son's daughter	ya ya	By Name
Daughter's son	Ja ya	By Name
Daughter's daughter	ya ya	By Name

VI

Livelihood of Savaras

Savaras lead a hard life. They live in a different environment. They are living in forests and hilly areas. They live in difficult terrain. Their habitations are filled with hilly tracts. Their locations are filled with wooded forests. Their dwelling places are not much useful for productive purposes. The other tribal groups are more advanced. They are also economically sound. Savaras are left out with nothing. They live in the sloppy areas where it is convenient for 'Podu' cultivation. They mortgage their own lands. At present, their economic position is very poor. Savaras mainly depend on agriculture, forest contract work, food gathering, collecting and selling of minor forest products, hunting, fishing and Podu cultivation, etc.

Agriculture is the main source of occupation for the Savaras. All members of Savaras work in agricultural fields. Agricultural activities of Savara families are confined to Podu terrace. They mainly depend upon dry and wet cultivation. Podu or shifting cultivation is one of the traditional occupations of Savaras. They perform Podu cultivation in the sloppy areas in the forest. Each Savara family possesses 2 to 3 acres of Podu land. They do alternative cultivation in their Podu lands. Savaras do not use a plot of Podu land for 3 years continuously. They cut trees in the forest for doing Podu agricultural activities. They do not cut fruit yielding plants like mango, jeelugu and other productive plants in their Podu lands. They cut bushes, thorns and wild plants. They burn branches, leaves, roots of forest plants during the month of the March. Savaras kindle fruits in two, three places in their Podu land. They burn the Podu agricultural land during the monsoon break. At the time of the first showers of monsoon, Savaras shower seeds in their Podu land. They approach the Desari for putting seeds in the Podu fields. The entire village of Savaras starts agricultural work on the same day. Men, women and children in Savara families participate in agricultural activity. The Desari fixes an auspicious day for putting grains in the field. On that day, all the Savaras visit their fields, pray to their ancestors and sow seeds. Savara women keep seeds in a corner of the field. They sprinkle grain and chant some words. They pray to gods and goddesses to give good crop that year. They also sprinkle fowl's blood on seeds. They sprinkle grain soon after praying to their ancestors. During the first year of Podu cultivation, Savaras prefer to put redgram seeds in their land. Savaras make small holes with an instrument (how-cum). They put some redgram seeds in the hole and cover them with sand/soil. Savaras plant 'Korralu' during the second crop. They go for a mixed crop during this stage of agricultural work. During the second year, Savaras raise a mixed crop such as Korralu, Udalu, Ulavalu, Sama, Gante, Chodi, Jonna and Nuvvulu. They also raise castor and cucumber in their Podu fields. Soon after rains seeds will sprout. Savaras cultivate their lands until the crop grows to 1 to 1½' height. Later Savaras will undertake weeding operations.

Savaras first harvest Korralu. Later they go for Udalu, Gantulu, Jadumulu, Chodi and Jonna, etc. Savaras also cultivate ginger and turmeric in their hilly and sloppy areas. Savaras have adopted the cultivation of turmeric in recent times. Their contacts with non-tribals motivated them to take some commercial crops. Savaras allow ginger and turmeric pieces in their hilly areas for 2 years. Later they harvest these crops also. In the dry-lands, Savaras start their cultivation after the onset of monsoon. During the first showers of rain they till and sow seeds in their dry-lands. Later Savaras mix two varieties of redgram seeds and put them in agricultural fields. They put 40 seers of Nuvvulu and 20 seers of red gram per acre. When these plants are grown, they undertake weeding activity in fields. Sesamum, groundnut and redgram crops are harvested at the time of Dasara festival or during the time of Karthikam and Palakamma. They put Sama crop during the month of 'Mummulolli'. They undertake weeding activity at the time of Endra (July–August months). They harvest this again during the month of 'Karthikam'. Later, Savaras cultivate Udalu and Chodi crops. Savaras weed their lands in the month of 'Endra'. They harvest crops during the month of Dasara.

Savaras also perform wet cultivation. Savaras prepare seedbeds. They put seeds in fields during the months of 'Visakha'. They plough fields for better transplantation. They water fields. They conduct operations with spades. They make soil soft and loose. They plough their fields with a 'Nolla'. They remove all the weeds and other waste. They water fields regularly. They level the slushy soil of fields with the help of 'Sadu' seedlings. They transplant the seedling during the month of 'Aviti'. Weeding will be undertaken during the month of 'Bodra'. The paddy crop gets fully ripened by the end of Karthikam. The crop will be cut at the time of 'Palakamma'. They thrash paddy during the Sankranthi festival.

Savaras practise terrace cultivation. The terrace fields are found near hilly areas by the side of the streams. Water will flow from top to the low level areas. The fields are flat. The soil is fertile. The terrace fields are largely found in Seetam Peta Mandal in Srikakulam agency area. Savaras level their fields like steps of a staircase. There was a perennial flow of water. This assures Savaras very good harvest. They grow wet crops like paddy. They follow agricultural practices of the cultivators of dry land. Savaras use various types of hays in their paddy fields. They use some of the green plants as manure for field.

Savaras collect minor forest products. The minor forest product comprise varieties of vegetables, mineral products of forest, animals in forest and also firewood. Savaras make their subsidiary occupation through the collection, partial processing and the sale of minor forest products. The collection of minor forest products will help Savaras economically and commercially. Savaras are sustaining themselves through this activity. The earnings and turnout from Podu cultivation are very meagre to Savaras. They cannot sustain their families throughout the year with Podu cultivation.

Savaras collect minor forest produce like tamarind, hill-brooms, myroobalans, hill-jute fibre, adda-leaves, Mahuva flowers, Beedi leaves, etc. for sale. They sell all the products to Girijan Cooperative Society stores established in forest agency areas. Savaras weave ropes. They make ropes from the hill-jute fibre. They sell them in the weekly markets during the months of February to May. They collect Mahuva flower for domestic use. Thus, various economic activities of Savaras consist of agriculture, labour contract work, collection of minor forest produce, hunting, fishing, etc. Savara economics is purely a subsistence economy. They do not have surplus agricultural or forest produce. They face severe food crisis during the months of August and November due to depletion of food grains. Savaras face severe financial crisis at the time of rainy season. They spend all their money for cultivation and household expenditure. Savaras are constantly engaged in social and economic activities throughout the year. Every year during the month of April, they find leisure and actively engage themselves in celebrating festivals and marriages.

An analysis of the income pattern of Savaras establishes the fact that Savaras are one of the economically backward communities in the State of Andhra Pradesh. When compared with the per capita income of the Savaras with per capita income of the state, the per capita income of Savaras is very low. Savaras are practically at the lowest rung of income status. Savaras needs urgent rehabilitation measures to raise their income status.

In the Akkannaguda village of Seetampeta agency area, Savara people complain that they hardly get any loan for their agricultural work. They do not get bank loans. They take loans from moneylenders. Seeing the innocence of these tribes they take advantage. The moneylenders charge very high rates of interest for the money Savaras had taken. They collect grain and other goods from Savaras at the time of Podu or after Podu cultivation. Moneylenders charge 100 per cent interest for the money they have given. Government should take active steps to save Savaras from corruption. Even with such problems, Savaras save money in their traditional banking system. Savara men and women save their money with a trustworthy person without informing anyone. They keep on saving their money without anyone's knowledge. In case of death of Savaras the person with whom the money was kept will not be given to the relatives or to the kith and kin of Savara people. Thus, many of Savaras got cheated.

Savaras have their own herbal medicine for different problems. The Kudan or the Kundaboi are the experts in identifying plants and leaves. They know reasons for various kinds of diseases. They can cure any kind of bone fracture. They learn about their traditional medicine from their community members (*Yejjodu*). Seeing their elderly people, Savaras learn their art. Even today, Savara people know different types of medicine. Jammaraju was very good at giving medicine and solving problems of bone fractures. With their herbal medicine, Savaras cure bone fractures. Savaras call herbal medicine as '*Beradu*'. Savara doctor removes tender leaves from herbal plants and makes it into a paste. They call the paste as 'Paneramgada'. Savaras collect milk that comes out of branches and leaves of the herbal plants. Savara doctor makes the paste from leaves, herbs, milk and other products. They apply the paste on the fractured bones for ten days to set them properly.

VII

Cultural Heritage of Savaras: Dance, Music and Art (Painting) and Festivals

Savara Dance

Dance is rhythmic. It is a physical movement of humans with feelings and emotions. Man is born with certain feelings like joy, love, fear, sorrow, etc. He always expresses his feelings in movements. Dance is the oldest form of man's emotional expression. Man dances at every stage of his life. People dance in happiness, in sorrow, while sowing seeds, during the time of harvest or in healing the sick. Behind many rituals there are dances. Some dances are ritual dances. There is also a strong belief among people that through dance only they can directly talk to god. When people dance they break the barriers in ecstasy. They become part and parcel of nature and god. The ritualistic dance performs several functions. It is beyond the power of dance. It acts like a sacrificial site, a charm or a prayer. It becomes a prophetic vision. People dance in different styles. People also dance for different purposes. Some people dance for fun or for entertainment. Others perform dance as a means of communication. People dance to celebrate success, for good harvest, personal achievements, etc. Dance is performed while worshipping gods and goddesses. Dance creates the feeling of unity and togetherness. Dance is used for invoking spirits, demons and gods. Whatever maybe the reason for doing different varieties of dance, but dance is always an integral part of man's life.

James K. Ferbleman defined dance as 'all that which deals with the motion of the human body'. Dance is further defined as 'an art performed by individuals or groups of human beings existing in time, space, force and glow in which the human body is the instrument and movement of the body is the medium'. Movements in dance are stylized. In fact, the entire dance work is characterized by form and structure. Dance is commonly performed to musical or other rhythmic accompaniment. Dance has a primary purpose. It expresses inner feelings and emotions. Dance is always performed for socialistic, ritualistic, entertainment or any other purpose. Dances can be broadly categorized into two categories: first, Theoretical dance and second, Social dance. Theoretical dance is performed for the purpose of entertainment. This style of dance is not meant for self-satisfaction of the dancer. This type of dance is purely for the entertainment of others. This dance is meant for audience or spectators. Here dancers can always improve their dance performance to make it more attractive, beautiful and purposeful. In social dancing, participants dance for their own pleasure rather than for the entertainment of audience. These dances have specific steps, rhythm and meaning as well. Whatever the style of dance may be, it involves various movements, energy, rhythm and design. Organized movements, steps create dance. Energy in the body provides the required force. It also executes a particular movement. Rhythm is the pattern of time around which dance movement is organized. Design refers to visual patterns made by the body of dancer.

Dance is one of the most primitive art forms. Primitive man was satisfied with his basic needs such as food. He began to express his emotions through the most natural or immediate channel, the body. In a primitive society, dance plays an important role. It is part and parcel of every phase of human activity. Dance is linked with birth, marriage, death, harvesting, celebrations, hunting, war, fairs and festivals, rites and rituals, sickness, joy and sorrow. On all these occasions dance is performed by tribal groups. In simple terms, dance is the existence of life on a higher plane. There are many characteristic features of dance among the primitive tribal groups. The predominant characteristic features are:

- Dance seeks to identify initiative or emulative manner.
- Dance is a means to say something or to communicate something which cannot be expressed in any other form.
- In the primitive tribal communities, dance remains all-embracing. It is a strong binding influence in the life of tribal communities.
- Dance is a means of defining social identity of a group through the acceptance of the rituals right from the cradle to the grave.
- Dance is central to tribal life in health, sickness, joy, fear, birth, puberty, marriage, death, harvest and in every aspect of life.
- The dance among tribal groups celebrates tribal divinity.
- Dance is the basic response to emotional stimulus.

In primitive communities, dance is transcended everyday through action. It is merely by force of repetition. Dancers reproduce reality and truth of daily labour. They repeat the same steps and songs with the help of music. Primitive people have different steps and songs for different seasons and occasions. Tribal dance is performed in different forms. They are group dance, couple dance and single dance, etc. Among tribal groups there are various kinds of dances such as war and hunting dances, sacred and ritualistic dances and social dances, etc.

In the group dance, dancers are linked to one another. They move in a certain manner by joining hands with each other. They keep their hands on the waists or shoulders. These dances are found throughout the country. The best-known group dances are in the form of circle or columns. The circular dance is acceptable to males and females. The column dance is dynamic. Movements in this dance are more complicated. The tempo in column dance is more sustained. Couple dances are either through the formation of columns or without any special formation of columns. Generally, while revolving in the form of couples, females do pirouettes. Males make virtical movements. Among a coupled dances, the most important group is represented very frequently by Chhau and Yatra very frequently. This type of couple dance can be seen among Savaras. In single dance, performance is made by a single dancer. This is not common among tribal groups. Tribals play this dance in single by being a part of a group.

War and hunt dances among tribes are found in some Tribal Sub-Plan areas. Tribes while performing this type of dancers paint their body completely. They dance according to chanting of hymns. It is a group item. It reflects the spirit of the tribal community. Here, tribal groups initiate their actions. When tribal people are going to hunt animals, they perform this type of dance. This is a style in which tribals share their daily experiences. This dance helps young children among tribals to observe how to hunt animals. Sacred and ritualistic dance style perhaps is the most common dance among tribals. The object around which dance is performed is a sacred one. The sacred object may be an idol, a sacrificial thing, a holy tree or a well or a stone. Among forest tribes, a number of dances are ritualistic. These dances are devised mainly for the purpose of propitiating gods, goddesses and ancestral spirits. Social dances among tribal groups are mainly connected with seasons, festivals, marriages, funeral activities, etc. These dances are commonly found among tribal population. Tribal dances are associated with productive, preventive, promotive and destructive rituals and practices. Productive tribal dances are associated with the rituals of fertility of crops, plants, animals and human beings. Preventive ritual dances among tribals are associated with rituals and ceremonies performed to prevent an individual, family, a community or a village from diseases, illness and misfortunes. Promotive ritual dances are certain actions which are performed to promote health, growth and welfare of individuals, families, community and villages. Destructive rituals are performed to destroy the evils.

Amongst all the primitive dances, fertility dance is the most important one amongst tribes. Tribal population propitiates divinities like wind, sun, rain, fire and celestial bodies for progress and welfare of the community. Such dances are performed as prayers. These dances are called fertility dances. These dances are often in the form of sympathetic magic. This is a kind of a wish or fulfilment through a prophecy. It is called inspirational shamanism. Dance is intimately connected with all these activities. Occasions of integrated ritual dance comprise clay modelling, painting, designing on floor and cloth, recitation and singing. Life is an integrated picture in which dance is not an art or a part with appendages of costuming and diagramming which is added. It is one of the ingredients of a total life vision. It is something in which everything is woven together into a beautiful whole. All these traditions are commonly called tribal or folk tradition of Indian art. It coexisted for several years and continues to coexist forever. It lives with Shastric tradition of architecture, sculpture, painting, etc.

The speciality of primitive tribal dance and music is that it is never taught in a formal manner. When elders dance and sing, youngsters watch them and join them. Tribal dancing floors are schools of enculturation and socialization. Younger generations learn customs, traditions and manners through oral history. Dance is the base to disseminate traditions through the words of mouth. Actually, myths are recreated through dance formations and movements.

Among Savaras one can find a rich cultural heritage through their dance. Dance, music and painting are part and parcel of the life of Savaras. The dance of Savaras revolves around their lifecycle. They dance at the time of birth, marriage or at a funeral procession. Most of Savara dances are procession dances. When Savaras are escorting someone or bringing somebody to their home/village or celebrating a festival, they dance. They dance when a bride is going to a new house. They dance during harvest festivals. When the dead people's ashes are being brought to village in a procession, Savaras dance. They dance through streets. They dance when they visit a village or a funeral procession. Savaras carry something or the other in their hand. All Savaras dance in a single group or file. They arrange themselves into four groups in a particular row. Savaras do not know circle formations. They differ in their dance forms from Gonds or Oraons. Their dance appears as if they are assembling into a jumble. They neatly interlock their patterns. Desari, the priest leads the procession. They often fall into a trance. They torment themselves and show signs of convulsions. They roll on the ground, tear their hair and sway in all directions. They perform this type of act particularly when they celebrate ceremonies for their dead people or when appeasing gods and goddesses or to remove evil spirits from their villages.

Belongings of the deceased man or woman will be carried by Savaras on their heads. They perform the dance immediately outside their houses or in the open space. Desari dances with heavy heart on the death of a person in the village. Savaras dance at the time of proceeding for hunting or during the time of animal sacrifice. They perform better dances at the time of marriages. Savara girls and boys dance around musicians. Usually, they use a flute or a fiddle player at the time of their dances.

Savaras perform different steps in their dances. They involve footsteps and hand movements in their dances. Savaras living in Srikakulam district demonstrate their dances with two steps in their villages. Savaras in Devanapuramguda and Akkannaguda perform their dances in different styles. Among Savaras, both men and women dance together. The following are different types of steps involved while Savaras perform their dances:

1. Savara women while dancing stand in a straight line. They hold each other. They keep their hands on their waists. They move round in a circle by rotating themselves. They keep their feet very close while moving. They stand straight. While taking around they hit anklet of the leg with the anklet of another leg. Sounds of anklets play the role of rhythm in this form of dance. While making steps rhythmic sound attracts viewers. When they hit two anklets, they give a melodious sound. The anklets are sharp and metallic in nature. While hitting anklets Savaras jump slightly. They jump clockwise and anticlock wise. They complete one circle in four beats or counts. Savaras complete their clockwise and anticlockwise movements in eight beats. They perform

their steps with different speed movements. When they perform the dance in full speed their legs move apart slightly.

2. When Savaras dance in pairs, they change their hand movements. They raise hands up to the level of their foreheads. Savara woman holds an umbrella in her hand. She moves in clockwise and anticlockwise directions. While dancing they shout with words like hoy, hey – to show their happiness.
3. While performing the dance, males make steps. Male dancers individually perform the dance. They do not mix in the group. Male dancers also move around jumping slightly. They hit their legs jumping a little higher. They touch their ankles. Male dancers take rounds near the same place. They hold musical instruments in their hands. They dance like Kinnera.
4. Female dancers among Savaras make certain pairs. They hold the hands of each other. They stand straight. They shift their body weight from one leg to the other. They stamp the ground with one leg. They move the other leg forward and hit it in the air slightly. While dancing, Savara women form themselves into semicircles.
5. Various steps in Savara dance involve forward and backward movements. Dancers run forward and backwards. They hit or stamp their legs on the ground alternatively. In their steps, they first move forward and later go backwards. Later they take rounds in the same place. They decide the number of footsteps to take by themselves. They do all variations in four beats. While dancing, players bend their body parts in a proper sequence to forward movements and backward movements. They also step in pairs. Steps are performed invariably both by men and women. They hold each other's shoulders.
6. Some of the dance movements among Savaras are invariably enacted by the couples. They first stand straight. They face each other and hold their hands. They perform certain jumping movements. They jump and lift their right leg. They keep their left leg on the ground. They do it once. Later they take the round. They hold their hands above their heads. They never lift their hands when they take certain steps.
7. There are certain dance steps performed by couples. They join their right hand with the left hand. They run forward taking four steps by holding the right hand of a person joining with the left hand of another person. Later they leave their hands and take turns. They continue with their steps. After performing their dance for sometime, they join their hands again and come to their original position.
8. Some of the steps among Savara dancers involve group dances. They break into couples. Couples further breaks into single groups and start their dance. Here Savaras keep their left hand behind the backside of their body. They keep their right hand in the mushti hasta pose. They raise their right hand up to the level of their forehead. They jump keeping their feet together. They take circles both clockwise and anticlockwise.
9. Another dance form among Savaras is performed with any number of people. In this type of dance, Savaras thump on the ground. Heel of the other foot will be touched forward lightly. They move forward and backwards in eight counts each. They hold the shoulders of each other.

They move their steps very fast while moving forward. They slightly bend one of their legs. They keep their leg in front and bend slightly. They change their dances with certain variations as and when required. Sometimes, they dance on one leg hitting against the heels of the other foot.

10. Savaras make couple dances with their foot. Right hand of the girl will be held with the left hand of the another girl. They take a round among themselves in such a way that their backs face each other. After sometime, they turn back in the same direction. They join face to face. They take these directions alternatively. Sometimes, Savaras take circles between forward and backward movements. Even at that time they hold their hands together in front of their forehead. These steps will be made only during the time of couple dances. Young boys and girls while performing these dances hold musical instruments with them. They thump their feet on the ground. They come in between dancers. There is a group of instrumentalists performing music tunes while they are dancing. All the dance steps are performed at a fast pace. They perform their steps in *Tishra Nada* (Takita). The Nada helps us to understand/indicate that dancers make their movements very fast. The performance of steps by the older Savara people is entirely different from the younger generation of Savaras. Younger generation of Savaras have improved and modernized their dances. Older women reject wearing or using modern musical instruments while performing their dances. It is because of this reason that anklets and other traditional ornaments they wear are used by them for musical purposes. Their anklets provide the required music for their dances. But the younger generation has entirely changed their dances. They do not follow their older generation. They do not wear traditional anklets and prefer modern technology.

Among Savaras there are many professional artists. In Adduripeta village of Srikakulam district, Savara Chinna Jammayya was a very popular dancer. He is a professional dancer and singer. He is an expert in playing instruments. At a time he sings, plays the instrument and performs the dance. He shows different dance steps imitating various animals. He is highly respected and invited for all cultural activities and festive occasions.

Savara tribals are basically hunters. One of the methods used by Savaras while they go for hunting is the imitation of the animals. They imitate different steps of animals. It is also important here to observe that tribals learn their dances through imitation of animals. Sammayya dance had mentioned that they teach their younger generation different styles of their dances while they take them for hunting activity. Tribal children learn various techniques of the cultural activities from their older generation, whether they follow it or not in their later life. Savaras perform their dances at the time of festivals, agricultural activities, etc. Their worldview is entirely different from civilized people. Whatever they get, they first offer the same to their deities and ancestors. Later, the whole community shares and participates in various activities of their social life. Some of the important dance forms of Savaras are Puli Adugu,

Nagupamadugu, Elugubanti (bear) step, hyena, lion and peacock dance, elephant dance, Mamidikayapanduga and Tenkapanduga.

While performing '*Puliadugu*', Savaras keep their feet together very close. Then, they jump backward and forward. Depending upon rhythm of the song, Savaras make their own dance steps. They bend their knees downwards while performing this dance. While performing '*Nagupamuadugu*' dance, Savaras move on all sides by crossing their legs. While moving to the left, they keep their left leg in front. While moving to right side, they keep their right leg in front. While moving to the left, their to legs touch the ground. Similarly while moving to the right, they touch ground with their right legs. They form their movements in the form of 'S' shape. Savaras like performing Elugubanti/bear steps very much. First, they move their right leg very straight. They place right leg in front of the left leg. They also move their left leg in the same fashion. While performing this type of dance they move forward to six beats. They take another two beats as a pause. They bend their body and knees forward while moving. When the pause is given they will stand straight. Hyena is a normal walk which is conducted with bent knees. The dancer moves towards the front side and backside. They do it slowly, to begin with and increase the speed as and when required. When they move frontward they jump keeping both the feet front side. Savaras while performing lion dance they make bigger steps. Savaras perform the peacock dance both in clockwise and anticlockwise direction. They keep one leg in normal posture and move the other leg around it. They move around side to the centre and get back to normal position. In the elephant dance, Savaras lift their legs upwards and very high. They keep their legs in the front and in the same way backward also. While celebrating Mamidikaya Panduga (mango fruit festival) Savaras dance in circular form and jump with the help of two legs. They perform this dance in clockwise and anticlockwise directions. In Tenkapanduga, they form themselves into circles and semicircles and dance. In Kandikotta festival, they dance showing agricultural activity such as sowing of seeds with their hand movements.

Savaras are very artistic people. Other than dance and music they are experts in singing Savara songs and in painting. Savaras decorate their walls with paintings. They depict different kinds of pictures on walls in their houses. They also paint different pictures on cloth by using different colours. The paintings of Savaras depict their day-to-day life activities. In their paintings they depict animals which they are domesticating, grazing and also using for food, agricultural and forest work. Country liquor that they drink, festival activities, gods and goddesses, their different ways of life, day-to-day activities – all are depicted in their paintings. They use them as objects of worship. The animals which are drawn in their paintings represent their economic life. Their paintings are a number of small pictures done on a big piece of cloth or on walls. These paintings of Savaras have pictures showing how they draw water from wells or of mountains, what they fetch from forest and their duties and work-related activities. Their paintings also show their hunting activities, festivals and rites and rituals. Savaras live with their domesticated animals. They indulge in different kinds of activities every day. They relate their activities mainly to earth and forests. They represent all these work related activities in their paintings. They indicate their life in painting. This style of depicting their life pattern through paintings is a special feature of Savara tribe.

Savara Songs

Savaras are good singers. They sing songs on all occasions. They offer prayers to their ancestors, gods and goddesses, at the time of marriage, birth and death ceremonies, fairs and festivals, when they bring new bride and bride-grooms, agricultural and forest work, and during festive occasions. While offering something to their deity Savaras sing the following song:

> *Song-Kandeno khandenamma mambulu namkoni kandeno khandenamma musara namkoni Tilamdo Tillam Tillam Nimado Ninamde Namakama Tillam namma naotaram Tillam dumma. Mamulu namdo nati masare namdo nate Ammaronamma nathang niyanglo niyang naman Kandero KammaVillaved Kandero luyeng villaved Kandero mamulluna Kandero musa Saranam Ammaye Ammayendo fusudi Elang tillam Ammaye Ammayendo Paruye Elang tillam Khurgayol Panja yeenam tillam do ramma namam Urado panja yeenam tillam dorammanamam Ennango Yampam naman nannamma kampin nayendo Ennango Yampam naman nautaram lingnomanna Gangomai gangomaido nammadonamma naman.*

The song means that Savaras adorn their gods with pet animals like goat, sheep, hen and buffalo. They are asking the deity to be happy with the offering and bless them with her kindness.

Festivals

Savaras celebrate various festivals. The festivals which Savaras celebrate can be classified into three categories. They are: (1) festivals related to economic activities, (2) festivals related to social activities and (3) festivals related to religious activities. The festivals related to economic activities are connected with harvesting season and the first crops of their paddy field. They celebrate these festivals when their harvest comes to their house. These festivals are connected with agricultural and other allied activities. These festivals are known as Kondem Kothalu, Kandi Kothalu, Mamidi Kothalu, Tenka Kothalu and Korra Kothalu.

Festivals Relating to Economic Activities of Savaras

The *Kondem Kotha* festival is celebrated by Savaras during the month of '*Endwa*'. Savaras harvest Kondem in their Podu lands. They offer the crop to deities and ancestral spirits during the celebration of these festivals. Only after offering these crops to deities, Savaras eat them. The Buyya among Savaras fixes an auspicious day for celebrating the festival. Savara woman cleans her house. They bring Kondem from the field and its grains will be cooked. The 'Kudan' invokes deities and ancestral spirits. They keep some cooked rice in a small basket along with five-leaf plates. They also keep Mohuva liquor in a jug. They keep them in front of 'Lingor'. The figure of Lingor will be drawn on the wall. They recite some hymns. They sprinkle some liquor over it. They cut a goat or a hen. They cook heart and other parts of the poultry. They place the cooked food and meat on the adda leaf. Then they offer the food to deities and ancestral spirits. The rest of the food first will be served to 'Kudan'. Later they serve food to other members of the family and relatives. All of them freely eat 'Kondem' grains.

The *Kandi Kottha* festival is celebrated by Savaras soon after they receive red gram crop from their Podu fields. Savara woman first cleans up her house. They keep a bowl of the red gram grain which they had collected. They remove husk of the grain. They cook red gram and place it before 'Kudan'. They also place a 'Solla' of rice and some incense. The Kudan recites hymns. He invokes deities and ancestral spirits. He offers the special food prepared with red gram. They worship 'Goddalamma,' the goddess with the axe by beating drums. Buyya helps them with all facilities. After worshipping the goddess they eat and dance throughout the night. The next morning, they take Goddalamma on a procession to the nearby village. The villagers offer rice which was collected in a basket. All Savaras place Goddalamma in her original place – forest. Savaras collect rice and cook food for the deity. They offer food to the deity and later all of them eat food and return home.

Mamidi Kotha Festival

Savaras celebrate this festival during the month of 'Kothamasam'. They offer the first fruits to all their hill deities and ancestral spirits. During this festival, they get the mango crop. Savaras go to forest to fetch mangoes. They keep mango fruits in baskets to sell. Women cook 'bonam' and place mango baskets before the 'Kudan'. The Kudan sprinkles liquor on the offerings and recites hymns. After reciting hymns, the Kudan feeds fowl or a goat with rice. Later, he sacrifices the animal to the deity. Kudan sprinkles the blood on bonam and mangoes in the basket. Woman cooks heart and meat of the sacrificed animal and places it in front of the 'Kudan'. Kudan again recites some hymns and invokes deities and ancestors. He offers food to them. Later Savaras serve food to 'Kudan' and 'Buyya'. Later, all the Savaras celebrate the festival.

Tenka Kotha Festival

After eating mangoes Savaras store the kernels till the month of May–June (Munukolli). They offer kernels to the hill deities and ancestors. Later, they celebrate this festival. They purchase a buffalo for sacrificial purpose. Buyya fixes an auspicious day. He fasts on that day and cooks 'Bonam' with five seers of Sama grain in a new pot. He takes liquor and mango kernels. He goes to Jakari deity. The deity is represented by a stone idol. They place the idol 1 or 2 km away from the village. All the villagers accompany the Buyya for worshipping their idol. Bonam, mango kernels will be placed before the 'Jakari'. Kudan recites some hymns. He sprinkles liquor over it. He breaks kernel and again recites hymns. They sacrifice animals and sprinkle the blood on Jakari and mango kernels. They cook meat and place it in front of the idol. They take the idol for a procession by beating drums. The entire village participates in the procession. In the procession, some of the Savaras collect rice, dhal, etc. They place the idol again in the original place. They cook food with rice which was collected. They offer food to the deity and later, all Savaras participate in the celebration of the festival.

Korra Kotha Festival

Savaras celebrate this festival when they harvest the crop of 'Korralu' (Burroi). This is the first crop that Savaras harvest in Podu fields. Savaras grow this crop only after celebrating the Burroi-Kurrawal. They reap the harvest after the celebration of the festival. The Korra Kotha festival will be celebrated by individual families. Kudan and Desari propitiate 'Baru-Sonum'. They offer Korra grains to the deity and later they cook the grain as bonam. They keep a small portion of the food in nine adda leaves. Kudan and Desari recite some hymns. They feed animals with some rice. If the animal eats rice, it is said that the Baru-Sonum is pleased with their offerings. Then they sacrifice the animal and cook its meat. They place the cooked meat in front of Kudan Desari. They recite some hymns. Then Kudan and Desari offer food to the god. Later all Savaras celebrate the festival.

Festivals Related to the Social and Religious Activities of Savaras

The social and religious ceremonies of Savaras will be celebrated by them at the time of their birth, puberty, marriage and death. Savaras celebrate two types of religious festivals which are as follows: (1) Vijidigonyo festival and (2) Durga Puja.

Vijidigonyo

Savaras observe this ceremony after detecting an epidemic in their villages. They go round Savara villages and collect contributions to buy materials. The 'Kudan' propitiates the deities. Kudan cleans up particular places in villages. They draw lines with white flour. Kudan prepares turmeric rice. They keep leaves in a circular form with turmeric rice. They cover the leaf with a basket. They burn incense and invoke deities. Kudan uncovers the basket the next day. He notices direction to which the rice has moved. This was an indication that in that direction the epidemic had to be sent out. Immediately Kudan prepares a small cart with collected wood. He keeps the basket on the cart. A knife, bow and arrow and some figures symbolizing deities dressed in different coloured clothes will be prepared and kept in the basket. They pull the cart outside the village. While pulling the cart the Savaras collect rice, dhal, etc. from the villagers. They pull the cart in that direction, which turmeric rice indicated. Savaras leave the cart, rice and other materials taken along with them. They return home leaving all the materials outside the village. They keep food, clothes and other materials, leaves the deity there praying that deity of the epidemic should not come again into their villages.

Durga Puja

Jakari and Durga are two deities. Savaras worship these two deities during the month of Dasara festival. All Savaras in their respective villages celebrate this festival. Savaras propitiate their deities to ensure that wild animals do not spoil their crops. They also worship to protect them when they move in forests and to give better rains for their crops. The Desari propitiates Jakari and Durga deities. In some villages, instead of Savaras, Jatapu tribals propitiate the deity. The headman of the village collects contributions from villagers. From the collection, they purchase a buffalo or a pig. They sacrifice animals to Durga and Jakari. Desari and Buyya go to the outskirts of village with knives. They clean up near the trunk of a tree. They keep the knives there. Buyya sprinkles liquor. He enchants some hymns. He breaks coconut and places the pieces of coconut near the knife. They sprinkle turmeric and rice over them. They bring buffalo to the spot. Buyya sprinkles, liquor and turmeric rice on its head. Later, they sacrifice the animal. Meat of the animal will be cooked and later they take the meal near the spot. Savaras follow the same procedure for the propitiation of Jakari.

Savaras believe that every person has two lives: (1) Rup-Rup-Puradan and (2) Suda Puradan. The Rup-Rup Puradan was identified with heart. A person dies when Rup-Rup-Puradan stops. Savaras believe that a dead person will not be having a second life. Savaras identify Suda Puradan as the 'atman'. Savaras believe that when a person dies his/her atman enters into another person's atman at will. Suda Puradan leaves the body and wanders about while the person is asleep. Thus, Savaras believe in the existence of two types of souls. The wandering soul which leaves the body reappears in dreams of other persons and the other permanently dwells in the body. Its departure results in death. When a person dies, the Rup-Rup-Puradan also ceases automatically. Suda-Puradan is immortal. They believe that it only leaves the body after death. It is known as Kulban (spirit). Sudan-Puradan remains as Kulban until the last rites were over, i.e. 'Gaur' ceremony is performed by Savaras. When they get good crops after two years, again Savaras invoke Kulaban of the dead person and offer sacrifices to it. Savaras call this ceremony as 'Gaur' ceremony.

Savaras celebrate Gaur ceremony in a very interesting manner. Kudan fixes an auspicious day for husking paddy. He keeps rice in a winnowing fan. He recites Sermons. He keeps five seers of rice in 'Pallaki' or winnowing fan. He covers rice with adda leaves. Savaras purchase three copper rings on the auspicious day. According to the economic status, they purchase cattle meant for sacrifice. The Desari fixes auspicious day for the celebration of festival. Desari fixes ceremony on a full-moon day. Generally, festival is celebrated during the month of 'Palakamma'. All the relatives will be invited. They bring liquor, rice and some money. Savaras count dead persons in their family. They inform the same to Kudan. Each dead person will be offered with a Solla of rice. They keep rice near the doorway of the house. Kudan sprinkles liquor over it and recites hymns. Savaras call it as 'Dinaro'. A day before the ceremony, all the family members and Kudan take bath. Kudan keeps five kg of rice in a winnowing fan and recites hymns, falls into a trance. Savaras serve food to all the members. They spend rest of the day in singing and dancing. Kudan cooks three seers of rice the next day. They erect a memorial stone. They plaster the stone with cow dung. They apply turmeric paste to the stone. Savaras erect three stones for males and two stones for females. They keep a turban for stone for the male member and a saree for the female stone which is erected for the purpose of worshipping stones. They sacrifice a buffalo. Then Savaras cook meat. Liquor will be sprinkled. They also recite hymns to invoke Kulbans. They carry the food to the house. Cooked food will be served to all the people. The Kudan, Buyya, Desari, and Gamang will be served the food first. Later, food will be served to all members. Savaras clean their houses. Savaras cook 'Dinaro'. They entertain villages in the feast. Their individual families offer memorial services to their ancestors. They call it as *'Lathar'* ceremony. All the brothers perform this ceremony in a Savara family. Desari helps the Savaras in performing this ceremony. Savaras clean the house on a fixed day. One of the brothers in a Savara family go to forest and brings fruits, flowers, tamarind, creepers and other forest products. They make a garland with flowers and having it for their neck. They also adorn the new pot with flowers. They place adda leaves in another pot. They cook 'Sama' grains in another pot. They keep tamarind fruit, sweet potato and other vegetables in a basket. There will be three girls to carry the pot. Among the three girls, two girls carry one pot and one girl carries the winnowing fan. They carry it from the eldest brother's house to the youngest brother's house. While carrying the pot they enjoy whistling and dancing. They take materials to a stream and keep all of them there. Buyya keeps a cot near the flow. He sprinkles liquor and turmeric rice. He also recites some hymns. They sacrifice an animal. They sprinkle blood on the cot and keep the head of the animal near the cot. He recites some hymns and pushes the cot into the stream. They serve food to everyone and return home. Savaras offer memorial service to their ancestors once in every four to five years. They offer their prayers to their ancestors during the months of 'Palkamma' or 'Kothamasa'. They call this festival as Idee-Sung. In this celebration also, Savaras count the number of dead persons in a family. Equal number of leaf cups and baskets are prepared. Idee-Sung figure is drawn on the wall. Two bamboo sticks are equated. They tie another bamboo stick over the two. Kudan recites some hymns and sacrifices an animal. They invoke their ancestral spirits. They cook Bonum and serve it to all people. Later Kudan, Buyya, Gamang and Desari eat food. The rest of the day will be spent in singing and dancing.

Savaras are very hardworking people. They toil hard from morning to evening. They work from sunrise to sunset. Even though their work helps them very busy they maintain their rites and rituals promptly. They cannot lead their life without following their tradition. They are immersed in their culture. Today, many of Savaras in their tribal mandals are converted to Christianity. Christian missionaries gave them hope to improve their life. Savara tribal population lead an innocent life. The local moneylenders and local medical doctors (*Addai* or *Yejjodu*) always deceive them. Still, the government had not done anything to improve their social and economic life. Literacy rate is very low among Savaras.

VIII

Savara Culture in Flux

India occupies second position in the concentration of tribal population. With regard to tribal communities, its position is unique. There are about 535 Scheduled Tribes living in India. They speak 400 languages. According to 1981 census, there were 53.8 million Scheduled Tribe people. The tribal population constituted 7.85 per cent of the total population. In 1991 census, tribal population increased to 68.4 million constituting 8.08 per cent of the total population in India. Tribal population occupies 15 per cent of the total geographical area of the country. Andhra Pradesh has the largest hilly, agency and plain areas. There is 35 groups of Scheduled Tribes. They consist of 31.78 lakhs. There are about 5.91 per cent in 1981. It became 41.99 lakh constituting 6.31 per cent of the total Scheduled Tribe population in the country out of 41.99 lakh of the total Scheduled Tribe population of the state out of which 21,42,817 are males and 20,56,664 are females. During 1950s, the Scheduled Tribe population had grown to 51.59. In 1980s, their growth rate was 32.22. There is a fluctuating trend in the growth of Scheduled Tribe population in Andhra Pradesh. In the state, scheduled area comprises 29,683 sq km. The tribal area constitutes 10.7 per cent of the total geographical area of the state. It constitutes 11 per cent of the total scheduled area of the country. Tribal villages are inhabited by different groups of tribal population. There are 35 tribal groups in Andhra Pradesh and Telangana. Gonds, Andhs, Thothis in Adilagbad district; Koya, Kona Reddi, Naikpods in Khammam, Warangal and Godavari districts; Bagatha, Valmiki, Savara and Jatapus in the districts of north coastal Andhra Pradesh and Chenchus in the pockets of Mahaboobnagar, Kurnool and Prakasam districts. Their social structure resembles each other. They have similar clan organisation. Their social practices, customs, beliefs, code of conduct are very similar to each other.

The United Nations declared 1993 as the International Year of the Indigenous People. The United Nations emphasised on the protection of their interest for a better future for them. The contemporary position of Savaras in the Eastern Ghats has changed in nature. Several innovative Savara educational experiments have been initiated. The Savara art is more realistic or naturalistic. It remains more in a state of man versus nature. Savara art has the provision for artistic expression of psychoanalysis. Savara art has received a severe setback because of impinging forces of change. Savaras have experienced more impact of a cultural influence. This has partly happened because of their higher degree of contact and continuous interaction with plains people. The mechanisms of planned change have not operated among them. The missionaries penetrated deep into the areas of Savaras. They carried new ideas, technologies, schemes and programmes. But Savaras adhered to their native way of life. They resisted some of the elements of the missionaries and non-tribal agents.

IX

Rehabilitation

Savaras occupy a unique position among the 35 tribal groups in Andhra Pradesh. Their social organisation is very neat. In the social system, family is the lone unit. They distinguish themselves from the plains people and Hindu castes. They distinguish themselves from the hill dwelling tribal groups. The distinctive cultural traits of the Savara tribal people keep them in a unique position in the cultural configuration of tribal population. Savaras have a long standing cultural contact with other ethnic groups. This has resulted in some changes which are very visible in the social, material and spiritual life of Savaras. Savaras contact various people from everyday life. Their contacts with people have a profound bearing on their social and cultural life. Savaras daily contact the neighbouring tribal and non-tribal groups. They also contact agency people. Savaras participate in marketing and developmental activities. They sell their products to ST Cooperative Finance and Development Corporation and Tribal Development Agencies. For the advancement of tribal population, the government has established Integrated Tribal Development Agencies (ITDAs). Savaras also come under the purview of schemes initiated by the ITDA.

Today, we can see a lot of change in their social life. Their dress pattern has undergone a lot of change. This is also due to their shifting economic status. Nowadays both men and women instead of wearing their traditional pattern of dress are wearing shirts, full sarees, blouses and other modern outfits. They are imitating their counterparts in the larger society. Even in the naming ceremonies, Savaras are adopting new, modern and plain people's names. Traditional names like 'Sukku', 'Sombra' are being replaced by Ramaiah or Timmayya, etc.

Among Savaras, Kapu Savaras live in plain areas. They act as political and religious functionaries. But today their positions have undergone change. They have redesignated their positions. They have replaced and renamed their positions. For example, we do not see in most of the Savara habitations the religious and social functionaries such as 'Gamang', 'Buyya', 'Dasari', 'Kudan' and 'Kudanboi'. The designation of 'Gamang' has almost disappeared from the social position of Savaras. They are adopting respectable terms/ positions like 'Naidu'. Naidu is usually the designation of the headman in plain areas.

In the social front of Savara life, a lot of changes have taken place. Changes have taken place in the type and performance of conduct of their marriages, selection of bride and bridegrooms, acquiring mates and also conducting their rites and rituals. Marriage by capture and elopement has completely disappeared from Savaras as this type of marriage, generally, is not approved by plains population. While performing marriages erecting pandals, tying a 'Mangala Sutra' (gold ornament) have already crept into social practice of Savaras. Savaras have changed the custom of celebrating marriage from bridegroom's residence to bride's residence. Savaras choose vegetarian food instead of non-vegetarian food. Beef was considered as the choicest dish for

Savaras. But due to the influence of plains people, Savaras living in the top hill areas are slowly avoiding eating beef. Even eating of non-poisonous snakes, red ants have been abandoned by Savaras. Similarly, various varieties of edible roots, tubers, leaves and flesh of various forest animals which further supplement their diet have been slowly given up by Savaras. Restrictions imposed by forest department officials, ITDA and forest laws further debarred them from depending on forest products for their sustenance.

Savaras living in the top hill areas have retained some of their social practices. But the ritual practices of Savaras living in the plain areas have undergone a change. Pantheons of Savaras includes many gods and goddesses such as Shiva, Rama, Krishna, Simhadri Appanna, etc. They keep photos of these gods and worship them daily in their houses. There is also a change in agricultural practices of the Savaras. Some of them have abandoned shifting cultivation. They have adopted settled cultivation. Thus, they have stopped worshipping the hill deities such as 'Barusum' as there is no functional significance of worship in their changed mode of living. A large number of poor people in plain areas who could not eke out their livelihood, migrated to the lands of Savaras in search of their livelihood. These migrants are distillers of illicit liquor in Savara habitations. Further, petty traders, moneylenders are in continuous operation in their villages. They have occupied most of their lands and reduced them to the position of a tenant cultivator or a labourer working in his own lands. Moneylenders are preoccupied with business activities in Savara lands. The self-sufficient Savara colonies have become colonies of moneyed folk and businessmen. Savaras continue to live on labour work. They go to distant places from their original place of residence or to remote areas in the forest. Some of Savaras in the hilly areas continue to depend on traditional occupations such as shifting cultivation, minor forest products, etc.

Government has imposed restrictions on Podu cultivation. Collection of minor forest produce was prohibited. Hunting in the reserved forests was abandoned. Therefore, Savaras shifted their economic activity. Even in the unreserved areas, Savaras have to face harassment of subordinate forest officials. The forest officials impose reserve forest laws to harass innocent tribal folk illegally. Savaras were not allowed to do Podu cultivation. There are many protective legislations for the safeguard of tribals such as Andhra Pradesh Scheduled Areas Land Transfer Regulation, moneylenders regulation, concessions and privileges extended to tribal population in forest areas. Despite constitutional, legislative and judicial safeguards, Savaras are becoming victims in the hands of bureaucrats, moneylenders and rich people. This, to some extent, is because the poor Savara tribal people are not aware of the privileges extended by the government to them. There is no effective machinery to enforce protection of Savaras.

The traditional economy of Savaras has always been drained by the moneylenders (Shahukars). They lend money when Savaras are in dire need. Moneylenders collect compound interest every year. Thus, they become farm servants and lose their valuable land. Their agro-based economy is seriously affected not because of their unscientific production activities. This is because of poor marketing facilities or lack of marketing facilities for their products.

The tribal cooperative movement has failed in the state. It has not achieved expected results. This is not because of the defective structure or unsuitable philosophy. It is particularly due to its inefficiency and deficiency. The credit societies have miserably failed to realize the loan amounts given to tribals. Fresh loans were not granted to Savaras as the loans have not been repaid or huge amounts taken from banks are not repaid. It is also clear that Savaras do not disrespect repayment of loans. The societies are unable to collect money at an appropriate time. Savaras have to strive all their life to repay loans to Societies/banks. The amount of money given as loan is very small but the amount in turn collected from them is very big.

The Scheduled Tribes Cooperative Finance and Development Corporation is the oldest primary society. This has been functioning in the villages of Savara tribal groups as a marketing agency. They purchase minor forest products collected by tribals. The society also supplies daily requirements of tribal population such as rice, kerosene, oil, salt, cloth, tobacco, soaps, pulses, handlooms, food grains, etc. The society also provides short-term loans to Savaras.

Most of the agricultural, forest products of Savaras will be sold to moneylenders and business people. That is the reason why business people frequently visit tribal areas from the state and outside the state also. This clearly shows the persisting hold of private traders, business class, merchants and moneylenders on Savara agricultural markets (shandies). There is severe competition between cooperative society and moneylenders in Savara habitations. So far, there is no small scale or cottage industries worth the name that has been opened/established for processing, manufacturing the finished products of Savaras. These industries if established on specific aims and goals can make use of local forest products, mineral, agricultural materials available in the surrounding areas.

Savaras sacrifice and slaughter cattle to appease supernatural powers and domestic consumption. They sell skin and hides to private individuals. These things do not bring them attractive prices. There can be separate cooperative to buy skin and animal products which is the main source of economy for tribal people.

Savaras live in thick forest areas. The surroundings of their habitations are not generally hygienic. They face many health hazards. Malaria is a common disease in Savara habitation. Savaras predominantly depend upon their indigenous medicine to cure all their diseases. They believe in magico-medicinal treatment. This forms an important part of their diagnostic and curative methods of treatment. Savaras consider and believe that every disease is a result of evil spirits, angry ancestors or non-treatment of their deities. They believe that by pacifying their deities, ancestors or gods or goddess and spirits through sacrificial offerings and prayers, they can easily cure diseases or escape from health hazards. They trust this as the most effective method and practice of curing. Some of herbal medicines of Savaras are worth for scientific investigations. Introduction of modern medical practices has to be clubbed with their traditional, indigenous medical practices at least in the initial stages. It should be a process of supplementing the merits of indigenous medicines. Modern medicine should not uproot traditional medical practices of Savaras.

The primary healthcare centres opened by government in Savara habitations do not provide proper medical treatment. Doctors do not treat Savaras properly. They are even deceived by doctors working in their primary health care units. Medicines supplied to them do not reach them. Doctors sell them outside and earn money. Even for simple problems, like fever and other common problems, Savaras have to spend thousands of rupees. Corruption is rampant in medical facilities.

Education is an important tool for their development. But still, Savaras are not aware of educational facilities provided to them by the government. Savaras have to still realize the importance of education for them. Savaras perhaps are not convinced with the type of education that the government has provided for them. There are many drawbacks in the proper implementation of education programmes for Savaras. Savaras believe that education should give them some immediate gains or results. They are under the belief that they have to forgo earnings of their children, however, small the amount they fetch through their hard work. Therefore, they do not show much interest to send their children to schools. Instead, they take them for economic activities. Savaras believe that their children are an asset for their economic life. Therefore, opening Ashram, mobile schools with stress on craft-based education, skill-based education is an urgent requirement. The curriculum imparted in Savara schools is the same as followed in urban, state government, private schools. The curriculum does not reflect tribal culture, agriculture and forest activities. Their history, mythology, culture and other aspects of life should be included in their education system. The school timings, holiday pattern must be in tune with their social, economic and cultural activities.

Savaras are not still aware of their development programmes that have been initiated for them for their upliftment. They are unaware of the protective measures that guard them from the exploitation by outside people. The official machinery must be fabricated with judicial powers. Their cases such as land alienation, unauthorised moneylending must be detected. Easy and quick credit facilities have to be provided. Alternative sources of credit through cooperative societies or banks with easy repayment facilities have to be provided to Savaras.

X

Conclusion

Savaras have a rich historical, social, economic, geographical, cultural and demographic background. Their cultural heritage is unique. Savara tribe can be traced back to more than 2,000 years. Savaras are the oldest inhabitants. But still, primitiveness is haunting them. They are not successful in coming out from their primitive lifestyles. Today, modernization is increasing on one hand. At the same time, people are forgetting their ethics and moral values. In the globalized scenario, Savaras are unable to improve their lifestyles. They are also not in a position to enjoy the bare necessities of life. The Savaras are experts in agriculture, cattle rearing, medicine, art, but still, they are lagging behind. The main reason for their backwardness is illiteracy. Savaras are not properly educated. They are not in a position to express or voice freely their opinions. Savaras are exploited and deceived by plains people. Further, many of Savaras have converted to Christianity. The Christian missionaries have encroached their surroundings. Savaras have accepted the conversion for various reasons. Savaras say that to follow Hindu religion, they have to spend a lot of money. In the temples, they have to offer prayers, conduct fairs and festivals and organize puja. In order to conduct these programmes, they have to spend a lot of money and offer money to the temple priests, whereas in Christianity they have to light only a candle in the church. Savaras have lost their Hindu religious and social life.

Moneylenders, traders, government doctors, public officers, missionaries are fulfilling their ulterior motives in Savara habitations. This is due to lack of education among the Savaras. Due to lack of education Savaras are unable to reason out the things that are happening around them. Solution to the problem is expanding education in Savara villages. Oral education, education through their medium of instruction, with their mother tongue at least up to the primary stage, bilingual, multilingual education, providing evening classes, schools for adult Savaras, open school, distance education, mobile schools, are the need for Savaras. An itinerating agency will help government to go round schools and school complexes and strengthen the agency schools for effective functioning. Tribes who are studying in the agency schools should be given preference for getting jobs, higher incentives and facilities. Sincere efforts have to be made. Their programmes have to be properly planned and implemented. Their health and educational programmes have to be strengthened.

Savaras celebrate their social customs, rites, rituals, cultural activities, fairs and festivals, etc. in a very elaborate fashion. But nowadays, due to loss of income, Savaras are not in a position to perform all their cultural activities. This results in forgetting their own culture or customs. The younger generation, due to external influences is speedily forgetting their rich cultural heritage. Therefore, government should provide good, proper facilities, cultural centres, folk universities, music universities, sports clubs to help them preserve their social, traditional culture and customs.

Savaras are excellent singers and dancers. Their dances and folk songs help us to understand about the deep cultural heritage of Savaras. Although Savaras are socially, economically, politically and educationally backward, they are culturally very rich. However, they are now in contact with non-tribal people. They are exposed to different mass media. Their conservative ideas and isolation developed due to lack of awareness. This is shaking their rich cultural heritage. Some Savaras prefer education for their children. They are sending them to schools. A few Savara tribal children are also attaining higher education. But most of the youth do not like their own traditional life pattern or culture. For example, when a Savara youth was contacted and requested to perform their dances they did not participate in the dances with their elders. Perhaps they feel shy. Even to give information about their cultural life they show disinterest. Thus, the very functional aspect of their culture has been badly affected by generation to generation. The rich cultural heritage of Savaras is undergoing a gradual change under the stress of civilizational progress. If the same thing continues, within a very short span of time, their valuable cultural heritage, culture, language, dialects will be lost.

Factors like Christianity, urbanization, modernization, industrialization, education, communication, administration, community development programmes, tribal welfare organizational initiatives, agency administration are all responsible for brining an immense cultural change among Savaras. Their food, dress habits, social practices, behaviour, religious beliefs, traditions and practices, their natural attitudes and outlook all had undergone a tremendous change. The tools of modern civilization is becoming status symbols and developing a new consciousness uprooting their originality.

Savara arts, folk songs, myths and legends are preserved in the original form. They have acquired some new ones from outside. Savaras are keen to come in contact with people from modern society. Savaras are very keen to take modernity to their traditional pattern of society. The different dance forms of Savaras are the overt expressions of their entire society. Dance represents their aesthetic moods. It is created out of their interaction with environment. Dance is an occasion for them to come together. They re-emphasize their group solidarity and express gratitude and thanks to nature and mother earth for good yield. Their dances reveal that they have intimate relationship with nature. However, the freedom and liberty of Savaras have been amalgamated in the democratic life of Indian state. Any future developmental programmes initiated for them should take into consideration of their cultural dimensions. Without paying proper attention to the ethos, belief systems, social organization and rich cultural heritage of Savaras, there can never be a true development of Savaras in the tribal world of India.

References

Addai, B., 'Savara Culture Influx', *Man and Life*, Vol. 34, No. 1–2, 2008.

Arup Ray, 'Cashewnut Plantation Scheme and the Savara of Andhra Pradesh', *Vanyajati,* Vol. XLI, No. 3: 16–18, 1993.

Government of Andhra Pradesh, *A Handbook of Basic Statistics*, Tribal Cultural Research and Training Institute, Hyderabad, 1993.

Government of India, *Census of India,* 1931 and 1961, Manager of Publications, New Delhi.

Krishna Rao, M.V., 'Savaras of Andhra Pradesh', *Girijana Samskriti,* Vol. 1, No. 1, 1968.

——, 'Savaras of Andhra Pradesh', *Man and Life,* Vol. 20, Nos. 1–2: 109–29, 1994.

Mohammad, P.H., 'Child Rearing and Socialisation among the Savaras', *Man and Life,* Vol. 23, No. 3–4, July–December 1997.

Narayana, P.L., 'Saora Kinship Terminology', Folklore, Vol. XIII: 391–96, 1972.

Patanaik, Nityananda, 'Importance of Ethnographic Data in Administration: A Study of Savara community in the Scheduled Areas of Andhra Pradesh and Orissa', *Community Development and Panchayat Raj Digest*, 2 (2), 197–203, 1970.

Raghavaiah, V., *Tribes of India*, Vol. I, Bharatiya Adimjati Sevak Sangh, New Delhi, pp. 83–84, 1969.

Ramamurthy, Gidugu, *The Savaras* (Telugu).

Rao, K.S., 'Megalithic Religion Among Savara of Srikakulam District, South India' *The Eastern Anthropoligist*, Vol. 42, No. 3: 289–93, 1989.

Reddy, K.T. and Rao, S.K., 'Savara Art: A Model for an Interpretation of Prehistoric Rock Art', *The Eastern Anthropologist,* Vol. 45, No. 4: 385–94, 1992.

Sharma, B.V., 'Shifting Cultivation among the Savara Tribe', *Vanyajati,* Vol. XLII, No. 4: 24–30, 1984.

——, 'Formal Education among the Savaras: An Ethnographic Study (unpublished Ph.D. thesis), Hyderabad: University of Hyderabad, 1992.

Srikanth Prabhakar, K. and Narendra, B.D.J. 'Symbolism in the Marriage Rituals of Chenchus and Savaras', *Girijana Samskriti,* Vol. 2, No. 2. 1994.

Suryanarayana, M. 'The Significance of Games in the Savara *Culture' Folklore,* 5. 187–192, 1969.

Thakkar, A.V., Bharatiya Adimjati Samaj Sangh, New Delhi, 1948.

Thurston, Edgar, *Castes and Tribes of Southern India*, Vol. VI, Government Press, Madras, 1883.

8

Ethnographic Profile of Yanadis

The Yanadi are one of the major scheduled tribes of Andhra Pradesh. It is presumed that they are the earliest races of the Indian peninsula. Thurston suggested that they derived their name from the Sanskrit word *anadi* denoting those whose origin is unknown and noted that they were the natives of Sriharikota Island. Now they are predominantly spread over the districts of Nellore, Chittoor and Prakasam districts. The Yanadi live in symbiosis with non-tribals. Their population, according to 1991 census reports, is 3,95,739 in Andhra Pradesh. The total literacy rate among them is 14.78 per cent. The mother tongue of the Yanadis is Telugu. Their culture originated, developed and even today largely flourishes in the lap of nature. But with the passage of time, several negative interactive forces, especially deforestation, destroyed their environment which ultimately resulted in shattering the Yanadi life, particularly their economy. However, without suffering any social disorganisation, the Yanadi have successfully adapted themselves to the changing environment.

I

Ethnic Background: Name of the Tribe and Brief History

The Yanadis are also called as 'Yanadi' or Yenadi. Thurston opined that the Yanadis are a distinct tribe. They had the similar customs that of the Nakkalas of Palakonda taluk in Vishakhapatnam district. The Yanadis are essentially a jungle tribe. They call themselves as 'Yanadi Doras'. They are distinctly homogeneous. The Yanadis were divided into three main groups viz. (1) Dammala Yanadis (worshippers), (2) Kapu Yanadis (cultivators) and (3) Donga Yanadis (thieves). Dammala and Kapu Yanadis are very honest. They will not mix and dine with the Donga Yanadis. It was the Donga Yanadis who were registered as a 'Criminal Tribe' under Section 16 of the CT Act 1911.

Description of the Tribe

The Yanadi settlements are mostly found on the fringes of forest. Ethnically they are characterized by dark skin, curly to wavy hair, medium stature, long head, broad facial with a short chin, mesorrhine and depressed nasal feature, less prominent cheekbones, poor straggling beard over the fore part of their chins and their muscles are soft and flabby. Their dress pattern does not differ from that of neighbouring caste communities. The non-colonialized yanadi live in low, conical and circular huts rudely built with bamboo and palmyra leaves, grass or millet stock, thatched roofs consisting of a single room with a small entrance. Ventilation is very poor in their houses because of small windows. The house can accommodate only a few members. Cooking is usually done outside the hut during the rainy season.

Whether Nomadic or Settled

The Yanadis originally lived in the north-eastern corner of Sriharikota, in Nellore district of Andhra Pradesh. But some scholars believe that the Yanadis are originally from the Chenchu tribe of Nallamala hills and when they left the hills and came down to plains became Yanadis. They lived in 18 villages in Sriharikota with other ostensible means of livelihood.

The Manner in Which the Yanadis Earn their Livelihood

The Yanadis are very local in their habits. Women and children accompany the males for earning their livelihood. The Yanadis attend the marriage functions regularly and collect the food from the left out leaves. They help the people in domestic and labour work. The Yanadis does the allotted work sincerely. The Yanadis earn their livelihood by committing petty offences and housebreaking, etc. It was stated that 'although they were permanently settled in villages, they were already a semi-jungle tribe. Whenever the police tried to arrest them, they absconded into the hills, where it was almost impossible to arrest them. They bury their property in the jungles. Raid after raid had been made on the villages but in every case without success'. They also earn their livelihood by doing cultivation, cooli work, grazing cattle, village watching and domestic work and by stealing the cattle. They lead their lives in abject poverty. They support the large families and under these circumstances, they were notified as a CT (Criminal Tribe) in Madras Presidency.

Food Habits

They eat all kinds of vegetables that are available in their surroundings as also in the markets. They are non-vegetarians. They catch jackals and eat rabbit, rat, squirrel, fowl, goat, sheep, wild pig, fish and other small animals. They abstain from eating beef. Alcoholic consumption is a common feature among males and among the females during the festivals and at the time of celebrating rites of passage.

Marriage System

The Yanadi consider marriage as a necessary biological and social institution. They have their own rules and regulations which govern the choice of mates.

These rules also suggest not only the person whom one may or may not marry but also the person whom one ought to marry. They are tribal endogamy, subtribe endogamy, surname exogamy, incest taboos, and preferential marriages. The rules of endogamy compel the Yanadi to select a spouse within the tribe and within the subtribe but the rules of exogamy prescribe that an individual must find a spouse outside the surname group. There is also the custom of treating members of the surname groups as siblings, besides the custom of treating some groups as siblings of one another.

The rules, besides providing guidance as to from where spouse should be obtained, the Yanadi encourage preferences for certain categories of relatives. With regard to such relatives, symmetrical cross-cousin marriages are favoured, because the marriageable persons know each other and because of this, a better understanding is supposed to develop among them later when they marry. However, a person is free to marry either a patrilateral (father's sister's daughter) or a matrilateral (mother's brother's daughter) cross-cousin. If both the cousins are available for marriage, generally it is left to the discretion of the boy so that he can choose any one of them. In practice, matrilateral cross-cousin marriages occur in lower proportion than patrilateral cross-cousin marriages. Further, it can be observed that of all the preferences for certain categories of relatives, unrelated people are mostly preferred. Further, no child marriage has been noted among the Yanadi. Girls are eligible for marriage only after they attain menarche and boys are usually married after the age of 20 years. The payment of bride-price to the bride's parents is inevitable among the Yanadis. Marriage by negotiations, mutual love and elopement are usual modes of acquiring mates. The re-marriage of divorcees, widows and widowers is permitted. The nuclear type of family is more predominant.

Occupations

The Yanadi depend on a seven-fold subsistence pattern of the economy such as (1) gathering, (2) hunting, (3) fishing, (4) fowling, (5) farming, (6) casual or agricultural and cooli labour and (7) firewood selling. To earn their livelihood, today very few Yanadi families depend upon government service. The Yanadis pursue two or three occupations as primary and secondary ones. They gather fruits, roots, tubers, leaves, honey, firewood and other forest produce. They usually sell the forest produce in the neighbouring villages or towns. Honey collection is one of the important economic pursuits of the Yanadi during the months of March and April. Much of the honey is sold locally after storing the required quantity for their own consumption. With regard to hunting, they usually hunt cats, wild doves, mongoose, etc. Big game, however, is absent in the foothill zones on the one hand and on the other hand, forest laws forbid hunting in the reserved forest. However, they are traditionally proved to have hunted wild animals like Kaniti (*cerves unicolour*), Adavi Pandi (*susserota cristatus*), Kondagorre (*Muntiacus Muntjak*), Jinka (*Antelope*), and Kondamuchu (*presbytis Entellus*). Fishing activities are undertaken in seasonal as well as perennial aquatic zones by adopting different fishing methods. Similarly, for catching patridges and wild doves, both traditional and modern methods of fowling are adopted. Farming in small extents is the latest economic activity taken up by the Yanadis. They also work as farm labourers for the neighbouring peasants.

II

Social Life: Religion

Since the Yanadi have been living in close contact with the Hindu neighbours, they are subjected to Hindu influence through different sources such as affinity with (1) Hindu mythology, (2) Hindu shrines belonging to Saiva and Vaishnava cults. These sources of influence are working simultaneously and they usually combine together to bring about the change of life and culture among the Yanadi. The latter have borrowed several little traditional deities of the neighbouring agricultural castes such as Gurrappa, Muniswami, Patemma, etc. At different festivals, they utter the names of Venkateswara, Rama, Krishna, Siva, Anjaneya, Saraswathi, Lakshmi, Subramanya, Valliyamma and other deities of Hindu pantheon, especially those of agricultural castes. The impact of Hindu deities and the epics can be seen in the naming pattern of children who are named after Lord Venkateswara, Lord Subramanya, Lord Nataraj, Lord Ganesh and Lakshmi, Parvathi, Sreevalli, Bharathi and epic characters like Krishna, Dharmaraju, Bheema, Arjuna, Sahadeva, Dhananjaya, Yasoda, Sasirekha, etc. Nowadays, there is a growing tendency to give their children modern names among the Yanadi.

The Yanadis go on pilgrimage to the important pilgrimage centres such as Tirupati, Tiruttani, Palani, Melmaruvattur, Sabarimala, etc. offerings of money are made to the deities such as Lord Venkateswara, Subramanya whose temples are located at Tirupati and Tiruttani respectively for the bestowal of children, redressal of their day-to-day grievances, relief or cure from physical and mental ailments, etc. When their prayers are answered, they visit the said temples for offering worship. In case any child is born to them, it is christened after the deity in whose name the oath is taken. Thus, the numerous gods and goddesses that the Yanadis worship are conceptualized in different ways.

Rites and Rituals

Like all other Hindu castes, the Yanadis observe the rites and observances concerning the major crises of life with a view to leading the appropriate way of life so that they can enjoy prosperity and well-being of the family and have a desirable future for individuals after death. With the exception of lifecycle ceremonies and festivals, according to the calendar, there is very little spiritual activity in the Yanadi community. The Yanadis celebrate festivals such as Sankranthi, Sivarathri, Ugadi, Sriramanavami, Vanatamama Panduga, Adikrittika, Vinayaka Chavethi, Diwali, Om Sakthimala and Ayyappamala which reflect the Hindu impact in ample measure. The Yanadi institution is consisting of 'Rangam' and the entertainment form of 'Melam'. This goes into the worldview and structural linkages of their society. The Yanadi divide the world into visible and invisible worlds in which living human beings, gods, devils, plants and animals are both benign and malignant to them. They simultaneously live in these distinct worlds. There is no end for life because even after death in visible world, they do live in invisible world and interact with their kins of the visible world. Life is not even cyclic but is considered to terms of extension from visible world to invisible world. In the visible world, the human beings are broadly classified as non-Yanadi (Samsarulu) and Yanadi. The non-Yanadi are again divided into benign and malign non-Yanadi. In the invisible world, all things are considered powerful but are divided into gods and devils. This suggests a dichotomous nature of perception of the universe by the Yanadi. 'Rangam' is a very recurrent activity in the life of the Yanadi. This was made by them to understand the characteristic behaviour of the Yanadi. The views of the Yanadi about the world is very complex.

III

Economic Life of Yanadis

Every tribe has its own economic structure. The Yanadi economic system was divided into food gatherers, hunters, fishermen, bamboo workers, farm labourers, non-farm labourers, trappers, herdsman and cultivators. They were mostly hunters and food gatherers. The Yanadis could easily identify the footprints of their relative animals and birds that were caught by identifying their footprints and disturbing the shelter and chasing them with the help of dogs. From ten to twenty people may combine to follow the footprints of animals or birds. Working as daily waged labourers under the Forest Department and private contractors was another main source of livelihood for the Yanadis. The main activities in the forest were organized around bamboo forestation. The contractors used to pay them very low wages. Moreover, these middlemen and the colonial contractors encouraged the plantation crops that destructed the very essence of the livelihood of this Yanadis and maximized the profits for these contractors. The Yanadi economy should have been continuously based on a food collection pattern, e.g. collection of fruit, seeds, roots, hunting and fishing, their direct contact with nature was broken with the arrival of the British rule. Cash economy was introduced in the life of the tribe. The British state looked down upon the Yanadis as savage human beings. As a result, the Yanadi contradicted with the dominance of the British superiority. The tribal economy was based on forest produce. They could never cut any tree for their own interests. They treated it like a goddess and worshipped it before each hunt in case of the Garela Misemma of the Chenchus in modern Andhra. They could also gather several items of forest produce, including medicinal herbs, fuel, honey and housing material from the forests. The Yanadis know the forest flora well and used various trees and shrubs for various diseases. They have a wide and practical knowledge of the jungle. Every kind of tree, herb and vine have a name. The properties of each are as well known to them as the letters of our alphabets to us. They gather roots, fruits, leaves and honey for their food and know well the best season for each variety and where it grows best. They have learned by experience the properties and uses of herbs and roots in medicine. Every ache and pain has its supposed remedy in the jungle flora. However, with the entrance of the western medicines; the indigenous medical system was replaced.

The following list of minor forest products that are collected by the Yanadis, were given in the Nellore District Gazette. Namely, Chay root (*Oldenlandia umbellate*), which by a quaint imprint, appears as Chay root, Kanuga (*Pongamia glabra*), Sarasaparilla (*Hemidesmus indicus*), Nuxvomica (*strychnos Nux-vomica*), Tangedu (*Cassia auriculata*), Soap nut (*Sapindus trifoliatus*), Achilla weed (*Lichens*), Ishwarac (*Aristolochia indica*), Vishabuddi (*Sida carpini folia*), Kukkapala (*Tylophora asthmatica*), Honey, Rattan (*Calamus Rotang*), Tamarind (*Tamarindus Indicus*), Neredu (*Eugenia Jambolana*) and Surati bark (*Ventilago madras patana*). They know the forest well; this expert knowledge of the jungle led the government in 1835, when it took possession of the island, to employ the Yanadis in collecting minor forest products. In return for their labour the government at first paid them in clothing, grain and money. The Yanadis, a backward tribe, form the backbone of the labour force in the Sriharikota Island. They collect chiefly nux vomica, soap nuts, tamarind, rattans, sarsaparilla roots, barks that are still used in South India as dye-stuffs, and various leaves, roots, and bark that are marketed in India or elsewhere for medicinal purposes.

The Yanadis were the original inhabitants of the island. The headquarters of the Yanadis was the island of Sriharikota in Nellore district. Their primitive condition was noticed in 1835, when the island came into the fold of the colonial state that endeavoured to ameliorate their position by supplying them with a liberal allowance of grain, clothing, tobacco and money in return for the jungle produce for constructing railways and modern industries. The demand for the labour naturally rose, and the Government offered to pay to parents two annas six paise on the birth of a male and one-anna three paise on the birth of a female child. In this way, their labour was used and exploited for the colonial interests forgetting the economic needs of the Yanadis. The Mutta of Sriharikota came into the possession of Government in the year 1835 and saw these Yanadis were in a state of complete barbarism dependent on roots, fruits and other jungle products. They were employed in the collection of jungle products that was delivered to Government agents who economically benefited. From the eighteenth century up to 1815, Sriharikota Island was in the control of Kondaledu Muttadars or Poligars, of Chinglepat district, who were under the suzerainty of the East India Company. These Muttadars paid a tribute of ten thousand sticks or billets of wood to the Company per annum. The tribute was raised to 1,00,000 and the Poligars refused to pay the East India Company with the assistance of the Kalahasti and Venkatagiri Zamindars.

Before the colonial rule, the tribes enjoyed absolute freedom to carry on this specific economic activity. The Forest Department in late nineteenth century completely integrated the hill tribes and had forcibly usurped the right of collecting even the minor forest produce. It even tightened the collection of minor forest produce by keeping the contractors under the supervision of the colonial government. At some places, the rates were fixed by the state itself. Thus, the colonial government took a right to the minor forest away from the native tribes. This process of transformation led this Yanadi tribe to become coolie labourers in the capitalist structure that created a vast gap between the colonizer and the colonized in the terms of economy. These contractors and middlemen paid very low wages to these tribes to maximize their profits. Shri R.S. Malayappan, IAS, the then Director of Harijana Welfare, Madras Government, and an unhesitating champion of all oppressed people wrote in his Report dated 23.5.1953 that, 'Yanadis working under the forest manager are paid ₹ 0–12–0 per head or ₹ 1–8–0 for a couple. They cannot do the work allotted to them unless they engage their children also but nothing is paid to them separately, apart from what the parents are paid'.

In the Order No. 609 Ref. dated 5th September 1895, the government sanctioned the grant of eighteen cubits of cloth (to each male) and three tons of paddy (per annum), twenty cubit of cloth (to each female) and half ton paddy (per annum) as *inams* to Government of the Sriharikota island in return for their services in the collection of minor forest produce. This grant was subject to the provision that the total number of males or females to whom the inams are granted shall not exceed one twenty in any year and all the recipients should be adults. In his Ref. No. 357/Genl, 1922 dated 15.5.1922 the district Forest Officer in Nellore addressed to the chief conservator recommending to government the revision of the above rates as follows.

For many years part as seemed from a perusal of the previous records, inams do not appear to have been disbursed with reference to this G.O., but in the proportion of the amount earned by the Yanadis as wages for the year. The amounts, however, were sanctioned, but did not appear to have exceeded the correct amount advisable as per G.O. No. 609, 1895.

A circular emphasized by a forest officer read that the minor forest produce was collected departmentally through the agency of the Yanadi labour living in the jungle of Sriharikota. In addition to these, weekly wages were disbursed and 'inam batta' or rewards at the end of every half-year were disbursed. The work of collection of jungle produce was carried on from November to July. During the remaining months, the Yanadis had no other means of subsistence. According to a G.O., the District forest officer was allowed to grant inams at 50 per cent of the wages of the Yanadis with discretion to apportion inams to each Yanadi according to quantity of work turned out by him. The restriction that there should be only one twenty Yanadis in the list might be cancelled, as they wanted more Yanadis for their work. The present conservator and the then collector A.R. Cox who visited the Range during October 1921 expressed his willingness to the Range Officer to recommend to the government to increase inams. The district forest officer's proposal had the approval of the collector; Fischer. The conservator opined that the matter was within the conservator's competence to sanction the rate of inams as part of the estimate for the collection of produce. He, therefore, sanctioned the revised rates and did not forward the above reference to the chief conservator. The inams were being included in the collection estimate for minor forest produce at 45 per cent of the wages earned and there had been no objection hitherto. The G.O. numbered 5.9.1985 restricted the scope of the grant of the inams to be maximum number of one twenty individuals who should all be adults; and that the sanction accorded by the conservator, third circle varied from the terms of the Government order. It was only by compulsion that they could be induced to engage in this occupation by the colonial masters. Since the new agrarian methods and modernization forces entered into the society, these could not complete the colonial structures that always aimed at maximizing profits rather than developing the indigenous economies. In Nellore, the Yanadis were employed on the collection of minor forest produce and for casuarinas planting in the Sriharikota range. Some of the Yanadis appointed by the Government had also been engaged in watering the casuarinas plantation. As the area was to be fell annually for fuel, working circle had been reduced and there would be considerably less work for private villagers, they should be attracted to the casuarinas plantations for watering to release as many Yanadis as possible to collect the valuable items of minor forest produce like nuxyuomica, soap nuts, tamarind, etc. Yanadis would do watering under government control. It was found that a Yanadi could water one thousand plants per day working eight to nine hours and walking fourteen to fifteen miles. The rate per thousand plants would be three annas. Their labour was at the cheap rate and was misused for the colonial interests.

Whenever the government had induced the Yanadis to collect minor forest products, it introduced coolies from the mainland to cut firewood to be sent to Madras City and to teach the Yanadis the art. But they worked under protest. They preferred to be let alone to enjoy the wildlife of the jungle. Fishing was one of the important food procuring activities. There were instances of the Yanadi deciding to go to fishing and foregoing a day's work. The implements used for fishing were ootha mandam and galem (angler). There could be no doubt that the Yanadis were a great fishing race and used to embark on large scale expeditions even to distant places. The ideas of Yanadi's economy were primitive and simple. Therefore, the surplus was very low. The economy of the Yanadi was essentially one of hand-to-mouth existence. It seldom took note of non-essentials. It did not have much to do with money-economy. The institution of the market economy was seen in one form or the other among Yanadis. There were regular markets. Cereals, spices, meal salt, utensils, agricultural tools and implements, clothing, cosmetics, etc. were available in the market. Non-tribal traders were also interested in these markets in search of local produce at throwaway prices. However, the British policy of isolating the tribes resulted in exploitation. Zamindars, landlords, moneylenders and contractors exploited the tribes to the maximum, which led to the burden on tribal people.

The economy of the Yanadis was largely undisturbed until the beginning of the colonial state in Andhra. The intervention of an omnipotent Colonial state into a hitherto hunting and gathering community led to serious consequences. The colonial state in its attempt to access the rich natural resources of the area deprived livelihood of the Yanadis. This deprivation led to the migration of Yanadis to nearby villages and towns where they ultimately ended as agricultural labourers, who were treated as criminal tribes. The Forest Department could not do away with the expertise of Yanadis on forest matters. Some of them were employed by the colonial administration to collect various forests products for export. The economic structure of the Yanadis was based on the food gathering economy unlike the economies of the Savaras, Konda Reddies and Koyas based on the shifting cultivation. In this sense, the British differed the treatment of Yanadis with other tribes. The colonial state not only destructed the economic structure of the indigenous system of the Yanadis but also it disturbed the life of Yanadis and sources for their livelihood by creating the political, economic and cultural institutions like forest, economic and other departments. In order to get support of the local people, the colonial administration employed a small section of the tribal people to collect various forest products of export. But their policy of complete isolation took a reverse turn and the landlords, moneylenders and contractors exploited the tribes. The Yanadis were exploited and were provided with clothes, cigars and rice as remuneration by the British Government. Cash economy, which was introduced by the state in the agrarian sector, did not affect the economic transactions of Yanadis. Even after the penetration of the colonial state, they largely depended on the non-saleable forest foods and products for their survival. Industrialization, unlike modernization is a particular process of change. With the growth of industry in surrounding coastal areas, the Yanadis underwent a change in their economic life. They started migrating to industrial areas for more remunerative work. They imbibed the work-culture of an industrial complex and got acquainted with labour work.

Industrialization and urbanization, transformed the means of livelihood of Yanadis. The fascination of existing in a town or city constantly attracted the Yanadis to migrate to towns, where until now their inhabitants were living in the interior villages. They came to the cities as wage earners, particularly money-wages, and to work as manual workers in the erection of roads, buildings and a congregation of other activities. The Yanadis came in touch with the mainstream plains people, learned to adapt and accommodate themselves to the new economic relations; slowly shifting away from their traditional modes of sustenance, i.e. hunting, fishing and other natural habits. They learned to exchange their labour, for example, from the earlier barter system to this social money exchange. They also learnt to live with non-tribal communities, realized and recognized new job opportunities and working under government and non-government institutions. To conclude that from time immemorial, the Yanadis had their own social, economic, cultural practices and relations, and these relations had not remained the same in the historical process.

IV

Political Organization: Kulapanchayat

Regarding the system of customary governance in the Yanadi society, the political organization of the Yanadis falls under 'Stateless' system as it was not a formal government embracing the entire society, the political functions being performed by the settlements and there being no person or group with centralized authority applicable to the tribe as a whole. The principle of organization in the Yanadi society is based on genealogical or associational units. There is no headman for every clan. All classes enjoy equal status. In addition, there are no special associations such as military organizations, religious organization, etc. Hence it is appropriate to place the organization of the Yanadi settlement under the principle of territory as the main organization criterion. Thus, the territory unit is the settlement, the smallest unit of organization represented by family. The Yanadi inhabiting a number of settlements constitute the tribe. The system of governance resembles that of a political system with a hereditary/non-hereditary chief, assisted by a body of hierarchically placed officials. It, however, differs from feudalism to democracy in its functioning. The officials have no absolute power to enforce their decision without consulting the elders of the settlement. Further, in the Yanadi settlements, there exists no military organization which is an indispensable characteristic of any government. Hence, the system is comparable to the caste panchayat (Council). The Panchayat consits of a head with a body of elders. The Yanadi interpret their settlement officials in terms of officials of royal kingdom viz. Raja (King) and Mantri (Minister). The settlement has a permanent hereditary/non-hereditary headman called Yanadi Pedda (Raju) who presides over the traditional Panchayat (Council). The chief hails from a particular clan which is not the same in all settlements. In general, succession to the office of the Yanadi Pedda is hereditary. Upon his death, the eldest son succeeds him if he is intelligent, is known for his understanding and capability of managing the affairs of the settlement. Otherwise, the settlement people select one of the sons of the Yanadi Pedda. The succession to the office of Yanadi Pedda is not characterized by a special ceremony. He is not entitled to any type of regular or voluntary gifts, either in kind or in cash and compulsory dues such as tribute or tax. But there is a traditional obligation that when liquor is served at the time of dispute in the settlement the Yanadi Pedda is treated first. In the traditional political structure of Yanadis the Yanadi Pedda is assisted in discharging his duties by Kolukarudu (Minister) and a few elderly persons. The latter express their opinions on the merits of the case and assist the Yanadi Pedda in arriving at a decision. Ordinary disputes are settled by the Panchayat itself, whereas serious offences and complicated disputes are often settled by caste leaders at the village level or by the police personnel. The disputes are usually related to adultery, elopement, theft, divorce, abusing, etc. Of late, the culprits are punished as per severity of the crime. There are various rates of the fine within the range of maximum and minimum. The fines are imposed in order to compensate the loss and the punishments include an apology and ex-communication.

V

Criminality: Modus Operandi

Women and children accompany the males for committing crime. It was stated that the Yanadis were very local in their habits. All the crimes committed by them were within a day's march from their homes. They confine their operations to the neighbouring places in which they lived. The crimes committed by them were under the security sections of the IPC only. Housebreaking, robbery and cattle theft were the crimes frequently committed by them. Although they were permanently settled in villages, they were by nature a semi-jungle tribe. Whenever, the police tried to arrest them, they used to abscond into the villages and hills. It was almost impossible for the police to catch them under such circumstances. It was stated that 'Raid after raid has been made on the villages but in every case without any success. They were familiar with every path of the village to the hills where they easily evade the arrest'. The Yanadis used to earn their livelihood by the extortion of cattle owners. The owners used to pay to the local Yanadis a few rupees in order not to steal the cattle. If the owners refused to pay the money then the Yanadis used to steal the cattle one by one. The women and children used to act as spies and informants for the men. The Yanadis never reveal their movements. Under these circumstances A.M.A.G. Galletti, the then-District Magistrate notified the Yanadis as a criminal tribe under Section 10(a) of the CT Act. A draft notification was also issued by the then British Government declaring them as a CT in Madras. According to the draft notification it was stated that: 'Whereas there is reason to believe that the tribe of Yanadis known as Donga Yanadis are addicted to the systematic commission of non-bailable offences. The Government in Council in the exercise of the powers conferred on him by Section 3 of the CT Act VI of 1924 hereby declares that the Donga Yanadis is a criminal tribe for the purpose of the said Act. Further, under Section 10 of the said Act, the Governor in Council directs that every registered member of the said criminal tribe, report himself at fixed intervals and shall also notify his place of residence and any change or intended change of residence and any absence of intentional absence from his residence'.

VI

Yanadis Today

With a view to solve the poverty-stricken conditions among the Yanadi community, land colonization schemes were started during the colonial period. The same has been continued even after the post-independence period for reformation, reclamation and rehabilitation of the Yanadis. The Government of Andhra Pradesh has also introduced land assignment schemes to provide land for cultivation to the landless Yanadi community members. The District Administration has taken up two colonization schemes, one in Karvetinagar Mandal and the other at Kuppam Mandal. In Karvetinagar Mandal, land to the extent of one or two acres was allotted to a few Yanadi families. Loans to the extent of an amount of ₹ 4,000 were sanctioned under DWACRA. The Yanadis in Kuppam Mandal have been cultivating unassigned lands in the forest area. In addition to this, some of the Yanadi families were given sheep and buffaloes which were disposed off in the course of time to meet their financial exigencies. Besides, the developmental schemes under the sectors like education, housing, woman and child development, health and nutrition, roads, electricity, sanitation, etc. are also under implementation level for the benefit of the Yanadis. The expected results of progress and development of the Yanadi families in Andhra Pradesh could not be achieved despite of the efforts of the State and Central Government programmes. Therefore, a decision has been taken by the Government of Andhra Pradesh on 9.9.1997 to establish a separate Integrated Tribal Development Agency for the Yanadi inhabiting districts such as Nellore, Chittoor and Prakasam districts. A Yanadi development plan has been prepared for the improvement and development of Yanadis who were inhabiting in 166 Mandals in Nellore, Chittoor and Prakasam districts. The Government of Andhra Pradesh issued orders (vide G.O. Ms. No. 136 Social Welfare Tw. Bud. 2 Department, dated 19.12.2001) for establishing the ITDA for the Yanadis. The Project is headed by a Project Officer (IAS rank) assisted by Development Officer and other supporting staff to implement various developmental programmes. It is needless to state that the ITDA should take the responsibility of the development of the Yanadis who are still in a primitive stage in the states of Andhra Pradesh and Telangana.

References

Agarwal, Binod, C.N. Sudhakar Rao and P.C. Gurivi Reddy, *Yanadi Response to Change: An Attempt to Action Anthropology*, Concept, New Delhi, 1985.

Aiyappan, A., *Report on the Socio-economic Conditions of the Aboriginal Tribes of the Province of Madras*, Government Press, Madras, 1948.

Anthropological Survey of India, *Yanadis* (unpublished monograph), Mysore, 1980.

Gousia Begam, S., *The Yanadis: A Study in Marriage, Family and Inter-community Linkages* (unpublished dissertation), submitted to S.V. University, Tirupati, 1986.

Government of India, *Census of India, 1961, Vol. II, Andhra Pradesh, A Monograph on Rettamala*, Government of Andhra Pradesh, Hyderabad, 1961.

——, *Census Report, Special Tables for Scheduled Castes and Scheduled Tribes*, Government Press, New Delhi, 1991.

Government of Madras, *Administration Report of the Forest Department of the Madras Presidency, 15 October 1940*, Government Press, Madras, 1939.

——, *Administration Report of the Forest Department of the Madras State for the Year Ending 31 March 1952*, Government Press, Madras, 1954.

——, Forest Department, G.O. Miss. No. 72, dated 26 August 1925.

——, Fort St. George Gazettee, dated 15 December 1925, Notification No. 214, Judicial, dated 9 December 1925, Part I.

——, Fort St. George Gazettee, dated 30 August 1932, Notification No. 306, Part I.

——, Judicial Department, G.O. No. 28, dated 15 January 1926.

——, Public Works and Labour Department, G.O. No. 1764 L, dated 19 August 1932, G.O. No. 1962 L, dated 6 September 1932.

——, *Report on the Administration of the Madras Presidency for the Year 1935–36*, Madras, 1937, p. 102, Progress of Chief Conservator of Forests, Forest Department, G.O. No. 444, dated 11 October 1935.

Hasnain, Nadem, *Tribal India Today*, Harnam Publications, New Delhi, 1983.

Kumar, G. Stanley Jaya, *Tribal from Tradition to Transition: A Study of Yanadi Tribe of Andhra Pradesh*, M.D. Publications Pvt. Ltd., New Delhi, 1995.

Pratap, D.R., *Andhra Pradesh Adimajatulu (in Telugu)*, Director, TCR & TI, Hyderabad.

Pulla Reddy, A., 'Ethnographic Note on the Yanadi Tribe of Andhra Pradesh', *Vanyajathi*, Vol. XXXII, Bharatiya Adimjati Sevak Sangh, New Delhi.

Raghavaiah, V., *The Yanadi*, Bharatiya Adimjati Sevak Sangh, New Delhi, 1962.

——, *Tribes of India*, Vol. I, Bharatiya Adimjati Sevak Sangh, New Delhi, 1969.

Ramesham, *Andhra Pradesh District Gazatteers, Chittoor*, The Director, Government Press, Andhra Pradesh, Hyderabad, 1979.

Reddy, P.C., *The Yanadis of Madras Presidency* (unpublished Ph.D. Thesis), Lucknow University.

Saheb, S.A.A., 'Yanadies: Ethnographic Profile of the Tribes', in K.S. Singh (ed.), *People of India, Vol. 2: Tamil Nadu*, Anthropological Survey of India, Kolkata, 2004.

Sudhakar Rao, N., 'A Structural Perspective of Yanadi's Two Forms of Entertainment: Melam and Keelugurralu', *The Eastern Anthropologist*, Vol. 50, No. 1, 1997.

——, 'Rangam of Yanadi of Sriharikota', *The Eastern Anthropologist*, Vol. 36, No. 3, 1983.

Sudhakar Reddy, B.V., *Tradition and Transition: A Study of Socio-cultural Change among the Yanadis of Andhra Pradesh* (unpublished Ph.D. Thesis), S.V. University, Tirupati, 1982.

Sudhakara Reddy, P., *The Displaced Yanadis of Sriharikota Island: A Study in Socio-cultural Continuity and Change* (unpublished Ph.D. Thesis), S.V. University, Tirupati, 1981.

Sumner, Cushing W., 'Sriharikota and the Yanadis: A Sandy Island Off the East Coast of India and Its Inhabitants', *Annals of the Association of American Geographers*, Vol. 7, 1971.

The Working Plan for the Sriharikota Range (Nellore District), 1932–33 to 1941–42.

Thurston, Edgar and K. Rangachari, *Castes and Tribes of the Southern India*, Vol. VII, Cosmo Publications, New Delhi, 1975.

Thurston, Edgar, *Castes and Tribes of Southern India*, Vol. 3, Cosmo Publications, New Delhi, 1909.

9

Yerukulas

A Denotified/Nomadic Community in Andhra Pradesh and Telangana

In Andhra Pradesh, according to 1991 Census, tribal population accounted for 5.93 per cent that is 32 lakh in the total population of 5,35,49,679. In 1977, the Lambadis, Yerukulas and Yanadis were included in the categories of Scheduled Tribes. The tribal population increased substantially with the inclusion of these tribes. These people occupy 30,000 sq miles of area, i.e. 11 per cent of the total area of the State. They are spread over 6,197 villages. In South India, among the various tribes, Yerukulas occupy an important position. According to the 1981 census report, the Yerukulas occupy the fourth place out of 35 groups of tribes, and their number was 3,00,557. These Yerukulas were found in almost all districts in Andhra Pradesh. However, their number is higher in Rayalaseema, Telangana and coastal Andhra Districts.

I

Ethnic Background

The Yerukulas are spread all over India with different languages and dialects and are known by different names in different localities from the extreme South to the North Arcot district in Madras Presidency, they were called Koravas. From North Arcot district up to the ceded districts they are called Korchas or Korachas. From ceded districts, they are called Yerukula. Thurston found, in Calcutta, that these were practicing quack doctors. Writing about Yerukulas, Paupa Rao Naidu observes that 'as railways spread all over the country they readily adapted themselves to travelling by them and the opportunities afforded for going quickly far from the scene of a recently committed crime or for stealing from sleeping passengers, were soon availed of'. H.A. Stuart stated that he found Yerukulas, a vagrant tribe in Madras

Presidency as well as in many other parts of India. The Yerukulas, Koravas and Korchas were in fact branches of the large Korava community operating in different regions of Madras Presidency. Yerukulas lived and traded in Telugu districts, Koravas in Tamil districts and Korchas in coastal districts of Andhra Pradesh. In the Andhra region, these people were called *Yerukulavandlu* or *Korachavandlu* but they always speak of themselves as Kurru. In Nellore, they speak of one another as *Kurru* and *Kula*. It has been suggested that *yeru* is connected with 'Erra' meaning red.

In Telugu, *Yerukulavandlu* means fortune-tellers and Oppert suggests that this is the origin of the name Yerukula. He says, 'It is highly probable that the name and occupation of the fortune-telling Kurruvandlu or Kulavandlu indicated the Telugu people to call these people Yerukulavandlu'. He further connects the word *kurru* with the root *ku* a mountain, and Thurston informs that in a Tamil work of the 9th century (*Tirumurukairuppadi*) *Kurru* or *kuru* is given as the name of a hill tribe. Brown and Wilson, in their glossaries, used the word, Erukalavandlu or Erukulawaru, a plural in Telugu for Erukavadu. Both men and women have tattoo marks on their heads and forearms.

Each caste has its own subcastes and its own caste rules. Social customs, religious beliefs, omens, ordeals and standards of morality vary from tribe to tribe and from one social group to another. Their social customs and religious beliefs are perfectly in tune with their career. From times immemorial, the members of the nomadic/Denotified tribes have been following Hinduism in its crude form. Similarly, these Yerukulas also have their own way of living, customs, traditions, superstitions, rituals and ceremonies. These traditions separate them from other population.

Easily identified, traditionally, the men dressed only in a Gochi, or piece of cloth around the loins and possessed a bag called *vadi Sanchi* (made of striped cloth). The Yerukula women wore a black cloth. Necklaces and beads, made of variegated colours, were common to both men and women. Silver, glass or brass bangles adorned them from the wrist to the elbow. Silver rings on their fingers were also common. The new generation has gradually moved away from these traditional modes of dress and they are increasingly copying the Hindu women. Here we find the Sanskritization process which M.N. Srinivas talked about. The Yerukulas split up into infinite divisions, some criminal and some non-criminal. They wander over the districts of Nellore, Kurnool, Guntur, Krishna, Godavari and Hyderabad. They are divided into seven main divisions known as Criminal Investigation Department Gang Nos. IV, V, VI, VIII, X and XIII.

To check their criminal tendencies, the Madras colonial government established several criminal tribes' settlements in various parts of Andhra. Primary education is being imparted to children in these settlements. There are also graduates and post-graduates among them. Between 1910 and 1935 the Madras Government declared 30 tribes or castes as 'criminal' and among them were Donga Yerukulas, Donga Dasaris, Donga Waddars, Yanadis, Dommaras, etc. (Originally the Yerukulas were innocent temple servants. Subsequently, they took to petty trading and selling of agricultural products in several places. With the development of communications, the Yerukulas discontinued their trade. This disorganization in their social and economic life made them become petty criminals to make their both ends meet. Generally, they feel that it was an absurd thing to work a whole day for six annas. By courage and good luck, one night-adventure may bring in thousands of rupees.

II

Social Life: Family

The society among the Yerukulas was based on the patriarchal system. Women occupied a relatively important position. Women are treated well in general. Both the joint and the nuclear family system evolved. The decision-making power rested with man. The relationship between married children and their parents is good. Freedom was given to the married members of the family. Even now there are some traces of joint family system.

The society of Yerukulas consists of three types of families – nuclear, joint and single membered families. However, the numbers of nuclear families are more. The population is divided into four age groups, i.e. 1 to 13; 14 to 20, 21 to 59 and 60 above. The age group of 21–59 represents the highest number of people. Basically the houses of the Yerukulas are (1) *tataku itukillu* (thatched brick houses) and (2) Penkutillu (brick houses). The thatched houses are large in number because of the poverty stricken conditions of the Yerukulas. Both men and women are hard working. Both are busy with their work. Generally, men go for works like agricultural operations, rickshaw-pulling, cooli work and work in the Indian Leaf Tobacco Department and other private employment. Women, when not employed stay at home and look after household work.

Position of Women and Children

Traditionally, women were greatly oppressed and this has changed a little and for the better. They are expected to show respect to the male members of the family. In general, the brother-in-law or other children accept women as part of their family. They cannot call their husband by name. Some Yerukulas are particular about the reputation of their womanhood and consider it a serious matter, if any of them return home without an escort after sunset. Debauchery is considered to be the most sinful act and is severely condemned. The fortune-telling women carry a basket, winnow, stick and wicker tray in which coury shells are embedded in a mixture of cow dung and turmeric. The basket represents Kolapuriamma. The women go about the streets calling out 'Yeruko Amma yeruka' which means 'prophecy, mother, prophecy'.

Clans or Gotras

They have their own Clans or *Gotras*. They are Sathupati, Kavadi, Manepati, Mandragutti. These are all corrupted Tamil words. Sathupadi is a corruption of *Sattupadi* which means adorning a Hindu deity with flowers, jewels and vestments, Kavadi means a pole carried on the shoulders with two baskets, pendants hanging from both ends. Manepati is a corruption of *manpadi* which means stitching a pair of shoes and presenting them to the temple. In earlier days, these people were very particular about their gotrams. Of these four major divisions, *Sathupati* and *Kavati* gotrams are considered superior. A *Kavati* man (styled as *Pothuvadu* in Telugu), according to the tradition, can marry into a Sathupati family as they are endogamous. However, the reverse is not generally acceptable, though there are a few exceptions.

These tribes are said to have many subdivisions but these refer chiefly to the various occupations they follow. Some of them are, Kavali Yerukulas, Uppu Yerukulas, Dabba Yerukulas, Karrepaku Yerukulas, Parigimugga Yerukulas, Koot Yerukulas, Kotulas, Bhazantri Yerukulas, Ram Yerukulas, Nagi Yerukulas, Suvva Yerukulas, Kunchapari Yerukulas, Sathupati Yerukulas, Kuddikatti Yerukulas, etc. Some men who were appointed as watchmen were called Kavali Yerukulas. Some men who maintained their livelihood by taking the business of salt were called *Uppu Yerukulas. Dabba Yerukulas* were those who prepared bamboo baskets. The people who sell karvepaku leaves were called Karvepaku Yerukulas. Pamulas were those who catch snakes and exhibit them in the villages to earn a living. *Parigamuggalas* were those whose profession is tattooing. The people who obtain their livelihood by prostitution are called *Koot Yerukulas*. In Telugu areas, these people were called Bogamuvaru. They also kidnap and sell children; *Kotulas* were those who trap monkeys and perform. The people who play the orchestra at the time of festivals, marriages and other cultural proceedings were called *Bhazantri Yerukulas*. Ram Yerukulas were those who live on the profession of working on rocks. The people who eat monkeys are called Nagi Yerukulas. Some gather roots in forests and make them into long brushes. They are excellent hunters. They are called *Kunchipuri* Yerukulas. *Satupati* Yerukulas were those whose main source of livelihood is preparing baskets. *Etapulla* Yerukulas were those whose main occupation is net weaving. *Suvva* Yerukulas were those whose main occupation is the basket making with iron rods.

Among the Yerukulas, there are basically three religious groups viz. Hindus, Christians, and Muslims. But the number of Hindus and converted Christians are large in number. The Hindus worship Venkateswara, Lakshmi, Siva and other gods of Hindu pantheon. The Christians attend the church service. But due to the influence of the American Baptist Telugu Mission, Canadian and the Salvation Army there are a good number of people who go to the church though they are traditionally Hindus. Both Hindus and Christians used to celebrate their festivals like Dasara, Deepavali, Pongal, Christmas and the New Year Day. Some of the people who engage in criminal activities are *animists*. They believe in natural forces and worship all kinds of idols, animals, birds and supernatural forces.

The *Kula Dharma* (caste duty) of Yerukulas was dongatanamu (that of thieving). Before going out on a house breaking excursion or a raid on a peaceful village they used to pray to the Modevi (goddess of sleep). The contents of the prayers being that they themselves might be kept alert and heavy sleep might fall on their victims and that the police would not interrupt their operations. When the Yerukulas were first brought to the settlements it was not easy to get them to attempt ordinary honest work.

Language

Yerukulas have their own language but no script. The words of Yerukulas and Koravas appear to be taken mainly from other South Indian languages such as Tamil, Telugu and Canarese. The wandering tribes speak more than one language to make friends with others. But the settled people speak the language of the locality. Those Yerukulas who were spread all over the Andhra region speak only Telugu language. They use slang expressions which are unintelligible to the outsiders.

The Yerukulas in the settlements have their own language. Parents generally talk in Yerukula language. Some of the children learn this from their parents. Language is the factor which contributes to their unity and they recognize the non-Yerukulas very easily. In the settlements, the people observe their gotrams or kinship relations very strictly while performing marriages. They identify a certain person by his house name. Thus, they follow endogamous rules. Today, inter-caste marriages are taking place among the Yerukulas.

Food

Cats, fowls, monkeys, jackals, field rats, deer, goats, sheep, antelope and all sorts of birds, crows, sparrows, squirrels, parrots, etc. serve as articles of food for these people. They are totally non-vegetarians and love hunting. But due to their economic scarcity, they are tuning into vegetarians. They drink toddy heavily. They also take drugs. They eat all varieties of vegetables. They are restricted to eat with other communities like pariahs and Muslims.

Marriage System

The type of marriage that prevails among Yerukulas is polygamy. But it is weakening now. They are favouring monogamy. Elders arrange their marriages. They freely admit other caste women into theirs, except those of the lowest order, such as Malas, Madigas and the like. At present, they are admitting these women also into their fold. A marriage is generally negotiated between the parents of the bridegroom and the bride and the former promises to pay a *voli* or bride price of ₹ 3.50 for the first marriage and seven rupees for the remarriage of a man or woman. Child marriages are not allowed. Dr Shortt stated that 'A custom prevails in the tribe whereby the maternal uncle may claim the first two daughters of family as wives for his sons'. Generally, the selection of a match was followed in the following manner. First, they select a suitable bride and the parents of the bridegroom visit the bride's house with all elderly persons. The village head was the mediator between the two parties. If they find that the girl is suitable to their bridegroom, they give their acceptance. Instead of bride-price, the dowry system slowly stepped into their life due to the sanskritization process. People take dowry according to their social status. It is taken in terms of fields, cash, gold, vehicles and other luxurious goods.

Soon after the selection, they celebrate the occasion with the drinking of toddy in the presence of the village head. Parents of both the parties exchange toddy and also supply one vessel to the head of the *kulapanchayat*. Feast will follow after drinking. After the betrothal ceremony is over, the parents of both the parties are bound by the contract. Otherwise, a meeting is called for and explanation is given accordingly for the breach of the contract. The *kulapanchayat* gives its judgement and it will be followed strictly.

Generally, for those that follow Hindu customs, a brahmin priest fixes the marriage *muhurtam* (auspicious time) and performs it. A Pastor performs the marriage for converted Christians. The Tali consists of black beads and *Talambralu* (rice grains over the heads of bride and groom) will follow. Widows are not allowed to participate in the function. Another custom that exists in their family is to make a contract between two individuals before the birth of their children. They say to one another: 'If your wife should have a girl and mine a boy or vice versa they must marry'. But if a brahmin objects, then there is a scope for its breach.

Puberty

Puberty is a happy occasion to the tribals. If the girl attains puberty, the news is sent to her maternal uncle. The girl 'sits' for five days and observes pollution. Her uncle gives her new clothes, comb, mirror, flowers, *kumkum* (coloured powder), nuts and bangles, etc. and also arranges for a feast to her. Sweets are distributed to celebrate the occasion.

Divorce

Divorce is rare and, if it takes place, the divorced parties may rake up their differences and become enemies. In the case of elopement, the father of a boy or girl summons a meeting at which the accused is penalized. The man who elopes with the girl is forced to marry her. If a married person elopes with another girl, both woman and man are strictly punished by the village elders in the *kulapanchayat*. Certain amount is also fixed on the accused. This system is also implemented on those who have illegal contacts. If a man, already having a wife, does not have children, then he is eligible to take a second wife. Otherwise, he is punished. He is obliged to pay for the maintenance to the first wife.

Widow Marriage

Widow marriages are quite common in this community. It is said that a widow can marry seven times. A woman who marries seven times is called Peddabeyasani. She is considered to be a sacred woman in marriages and other religious ceremonies. A person who wishes to marry a widow will buy a new saree and accepts her as a wife in the presence of others. This is what is called (wearing the saree) *cheerakattukovadamu*. The head of the village acts as a mediator. They celebrate it with drinking toddy. Another custom prevailing among them is that in the absence of her husband who is in jail, his wife lives with another person. On his return, the husband again accepts her along with the newborn children.

Birth Ceremonies

In earlier days, immediately after the birth of the child, they burn incense in front of the hut. They purify the hut with cow dung. After this purification, everybody is allowed to see the newborn baby. They also follow certain practices for the safety of the child in order to escape from a supernatural force. They bestow attention on mother and child. They take a bath on the 9th day. Toddy and dinner are served. Naming the child will take place after a few months. These names are most probably selected from their ancestors, sometimes their heroes or from their gods and goddesses. Generally, the names are Venkatigadu, Gangadu, Nagi, Ankali, etc. After a name is given, a black string is tied to the wrist of the infant. The maternal uncle takes an interest in the newborn child. They consider it a good omen if the child is born on the new moon night. If the child is born with an umbilical cord twisted around his neck, they take it as a bad omen and expect death of the father or the maternal uncle. They would like to overcome this by killing a fowl and wearing its inner parts round the neck and afterwards burning them along with the umbilical cord. The Yerukulas teach their children to answer negatively to whatever questions are put to them and also teach them all sorts of methods of committing crime.

Disposal of the Dead

If a wandering Yerukula dies, he is buried as quickly as possible, by keeping the head to the north and feet to the south. They cover the corpse with new clothes and he is given a bath and a coin is placed in one corner. They invite crows thinking that the spirit of the dead is moving around. Exactly after one year, they perform a function and that completes the major death ceremonies. More or less, the procedure is followed by converted Christians with minor changes. Some Yerukulas used to plant a *Tulasi* plant at the place where the body is burnt.

Superstitions

Falling of a lizard in front of them is considered bad luck, and if it chirps; on otherwise, it is taken as a sign of good luck. While starting, if any member of his family sneezes once, it is considered to be bad luck but if it is done repeatedly, it is considered to be good. It is inauspicious to them to see an oil-man, a barber, a police constable and a cock-eyed man while they are going out. A crow flying towards the right-hand side is considered a good omen, but if it flies over the head of a person, it is considered a bad omen. If the crow cries, it is supposed that somebody is coming to their home for a visit. It is unfortunate, when starting on a journey, to see widows, pots of milk, dogs barking, a man leading a bull. Number three is considered ominous and an expedition never consists of three. Sundays are auspicious for weddings while they are inauspicious for crime. Mondays, Wednesdays and Saturdays are unlucky. It is a bad omen to meet with a bundle of wood or cow dung cakes. If they meet a well-dressed widow or a cat it is considered as serious and bad omen.

Weapons

Most Yerukulas possess knives and a kind of 'billhook', called *Kodavali*, which is a sort of compromise between a sword and a sickle. The back of the blade is heavy and renders it capable of dealing a very severe blow. With this implement, animals are slaughtered, murders committed and bamboos split. For the purpose of committing burglaries they use an iron instrument called *gadikolu* or *sillukolu*.

Kulapanchayat

In the past, the village head played a very important role in tribal communities. He was the person concerned with register for the births and deaths and new arrivals into the settlement. All the settlers were controlled by him. He was elected on the basis of his popularity, age and the ability to deal with the cases of various types. The Panchayat comprises of five persons. These five elders of the tribe are called *Berumanusom*, big people or elders from the council. All the individuals respect their unwritten law and obey the will of *kulapanchayat*. Any violation of these conventions is seriously dealt with. The meetings of the panchayat are held at a common meeting place. The alleged culprit and his people usually sit on the left side and the aggrieved party on the right side or vice versa while the elders sit in between the two parties. The elders secretly decide the type of ordeal to test the guilt of the culprit. It is customary that the accused should dip his fingers into the boiling oil and it is an indication to prove his innocence or guilt. Still there are some traces of this custom. The other system of this sort is lifting a red-hot crow bar from the fire and carrying a pot filled with water to its brim without slipping a drop. The tribal panchayat usually deals with (1) cases of immorality within the members of the tribe. If any woman is caught red-handed when she is involved in adultery, the husband brings the case to the members of the *kulapanchayat*. On an enquiry, the *kulapanchayat* decides the punishment. The culprit is expected to bear the cost of it. (2) persons who violate the social custom, (3) property disputes, (4) marriage disputes, (5) disputes were pertaining to the division of the parental property, (6) to admit new persons, and (7) disputes of stolen property, etc.

III

Criminality – A Modus Operandi

In the Criminal Investigation Department (CID) records, for the verification of crime, they divided them into several gangs. The names of these gangs are as follows: 1st gang, also called store gang for Gadida Yerukulas. 2nd gang for agriculturists, 3rd gang for labourers, 4th gang also for labourers, 5th gang for the workers in Indian Leaf Tobacco Department (ILTD) Company at Chirala, Prakasam District and other traders, new gang for Uppu Yerukulas, Kella gang for Yeddu Yerukulas (Traders), Ettapuram or Mitrapuram farm labourers. We get a fair account of their crimes and causes through the interviews conducted with some of the Yerukala Tribal families in Andhra Pradesh (Sitanagaram,

Stuartpuram, Kapparalla Tippa, Lingala and Bitragunta villages in Andhra Pradesh) in the settlement. The types of crime they generally commit are: (1) Pickpocketing (2) Dacoity (3) Housebreaking (4) Animal theft (5) Railway robbery (6) Bank robbery (7) Shop snatching (8) Chain snatching and, (9) Rafu (placing artificial gold instead of real gold and pass it to the customer in the process of bargaining), etc. The following five factors prompt the Yerukulas in the 5 settlements to commit crimes. They are (1) Lack of alternative avenues of livelihood. (2) Lack of prcper upbringing of children. (3) Their poor economic conditions. (4) Laziness in work, and (5) The harassment of the police department even after giving up criminal activities. When interviewed, one criminal among the Yerukala family in Stuartpuram said, 'My parents from the beginning belong to Stuartpuram settlement. My father used to commit petty thefts since my childhood and was a drunkard. He died of tuberculosis. My mother died after that. After the death of my parents, I faced acute financial troubles. Then started my criminal life and in the course of time, I grew into a notorious criminal. Another Yerukula family member in Sitanagaram settlement revealed that, the police would arrest even the children of the ex-criminals. This police harassment of the children and the parents will leave strong impact on the tender minds and it would sometimes forcibly make them take to crime. In the interviews, the 'criminals' narrated several ways of committing crimes. To start with, they choose the place of their operation and gather information through the local people about the potential rich homes. Generally, they go in batches to commit theft. They steal money, gold, silver and other costly goods. Sometimes, they act like rich people and go hired cars to commit robberies. They never return to their homes without stealing. They have their own code language when they are doing the crime. Some of the words they use are listed below.

Word	*Meaning*
Oluku	Torchlight
Sonapam	Gold
Kanchakam	Money
Bokollu	Police
Berikeda	Sub-Inspector
Pullakollu	Leader of the gang
Ellavi	Assistant leader
Nemati	Man
Tella Belupu	Silver
Ulli Mukka	Knife or screwdriver

The nature of the criminals among the Yerukula tribe is that they never reveal the secrets of their gangs. Whenever they feel the threat to their lives, they even kill people in order to escape from the danger. The fact is that there are nearly 20–30 batches in the 5 settlements and each batch is consisting of four to five members. People in one batch should not join another batch until their operation is over. Each batch has its own leader and an assistant. No batch reveals the secrets of the other batches. They commit crimes only in the late nights between 12 o'clock at midnight and 3 o'clock in the morning. They enter by making big holes in the walls, breaking locks and windows. They cleverly escape when they find any problem in committing thefts. They call this type of crime as *Chori*. They call it dacoity when they rob the house in front of people in the house by threatening them. The number of women criminals among the Yerukula tribe are also large in number. There are twenty families in which women go for thieving in all the settlements. The crimes they indulge in are pocket-picking, suitcase lifting, snatching both from the railway passengers and busy shopping centres. The main reasons for these women to commit crime are, more or less, the same as that of their menfolk. However, in some cases, these women, divorced and widowed, both categories going without subsistence, along with other women who are undergoing imprisonment, take to these criminal activities. The criminals in the settlement have links with some of the other notorious criminals in the state and sometimes even outside. One criminal in Stuartpuramhas narrated how they robbed a rich temple in Simhachalam. They went in a gang consisting of twelve members and planned to steal precious jewels and ornaments from the temple. They went to Visakhapatnam and gathered information about the temple. After a week, they went to that place with all kinds of weapons. First, they went to visit the temple for 'Darshan' and returned. The next day they entered the temple and threatened the priest and looted money and jewellery. Soon after finishing the temple robbery, the priest was killed in the operation but the police got information about them and all of them were nabbed in the settlement and were kept behind bars. It was reported that the police were responsible for perpetuating crime in the five settlements. The police encourage crimes and they claim a lion's share in the looted property. In return, they rescue them in times of need. It is a matter of routine that the police demand money from them. Unable to bear the police harassment, the criminals give false names. When interviewed, a woman criminal in Kapparulla Tippa (Bitragunta Settlement) stated that police never allow them to stop thieving. They want their *mamullu* (bribe). In order to escape the harassment of the police, some criminals are forced to dispose off their property and other belongings such as grain and vessels to bribe the police. In this context, a criminal stated, there were no minimum facilities in the jail. Moreover, the police used to ill-treat his relatives whenever they visited him. They even extorted money from his relatives and sometimes committed rapes on their women. In the prison, he was beaten severely with lathis three times a day.

The mention of a dacoity anywhere in the state makes the police to involve the Denotified Tribes particularly Yerukulas even though they are not involved in it. Radio, T.V. or the newspapers also emphasize the same. It is a pity, however, that real culprits are never punished. An ex-criminal in Sitanagaram settlement in an interview gave a graphic account of this. 'In *Eeenadu* (Telugu daily) there was a statement twenty days back that a theft took place at Mangalagiri (Guntur District), and in that crime, it was reported that two young persons by name Golla Sreenu and Venkaiah were involved. It is also reported that both of them belong to Sitanagaram settlement'. But these two people do not belong to the same place. Unfortunately, the very mention of the place Sitanagaram is associated with criminal activity and this shows the notoriety it has assumed over time. An ex-criminal in Bitragunta explained that, in Tirupati, a police officer reported to the newspapers that a dacoity and murder was committed by Bitragunta Yerukulas. Consequently, they were arrested. But what actually happened was quite contrary to the police officer's public pronouncement. In the CBI enquiry, it was later revealed that the ex-criminals of Maharashtra were involved in the crime. He further elaborated on how the police used them as pawns in their game. It is true that the Yerukulas in the 5 settlements produced a good number of criminals. Among them, a notorious criminal who was their hero, gained popularity in Andhra Pradesh. He was the local Robin Hood and spent a major portion of the stolen wealth on his fellow-men, i.e. the poor people. Being an orphan himself, he gave shelter to orphans. This 'hero' was Tiger Nageswara Rao from Stuartpuram Settlement. He become so legendary in his own lifetime that songs were composed extolling his philanthropy, kindness, etc. In one of the songs, the atrocities committed on him by the police, who killed him later, were also vividly mentioned.

IV

Yerukulas Today

The Yerukulas consists of both criminal and non-criminal families. The section of non-criminal families is employed in government jobs, industrial establishments, agricultural operations and petty trade. Among the criminal families, there are two categories, 'white-collar' and 'blue-collar' criminals. These people have a criminal background, but they are averse to committing the crime. The reasons are obvious viz. (1) Some of their kinsmen are killed by the police. (2) They are unable to bear the ill-treatment and harassment either by the police or from the public. (3) Education has enabled them to realize their folly. (4) They are interested in the future of their children, and (5) They want to lead a respectable life by joining the mainstream of life. Gradually, they are taking to small jobs and business and changing their lifestyles. But there are not many opportunities either in the private or public sector to provide them with some meaningful occupations, even though the government is providing some succour in the shape of small loans, cattle, rickshaws, etc. It is needless to state that such measures are inadequate.

References

Government of India, *Census of India, 1981, Special Tables for ST's, Series 2*, New Delhi.

Government of Madras, *Administration Report on Kallar, Koravar Reclamation and Criminal Tribes Settlements and Yanadi Reclamation for the Year 1947–48*, Madras, 1949.

——, *Administrative Report of the Inspector General of Police*, Madras, 1951.

——, *Administrative Report on Habitual Offender's Settlements for the Year 1951–52*, Madras, 1953.

——, *Hukumnamas and Papers Relating to Sriharikota Yanadis, Vol. 1: A Selection of Papers from the Old Records of the Nellore District*, Nellore, 1915.

——, *Madras Government Bulletin, Vol. V, No. 1, Anthropology Vision of the Uralis and Sholagas: More Marriage Customs in Southern India, Hook-swinging, Paliyans*, Madras, 1903.

——, *Madras Government Museum, Bulletin, Vol. IV, No. 3, Anthropology*, Madras, 1903.

Hatch, W.J., *The Land Pirates of India*, OUP, Delhi, 1928, p. 62.

Lalitha, V., *The Making of Criminal Tribes: Patterns and Transition*, New Era Publications, Madras, 1995.

Naidu, M. Paupa Rao, *The History of Railway Thieves*, Higginbotham, Madras, 1904.

Oppert, Gustav, *On the Original Inhabitants of Bharatavarsha or India*, A. Constable and Co., New York, 1978.

Pratap, D.R., *The Tribes of Andhra Pradesh*, Government Press, Hyderabad, 1974.

Radhakrishna, Meena, 'The Criminal Tribes Act in Madras Presidency: Implications for Itinerant Trading Communities', *Indian Economic and Social History Review*, Vol. XXVI, No. 3, July–September 1989.

Rao, Kamala Manohar, *Bulletin of Tribal Cultural Research and Training Institute*, Madras, 1901.

Salvation Army Monthly, 'The War Cry', World International Heritage Centre, London, April 1937.

Satyanarayana, Chalavadi, *Yerukulas: An Ex-criminal Tribe of Andhra and its Settlement, Stuartpuram* (Unpublished M.A. Dissertation), Sagar University, Agra, 1950–60.

Sherring, M.A., *Hindu Tribes and Castes*, Vol. 3, Cosmo Publications, New Delhi, 1974.

Simhadri, Y.C., *The Ex-criminal Tribes of India*, National Publishing House, New Delhi, 1979.

Siraj-ul-Hassan, Syed, *Castes and the Tribes of H.E.H. the Nizam Dominions*, Vol. 1, Government Central Press, Bombay, 1909, p. 185.

Thurston, Edgar and K. Rangachari, *Castes and Tribes of Southern India*, Cosmo Publications, Delhi, 1909.

10

Issues Relating to Denotified and Nomadic Tribes of Andhra Pradesh

The main purpose of the present chapter is to bring awareness about the existing public policies in respect of Nomadic Tribes/Denotified Tribes (NT/DNT) communities. This will enable them to properly implement the policies of the government. After going through this module, the trainers will be able to know and understand the following issues about NT/DNT communities in Andhra Pradesh: (a) Understand the past and present conditions of NT/DNTs, (b) Understand the origin, development, nature and character of the Criminal Tribes (CT) Acts and its impact on NT/DNT communities, (c) Awareness of public policy interventions with regard to NT/DNTs and (d) Suggestive measures for the overall development of NT/DNT communities. *Nomadic Tribes* are the people who are continuously on the move and have no permanent place of residence. *Semi-Nomadic Tribes* tend to have a fixed habitat for a part of the year and are itinerant during the rest of the year. *Denotified Tribes* or DNTs are also known as Vimukta Jatis. They are the tribes/communities that are originally listed under the Criminal Tribes Act 1871, as 'criminal tribes' and addicted to the systematic commission of non-bailable offences. Nomadic, Semi-Nomadic and Denotified Communities are the categories of communities identified by the colonial government as against the settled caste communities. These are mobile communities, characterized by a distinct culture that is reflected in their customs, beliefs and traditional practices. They were and are present in almost all parts of India and more so in the states of Andhra Pradesh, Tamil Nadu, Karnataka, Maharashtra, Madhya Pradesh, Gujarat, Haryana, Punjab, Uttar Pradesh and so on. The impact of British colonial policies on Indian society, polity and economy have been devastating and resulted in cataclysmic changes particularly the nomadic, semi-nomadic and denotified tribal communities. During the early part of the 19th century, trading practices of various communities, in particular the nomadic economic routines of tribes were destroyed by the economic policies such as 1876 Forest Act and Revenue policies of the British Government. In post-independence period certain of these communities were reclassified as scheduled tribes, scheduled castes and castes under backward class; others continued as notified and denotified tribes. While the farmer obtained certain benefits under such reclassification through the policy of reservations, the latter did not get any benefit after the independence. Therefore, it is argued that the latter deserves special attention for their upliftment.

I

Impact of British Colonial Policies on Tribes

Impact of British colonial policies on Indian society, polity and economy have been devastating and resulted in cataclysmic changes. During the early part of the 19th century, trading practices of various communities, in particular the nomadic economic routines of tribes were destroyed by the economic policies of the British Government. The introduction of railways, roads, establishment of police constabulary, and repeated famines in 1823, 1866, 1876, 1895, and the forest policies of colonial government crippled the traditional occupations of a number of communities. Cattle possessed by them perished in large numbers. Forest officers did not allow them to depend on forest produce. The police and forest officials prevented their business, cattle to multiply and trading possibilities. The worst affected people out of these policies were men, women and children among these communities.

The Tribewise occupational status can be summarized as follows:

Community	*Occupation*
Dasaris	Traditionally employed as village watchers. They used to collect roots, tubers, vegetables, etc. They often performed tasks like domestic labourers, village servants and cattle rearing. Dasaris used to sell fancy goods, cosmetics, wigs, and trinkets. The women accompanied their males when they went around villages for begging.
Pedditi Gollas	Performing magic was the traditional occupation of Pedditi Gollas. They were experts in tattooing.
Jogis	Experts in indigenous medical care. They were aware of many varieties of herbs and shrubs. Traditionally they were mendicants.
Katipapalas	In addition to household work they used to sell combs, beads, and aluminium wear in the surrounding villages.
Konda Doras	They used to participate in agricultural operations like threshing, animal husbandry and collection of minor forest products.

Cont'd...

...*Cont'd*

Community	*Occupation*
Korachas	Participated in agricultural activities like sowing, transplantation, weeding, harvesting and other activities. They used to collect Palmyra leaves, bamboo and made mats, ropes and toys. They used to collect minor forest produce like tamarind, soap nut and sold their items in the market. They were experts in fortune-telling and collecting food grains. They maintained close relationship with their customers.
Banjaras	They were experts in colourful prints and embroidery work. They supplied their products, transported grain, salt and other items from plains to the inland areas.
Mandulas	They used to collect herbs and roots to prepare herbal medicine.
Muttarasis	They worked as contractors, mill workers and manufacturers.
Manggarudis	They used to sing folk songs and tell folk tales.
Nakkalas	Experts in making snares, stuffed animals and colourful necklaces. They were treated as expert saleswomen. They derive income from selling bangles, mirrors, combs, safety pins, needles, etc.
Parika Muggalas	Experts in sorcery and black magic and fortune telling.
Pitchiguntalas	They were traditional bards, folk singers, genealogists and wandering mendicants.
Veera Mushtis	They used to work as casual labourers. They used to prepare artificial pigtails (savaralu) to supplement their family income.
Yatas	Experts in toddy-tapping, making umbrellas and other house articles. With the enactment of Criminal Tribes Act of 1911, the local police authorities forwarded concocted reasons for their alleged involvement in different kinds of crimes in the Madras province and declared them as criminal tribes under Section 10 and 12 of the CT Act 11. Since then, they lost their traditional occupations and led a poverty stricken life.

With the enactment of Criminal Tribes Act of 1911, the local police authorities forwarded concocted reasons for their alleged involvement in different kinds of crimes in the Madras province and declared them as criminal tribes under Section 10 and 12 of the CT Act. Since then, they lost their traditional occupations and led a poverty stricken life. The colonial government imposed the following Criminal Tribes Acts on certain communities in India and branded them as criminal tribes. The *Criminal Tribes Act–1871*: This Act was applied to north India. *Criminal Tribes Act–1911*: This Act was applied to all provinces in India. The main provisions of the Act was registration, restriction, segregation of men, women and children and confining certain sections in penal, reformatory, agricultural and voluntary settlements. *Criminal Tribes Act–1924*: The CT Act of 1911 was revised in 1924 and of some of the provisions of the CT Act–1911 and repealed by the Criminal Tribes Laws (Repeal Act) in 1952. Providing passes, confining people to settlements, strict police supervision were some of the provisions of 1924 Act. *Criminal Tribes Act–1946*: Repealation of Criminal Tribes Act 1924 took place in 1946. The Criminal Tribes Act was finally repealed during the year 1952 with the initiative of the freedom fighters like N.G. Ranga, Jawaharlal Nehru, Dadabhai Nowroji, Vennalkunti Raghavaiah, K.N. Katju and others. In the state of Andhra Pradesh the Criminal Tribes Act was finally abolished during the year–1965 (abolition of Habitual Offenders Act–1965).

II

History of Criminal Tribes Acts: The Need to Bring the Criminal Tribes Acts into Force

The Colonial government used to deal with the individuals caught in criminal activities individually or collectively, first under the Regulation XXVI of 1793, then under the Act XXX of 1836 and later under the Indian Penal Code of 1860. Legally, until the year 1871, no tribe as a whole was dubbed as a criminal tribe. The control of criminal behaviour on the part of certain tribes became a problem for the British Government; the colonial authorities felt it was necessary for preventive and deterrent purposes to treat the entire tribal group legally as criminal tribes. All the members of the tribes were kept under continuous watch and vigilance. The first Criminal Tribes Act was passed in 1871 in Sind, Oudh, Berar and other provinces in North India. The Act was only confined to North India. The main aim of the Act was to keep an eye on the activities of certain communities wandering like gypsies. A constant surveillance over and vigilance about their activities was planned. This Act gave wider powers to the provincial authorities. The provincial authorities were authorized to declare any group of people whom they suspect as incorrigibles as criminal tribes. As a result of the experience gained, the authorities found that the criminals who were released from prison were worse than before. Therefore, the Act was amended in 1897 and the power of notifying tribes was delegated to Inspector General of Police. The colonial government declared another Criminal Tribes Act in 1908. It permitted the various provincial police authorities to make plans whereby tribes suspected of living by crimes could be registered and supervised by local police. Those members arrested and kept in jails on proving good conduct or behaviour could be released and were placed in settlements (open jails fenced with barbed wires). In these settlements these people were taught to work. Instructions were given to lead an honest life. It was hoped that such steps would bring complete reformation among them. As the desired goals could not be achieved by the Act of 1908, another Criminal Tribes Act was passed in 1911. The main features of the Act were if the local government had reason to believe that any tribe, gang or class of persons or any part of the tribe a gang is addicted to systematic commission of non-bailable offences, it may, by notification in the local official gazette declare that such persons or group was a criminal tribe as the term used in the Act. Such tribes under the government notification were called Notified Tribes. There are two methods of dealing with these people – registration and settlement. Registration attempted to keep track of them under police surveillance in the communities where they lived. Settlement means locating communities in a special place provided with fencing. In the settlement they were under the control of the settlement officers. On the recommendations of the Indian Jails Enquiry Committee, the Criminal Tribes Act was again amended in 1923 and it was applied completely to the whole of British India. In many aspects, the Act was found defective and contained loopholes. There was no attempt to reform and rehabilitate these communities. There were practical difficulties of separating children from their parents in order to bring them up in a wholesome atmosphere and educate their children. Notification, registration, unjust punishments and sentences were some of the main problems faced through this Act. Therefore, the Criminal Tribes Act 1924 was repealed and the Habitual Offenders Act came into force on 29th April, 1948. It aimed at controlling criminals who took crime as their profession. The Government of India appointed a committee in 1949 to study the usefulness of the Act. It expressed the view that the Act was against the spirit of the law of the land and the constitution. The public, National leaders and Social reformers moved in a big way and as a result the Criminal Tribes Act was finally repealed in 1952 and in its place the Habitual Offenders Act was enacted in 1956. Such of the tribes deleted from the notification under the CT Act were called Denotified Tribes. With the repeal of the Act about 22,68,348 people in the country were legally set free. However, the status of majority of the members of 198 communities in India is the same as that of the colonial era. The stigma of criminality is still haunting them in all walks of life. With the enactment of the Criminal Tribes (CT) Act 1911, many tribes in all the Presidencies were kept in agricultural, reformatory, penal and voluntary settlements (settlements are like open jails) opened by the colonial government. Men, women and children were placed in these settlements. In reality, they were not criminals. Men, women and grown-up girls, who are very averse to manual labour, were taught by the Salvation Army how to make a living by practising vocational trades. The government had stated that in Godavari, Kistna, Kurnool, Bellary, Anantapur and Cuddapah and the other districts in Madras Presidency, members of these communities were confined to various kinds of settlements due to suspicious operations. Men, women and children among these communities had a checkered life. The police used to investigate and detect ordinary and non-professional crime among criminal classes in the Madras Presidency. It had a great hope on men, women and children in the settlements as a means of reducing crime, as instruments of reformation, rehabilitation and reclamation of criminals. Nowadays changes are taking place in the society of NT/DNTs. They are following traditions, customs, language and habits of the mainstream society. There is a lot of change in dress pattern, language, dialects, customs, ceremonies, etc. Many NT/DNT members in the colonies feel that their tale of misfortune as wrought upon them continues even after they changed their ways of past life. Efforts should be made by the government to educate and orient them in order to make them realize the importance of the programmes initiated for their development. They must be persuaded to make use of these programmes for speedy development. It is argued that the problems of these communities should be handed over to non-governmental organizations. There is also an urgent need to study and review the existing conditions of NT/DNTs and also the policies and schemes, implementation strategies by independent bodies for ensuring speedy and quality delivery of government programmes and schemes. Opinions of educated members of these communities must be heard and considered while planning for any programme in favour of these communities.

III

Disintegration of Tribes into Communities and Family Units

With the enactment of the CT Act 1911, many tribes in the country were declared criminal tribes and were placed in the settlements though they were not criminals. The local moneylenders demanded free labour from men, women and children. Prejudices of the British administrators also played an important role for the suppression of these communities. It is a recognized fact that women and children among these communities were burdened with their men. Women as wives, mothers, daughters, and sisters worked hard to take care of their families when their husbands were in police custody or in jail. Contribution of women for the family welfare and giving economic support among these communities was very critical. Women and grown-up girls, who were very averse to manual labour, were being taught how to make mats. Salvation Army was asked to introduce lace and other industries in order to discipline the womenfolk. The government stated that in Godavari, Kistna, Kurnool, Bellary, Anantapur, Cuddapah and the other districts in Madras Presidency, members of these communities were confined to various kinds of settlements such as agriculture, penal, reformatory and voluntary settlements in Andhra Pradesh due to their operations. There was an increase in crime rate under dacoits, robberies and housebreakings in the Godavari and Krishna districts, which was attributed to men, women and children of criminal gangs viz., *Pamulas*, *Konda Doras*, *Donga Waddars*, etc. who were not settled and who escaped from the settlements. The increase of crime in Kurnool was attributed to *Chenchu* women and Yerukulas who were not settled yet. The employment of *Donga Waddars* prevented crime on their part. There was a slight increase of dacoits in Bellary district for which the members of Yerukulas and the out-of-view members of Rudrapad *Korchas* were said to be responsible. The increase in dacoits in Anantapur district was attributable to the escaped women members from Bhumannagadda settlement, while the marked decrease of crime in Cuddapah district was due to the settlement of women members of *Korchas* in Chittoor and Nellore districts. Settlements established for Notified Tribes in Madras Presidency came in Andhra Pradesh after Independence. (1) Kalichedu Settlement, established in Nellore District, during the Year 1912 as an Industrial Settlement for Dasaris, Dommaras, Yerukulas, Jogulas by Mr. Ludwig. (2) Kavali Settlement was established in Nellore district by American Baptist mission during the Year 1912 as agricultural settlement for Yerukulas. (3) Sitanagaram Settlement was established in Guntur district during the Year–1913 by the Salvation Army as agricultural settlement for the Yerukulas. (4) Siddhapuram Settlement was established in Kurnool district in 1913 as a voluntary settlement for Woddars and Chenchus by the then Government. (5) Yanadi settlement was established in Bapatla for reforming the Yenadis as a voluntary settlement during the year 1913. (6) Bhumannagadda Setttlement was established in Chittoor district by the Salvation Army during the year 1914 as agricultural settlement for Korchas. (7) Stuartpuram (Bethapudi) Settlement was established during the Year 1914 by the Salvation Army as agricultural settlement for Yerukulas. (8) Chintal Devi Settlement was established by the American Baptist Mission during the year 1914 as agricultural settlement for Kanjar Bhats. In the colonial period some communities referred as tribes such as Boya, Relli, Paidi, Pirikimuggala, Yatha, Golla, Chenchu, Yerukula, Budabukkala, Yanadi, Sugali, Dommara, Nakkala, Shikari, Waddera, Poosala, Mala, Madiga, Reddika, Uppara, Kepmari, Koracha, Konda Dora, Jogula, Mandula, Mutharacha, Dabbala, Mondivagula, Nirshikari and Kanjarbhatetc, were living as hunter-gatherers and inhabited both uplands and lowlands. Some of them were riverine fishing communities and some followed traditional, subsistent occupations, both big and small. Some of them lived by cattle breeding and dealt in all kinds of forest and agricultural produce. Most of them were acrobats, following different types of occupations such as monkey trapping, bird snaring and snake charming. Tribes/Communities Under CT Act (in the past) Boya, Relli, Paidi, Pirikimuggala, Yatha, Golla, Chenchu, Yerukula, Budabukkala, Yanadi, Sugali, Dommara, Nakkala, Shikari, Waddera, Poosala, Mala, Madiga, Reddika, Uppara, Kepmari, Koracha, Konda Dora, Jogula, Mandula, Mutharacha, Dabbala, Mondivagula, Nirshikari, and Kanjarbhat. Caste Panchayat (a hereditary body of the caste elders) constitutes the primary political organization. Its primary responsibility is settling various categories of disputes, overseeing the observance of community norms relating to marriage, divorce, property distribution, economic transactions, community disputes, etc. The *Kula Panchayat* system that prevailed among these communities degraded their positions with various ordeals conducted. Society among nomadic, semi-nomadic and denotified communities is based on patriarchal system.

New Professions

In places like Maharashtra, women from these communities such as Pardhies, Kaikadies and so on became bar dancing girls. They were traditionally from dancing communities and entertainers. As dancers and entertainers, they received patronage from feudal classes. However, in due course of time, with the introduction of television and cinemas their performances were not entertained. These dancers and entertainers took to street performances. There was no other alternative for these women to eke out their livelihood. They were forced to send their grown-up girls to dance in bars. In the bars these women bore the brunt of exploitation. They had no support to run their families. Their males were often left out without any work. With the loss of traditional livelihood, their skills and occupations were lost.

IV

NT, DNT Tribes: Developments in Post-1947 Era

Independent India envisaged building an egalitarian society in which people with diverse sociocultural and economic backgrounds can have equal opportunities in various fields with dignity and honour. In order to achieve a cohesive society, some sort of social engineering is imperative for bringing the historically neglected people at par with privileged sections of the society. Positive discrimination along with developmental interventions and capacity building were considered essential to social engineering. In order to achieve a state of social and economic equality, builders of modern India had undertaken certain measures since country's independence. The communities that were historically disadvantaged were kept under different social categories such as Scheduled Castes (SCs), Scheduled Tribes (STs) and Other Backward Classes (OBCs). Certain privileges were given to them to overcome socio-economic disabilities. As a part of the categorization, communities who were wandering, nomadic, and semi-nomadic, ex-criminal were included in the list of SC/ST and OBC categories. However, their categorization was not logical and uniform. A large number of communities were not included in any category of SC/ST/OBC. They were placed at par with the general sections of people. These communities have a long history of marginalization. They were neglected and oppressed during the colonial and post-colonial independent India. The development schemes designed for SC/ST categories have not benefited the NT/DNT communities. They are denied, segregated and pushed to the walls on account of stigma of nomadic and gypsy way of living. They are identified as wanderers, following customs such as earth digging, fishing, salt-selling, scavenging and basket-making, and leather-tanning, etc. In India there are 192 NT/DNT communities that comprise around nine per cent of the tribal population. In the erstwhile Madras Presidency, 43 denotified tribes were listed. Andhra Pradesh government declared 56 communities as NT/DNT communities in the state. The NT/DNTs are very poor and economically backward. Most of them are living with meager income and are engaged in petty business and government jobs.

V

Challenges Today: Changing Perceptions

The welfare measures initiated for these communities bear a resemblance of the efforts at squeezing oil from the sand. Their development is a real challenge to the present government. Policy formulation and its execution most often fall apart. Therefore, the gaps and problems faced by these sections of the people need urgent focus. Gaps and problems faced by NT/DNT communities are:

- Issue of land
- Alternative livelihoods
- Bank linkages through government
- Educational development with focus on Secondary and Vocational Education
- Filling up of backlog vacancies with STs
- Dossier Criminal Sheets (DC Sheets) still in operation (These sheets are not cancelled even in the case of reformed criminals in the settlements. There has been a long standing demand from the reformed ex-criminal families to do away with the DC sheets)
- Verification of caste status, some are still under BC-OBC category
- Problem of enumeration
- Alternative life skills and livelihood education
- Census and enumeration
- Wandering (nomadism) still persisting (Chenchus, Nirshikaris, Nakkalas etc.)
- Migration
- Police harassment
- Health related problems: Nutrition
- Stigma reduction is still a far cry

Nowadays changes are taking place in the society of NT/DNTs. They are following traditions, customs, language and habits of the mainstream society. There is a lot of change in their dress pattern, material things, language, dialects, customs, ceremonies, etc. They are imitating others in this respect. Communities which are better off are not allowing their women folk to work outside. They are particularly confined to the four walls of their household work. The custom of demanding dowry in the form of gold, silver, money, vehicles, land and other items at the time of marriage is taking place. This is replacing their custom of bride price. In the earlier days they used to fully recognize abilities of their women. There has been a clear shift in the perception and treatment. Nowadays, women among NT/DNTs are seen as an economic liability. The literacy rate among girls and women among these communities is highly insignificant. The important aspect of inequality among NT/DNTs is gender discrimination. Indian society is patrilineal and patriarchal. Women among these communities are denied several basic rights. They suffer from several social, cultural and economic handicaps. Poverty increased due to loss of their traditional means of livelihood. Their natural habitations were destroyed and no pro-active measures are being undertaken for their gainful employment. Women are greatly oppressed in sharing of power, education, health, nutrition and political process. They are unable to take their representations to government and fight for their basic rights. The sufferings of women among these communities are several times higher than that of women of other communities. They are the victims of cumulative inequality. Under these circumstances, they deserve immediate policy intervention. They are still leading a wandering life. The administration is often indifferent to their problems. Women were specifically targeted for sexual abuse and the pathetic situation is that neither the administration nor the police take serious note of the problems of women. They were subjected to severe atrocities, violence, rape and custodial deaths. Some of the women in settlements said that their children could not get jobs and womenfolk in the colonies are compelled to work instead. Efforts should be made by the government to educate and orient them in order to make them realize the importance of the programmes initiated for their development by the state and central government organizations in India. They must be persuaded to make use of these programmes for speedy development. Several schemes are initiated for the development of women among Scheduled Tribes and Scheduled Castes. There should be strict monitoring on the implementation strategies, time for implementation, utilization, advantages and disadvantages of the programmes. The village councils have to be empowered. Counselling centres need to be opened in all the ex-settlement colonies to provide proper guidance to reclaim their social, cultural, economic rights and needful employment opportunities. In this connection, efforts made by *Samskar* (founded by Gandhian and Atheist social activists, Hemalata and Lavanam), a voluntary organization in Betapudi, headquartered at Vijayawada is noteworthy. They provide skills, guidance and counselling, moral enlightenment, removal of stigma and protection from the police and public for these communities. Similarly, *Asmita*, another important organization is very actively working to solve the problems of women among Scheduled Castes, Scheduled Tribes and Minorities with regard to protection of the girl child, women's education, land rights, research and training, etc. Similar organizations have to be brought to the common platform in order to exchange and share experiences and speed up the process of development in the state.

VI

Recommendations

Notified and Denotified Tribes including the scheduled tribes are very poorly represented in the high paid and high skilled jobs. Their percentage in the police, judicial, educational and medical sectors is very insignificant. They are mainly concentrated in the low paid, minimum skilled, labour incentive, traditional, unproductive, menial and low paid jobs. They are seen in the highest numbers as housemaids, rag pickers, earth diggers, fortune-tellers, acrobats, and other types of labour works. Self-employment and credit facilities must be extended to NT/DNTs. Local self-help groups, banking institutions and credit organizations must be encouraged to come forward extending support for the development of these communities. Governments should allocate resources in order to tackle problems of these communities. The budgetary provisions are often ignorant of the problems of NT/DNT communities and public welfare programmes reinforce caste, class and gender discrimination during implementation. Most of these communities have no access to primary, secondary, technical, vocational and medical education. They do not come under Tribal Sub-Plans and Special Component Plans, etc. Positive discrimination is very much necessary for development of NT/DNTs. Their accessibility to employment, land and credit facilities needs to be improved. Wages under the national wage policy must be improved. Social security mechanisms such as *Rashtriya Swasth Bheema Yojana* and *Rashtriya Vimuktajati Mahila Yojana* must be initiated. The educated youth among NT/DNTs must be supported with supplementary coaching facilities for clearing competitive examinations, entrance examinations and entry into professional courses. Infrastructural facilities like community halls, information and communication technology and other fast growing sectors must be strengthened. There is a need to ensure gender perspective and gender budgeting programmes in all policy matters of the government. Private sector institutions should come forward to tap the skills possessed by NT/DNT communities. There is also an urgent need to study and review the existing conditions of NT/DNTs in India and also the policies and schemes, implementation strategies by independent bodies for ensuring speedy and quality delivery of government programmes and schemes in the state of Andhra Pradesh. Opinions of women and educated members of these communities must be heard and considered while planning for any programme in favour of these communities. Results of the findings of the state and central government programmes must be widely publicized in the websites, newspapers and media. Periodic surveys must be conducted to understand the effectiveness of government programmes, policies and also problems of these communities and their specific needs. A few important questions that need to be debated and understood today with regard to the development of NT/DNTs are:

- Should NT/DNTs in the settlement colonies be treated as habitual criminals?
- What is the fate of women and children whose male members and bread-winners are sentenced to life imprisonment?
- Should women in NT/DNT colonies be left destitute and to fend for themselves?
- What measures the state and the central government organizations had taken so far for the development of NT/DNTs, their women and girl children?
- What are the current needs to improve conditions of NT/DNT communities in India and in the state of Andhra Pradesh?

References

Banerjee, Nirmala, 'Trends in Women's Employment, 1971–81: Some Micro Level Observations', *Economic and Political Weekly*, Vol. XXIV, No. 17, April 1989.

Booth Tucker, Frederick, *Mukti Fauj or 40 Years with the Salvation Army in India and Ceylon*, Marshall Brothers, London, 1910.

Deccan Chronicle, Vijayawada Edition, 'Cops Driving Them to Crime', dated 19 June 1984.

Gandhi, Malli and V. Lalitha, *Tribes Under Stigma: Problems of Identity*, Serials Publishers, New Delhi, 2009.

Gandhi, Malli, *Denotified Tribes: Dimensions of Change*, Kanishka Publishers, New Delhi, 2008.

——, *Development of Denotified Tribes: Policy and Practice*, Sarup & Sons, New Delhi, 2006.

Ghani, Muhammad Abdul, *Note on the Criminal Tribes of Madras Presidency*, Provincial Police Training School, Vellore, 1915.

Government of Andhra Pradesh, Department of Social Welfare, *The Tribes of Andhra Pradesh*, Tribal Cultural Research and Training Institute, Hyderabad, Andhra Pradesh, 1964.

——, *Report on Denotified Tribes of Andhra Pradesh* (unpublished report), Tribal Cultural Research and Training Institute, Hyderabad, 1964, pp. 1–10.

Government of India, *Report on National Commission for Denotified, Nomadic and Semi-Nomadic Tribes* (unpublished report), Vol. II, Ministry of Social Justice and Empowerment, New Delhi, June 2008.

Government of Madras, *Administration Report of the Labor Department for the Year 1927–28*, Madras, 1928.

——, *Administration Report of the Labor Department for the Year 1930–1931*, Madras, 1931, p. 7.

——, *Madras Criminal Tribes Manual, Criminal Tribes Act VI of 1924, Brought up to 31 March 1927*, Government Press, Madras, 1927.

——, *Memorandum on Donga Yerukulas Prepared by the Deputy Inspector General of Police and Criminal Investigation Department*, Madras, 1918.

——, *Note Showing the Progress Made in the Settlement of Criminal Tribes in the Madras Presidency up to January 1916*, Madras, 1917.

——, *Note Showing the Progress Made in the Settlement of Criminal Tribes in the Madras Presidency up to January 1925*, Madras, 1927.

——, *Stuartpuram Administration Report 1920–21*, Tamil Nadu Archives, 1921.

Government of Madras, Development Department, G.O. No. 1315, dated 27 October 1933, Commissioner of Labor, Letter to Secretary to Government of Madras, dated 1 October 1933.

Government of Madras, Home Department, G.O. No. 1544, dated 20 March 1939.

Government of Madras, Home Judicial Department, G.O. No. 1140, dated 1 May 1920.

——, G.O. No. 1534, dated 14 June 1916, pp. 1–2.

——, G.O. No. 1649, dated 19 July 1919, pp. 1–4.

——, G.O. No. 2497, dated 29 October 1919.

Government of Madras, Judicial Department, G.O. No. 110, dated 27 April 1921, p. 3.

——, G.O. No. 1161, dated 12 June 1913.

——, G.O. No. 917, dated 10 May 1913 (Mis).

Government of Madras, Public Works Labor Department, G.O. No. 1313L, dated 17 June 1932.

——, G.O. No. 1313L, dated 17 June 1932.

——, G.O. No. 1654L, dated 6 July 1928.

——, G.O. No. 2338L, dated 19 August 1930.

——, G.O. No. 2671L, dated 6 December 1934.

——, G.O. No. 2726L, dated 17 December 1935.

Hatch, W.J., *The Land Pirates of India*, Seeley Service and Co., London, 1928.

Indian Express, Vijayawada Edition, 'Raw Deal to Residents of Settlement Colonies', 16 June 1984.

Krishnan, P.S., *Dalit Manifesto, Incorporating the Rights and Entitlements of Scheduled Castes, Scheduled Tribes and Backward Classes*, National Action Forum for Social Justice, New Delhi, 1996.

——, *Report of the Working Group on the Empowerment of Socially and Educationally Backward Classes in the IX and X Plan* and *Empowering Dalits for Empowering India*, Manak, New Delhi, 2009.

Lalitha, V., *Making of Criminal Tribes: Patterns and Transition*, New Era Publications, Madras, 1995.

Lavanam and Hemalatha Lavanam, *Notes on Reformation of Criminal Tribes People*, Atheist Centre, Vijayawada, February 1976.

News Time, 'Reformed Criminals to Take Part in the Meeting', dated 12 June 1984.

NT/DNT Rag, *Technical Advisory Group Report 2005*.

Radhakrishna, Meena, 'From Tribal Community to Working Class Consciousness: A Case of Yerukula Women', *Economic and Political Weekly*, Vol. XXIV, No. 17, April 1989.

——, *Dishonored by History: 'Criminal Tribes' and British Colonial Policy*, Orient Longman, Hyderabad, 2001.

Ranake, Balakrishna, Ministry of Social Justice and Empowerment, *National Commission for Denotified, Nomadic and Semi-Nomadic Tribes, Report*, Vol. I, Government of India, New Delhi, 2008.

Sastri, E. Ramachandra, *History of Criminal Tribes in Madras Presidency*, Sri Rama Press, Madras, 1929.

Singh, K.S., *People of India, National Series, Andhra Pradesh, Vol. 4–6*, India's Communities, Anthropological Survey of India, Calcutta, 1988.

The Hindu, 'Thirteen Criminals Surrender', March 1999.

The Hindu, Hyderabad Edition, 'High Court Judge Fours Sending Juvenile Offenders to NGOs', dated 3 October 2001.

——, 'Reform Process a Pace at Stuartpuram', Saturday, 13 March 1999.

The Hindu, Vijayawada Edition, 'A Change for the Better', dated 19 June 1984.

——, 'Reformed Criminals Want the Government to Lift Ban on Employment', Wednesday, 20 June 1884.

The New Indian Express, Hyderabad Edition, 'Twenty-five Hardcore Dacoits of Guntur Surrender', Tuesday, 30 March 1999.

Tucker, F. Booth, *Criminocurology or the Indian Crime and What to do with Him: A Report of the Work of the Salvation Army among the Criminal Tribes, Habituals and Released Prisoners in India*, London, n.d.

Unni, Jeemol, 'Changes in Women's Employment in Rural Areas, 1961–63', *Economic and Political Weekly*, Vol. XXIV, No. 17, April 1989.

11

Reformation and Rehabilitation of Yerukulas in Andhra Pradesh and Telangana

For long periods in history, tribes had little or no intercourse with people in the plains areas and were unaffected by the so-called civilizing influences. The relative isolation led to their backwardness, as the agents of development deployed by the mainstream state could not penetrate into the deeper forest regions. The situation underwent a change with the advent of the British who saw great opportunity of exploiting the forest wealth by intruding into the private spaces hitherto inhabited by Adivasis. To avoid the problems posed by tribes, the British Government passed the first Criminal Tribes Act in 1871 under the pretext of controlling the rate of crime. Under the Act, several tribes were declared criminal and settlements were started where tribesmen and women were lodged. The task of their management was entrusted to voluntary agencies such as Salvation Army, Chief Anjuman Islamia, Arya Samaj, etc. In addition, the government too at some places was directly involved in organizing reformatory settlements. Settlements were classified under agricultural, industrial, reformatory and penal settlements. Yerukalas and Katheras are two ex-criminal tribes of Andhra Pradesh. These two groups are stigmatized as dacoits, burglars, pilferers, thieves and railway wagon breakers. Stuartpuram is one of the settlements established in 1914 by the colonial government. It was an agricultural settlement put under the management of Salvation Army. The organization executed monumental development programmes for the benefit and welfare of the settlers. They included agriculture, education, health and vocational training activities. Salvation Army enjoyed judicial powers while managing the settlement. Basic approach to change and reform of the settlers adopted by the organization was religious in nature which as such had some inbuilt limitations. The Salvation Army was active for almost four decades before the tribal welfare department took over the settlement after independence. The organization continues its religio-social work till date. The second major attempt at reforming and mainstreaming inhabitants of Stuartpuram settlement was initiated in the year 1974 by a group of secular and a religious humanists from the Atheist Centre, Vijayawada. Criminal reformation is a three dimensional process involving different kinds of actors and characters: criminals themselves, the state machinery including police/government officials and finally society at large. Of these variables, surrounding society plays a major role, either to accept or deny reformed criminals into the mainstream ways of life. When this variable is in place, rest of the variables follow the suit. Samskar (NGO) represented this important social variable in the process of social reform and rehabilitation of members of Stuartpuram colony. The organization executed its work in five phases through a strategy known as Three Generation Approach. Major emphasis of social reformers during the process had been on social integration and area development through 3G Approach. Social reform experiments in a DNT colony hint at one important historical lesson that traditional approaches to the problem of despised social heritage has reduced scope for reform of diehard avocations of hardened criminals. On the other, humanist and democratic interventions provide enough social space for bringing about the desired change.

I

With the introduction of modern means of transport and communication, the land grabbing greedy plainsmen entered the forest areas and populated them. Adivasis continued to be the easy prey of the Hindu and Mohammedan feudal and British colonial oppression down to the 20th century. They lost much of their land and were destined to swell the ranks of the depressed classes. The colonial exploitation combined with the tyrannical oppression forced the Adivasis to stage revolts over different periods of history.

Crime as a social phenomenon is an age-old problem faced by mankind. It is commonly held that social structure of any given society is responsible for criminal propensities of crime-inclined people. Social scientists propose that social banditry is a universal and virtually unchanging phenomenon. Hindu Dharmasastras and Kautilya's Arthasastra mentioned about theft and ways of curtailing it. Not only the preventive steps but punishments of different nature for variety of crimes were also specified in them. Appropriate legislation has been made from time to time to curb crime and punish culprits. It is increasingly realized that economic deprivation and inequalities promote crime. Humans are not born criminals, but it is social environment that generally nurtures crime. In the Indian subcontinent, we come across certain tribes and castes taking to crime due to variety of reasons under different circumstances. They were dubbed as criminal tribes by the British.

Several theories are put forward discussing the origins of criminal tribes. Research studies declare that they are descendants of gypsies of India. Some of these tribes claim their descent from Rajputs and bear Kshatriya clan names. Under the impact of successive Muslim invasions, they became nomads and habituated to crime as their livelihood. To name a few of them from North India are Kanjar, Bhantu, Meena, Tagu, Sansiya and Lodhas. In South India they are known by the names of Lambadas, Koravas, Dommaras, Kallars, Waddars, Yerukalas – to name only a few. The term criminal tribe is a misnomer, because both tribe and caste as also several other communities are classified as criminal tribes. Criminal tribe has been a label to mark a few groups as habitual rather than natural offenders. Criminal tribes are distributed in different parts of India. Yerukalas, Koravas and Korachas are different branches of the large Korava community living in different parts of South India. Yerukalas are mostly seen in Andhra Pradesh and live mainly in the coastal and Rayalaseema districts. They are also sparsely found in other parts of the country. In the Telugu-speaking areas they are called *Yerukalavandlu*. It is reported that they are fortune-tellers and through this profession came their name, Yerukala. Yerukalas like other tribes have specific customs, traditions, beliefs, superstitions, rituals and ceremonies.

The British Government passed the first Criminal Tribes Act in 1871 ostensibly to check the rate of crime. Several settlements were started where tribesmen and women were lodged. The task of their management was entrusted to voluntary agencies such as Salvation Army, American Baptist Mission, London Mission, Canadian Mission, Chief Khalsa Diwan, Deo Samaj, Anjuman Islamia, Ahmedia Society, Sanatan Dharma Sabha, Arya Samaj, Punjab Hindu Sabha and Adimajati Sevak Sangh, to mention only some well-known organizations. In addition, the government too at some places was directly involved in organizing reformatory settlements. Settlements were classified under agricultural, industrial, reformatory and penal settlements. Inmates of these settlements were provided employment of different kinds for an honest living. Their children were given training in special skills in the schools established for them. The whole idea was to wean them away from crime and to lead an honourable life on their own. The Madras province repealed the C.T. Act in 1947 and Bombay in 1949. The All India Criminal Tribes Enquiry Committee in 1949 evaluated the problems of criminal tribes and recommended for repealing the Act. After the repeal of the Act many were freed from the stigma of criminality. However, a sizeable section of inmates of the settlements could not escape from the stigma of theft and, in fact, they were not totally reformed belying the hopes of the government. It became known that they continued their criminal activities of robbing and other petty crimes of pocket picking, shop lifting and stealing passengers' luggage in trains and buses. The reasons are not far to seek – alternative means of livelihood offered to them were meager and it was an age-old crime culture that became a part of their psyche which could not be eradicated so easily.

II

Yerukalas and Katheras are two ex-criminal tribes of Andhra Pradesh. These two groups are stigmatized as dacoits, burglars, pilferers, thieves and railway wagon breakers. They are registered under the Criminal Tribes Act. One of these tribes, Yerukalas was nomadic and used to move around in the Rayalaseema districts of Anantapur, Kurnool, Cuddapah and coastal districts of Guntur and Nellore. It is believed they acted as spies or espionage staff who collected secrets from the enemy and passed them over to rulers who employed them. Consequent upon the British conquest of these territories, they lost their livelihood as spies and looked to alternative occupations such as agriculture, petty business and rope/basket/mat making. Some of them were employed as night watchmen in villages. Regular loss of livelihood in the wake of British occupation left them in total disarray and a significant number of them took to crime for their livelihood.

Stuartpuram is one of the settlements established in 1914 by the colonial government. It is located in Guntur district on the Madras-Howrah railway line. It was an agricultural settlement put under the management of Salvation Army. Captain H. Robbiliard was the manager. The total inmates, to start with, were 691 in number. There were Hindus, Christians and Muslims and among them Hindus formed the majority. Under the influence of Salvation Army, a large number of settlers were attending Church service. The *kula panchayat* system worked as arbiter of disputes among the Yerukala settlers. The tribal head, a senior member endowed with ability to arbitrate, generally chosen by the whole community, is assisted by five other elders of the community. The decisions of *kula panchayat* are rarely disobeyed. Prior to their life in settlement, Yerukalas along with others depended upon forest produce for their living, in addition to some petty business activities. They were known for their skills in basket and mat weaving, rope-making and so on. They traded in salt and grain and transported merchandise to distant places on the backs of animals such as donkeys and horses. While trading, they used to indulge in thefts and exchange of stolen property with other gangs involved in trade. These minor and need-based acts of crime gradually drove them to become professional robbers and dacoits.

To provide inmates of Stuartpuram settlements with regular and fixed incomes, the Salvation Army organization introduced agriculture. About an extent of 2,000 acres of land was made available to the settlers. Each household was given 2/3 acres of land. The settlers were introduced to methods of cultivation as most of them were alien to agricultural operations. Though they were reluctant to learn the new trade, they were, however, persuaded to adopt them and in course of time were able to extract reasonable yield. Agricultural income was supplemented by manufacture of mats, baskets and horticultural products. In addition to these, they were also drafted to do road laying work, quarrying and related works. It was also thought necessary to start a subsidiary industry to augment their incomes as well as engage them throughout the year. Steps were taken to set up schemes for casuarinas and tomato canning. Coconut plantations along with eucalyptus were set up which became successful ventures in course of time. Gradually, over a period of time, irrigational facility was provided by constructing a dam across Romperu drain in 1919 near Stuartpuram. With the availability of water, the settlers were now raisings crops like groundnut, pulses, ragi along with cashew nut, coconut and mango plantations. After careful consideration of the behaviour of settlers and their zeal for cultivation of land, they were granted permanent pattas on the condition that lands should neither be mortgaged for a period of ten years nor be ever sold to non-Yerukalas. Improvement of settlers was slow but steady by 1964 while the total extent of cultivable land was 2,007.71 acres out of which 1,772.58 acres were actually cultivated.

A major development in the history of Stuartpuram settlement was the opening of a railway station in 1921. Horticultural produce like tomato was now transported to distant markets. Additional employment avenues were opened when the Indian Leaf Tobacco Development Company (ILTD) was established near the settlement. Despite several measures to ameliorate the financial difficulties of settlers, the number of absconders from the settlement increased. The main reason was that they were not happy with farm-oriented professions. A cooperative society and the stores to supply food materials at cheaper prices were also started.

In matters of education, the Salvation Army was convinced, from the beginning, that settlers should be provided schooling facilities. To this effect, an elementary school was started in 1916. It was compulsory for school going children to attend the school. Three 'R's were taught along with a bit of science, gardening, English and physical education. Bible was a compulsory subject at the school. Training in agriculture and industrial crafts was imparted to pupils of higher classes. Adults among settlers had night schools. Teachers from Yerukala tribe, as far as possible, were appointed in the school with a view that they would be able to work with commitment for the children of fellow tribal families. Teachers were paid well and mid-day meal (ganji, the boiled rice liquid) was served to children. In addition to the elementary school, a boarding school was established for the sake of orphan children and children whose parents were either absconding or languishing in jails. It was believed that separate climate, away from their homes, would help children grow up in non-criminal atmosphere. Separate hostels were built for boys and girls and peons were appointed to visit settlers' homes to enrol children into the school. Children were practically segregated from their parents except for occasional visits. Those who finished their schooling in Stuartpuram, later completed school final examination in Bapatla and after that were admitted in the Industrial School at Perambur, Madras (Chennai). A separate school for girls also functioned for some time. Nursing and sewing were specially taught besides the conventional subjects.

Further developments such as the post office, general library and high school took place which contributed to the general enlightenment of settlers. For the children of Yerukala settlers and a few of the converted Christians and upper caste Hindus, a new school was opened in 1958, under the joint auspices of the Salvation Army and the Police Department, which was converted into a middle school and then into a high school. It is noticed that by 1960s a good number of youth got educated even up to the university level and secured government jobs at the central and state levels. The long drawn out efforts of the Salvation Army bore fruit. Health and hygiene of the settlers was far from satisfactory. The settlement had no adequate health facilities and it was often infected by diseases like malaria and influenza. The Roman Catholic Mission disbanded its activities and left for the fear of frequent epidemics and lack of health care. Hospitals in the nearby towns, Chirala and Bapatla were too small to take care of large number of patients. Dispensary in the settlement was starved of sufficient funds and suffered irregular supply of medicines by the government. In 1930, a maternity ward was established and a full-time medical officer was appointed along with a nurse. Their visits to the hospital were infrequent. In 1930s some settlers were found affected with leprosy. They were treated as outpatients in the Bapatla Salvation Army leper colony.

Due to constant in-fights between settlers, peace and order became causality. With the increase of such infighting the number of criminal cases increased. Those who were involved in such cases were booked under restrictions and penalties Section 10 of the Madras Habitual Offenders Act of 1948. In addition to internal feuds, regular and routine types of crime the settlers used to commit are viz. dacoity, housebreaking, railway property robbery, bank looting, chain snatching, pocket picking, etc. What prompted them to commit crime was mainly the lack of alternative means of livelihood and poverty. Their antipathy towards hard work was another reason. Police harassment, sometimes meted out to innocents drove them towards committing crime. There are about twenty batches of criminals in the settlement, each batch consisting of four to five members with a leader and an assistant. Women do indulge in crime or assist men in criminal activities and a fairly large number of them are there in the settlement. Among women criminals, many are those who are either divorced or widowed and whose husbands are in prison. Contacts with criminals of other settlements and sometimes with the notorious robbers from outside the state are maintained by the inmates. That the police department abets crime and claims a lion's share in the stolen property is attested by those involved in criminal activities. It is a vicious circle from which they can seldom get out. Stuartpuram criminals are so notorious that whenever a serious dacoity or robbery takes place anywhere in the state, it is often attributed to them.

After 1948, the settlement was handed over to the Tribal Welfare Department. The Salvation Army's management officially came to an end. However, it continued its welfare activities through the dispensary, schools, church and hospital and provided financial assistance and clothing to the needy students.

III

The second major attempt at reforming and mainstreaming inhabitants of Stuartpuram settlement was initiated in the year 1974 by a group of secular and a religious humanists under the leadership of Gora of Atheist Centre, Vijayawada. The reform movement that began as a modest attempt was later on shouldered by Hemalata and Lavanam for the next three decades or so. By the time the reformation work began in the Stuartpuram settlement, the atheist social reformers had some theoretical and philosophical understanding of the problems of criminal tribes. Some of the people belonging to other social categories involved in crime do not have the stigma of criminality unlike the Stuartpuram's denotified tribes. When the British Government branded certain castes and tribes as criminals it meant that those thus branded would be so considered by birth and profession. The Criminal Tribes Act had an implicit assertion that a woman from criminal family would necessarily conceive a criminal embryo. Stuartpuram's inhabitants have been included in this category whereas other criminals escaped the branding.

Among the Yerukala tribe, there are two major divisions – those engaged in criminal acts and other non-criminal families. They do not mix among themselves. After the promulgation of the Criminal Tribes Act the non-criminal families were afraid that they might be suspected for underhand dealings if they had any kind of relation with the criminal families. As a result, even within the tribe, there was no interaction between criminal families and non-criminal families. In due course, criminal families were segregated socially and culturally. When external social relations were totally cut off, a culture of crime struck deep roots among the criminal families. Remnants of this inherited mentality are visible in certain respects even today. Yerukala tribe was brought into social and political structure by the ancient and medieval rulers to work as intelligence agents in the army. During the freedom struggle the British Government tried to humiliate the educated upper middle class. Congress leaders by placing them in the prison cells along with the criminals of criminal tribes. Devara Raju of Stuartpuram was the most notorious criminal in the eyes of the colonial government. He was famously called *Sardar* as he was believed to have perfected the art of crime and the act of stealing. When in jail he could meet and interact with the leaders of freedom struggle when the latter were placed in his cell. Some of the leaders took advantage, interacted with the habitual criminals and promised them that they would help in the repeal of Criminal Tribes Act after independence.

Devara Raju was one of those who was attracted towards freedom struggle and freedom fighters like Gandhi. He was the first person in Stuartpuram settlement who shaped himself as a nationalist while in jail. After his release from the jail he started enlightening Stuartpuram inhabitants on the nature of freedom struggle. He unsuccessfully tried to organize a meeting of leaders of freedom struggle in the settlement. Raju's episode was a vainglorious attempt, a non-starter and forgotten over a period of time. Under the influence of freedom struggle, Raju took a pledge that he would not commit crime again. Also, he took a resolve to educate his children and pave them a non-criminal way of life in future. Devara Raju was alive in his late 80s with failing memory when the criminal reformation process was initiated in 1970s. The reformers had an opportunity to talk to him patiently and gather information from him about how he transformed himself from a hardcore criminal to a staunch nationalist.

In the culture of crime, mutual distrust and harshness in personal and social relations are glaringly visible. As criminals, the male members of families are always haunted by the fear of being caught by the police. They cannot afford to live in peace. Neither can they spend time with their families happily. When they are at large and when they are away on thieving spree, they are aloof from family members. When in jail, they cannot meet anyone and talk to them. Lack of familial love and intimate human bondage make the criminals very harsh. They generally do not trust anyone which indicates the fact that social workers need to be kind with them, irrespective of their response. They are expected to trust the criminals on face value even if they mistrust everybody they come across. This process has to continue till a time when the criminal members start mending themselves. The reformers followed this principle through their interactions. By 1960s, Stuartpuram settlement had both criminal and non-criminal families. The non-criminals are employed in government service, private industrial establishments, petty business and agricultural operations. However, opportunities for employment are limited. The stigma of crime makes them suspects in public view. Added, the steps taken by government are not enough to provide them sufficient succour. Ultimately, the Stuartpuram settlement remained a place of criminals, semi-reformed and unreformed.

During the month of December 1973, women members of criminal families in Stuartpuram settlement beat a police constable that immediately attracted the attention of district police head, M.V. Thomas. The incident brought the police officer to the settlement when he had to face many uneasy questions about the treatment meted out to women and children when male members are in the cell. Though initially reluctant, the police head inspected the local Vedullapalli police station where he found women dresses and household utensils. The Superintendent of Police was very much ashamed and apologized to women on behalf of the police force. He went off, but the incident made him think. The next day he again came to Stuartpuram colony in civil dress and without escort. He met women members and said he did not come as a police head but as a fellow human being and will try to help them. That was the beginning of a new era of social relations in the hardcore settlement of Stuartpuram. That was the first time when a high-ranking police official exhibited interest and sympathy. Both men and women took the cleve and started exploiting the police officer to their advantage. They demanded that no police force, whether from Guntur district or any neighbouring district, should be allowed into Stuartpuram colony and take away their men at will. The Superintendent of Police posted a village police post at the entrance of the village and ordered that without his permission, no policeman should enter the village. This sympathetic and decisive act of the Superintendent of Police endeared him to both men and women. But the top-level police officers at the state level felt that Stuartpuram settlers were taking undue advantage of the goodness of the police officer and trying to save themselves from being investigated and prosecuted for the crimes they committed.

The Superintendent of Police realized the internal problems of policing and suggested to Gora and members of Atheist Centre that they might continue the work as they were not bound by any strict rule books of conduct and operations. On the other hand, government officers would be periodically transferred from place to place. Once the officer gets transferred, there is no guarantee that the succeeding officer would continue the efforts of the predecessor. If continued, the original zeal and sympathy may not be seen. There was a gut feeling among police administration that soft-peddling in Stuartpuram would not romp home cherished results. The Superintendent of Police, Gora, Hemalata and Lavanam convened a meeting at Vijayawada whose proceedings received wide coverage in the press with the All India Radio, Vijayawada broadcasting a special programme on the meeting. The theme of the meeting was *crime is no profession*. Subsequently, Gora wrote to the Chief Minister of Andhra Pradesh requesting him to allow the representatives of the Atheist Centre to take up the criminal reformation work in the colony. With the approval of the state government, Gora, Lavanam and Hemalata chalked out their programme strategy and carefully implemented the same in the colonies of Stuartpuram, Seethanagaram (Guntur district) and Kapparalla Tippa (Nellore district) settlements. By that time they had rich experience of taking part in the surrender and rehabilitation programmes of Chambal valley dacoits under the leadership of Vinoba Bhave in 1960 and Jayaprakash Narayan in 1972.

IV

In 1973, the social reformer couple, Lavanam and Hemalata conducted a novel camp as a part of national programme, *Youth Against Famine* at Bayyavaram in Visakhapatnam district which included 50 students of Mrs. A.V.N. College, Visakhapatnam and another 50 Borstal school inmates (juvenile delinquents). The programme was to mix student youth and non-student youth together in a two-week camp to promote responsible social awareness/citizenry. The local jail wardens had supervision over Borstal school inmates. Altogether fifty pairs of students were created, each pair having one Borstal school boy and one student of A.V.N. College. They were allowed to act free and work together in the camp from 6.00 A.M. to 9.00 P.M. after which the Borstal school inmates would go to the control of the wardens. All the youth lived in the local elementary school for fifteen days. Towards the end of the camp three of the fifty Borstal school boys ran away. They were immediately caught. The rest of the boys behaved very well and got six months to one-year remission in their jail terms. It was rated a very successful experiment by the government of Andhra Pradesh. The authorities were full of praise for social reformers for their humanist, reformist and Gandhian approach to the entire experiment.

The next major initiative was that reformers conducted a student N.S.S. camp in the Stuartpuram settlement. Fifty boys from the A.N.R. College, Gudivada were in the colony for fifteen days as a part of the camp. They helped in laying a road and a small bridge with branches of Palmyra trees. They visited every house in Stuartpuram and interacted with members of the families. This was the first ever opportunity for social interaction on a large scale with members of mainstream society. Students planted hundred coconut trees in the colony and the saplings were supplied by the government. The camp brought a tremendous change, particularly among the youth in the colony. Some of the ex-criminal youth of Stuartpuram, when they went to Gudivada, they visited the N.S.S. students to their great surprise. Reformers used to bring prominent citizens to Stuartpuram to promote a sense of belongingness with the rest of the society. A big cosmopolitan dinner was arranged by the reformers wherein the then police officials along with their families and several government officials participated.

One more effective public programme of the social reformers was introduction of sports and games for the inhabitants of Stuartpuram. Traditionally, families in the settlement were used to indulging in gaming activity at night (crime!). The current plan provided them two advantages: first, to participate in daylight gaming activities and secondly to interact with others from local society. Local police officers as well as district officials were invited for the activity. This programme encouraged reformed families to take active participation in a different programme of new social genre. These experiences came handy to the reformer couple in Stuartpuram when they were trying to establish rapport with the residents colony from day one. At this juncture, they forwarded two important decisions that would guide their work with the Stuartpuram criminals. They are not to accept anything except drinking water from the criminals' households in Stuartpuram. For, even a drop of tea offered by the criminals might be a part of the proceedings of the stolen property. Second condition was not to talk to any male member of criminal households if they approach in an inebriated condition. These two decisions had an electric effect on people. But three major crimes took place when the couple was interacting with the criminal families – bank robbery at Banaganepalle in Kurnool district, a big theft at Lakkavaram in West Godavari district and housebreaking venture in Chirala town near Stuartpuram. Soon Banaganepalle bank robbery suspects surrendered along with the booty with the help of social reformers. Initially, all of them agreed not to set up defence in the courts, but to plead guilty and accept the sentence with a sense of repentance. But when the police went back on their oral promise, the criminals too hardened their stand. They hired lawyers to argue their case. Finally, they voluntarily surrendered the booty to court. Criminal reformation demands a highly reasonable civilian attitude from the police in dealing with the criminals.

Reformer couple classified criminals of Stuartpuram settlement into three categories: first category comprised all those who commit crimes, prosecuted and jailed. For these people, one cannot provide public employment. They are to be encouraged for self-employment like rickshaw-pulling, agrarian activities, petty business; second category consisted of people who committed crimes, but not yet convicted. Not knowing whether they would be convicted or acquitted, one cannot get any public employment for this category also. They too are encouraged for self-employment; the third category had people who did commit crimes, but by bribing the corrupt officials, are never charge-sheeted. For them, the reformers pleaded with the police that since no action was taken they should be let off so as to reform themselves and settle down in civil society. With some difficulty, reformers could get public employment for some of them along with the non-criminal members of their own families. Public employment became an incentive for the changed criminals in distancing themselves from the old profession.

Rehabilitation of criminals was not only economic, but also social and cultural rehabilitation. It is difficult to compensate for their earnings through crime. Avenues can be shown for them to earn through socially and culturally accepted means. Alternatives may be few, but they need to be explored with all the force of social conviction needed by the venture. Perhaps, here the role of reformer or social worker or civil society members becomes extremely difficult. Also this is the junction between '*us*' and '*they*' where a comprehensive development approach to fellow delinquent children of an inherited avocation is to be pursued. Criminals have been accustomed to an easy way of life and easy money. Even some women members of the criminal families were involved in small-scale crime and thefts. Stopping of crime was very difficult for the earning members of these criminal families. Often it becomes extremely difficult to make them shift to other avocations where hard physical labour is the norm. When the district administration, acting at the behest of reformers distributed set of agricultural implements, within no time more than one-third of them sold off their implements to purchase liquor or cigarettes. The reformers took advantage of the fact that the criminals are scheduled tribes as they come under the reservation category of the Indian Constitution. They pushed all those who had a minimum of 8th standard qualification into government services, particularly Indian railways as class IV employees. The effort had its effect. Not even a single person thus employed had committed any criminal act after getting employed. This was a great boost for the continuation of the reformation work.

Crime is a cobweb. Along with the criminal, the stolen property dealers, the investors in crime, the criminal lawyers and the corrupt officials used to share booty of crime. Very often individual criminal is left with a meager amount for his anti-social labour, the major share of his booty being cornered by white collar people outside. As long as criminals were committing crime, there was an assurance for the investors that they would get back their investment. They were ready to finance for criminal families, the loan amount often being used for household consumption. Once the criminal stops the act of crime, there was no readiness on the part of investors as there could not be an assurance on repayment. Stoppage of crime means an impending poverty for the criminals. Hence, it became very difficult for the changed criminals to get even a small amount of loan from others including their own relatives. Popular perception has been that all crimes are committed by the criminals of Stuartpuram settlement. To dispel the misinformation, reformers suggested an innovative plan to the local police. Following the input, the police suggested that if the history-sheeted criminals were willing to sleep in the local school from 8.00 P.M. to 5.00 A.M. under supervision and willing to sign or give thumb impression at 8.00 P.M. it could be the recorded evidence that they did not go for crime. The reformed criminals agreed to the suggestion. They started sleeping on the floor of the local school. Reformers too slept with the reformed criminals and the act had an immense psychological effect.

Even though the Criminal Tribes Act was repealed in the post-independence era (in the year 1947, in Madras Presidency), nobody took a keen interest in the execution of the government decision in making the criminal settlements as free colonies. All the five settlements in Andhra Pradesh viz. Stuartpuram, Sitanagaram, Kapparallatippa, Siddhapuram and Lingala remained as ex-criminal settlements. Out of these five, Salvation Army had its major influence in Stuartpuram for a long time to come. The other four were completely taken over by the government towards the end of the colonial rule. They were put under the revenue jurisdiction or police jurisdiction. After independence the Madras Government appointed a committee under the chairmanship of Vepa Ramesam which recommended that all ex-criminal settlements be declared as free villages and distribution of land to all those bonafide inhabitants who have been living there. But the recommendations were not implemented. This anomaly was brought to the notice of Andhra Pradesh government by the reformers. Very soon, after this appeal, Secretary of Social Welfare, S.R. Sankaran notified through a G.O. in 1976 that all the ex-criminal settlements would be considered free village communities. Consequently government departments took control over all lands in the settlements and distributed the same in the name of local inhabitants with ownership rights. This act had left a deep impression on the minds of the settlement dwellers and they started enjoying self-respect as the rightful owners of property at par with other members of the mainstream society.

Government waste land on the left bank of the local drain, Romperu was given to 146 families, each family getting land measuring 90 cents. The then Chief Minister, J. Vengal Rao cleared the decks for land distribution. Social reformers personally supervised division of the land. Irrigation facilities were provided by the reformers. The land thus distributed was organized into a tribal co-operative society with individual members having the right to property. Seed and fertilizer were supplied in the first year, free of cost. Reformers convinced the government to give manual wages to all those criminal families who would work on the distributed lands. As the land was fertile, the first year's yield gave a great satisfaction to the reformed criminals and to the social workers. Within a couple of years they could not retain the same interest in agricultural operations. Slowly, the yield was reduced as it ought to be. A lot of time was required to be allowed for the reformed criminals to settle down in the new social roles. For generations together they were taught the family art of necessitated thieving and robbing. Also they were indoctrinated into a firm belief that they were born to rob and that crime was their natural attribute by birth.

Social reformers periodically communicated with those who were in jails. This was a part of a strategic counselling exercise. The jailed criminals used to write letters to the reformer couple regularly. Some of these letters written from jails by remanded criminals vouchsafe for the efficacy of the reformation process. In most of these letters the changed/reformed criminals used to reiterate their abiding faith in the reformation and the efforts of social reformers who in their turn used to educate jail wardens about the need for being reformative in their outlook during the entire process.

V

Criminal reformation is a three dimensional process involving different kinds of actors and characters – criminals themselves, the state machinery including police/government officials and finally, society at large. Of these variables, surrounding society plays a major role, either to accept or deny reformed criminals into the mainstream ways of life. When this variable is in place, the rest of the variables follow the suit. Social reformers represented this important social variable in the process of social reform and rehabilitation of members of Stuartpuram colony. Since religion and tradition always tend to promote social status quo syndrome, the reformers adopted a religious and rationalist/atheist approach to the entire problem wherein references to god, fate and religious observances had no place. It was only a saga of humanist programming and the central objective was human free will. The reformers executed their work in five phases and evolved a strategy known as 3G Approach/Three Generation Approach. Being aware of the shortcomings of earlier social reform trends of 19th century colonial India, they meticulously devised the current strategy.

Major emphasis of the organization during the entire process had been on 3G Approach and on social integration and area development. According to the understanding of social reformers a civilian/voluntary effort in reforming a diehard tradition or customary practice should ideally engage members/families of three generations. Members of the first generation form the direct victims who require an immediate counselling and a helping hand to break away from the despised avocation/custom. This process is expected to result in a smooth socialization and break away from the isolated past. Mainstreaming the reformed criminals and members of their families is an issue in the post-reform period. The second generation children of the reformed families need the social attention so that they would shape a non-criminal future for themselves. This would enable them to slip out of the despised avocation of their forefathers. Social and formal education was the focus area during this phase. Their children, representing the third generation are free from social memory and stigma. These members provide a conclusive verification on the veracity and efficacy of the reform efforts and their legacy. The change is generally slow, abstract and unconscious. It can be more perceived than realized in material terms.

During the first phase of reform activity during 1973 and 1974, the social reformers concentrated on establishing rapport with the criminals and their families. Reformers requested the charge sheeted criminals not to move bail petitions and to plead guilty before the judges so that their cases are disposed of very soon. The reformers assured them that they would work for their rehabilitation. When the criminals were in jail the reformers were in constant touch with the families of those jailed.

Efforts during the second stage (1975–1979) endeavoured to procure public employment for the non-criminal members of the criminal families. They were involved in programmes like land reclamation process of the Romperu lands, provision of irrigation facilities, encouraging agricultural operations and consolidation of the efforts of reformation. They made regular visits to jails, wrote letters to the jailed criminals, convened periodical meetings with the families of the criminals, organized a two-week student camp in Stuartpuram, built interfaces between the older family members of the criminal families and the government officers, helped to make Stuartpuram a free colony, explored methods for socio-economic rehabilitation of the reformed families. These programmes almost lasted for three years. Towards the beginning of stage II, the government constituted a Stuartpuram Rehabilitation Committee under the chairmanship of the District Collector with other district officials and the reformer couple as members. The committee was asked to look into the development aspects of the colony. It met twice a year. As the members on the committee were already involved in the reformation and rehabilitation process, formation of the committee did not either have an add-on value or delimit the pace of present process. It soon lost its importance and became defunct.

The third stage (1980–1995) was used to soften the process of reform and rehabilitation. It was observed that 30 per cent of the surrendered criminals took recourse to crime again, mainly due to non-availability of work/job opportunities and unnecessary police harassment. To address the problem, reformers focused on development of social leadership from among changed criminals who could go to the government offices and get their work done. Along with education of children and emergence of social leadership, womenfolk asserted their role and place in the process of transformation. During this period, three major developments were witnessed in terms of 'process consolidation'. They are: founding of the NGO, Samskar in 1983 under the Societies Registration Act XXI of 1860 (No. 157 of 1983); publication of a periodical, Samskar to propagate ideas of reform among the members of civil society and organizing the first-ever criminal reformation conference in 1984 at Vijayawada.

During the stage four (1995–2000) reformers had to deal with the emergence of *new generation criminals*. A few of the youngsters from non-criminal families of the colony tried to eke out their livelihood through crime. The organization tried its best to grapple with the new generation problem and took much time in counselling the families of new converts to crime. The second surrender of criminals took place during this phase and interestingly reformed criminals from the colony shouldered the responsibility of counselling the newly-developed criminals and surrendering them before the government. Samskar and its founders had enjoyed the first modicum of success as the current surrender hinted at the downward filtration of the spirit of reform in the Stuartpuram colony. Success followed *second surrender* of criminals voluntarily in the year 1998. With this, the circle of reformation had one full revolution completed. From 1995 onwards work of the organization became structured and fructified into programme-specific interventions. The organization executed various development programmes for children, youth, reformed criminals and their families with support from donor agencies. Various vocational programmes were launched during this period. Supplementary education, typewriting and tailoring were designed and implemented for the children and family members of the reformed criminal families. Seeds for a healthy social integration were sown during this period. The vocational and other training programmes were used by Samskar to admit youngsters from other non-criminal families in the surrounding villages like Betapudi. This was the beginning of an attempt at social integration through programme ventures.

The last stage (post-2000) witnessed exclusive focus on social integration through area development approach wherein programmes involving poor from Stuartpuram and surrounding villages were implemented. Integrated approach to the programmes where the benefits would be shared by reformed criminal families and other families were immediately welcomed by people as well as civil society. Young leaders who emerged on the scene began managing common functions like games and sports. The net effect of various interventions by the social reformer couple, Hemalata and Lavanam was a discernable reduction in the rate of crime and change in the attitudes of families towards life and living. A baseline survey conducted in 2002 under the leadership and monitoring of reformed criminals from the Stuartpuram colony painted an encouraging picture on the four decadal social reform activities.

The Baseline Survey–2002 presents the following picture:

Population	3,559
Male	1,119
Female	1,215
Children	1,225
Reformed Families	119
People in Crime	12

The 10-day intensive field survey and interviews bring out glaring differences between the pre-reform and post-reform period during which efforts of social reformers and their frontal organization, Samskar was actively engaged.

General Routines

Pre-Reform Period	*Post-Reform Period*
Addiction to alcohol and fear-stricken lifestyle	Peaceful life
Rough life	Smooth life routines
Scattered families	United families
Always on tenterhooks due to the fear of arrest by police	Settled life
Often away from homes	At home
No control over time	Relaxed time schedules

Social Status and Respect

Pre-Reform Period	*Post-Reform Period*
They are always suspected	They are respected now
They never come out under open sun	Moving freely at present
Solitary life in isolated and haunted places	Mixed with surrounding society
People are afraid of us	People now mingle with them
They are branded as criminals	They are now ordinary human beings
They are puppets in the hands of police	Police personnel still haunt and harass them

Family Life

Pre-Reform Period	*Post-Reform Period*
Relative prosperity while being thieves	They are happy though they are not economically comfortable
Mostly disorganized life given to vices	Life routines are satisfactory at present
They are vagabonds most of the time	They are with their wife and children now
Crime is the only known source of income	They are working now on other avocations
They had only night life – profession as well as family visits	Living together without any fear

Financial Status

Pre-Reform Period	*Post-Reform Period*
Discouraging	Leading hand to mouth existence
They had money in their hands (due to criminal acts)	They struggle for resources now but, are happy
All forefathers are in crime for family sustenance	Children are now safe; are free from crime; going to schools/colleges

The process of change and reform was a witnessed on the whole by two major players in the DNT settlements of Andhra Pradesh. While the Salvation Army's efforts were conceived through religious and traditional modes in pre- and post-independent era, Samskar's efforts were couched in religious and rationalist modes. The Stuartpuram experiment of social reform hints at one important historical lesson that religious and traditional approaches to the problem of despised social heritage has lesser or reduced scope for reform of diehard avocations of hardened criminals. The limitations of traditional methods as embedded in religious norms often act as hurdles in the process of social change or social reform. Table below presents dichotomy between the approaches of two major players in Stuartpuram colony in respect of reform and rehabilitation:

Salvation Army (Colonial)	*Samskar (Post-Colonial)*
Religious Social Work	A religious and Atheist Social Work
Faith-based	Humanist intervention/right-based
Conversions on religious lines	Changes based on human free will
Interpersonal relations hierarchical	Interpersonal relations at par
Institutional approach (top-down)	Three Generation Approach (bottom-up)
Armed with magisterial powers	Voluntary efforts engaged at peaceful conflict resolution
Advocacy and networking with appropriate bodies/institutions absent	Networking with policy makers, bureaucrats and philanthropic organizations very strong

Salvation Army (Colonial)	*Samskar (Post-Colonial)*
Scripture reading as part of the effort	Counselling sessions as the key intervention
Strong material resources at command	Weak material resource base
Impact at material development level	Impact at individual and psychological level
Interface with civic governance rare	Interface with democratic governing bodies always strong and continuous
Criminal reform often elusive	Change is discernible
Mainstreaming efforts partial	Mainstreaming efforts successful
Efforts in shaping second line leadership are few	Development of second line leadership from among the reformed criminals emerged in a span of 15 years

Though the efforts of Salvation Army are monumental at material level, one of its main objectives of social change among the criminal families remained elusive, despite best intentions. Whereas religious, rationalist and humanist approaches of Samskar did away with traditional approaches to the problem, the organization's *Three Generation Approach* with exclusive focus on monitoring reform efforts through three generations and building bridges between isolated colony and mainstream democratic governance systems helped in the speedy progress of reform and rehabilitation, spanning over four decades in the post-independent era.

References

Aiyappan, A., *Report on the Socio-economic Conditions of the Aboriginal Tribes of the Province of Madras*, Government Press, Madras, 1948.

Bhowmick, K.L., *Tribal India: A Profile in Indian Ethnology*, World Press Private Limited, Calcutta, 1971.

Bose, N.K., *Tribal Life in India*, National Book Trust, New Delhi, 1971.

Bruce, George, *The Stranglers: The Cult of Thuggee and its Overthrow in British India*, Harcourt, Brace and World Inc., New York, 1969.

Cecil Walsh, K.C., *Crime in India*, M.W. Books, Great Britain, 1930.

Chenchu, Raju, *Stuartpuram Girijan Settlement: A Rehabilitation Centre for Ex-convicts*, Government Press, Hyderabad, 1981.

Chetty, N. Gopalakrishnama, *Manual of the Kurnool District in the Presidency of Madras*, People's Publishing House, New Delhi, 1992 (first edition 1886).

Edwards, S.M., *Crime in India*, OUP, London, 1924.

Furer-Haimendorf, C. Von, *The Aboriginal Tribes*, Vol. 1, OUP, Hyderabad, 1943.

Gandhi, Malli, *A Historical Survey of Ex-criminal Tribe Settlements in Andhra: A Case Study of Stuartpuram Settlement (1914–1990)*, M.Phil. Dissertation, University of Hyderabad, Telangana, 1993.

Ghurye, G.S., *Aborigines So-called and Their Future*, Popular Book Depot, Bombay, 1969.

Government of Andhra Pradesh, *Andhra Pradesh State Administration Reports, 1953–1977*, AP State Archives (APSA), Government Press, Hyderabad, 1978.

Government of Madras, *Administration Report on Habitual Offenders Settlements from 1950–1955*, TNA, Government Central Press, Madras, 1956.

——, *Administration Reports of the Inspector General of Police, 1904–1940*, TNA, Government Central Press, Madras, 1941.

——, *Judicial Department (Confidential) Proceedings, 1920–1940*, TNA, Government Central Press, Madras, 1941.

——, *Police of the Nizam's Government*, Tamil Nadu Archives (TNA), Government Central Press, Madras, 1931.

——, *Reports on the Administration of the Criminal Tribe Settlement and Kallars and Yanadi Reclamation for 1940*, Government Central Press, Madras, 1905.

Gupta, Mithilesh, 'Rehabilitation of Criminal Tribes', *Eastern Anthropologist*, Vol. 17, No. I, 1964, pp. 39–48.

Haikerwal, B.S., *Economic and Social Aspects of Crime in India*, George Allen and Unwin Ltd., London, 1934.

Hardiman, David, *The Coming of the Devi: Adivasi Assertion in Western India*, OUP, New Delhi, 1987.

Lalitha, Vakulabharanam and Kompalli Sundar, *Hemalata Lavanam* (Biography in Telugu), National Book Trust, New Delhi, 2014.

Lavanam and Hemalata Lavanam, *The Problem of Denotified Tribes: An Experiment on Stuartpuram*, Gandhi Peace Foundation, Vijayawada, 1975.

Lavanam, Hemalata, *Mrityorma Amritangamaya* (Autobiography in Telugu 2005), Vishalandra Book House, Hyderabad.

——, *Nerasthula Samskarana* (Telugu 1985), Gandhi Peace Foundation, Vijayawada.

——, *Notes and Reflections of Our Work in the Rehabilitation of Ex-criminal Tribes People in the Settlements*, Gandhi Peace Foundation, Vijayawada, 1976.

Mullaly, Frederick S., *Notes on Criminal Classes of the Madras Presidency*, Government Press, Madras, 1912.

Native Newspaper Reports, 1872–1885 and 1908–1912, TNA, Madras.

Parthasaradhi, Jakka, *The Yerukala Ethnographic Study*, ASI, Calcutta, 1988.

Paupa Rao Naidu, M., *Notes on Criminal Tribes*, Higginbotham, Madras, 1904.

Raghavaiah, V., *The Problem of Criminal Tribes*, BASS, Nellore, 1943.

Sarma, Marla, *Samskar: A Profile*, Gandhi Peace Foundation, Vijayawada, 1992.

Simhadri, Y.C., *The De-notified Tribes: A Sociological Analysis*, Classical Publishing Company, New Delhi, 1991.

Singh, Sher, *The Sansis of Punjab*, Munshiram Manoharlal, New Delhi, 1965.

Stuartpuram: Baseline Survey 2002, Samskar, Gandhi Peace Foundation, Vijayawada (unpublished survey report).

Sundar, K.H.S.S., *Exclusion and Inclusion: Social Response Strategies during Colonial and Post-Colonial Andhra*, Paper submitted in the National Seminar on *Socio-religious and Cultural Responses of India to the Colonial Rule in the 19th and Early 20th Century*, Andhra Loyola College, Vijayawada, Andhra Pradesh, 17–18 August 2012.

Vakulabharanam, Ramakrishna and K.H.S. Sundar, *Legacy and Continuity: Social Reforms in Andhra Pradesh, 1850–2000*, Vijayawada, Andhra Pradesh, 2006.

Venkata Rao, V., *A Century of Tribal Politics in North East India 1874–1976*, S. Chand, New Delhi, 1976.

12

Education of Scheduled Tribe Children

Issues and Concerns

India achieved about seventy per cent of literacy according to the latest survey reports. Though the progress could have been better, considering several constraints, it is not a mean achievement. However, the rate of literacy among the marginalized sections, in particular, Scheduled Caste, Scheduled Tribe, Other Backward Classes and Minorities is much lower when compared with the non-SC, ST and forward sections. Further, the type of education provided to these sections of children is quite conventional. Even after six decades of independence, steps are not properly initiated to provide purposeful and meaningful education to these sections of children. Education of these children should incorporate their socio-economic and cultural genius. They should be sensitized with their rich cultural heritage. The present chapter is an attempt to examine the problems associated with the education of ST children, their culture specific curricular, pedagogic aspects, monitoring of their learning in schools, learning materials, multilingual education and socio-cultural aspects in tribal education. The chapter is an attempt to focus on the current needs of Adivasi children at all stages of school education. The specific aims and objectives of the chapter, however, is to identify the gaps and problems affecting the education of Adivasi children and to provide a road map to bridge the gaps in order to provide better and quality education to these children and also to focus on the educational issues relating to educational development of Adivasi children, their access to schools, quality, availability, grievances, governance and systemic reforms in school education. It is expected that the present chapter will help the policy makers, government authorities, teachers, teacher educators, researchers, and apex educational organizations to plan and organize effective, qualitative educational programmes for the overall development of ST children in general and their specific educational needs in particular.

I

Article 366 (25) of Indian Constitution refers to scheduled tribes as those communities who are scheduled in accordance with Article 342. Owing to a plethora of reasons they have been reduced to minorities in their own homeland. This process has acquired precarious dimensions in the post-independent era. Scheduled tribes (STs) constitute about 9 per cent of India's population. Each of the 705 scheduled tribes has their own language, which differs from the one mostly spoken in the State where they reside. Tribals are not a homogenous group. To look into tribal development issues *Integrated Tribal Development Projects* were conceived during the Fifth Five-Year Plan. During the Sixth Plan, *Modified Area Development Approach* (MADA) was adopted to cover smaller areas of tribal concentration and during the Seventh Plan, the TSP (Tribal Sub-Plan) strategy was extended further to cover even smaller areas of tribal concentration and subsequently *clusters* of tribal habitat locations were identified. In order to give more focused attention to the development of Scheduled Tribes, a separate Ministry, carved out of the Ministry of Social Justice and Empowerment, known as the Ministry of Tribal Affairs was constituted in October 1999.

Tribal education has recently witnessed a rapid transformation, particularly in the areas of access, pedagogic reform and community participation in tribal areas. The National Policy on Education (1986, 1992) and its programme of action (1992) have identified special measures for fulfilling the constitutional commitments to Scheduled Tribes. But recent studies on school management practices throw light on many grey areas in the realm of education of tribal children across the country. Inclusion of children in border areas and tribal/forest areas remains weak even today. Transition rates from primary to upper primary and secondary show significant dropout rates and there are significant gender differences. Serious issues of pedagogical problems have been reported by studies and gaps in educational administration are still plaguing the unhindered growth of tribal children and students. Systemic issues like discrimination, lack of schooling facilities, poor infrastructure, defective Teaching Learning Materials (TLM), etc. are brought to the notice of policy makers. The problem is more pronounced in case of Nomadic, Semi-Nomadic, Denotified Tribes and Primitive Tribal Group (NT/SNT/DNT/PTG) communities. The stigma of criminality is still one of the major impediments in the smooth run of educational progress of children and youth. Children often faced a kind of social alienation in most of the walks of social life. Social alienation particularly in young age hampers the growth of psycho-social faculties of the children. Although school coverage has increased, STs continue to lag far behind the rest of the population. Full implementation of legislative measures like Forest Dwellers Act (FRA) 2006, the Panchayats Extension to Scheduled Areas Act 1996 (PESA) and Non-Timber Forest Product (NTFP) shall be taken up on priority. STs face problems in securing the benefit of reservation due to the inclusion of certain non-tribal communities in the list of STs, leaving scope for non-tribals to pass off as STs. Tribal autonomy can be promoted better by bringing all tribal areas under the Sixth Schedule. The Dilip Singh Bhuria Commission's Report (1995) in this regard has not received practical attention. It is imperative that there needs to be more philanthropic investment in building community cultural wealth outside the classroom too. This would provide a solid foundation that leverages these assets and develops stronger individual potential that can transcend the barriers experienced by STs today. Thus, the chapter intends to focus on the educational problems of Scheduled Tribe children. The broad scope of the chapter is to analyse certain issues like problems faced by the Adivasi children in the school education scenario, constitutional goals and aspirations, effective tribal education system, barriers that prevent the tribal groups from taking advantage of the schools offered, issues relating to language, ashram, residential schools, culture specific curriculum, teachers, tribal ethos, life skills, home, school and community relations.

II

The Problems of Education of Scheduled Tribe Children: Background

Scheduled Tribes (STs), once proud masters of their traditional territory have been reduced to minorities in their own homeland. This is a historical process that has been going on for centuries and has acquired precarious dimensions in the post-independence era. This process has become virulent in recent times, when the mineral wealth of the tribal land has become much more valuable. The lands that still remain with them are poorly developed, are rarely irrigated and are poorly integrated with the market, leaving the field open to middlemen from outside. Irrigation projects that have been undertaken by governments in the tribal areas are typically programmes for building dams in tribal areas, submerging tribal lands, scattering their settlements and people to the wind and taking water to non-tribals outside the tribal areas. Public expenditures incurred on such projects are gratuitously shown as part of the Tribal Sub-Plan. No wonder increasing numbers of STs are forced into wage-labour and the proportion of STs among agricultural wage-labourers has increased in recent decades. Traditional tribal rights in forests which they have been enjoying through traditional symbiotic relationship with forests were unilaterally abrogated by the colonial government, making the STs dependent on others for their elementary requirements and very survival.

The term Scheduled Tribes first appeared in the Constitution of India. Article 366 (25) refers to scheduled tribes as those communities who are scheduled in accordance with Article 342 of the Constitution. According to Article 342 of the Constitution, 'the Scheduled Tribes are the tribes or tribal communities or part of or groups within these tribes and tribal communities which have been declared as such by the President through a public notification'. In pursuance of these provisions, the list of Scheduled Tribes was notified for each State or Union Territory with the proviso that it was valid only within the jurisdiction of that State or Union Territory and not outside. In other words the list of Scheduled Tribes is State/UT specific and a community declared as a Scheduled Tribe in a State need not be so in another State. The inclusion of a community as a Scheduled Tribe is an ongoing process. The essential characteristics first laid down by the Lokur Committee (1965) are: indications of primitive traits; distinctive culture; shyness of contact with the community at large; geographical isolation; backwardness. These characteristics are not spelt out in the Constitution but have become the important referral points as they subsume the definitions contained in 1931 Census, the reports of first Backward Classes Commission 1955, the Advisory Committee (Kalelkar) on Revision of SC/ST lists (Lokur Committee, 1965) and the Joint Committee of Parliament on the Scheduled Castes and Scheduled Tribes Orders (Amendment) Bill 1967.

III

Scheduled Tribe Development: An Overview

Scheduled Tribes (STs) constitute about 9 per cent of India's population. Each of the 705 scheduled tribes have their own language and differs from the one mostly spoken in the State where they reside. Tribals are not a homogenous group. Different tribes, even if living in the same village, maintain exclusive identities. Socialization is generally endogamous and they identify more with people belonging to their tribe rather than to those living in the same village or area. The recent history of tribals is filled with stories of forced displacement, land alienation and increasing marginalization, eruption of violence and the counter-violence by the State. Going by any parameters of development, the tribals always figure at the tail end. The situation of the communities that have been pastoral or nomadic is still worse. Tribal communities continue to face economic deprivation and lack of access to basic services, including education. Due to the absence of rehabilitation in post-independence era tribals are dispersed across the country, and live away from urbanization. As industrialization and urbanization flourish, infrastructure such as roads, water, electricity are not reaching these tribal localities. Reduced accessibility and connection have further deprived tribals from improving their lives. Adivasis often migrate to cities in search of a job within the mainstream for their survival. However, they are often unable to find a place in city slums due to various reasons. Realizing the need to improve the overall status of tribals, their education has emerged at the forefront of recent development efforts. Acknowledging that tribals comprise the most deprived and marginalized groups with respect to education, a host of programmes and measures have been initiated since India's Independence.

The tribal situation in the country presents a varied picture. Some areas have high tribal concentration while in other areas the tribals form only a small portion of the total population. There are some tribal groups which are still at the food gathering stage, some others practise shifting cultivation and yet some others are pursuing primitive forms of agriculture. The Constitution of India provides for a comprehensive framework for the socio-economic development of Scheduled Tribes and for preventing their exploitation by other groups of society. A detailed and comprehensive review of the tribal problem was taken on the eve of the Fifth Five-Year Plan and the Tribal Sub-Plan strategy took note of the fact that an integrated approach to the tribal problems was necessary in terms of their geographic and demographic concentration. Accordingly, the tribal areas in the country were classified under three broad categories: states and union territories having a majority scheduled tribe population; states and union territories having substantial tribal population but majority tribal population in particular administrative units, such as block and tehsils; states and union territories having dispersed tribal population.

It was decided that tribal majority States like Arunachal Pradesh, Meghalaya, Mizoram, Nagaland and UTs of Lakshadweep and Dadra & Nagar Haveli may not need a Tribal Sub-Plan, as the entire plan of these states/union territories was primarily meant for the ST population constituting the majority. For the second category of states and union territories, Tribal Sub-Plan approach was adopted after delineating areas of tribal concentration. A similar approach was also adopted in case of states and union territories having dispersed tribal population by paying special attention to pockets of tribal concentrations. To look after the tribal population coming within the new Tribal Sub-Plan strategy in a coordinated manner, *Integrated Tribal Development Projects* were conceived during Fifth Five-Year Plan and these have been continued since then. During the Sixth Plan, *Modified Area Development Approach* (MADA) was adopted to cover smaller areas of tribal concentration and during the Seventh Plan, the *TSP strategy* was extended further to cover even smaller areas of tribal concentration and subsequently *clusters* of tribal concentration were identified.

At the time of delineation of project areas under the Tribal Sub-Plan strategy, it was observed that the ITDPs/ITDAs are not coterminous. The Scheduled Areas as per the Constitutional orders have been declared in eight States viz. Andhra Pradesh (AP) (the erstwhile combined state), Bihar, Gujarat, Himachal Pradesh (HP), Maharashtra, Madhya Pradesh (MP), Odisha and Rajasthan. As per the provisions contained in the Fifth Schedule of the Constitution, various enactments in the form of Acts and Regulations have been promulgated in the above states for the welfare of scheduled tribes and their protection from exploitation. Since TSP strategy also has twin objectives, namely socio-economic development of Schedule Tribes and protection of tribals against exploitation, the Government of India (August 1976) had decided to make the boundaries of Scheduled Areas coterminous with TSP areas (ITDP/ITDA only) so that the protective measures available to Scheduled Tribes in Scheduled Areas could be uniformly applied to TSP areas for effective implementation of the development programmes in these areas. Accordingly, the TSP areas have been made co-terminus with Scheduled Areas in the states of Bihar, Gujarat, HP, Maharashtra, Madhya Pradesh, Odisha and Rajasthan. The state of AP where the TSP areas are not coterminous with

Scheduled Areas has also furnished a proposal to this effect which is under examination.

The ITDP/ITDAs (Integrated Tribal Development Projects/Agencies) are generally contiguous areas of the size of a Tehsil or Block or more in which the ST population is 50 per cent or more of the total. On account of demographic reasons, however, ITDPs in Assam, Karnataka, Tamil Nadu and West Bengal may be smaller or not contiguous. Andhra Pradesh and Odisha have opted for an agency model under the Registration of Societies Act and the ITDPs there are known as ITDAs. There are now 194 Integrated Tribal Development Projects (ITDPs) in the country spread across the states of Andhra Pradesh (Telangana and AP put together), Assam, Bihar, Gujarat, Himachal Pradesh, Karnataka, Kerala, Madhya Pradesh, Maharashtra, Manipur, Odisha, Rajasthan, Sikkim, Tamil Nadu, Tripura, Uttar Pradesh, West Bengal and Union Territories of Andaman & Nicobar Island and Daman & Diu where the ST population is more than 50 per cent of the total population of the blocks or groups of blocks. In eight states having scheduled areas the ITDPs/ITDAs are generally coterminous with TSP areas. The ITDPs/ITDAs are headed by a Project Officer though they may be designated as Project Administrators or Project Directors.

During the Sixth Plan, pockets outside ITDP areas, having a total population of 10,000 with at least 5,000 tribals were covered under the Tribal Sub-Plan under Modified Area Development Approach (MADA). So far, 259 MADA pockets have been identified in the various TSP states of the country. Generally, MADA pockets do not have separate administrative structures to implement development programmes. The line departments of the state governments are expected to implement development programmes in MADA pockets under the overall control of the District authorities. Clusters (of tribal population) are no separate administrative structures like MADA. So far, 82 Clusters have been identified in various TSP states of the country. Primitive Tribal Groups (PTG) are tribal communities among the STs who live in near isolation in inaccessible habitats. They are characterized by a low rate of population growth, pre-agricultural level of technology and extremely low levels of literacy. So far, 75 PTGs have been identified. In order to give more focused attention to the development of Scheduled Tribes, a separate Ministry, carved out of the Ministry of Social Justice and Empowerment, known as the Ministry of Tribal Affairs was constituted in October 1999. This is the nodal ministry for overall development of Scheduled Tribes. The mandate of the Ministry includes social security and social insurance with respect to the Scheduled Tribes, tribal welfare planning, project formulation, research and training, promotion and development of voluntary efforts on tribal welfare and certain matters relating to administration of the Scheduled Areas. Ministry of Tribal Affairs supports and supplements the efforts of State Governments/UT Administrations and the various Central Ministries/Departments for the holistic development of these communities.

IV

Education of Scheduled Tribe Children

With education viewed as a crucial input for total development of tribal communities, elementary education has been made a priority area in the tribal Sub-Plans since the Fifth Five-Year Plan (1974–79). As a result, there have been marked improvements in access, and to some extent in quality of primary education in tribal areas. Education has recently witnessed a rapid transformation, particularly in the areas of access, pedagogic reform and community participation in tribal areas. Emphasis has been on improving access to elementary education through the schemes of alternative education, training of teachers, appointment of local teachers, adapting curriculum to their needs, and providing locally relevant teaching-learning materials to schools.

Owing to determined efforts of the government, the Gross Enrolment Ratio (GER) of ST children has increased considerably at elementary levels of education, even more as compared to their non-tribal counterparts. The GER of ST children at primary stage is 137 as against 116 of their non-tribal counterparts. Participation of these children is now more or less in proportion to their share in population at the elementary school level. Dropouts, though declining over the years, are significantly large at this level: the dropout rate of ST children at primary school level is 35.6 per cent as against 27 per cent of their non-tribal counterparts. The corresponding figures for elementary school stage are 55 per cent as against 40.06. The general factors responsible for the high rate of dropout among the ST are: teacher absenteeism, lack of adequate teaching-learning materials in schools, irregular supply of mid-day meal, lack of participation of Village Education Committees/School Monitoring Committees (VEC/SMC) in school programme and poverty, and illiteracy of parents. These findings have immense implications for designing education of the tribal children in the Tribal Sub-Plan (TSP) regions of the country. Most of the students, as they come from socio-economically disadvantaged communities like the Scheduled Castes and Scheduled Tribes, are scared of the teachers and do not find anything interesting to hold them on to the schools and gradually they start withdrawing from the schools.

Education continued to receive high priority in the Eleventh Plan to facilitate educational development among STs by providing educational facilities, incentives and support, especially focusing the ST girls. Some Special Schemes for the development of education amongst STs are: Post-Matric Scholarship (centrally sponsored scheme providing financial assistance to the Scheduled Tribe students pursuing higher education beyond matriculation levels); hostels for ST girls/boys (to facilitate ST students to continue their studies at distant places by extending hostel facilities); upgradation of merit of ST students (to upgrade the merit of Scheduled Tribe students in classes IX to XII by providing them with facilities for all round development through education in residential schools); free coaching for STs (in operation since the Sixth Five-Year Plan and provides free coaching to ST students to enhance their competitive capabilities to face various competitive examinations);

scholarships scheme of Top Class Education (launched in 2007–08 with the aim of promoting quality education amongst ST students); Ashram Schools (cover 22 States and 2 Union Territories and the objective is to promote and extend educational facilities to Scheduled Tribe students including PVTGs in tune with their social and cultural milieu); strengthening education among ST girls (the scheme of educational complexes in the low literacy pockets was revised in 2008–09 and renamed as strengthening education among ST girls in low literacy districts); Rajiv Gandhi National Fellowships (launched in 2005–06 as a special incentive to extend scholarships to ST students to pursue higher studies and research degrees); National Overseas Scholarship (launched in 1954–55 providing financial assistance to meritorious ST students for pursuing higher education abroad at the level of Masters and Ph.D); Tribal Research Institutes (there are 17 Tribal Research Institutes located in various states and UTs conducting relevant research, student surveys and training).

A number of development projects viz. industrial, power or irrigation facilities are to be set up in the tribal areas during the Twelfth Five-Year Plan period. Though these projects offer tremendous opportunities for the economic advancement for the tribal people living in these areas, very little of the benefits actually accrue to tribals due to lack of adequate and eligible candidates for the jobs created. Tribal youth must be equipped with necessary education and skill abilities to take advantage of job opportunities in their areas and elsewhere. Otherwise, the opportunities will go in favour of outsiders, leaving a feeling of deprivation and discontent among the tribal youth.

The current focus is to review the educational needs of *Scheduled Tribe* children in the schools in the country. Provision for quality education for these children through improvised pedagogy, mother tongue instruction, types of action plans for implementing multilingual education, contextualization of the content of the school text books, support materials required, provision for support materials in tribal dialects, contextualization of classroom transactions, integration of life skills with the curriculum, overall need for modification of pedagogic routines in tribal context, in-service teacher training programmes, etc. are some of the emerging issues that need urgent action in India. Various recent studies on education of tribal children (from the perspective of social inclusion) throw light on the poor state of affairs. A recent study on school management practices under SSA supported by European Union states in its report that the prescribed curriculum and related teaching learning material (TLM) are top-down in nature; do not create opportunities or the administrative space and scope for need-based development of material and need-based planning at the school level; inclusion of children in border areas and tribal/forest areas remains weak. Similarly, transition rates from primary to upper primary and secondary show significant dropout rates in case of marginalized sections and minority religions, and there are significant gender differences.

Literacy rates among ST children still lag behind in many states. Though decentralized community mobilization efforts have improved enrolment, this cannot be said for inclusion of the most deprived communities or social groups. The Constitution of India prohibits discrimination on grounds of race, religion, caste, sex or place of birth. It stands for equity and equality of opportunity in matters of public employment. Inequitable circumstances leading to socio-economic and educational deprivations have created imbalances in society and lack of resources has tended to make it remain backward. The Constitution has made provisions for certain safeguards (social, economic, educational, cultural, political, service) and protective measures to ensure all round development of weaker and disadvantaged sections. It also provides that States will promote educational and economic interests of weaker sections of society, in particular, to scheduled castes and tribes.

The National Policy on Education (1986, 1992) and its programme of action (1992), have identified special measures for fulfilling the constitutional commitments to Scheduled Tribes which include opening of primary schools, *Anganwadis,* non-formal and adult education centres, construction of school buildings in tribal areas, development of curricula and instructional materials in tribal languages so as to render tribal students switch over to regional languages in course of time. The priorities also include establishment of residential schools, formulation of incentive schemes and scholarships for higher education, and designing curriculum at all stages to create awareness of the rich cultural identity of tribal people and their enormous creative talent. Various short term and long term measures as indicated in the programme of action on National Policy of Education (1992) has been identified for this purpose. A number of welfare, administrative and educational provisions have been made to improve the situation in respect of scheduled tribe communities. Funds have also been earmarked for the educational upliftment of this group under various sub plans. The major programmes of elementary education viz. District Primary Educational Programme, *Sarva Siksha Abhiyan*, *Lok Jumbish*, *Shiksha Karmi*, Education Guarantee Scheme and Alternative and Innovative Education and the National Programme for Nutritional Support to Primary Education have accorded priority to areas with concentration of scheduled tribes.

The scheduled tribes deserve a high priority in any programme of education and the main reason is that a large majority of the tribal children who are not part of the formal system of education come from this group. The Working Group Report on Education of the disadvantaged sections during Tenth Five-Year Plan (2002–2007) brought out by the Ministry of Human Resource Development in November, 2001 has mentioned that 'despite the fact that there has been an increase in the literacy rate of the STs since independence, the present position is still far from satisfactory. The overall increase in the literacy rate in the country during the period 1961–91 was 28.19 per cent against which increase in literacy rate for Scheduled Castes and Scheduled Tribes during the same period was 21.07 respectively'. The situation in respect of these sections of people is still far from satisfactory and greater efforts are required to bring them on par with the general population.

The Tenth Five-Year Plan has also recognized the need for increasing their retention and reducing their dropout rate as one of the measures to empower them. Therefore, there is a need to identify issues, which need to be addressed through carefully devised methodology of teaching these children, so that they are in a position to derive full benefit from the education system. The National Curriculum Framework for School Education (NCF 2000 and 2005) recognized the need to respond to the specific educational needs of the learners from various sections of society by integrating socio-cultural perspectives in the educational programmes, partly by showing concern for linguistic and pedagogical requirement of socially disadvantaged groups. This is more relevant to scheduled tribes as they exhibit different culture and use different languages. Some of the languages do not have their own script and use scripts of other languages. India is a multicultural and multilingual society. Tribal population constituting 8.1 per cent of the total population comprises different social systems and dialects. Contextualization of curriculum and incorporation of fundamental rights of the disadvantaged groups are the right kind of steps to be taken up for promoting respect for all cultures, equity and democratic values.

The subject matter and pedagogy are the important components of tribal education. Tribal children bring with them rich experiences and perspectives of different cultures, which are different from other groups. This diversity is at times confused with multiculturalism. While diversity refers to individuals/ people that exemplify all cultural and congenial differences, multiculturalism means inclusion of theory, fact, values, and beliefs of all cultures. Therefore, the pedagogical strategies used for teaching in the tribal context ought to be different. There needs to be synchronization between school activities and lives of students contextualizing curriculum and its transactions by linking them with the experiences and skills of students.

A uniform teacher-training package is being used for teachers of both tribal and non-tribal areas. There is almost no emphasis on understanding psychology of children from tribal areas, their specific socio-cultural milieu, learning environment and the indigenous learning styles at home and community. Some of the training packages include a small module on tribal education, which often deals with macro issues mainly due to the paucity of time and space. The composition of Indian society calls for specific pedagogical inputs in teaching the tribal communities. This requirement is also supported by the recommendations of NCFSE 2000 and NCF 2005 which state that internationally, pedagogy is perceived not merely as a science of instruction but as a culture or as a set of sub-cultures as well, which reflect different contexts and different teaching behaviours – inside and outside the classrooms. The issues related with development of pedagogy of tribal education can be divided into six categories viz., medium of instruction; contextualizing textbook content and preparation of material; contextualizing curricular transaction; integrating life skills and entrepreneurship skills, information technology with curriculum; changing timings and holidays of tribal area schools and improving organizational climate in residential schools.

V

Pedagogical Requirements

Education through mother tongue has been emphasized both in the Kothari Commission Report (1964–66) and the National Policy on Education (1986, 1992) and its programme of action (1992). Various cognitive processes like perception, comprehension, responses and creative expression are maximally developed through the medium of mother tongue; the medium of instruction, therefore, ought to be the mother tongue of children enrolled in schools. Smooth transition from students' operations in the mother tongue to those in the regional language is to be ensured. The transition from mother tongue to regional language is very crucial to language learning. There is a need to take up studies on use of mother tongue as the medium of instruction in schools serving the tribal population.

In most of the states in India, tribal children have to learn from those text books which are being used for the non-tribal children of the state as a whole. The contents of these books deal with subjects/topics unknown to the tribal children. The tribal children, who live in isolated and remote villages, may not be able to identify themselves with these text books because of their urban-based non-tribal contents. Besides, the illustrations used in these text books are also from the world alien to tribal children. There is an imperative need that these text books are revised on a state-to-state and district-to-district basis so that necessary changes in them could be made to suit the socio-cultural and linguistic requirements of children from various tribal communities. At present, there is dearth of learning materials in the tribal dialects which is a strong factor contributing to high dropout rate of tribal children. Even the text books written in the regional languages do not permit the child to identify it with the content and its context. Besides the difference between the home language and the school language, non-inclusion of folk literature and culture specific stories, dialogues, etc. also hamper the interest of tribal children's learning.

There is a need to revise the prescribed text books on a state to state basis, which needs to be supplemented by development of culture specific material through District Institutes of Education and Training in collaboration with voluntary agencies working in the tribal areas. There is a need to develop specific support materials at the district and grassroots level to support learning by tribal children in their own mother tongue. Some concrete steps in this direction have been taken by states under SSA programme. Culture specific teaching-learning materials have been prepared by the state governments such as Gujarat, Himachal Pradesh, Maharashtra, Tamil Nadu, Uttar Pradesh, West Bengal, Bihar, Karnataka and Andhra Pradesh. This includes language books, glossaries, supplementary reading materials, bridge inventories, learning kits, etc. The *Anada Lahari* developed by the state of Andhra Pradesh under the *Janasala* programme is exemplary in this regard.

Formal schools often emphasize on discipline, routine norms and teacher centred instruction. This is a contradiction and poses problems to the free environment of tribal culture. This has led to sharp difference in the surrounding social environment of home and school. This difference in two environments is to a great extent responsible for high dropouts of tribal children from the school. This can be solved by the use of alternative teaching methods, taking into account the capacity of tribal children, availability of resources in tribal schools and the physical environment in schools. Teachers working in tribal schools are expected to know cultural values, practices, traditions and communication style of tribal children as well as the factors affecting their achievements in schools and learning difficulties. Adivasis lay a great emphasis on learning by memory because of their oral traditions. They are very fond of riddles and narratives of personal indulgences. All these issues are essential not only for a contextualized teaching-learning transaction but also for adopting appropriate evaluation procedures for the continuous and comprehensive evaluation of the tribal children in their environment.

One of the objectives of education for life is development of life skills relevant to the target group and their local contexts. These skills are basically local specific. These life skills are important for individuals to face challenges in their life. These life skills can be classified into four broad categories: universal life skills, teacher oriented life skills, student oriented and subject oriented life skills. Student oriented skills need to be addressed in the specific socio-cultural context of Adivasi children. Schools in tribal areas, due to their geographical isolation are deprived of emerging educational support systems. Education has to address both globalization and localization so that a balanced personality is developed. This task is more difficult in the tribal context where information technology facilities are very limited. It has also been advocated by many scholars and research studies that along with the academic studies, vocational training courses should also be part of the education system and curricular practices of Adivasi children. At least a few hours in a day may be allocated for vocational training of Adivasi children in their schools.

In tribal areas there is a vast networking system of residential, welfare and ashram type of schools which have been established and functioning for the overall development of Adivasi children. These schools are under the management, supervision and control of tribal welfare departments and integrated tribal development agency organizations. Reports on functioning of these schools across the country reveal mixed stories. While some schools are effectively functioning, other schools have not exhibited satisfactory results due to variety of reasons. Insensitive nature of supervision, lack of effective monitoring system, teacher absenteeism, poor motivating factors and poor residential conditions in these schools have a potential bearing on the socio-cultural practices of the Adivasis. Teachers working in the tribal schools are generally not mentally geared towards serving tribal children. They perform sensitive activities like teaching in a mechanical and routine manner. It is important to develop a specific training component for teachers and wardens who work in tribal schools. Moreover, teachers need periodic motivational training and field placement to become familiar with home environment of children and also their psychology. Experts and field functionaries suggested a few measures for the betterment of the existing situations: a few more schools may be established and should be provided with necessary infrastructural facilities; free coaching centres should be opened in the tribal villages for the educated and unemployed youth, physical education should be improved and special training facilities should be provided to make them national and state level players; universalization of ICDS with secured *Anganwadi* workers; compulsory elementary education for PTG and Hill Tribes' children; reduction of dropout rate among PTG children; availability of Upper Primary and High Schools in hilly tribal villages; girl-child friendly toilets in tribal schools; strengthening of District Institutes of Teacher Education (DIETs) to ensure availability of local teachers who are able to teach in their mother tongue; Nagaland model for strengthening the system of governance in tribal schools; for migrant workers among the Adivasis' alternative schools/tent schools/mobile schools; Kasturba Gandhi Balika Vidyalayas for tribal girls and effective skill development norms for girl child's education in tribal villages; child survival and health issues affecting tribal children under the age of 18 need remedial action; tackling of high levels of malnutrition in tribal villages; access to public services (health, PDS, etc.) to be improvised.

VI

Systemic Issues

Children coming from ST groups sometimes do not have access to government schools on par with others. There are state-wise variations with regard to this issue. The attendance rates among these sections of children are uneven. There is a gap between attendance reported in school records and the number of children present on all working days in the schools. Children from extremely poor families, landless daily wage labourers, and seasonal migrants among the STs tend to miss school more often. Most importantly, girls from very poor families were irregular and many children from such families reach school very late. Adivasi children are often ridiculed and ignored by the teachers. The combination of being poor, first generation school goers, being absent frequently due to circumstances and compelling reasons, children are often ignored. Tapping of their full energies in the schools is not taking place.

Like in the case of scheduled caste children, it is observed that children from ST communities, regularly participate in the tasks that were assigned to them by the teachers in government institutions. Teachers decide the roles and tasks to be performed by ST students both in the classroom and around the school. These include routine duties like sweeping the playground, classrooms, toilets and the place where the mid-day meal is served. Children of Adivasi families drop out of schools in large numbers as compared to the children of forward sections. Their experiences in schools are not very positive and encouraging as they come from diverse social and poor background. The educational institutions, particularly, the Adivasi children attend are mostly the government run schools. It is an established fact that the quality provided in these schools is anything but satisfactory. There are significant variations in education among ST children.

In the states like Assam and Odisha the habitations/villages/blocks where the children of Adivasi groups reside are quite far off. Their children cannot attend the school due to the barriers of distance from their school to home. For example, Bodos, Karbis, Mishings and Chakmas in Assam live in remote areas where it is always difficult for children to commute the distance to school. As these communities live in distant habitations/villages, their children often go to schools that are fairly homogenous. The social norms in Indian society with regard to the treatment of Adivasis are by and large discriminatory. The availability of school buildings, toilets, bore well or hand pumps are not ensuring easy access for ST children. The status of working of such facilities needs to be identified. There is a huge gap existing between the availability of such infrastructure facilities and the conditions of its usage and usability. Building infrastructure in ST schools needs to be upgraded. Ashram/Tribal welfare/Residential/KGBV/Madrassa schools should be modernized.

The Adivasi communities have started playing a significant role in politics due to social mobilization in the last 2–3 decades. The educational attainments and status of some of the Adivasi groups are better when compared to OBC groups/forward sections where the community participation, assertive political movements, social mobilization and urban proximity are better. There are however, two constraints. Intense activity is confined to pockets where density of tribal population is high (like in Madhya Pradesh where land right movement of tribal families under the auspices of Ekta Parishad is of great contemporary relevance). When compared to the SCs and their assertive social movements, the tribal social activism is at a lower ebb, still.

VII

Systemic Reforms

SC/ST/OBC children often face coercive conditions in schools. Teachers make use of them for different purposes like fetching water, roll call sheets, attendance register, and for personal causes. These conditions are often retarding the interests of ST children in schools. In some schools the scholarships these children get or incentives they get are rebuked by the teachers in the school assembly and classrooms. Schools should have the ability to tap the energies of ST children.

Infrastructure facilities are another important concern in SC/ST/minority schools. The infrastructure facilities that are available in these schools are poor in almost all the states. There are inadequate classrooms for children. Usable toilets are almost absent. In fact, toilets are available in majority of the schools but their usage is very little. Serious attention should be paid to ensure that they are brought into serviceable conditions with running water facilities and cleaned regularly. Toilets should be girl-child friendly. Girls mostly from the poor sections are frequently asked to clean the toilets.

Teachers working in tribal schools are not well versed in local languages. Among the problems on education of tribal children, language is an important barrier. Medium of instruction is an important indicator for education of ST students. This needs to be explored in detail since a large number of studies have focused on this issue. For instance, in Assam the main medium of instruction is very different from the mother tongue of tea garden workers or of workers who come from Hindi speaking areas of the country. Similarly, in the border areas of Andhra Pradesh, the medium of instruction is different from the mother tongue of the Adivasi children. In Rajasthan, local dialects vary in each district and children may not be familiar with the standardized Hindi used in schools.

Discriminatory practices are in vogue in many schools where ST children are either assigned less important and menial tasks in the schools or used for personal errands of school teachers. The social discrimination is conspicuous by its presence in matters of fetching water and cleaning toilets. These are often assigned to children form ST or SC categories, whereas kids of forward castes get refined school routines like conduct of assembly, reading prayers and speaking on chosen subjects. It is a case of intellectual dishonesty and negation of knowledge-acquisition where learning tasks are often given to upper caste children and are denied to others. This social denial results in psychological aberrations and prone to develop introvert thinking among children drawn from those social rungs of society other than upper ones. In some states, most of the schools allow the forward caste children to eat, drink water and wash mid-day meal plates first (Rajasthan). Another humiliating example is a case where students from ST/SC categories are *given water*, but not allowed to *take water*. In addition, there is overwhelming evidence of gender as well as caste-based discrimination in practices around cleaning of toilets. Wherever toilets are being used, children clean them using water from the hand pump or tap.

There are no sporting facilities for children in the ST schools. Culture specific sports are not a priority in ST schools and children were seen playing with their friends. Their culture specific sports, games are losing sheen. Like sports facilities, libraries also are absent. Even if the schools had books, they were not given to the children. Library books are never allowed for ST children. Teachers do not allow borrowing of books for home work particularly to ST students because they are considered low caste people and likely to spoil the books.

ST students regularly complain of punishment in schools. Children are prone to verbal abuse with caste and community identity. Often ST children are being abused. Teachers often complain about the ban of all forms of corporal punishments. They feel that this ban is the main reason for lack of discipline among ST children in schools. It is generally observed that ST children are slapped in schools. In many places children report that physical punishment is very common. The disciplinary measures thrust upon ST children are severe and complex. The RTE Act notwithstanding, teachers and parents were quite vocal about the need for punishment. The verbal abuse using caste/community identity is sensitive to STs in several schools. The attitude towards girl ST students and the kind of punishment meted out to them is very severe. After puberty, touching the girls is a taboo and therefore in some schools teachers resort to scolding the girls. Some schools report sexual violence on girls.

The mid-day meal (MDM) is one area which needs special attention. Social and community prejudices invariably surfaced in recent times. The cooks appointed in Adivasi schools are mostly from other caste category where there is every possibility that their performance is too poor. The seating arrangements for eating the food and access to water for cleaning the plates are poor. In almost all the states, ST children are attracted towards mid-day meals. Children from forward sections generally go home for lunch. The food items in ST schools are prepared and served by non-ST staff. Therefore, ST children do not prefer to take mid-day meals (for example, *Gondi* and *Sugali* communities). The adolescent girls due to several constraints are not able to eat mid-day meals. The ST children are observed sitting in their own community groups. Children are separated based on gender, caste, sect and community.

In schools at least three seating arrangements are practised. The brightest/most active/disciplined students are allowed to sit in the front rows. Academic performance of children matters much. They get their role numbers according to the academic performance. Normally, ST students were asked to sit at the back. Children from the forward sections even if their performance is found defective, would be allowed to sit in front rows. In most of classroom activities, it is observed by researchers that teachers attribute the poor performance of ST children to lack of interest towards the education. Majority of upper caste teachers exhibit a strong bias against ST students and brand them as underachievers/poor performers. Only a few teachers encourage ST children to develop academically and perform equally with other category children. Majority of the teachers are of the opinion that ST children's parents are often not educated and they eventually drag their children out of school and do not ensure regular attendance. In most instances, parents are by and large unaware of what is happening inside the schools and the condition of their children. Parents have nothing to say about what their children learn and do in the school. They believe that everything is quite alright. Awareness levels with regard to the benefits of education are very little. They do not expect much to happen in schools due to their constant fight for their survival. There is common perception that ST children do not perform better in schools. Interestingly, school records in some places reveal that academically these children perform better than many others. There is a distinction between the teachers' perception and reality. The teachers have their own prejudices and traditional stereotypes about the academic achievements and attainments of ST children.

Ensuring teacher regularity in ST schools needs a mention and attention of those concerned. One of the biggest challenges that needs to be tackled is the availability of adequate number of teachers to cater to various needs of ST children. There is acute shortage of teachers at all levels. Majority of teachers are not present in schools on every working day and do not come to school even though they are appointed on permanent basis. In some schools, contract teachers are being appointed who do not show serious interest in the quality education of children. Para teachers, contract teachers are not paid regularly. Community participation in ST schools is an important concern for promoting quality education for ST children. Another important aspect is the presence and functioning of School Management Committees (SMCs) or the Village

Education Committees have not been very effective to ensure involvement of parents, especially from the most backward communities. Majority of them admit that their voices are rarely heard and have no opportunity to participate regularly in school-level committee meetings. Both RTI and RTE should be linked to ST schools as RTI will supplement its strength to RTE. The qualification norms of teachers should be adhered to RTE norms for ST schools.

There is a need to study, understand and identify good school practices towards ST children with regard to their education. Some schools are following inclusive and positive practices in their classrooms. But these inclusive practices are very few and need further elaboration. There are a few initiatives launched by central and state governments for SCs like Tola Sewak (a volunteer in a village or habitation can take the responsibilities of getting children to school and interacting with them in school – practiced in Bihar) and Hunar programme for promoting and encouraging education for poor and marginalized sections. Such programmes need more attention and further extension to cover ST children.

It is important that the specific needs of special and needy children among ST groups are given separate focus. In majority of the cases such children are not included in the school system. The SSA framework clearly mentions that children with special needs should be provided education in an appropriate environment. They should not be left out of the education system. Child friendly infrastructure, positive and supportive attitude of the teachers and students, providing ramps and child friendly toilets form some important and immediate concerns.

Education of children of the Nomadic, Semi-Nomadic and Denotified Communities (NT/SNT/DNT) is a very important concern of the government. Despite provision for local habitation schools and mid-day meal, attendance was still not satisfactory and cherished results have not been achieved in the standards of education. The educational problems concerning these children should be tackled by the apex educational organizations as a part of their extension programmes. There is a need to study the educational pattern available to these children with a view to improving the achievement levels. The main focus should be to examine to what extent education has spread among these tribes in India. There is a strong objection raised regarding the pathetic conditions of education and educational institutions prevailing in the settlement schools. There are social and behavioural changes taking place among the members of the NT/SNT/DNT tribal settlement areas in India. The settlements in various states in the country constitute a major segment of the total scheduled tribe population in the country. In all these settlements NT/SNT/DNT tribes form a major part of population. Some of the settlers still suffer from problems of crime and illiteracy. One of the main problems identified by the field experiences and the field surveys is about the social treatment meted out to the families of these tribes. For generations together, the families and their members have been labelled as criminals, suffered dishonour and social negligence. The reasons are not far to seek, given the background of the socially despicable avocation as practised by some of the people belonging to these tribes. The children and women, in particular, have suffered ignominy from mainstream society.

The stigma of criminality is still one of the major impediments in the smooth run of educational progress of children and youth. Children often faced a kind of social alienation in most of the walks of social life. Social alienation particularly in young age hampers the growth of psycho-social faculties of the children. Social practices of the mainstream society have denied opportunities for the children coming from the so-called criminal families residing in the settlement areas. The approaches of the government often times remain impersonal with lack of human element in its approach. The school or the process of schooling in settlement areas or settlement schools may be used as instruments or tools to impart social culture, feelings of common fraternity, community approach, adjustment mentality, atmosphere of working and learning together and finally moral dynamics of social and cultural behaviour. The schools in settlement areas are to be treated or perceived from a different angle where they are expected to combine the role of an instructor and change agents. There is a need to conduct several qualitative and quantitative research studies in ST schools to capture the reality of conditions persisting in schools: gender equality, social equity dimensions, practices of social discrimination within the schools, classrooms and daily experiences. Modernization of these institutions with culture specific education is an urgent task. Any violation of the rights of ST children is a violation of their rights to equality, social justice and right against all forms of discrimination. Quality education should be provided to teachers working with ST children to attend to the needs of such children. Pedagogical and curricular issues need specific focus and attention so as to address the emerging issues in their proper social and cultural context.

VIII

Conclusion

Although school coverage has increased, STs continue to lag far behind the rest of the population. To deal with the low levels of literacy among tribals and to bridge the gap between dropout rates between tribals and non-tribals, there is a need to focus on elementary education. Therefore, there is a need to start a scheme of Pre-Matric Scholarship for all ST children across the country. The objectives of the proposed scheme are to support parents of ST children so that the incidence of dropout would reduce. There are strong recommendations for the scheme's continuance in the Twelfth Five-Year Plan that are tuned to the changing times. Some important recommendations are: the rates of scholarship and income ceiling should be revised at regular intervals in line with the price index; possibility of paying college fees directly should be explored; scholarships to students (day scholars or hostellers) should be paid on a monthly basis; it would be desirable that 100 per cent grant-in-aid is given for establishment of Ashram schools and hostels for ST Boys even in the non-Naxal areas; qualified teachers belonging to the local tribal communities should be trained and placed in position as teachers in Ashram schools; increase in the number of scholarships from 667 to 1,000 under Rajiv Gandhi National Fellowship Scheme; number of scholarship awards may be enhanced under National Overseas Scholarship (NOS), etc.

Education is the single most important means by which individuals and society can improve personal endowments, build capacity levels, overcome barriers, and expand opportunities for a sustained improvement in their well-being. In the context of education of ST children, finding a balance between preserving their cultural identity and mainstreaming for economic prosperity seems crucial. Recognizing that the education system is currently designed for the dominant group, there needs to be investment in creating support mechanisms that supplement the integration of the marginalized children into the formal education system. Some of the contemplated measures in this regard are: using both tribal and state languages during the pre-primary and primary levels; creating supplementary learning materials relevant to ST children; introducing monetary/non-monetary incentives for teachers in tribal areas; addressing the health and nutritional needs of children; improving community participation by training teachers and youth as peer educators; establishing and strengthening transitional education centres which focus on mainstreaming marginalized children and creating seasonal hostels and residential schools for children of migratory parents. These support mechanisms are expected to address some of the issues facing these children inside the classroom. However, it is evident that there needs to be more philanthropic investment in building community cultural wealth outside the classroom too. This would provide a solid foundation that leverages these assets and develops stronger individual potential that can transcend the barriers experienced by marginalized today.

References

Beteille, Andre, 'Access to Education', *Economic and Political Weekly*, Vol. XLIII, No. 20, 17–23 May 2008, pp. 40–48.

Annei, Zaidi, 'Death by Hunger, Malnutrition Deaths of Children in a Tribal Hamlet Point to the General State of Welfare Programmes in Madhya Pradesh', *Frontline*, Vol. 22, No. 9, 23 April–6 May 2005, pp. 49–52.

Banerjee, Sumanta, 'On the Naxalite Movement: A Report with a Difference', *Economic and Political Weekly*, Vol. XLIII, No. 21, 24–30 May 2008, pp. 10–12.

Barnhardt, Ray and Barbara Harrison, 'Developing Tribal Education Strategies in Indigenous Communities', *The Australian Journal of Educational Studies*, October 1993, pp. 1–15.

Das Gupta, K. Biman and Ajit K. Danda, *Tribal Education in India in Retrospect*, Anthropological Survey of India, Calcutta, 1984.

Das, A.R., R.V.K. Naidu and N. Sreedhar, 'Ashram Schools and the Education of Tribal Children', *Man and Life*, Vol. 29, No. 1–2, 2003, pp. 83–94.

Dreze, Jean and Amartya Sen, 'Basic Education as a Political Issue', *Journal of Educational Planning and Administration*, Vol. IX, No. 1, 1995, pp. 1–26.

Gandhi, Malli and V. Lalitha, *Educating Tribal Children: Issues, Concerns and Remedies*, Serials Publishers, New Delhi, 2014.

Gandhi, Malli, 'Educational Status of Denotified Tribes in Andhra Pradesh: Attainments and Challenges', *Journal of Rural Development*, Vol. 33, No. 2, 2014, pp. 133–45.

——, *A Study of Factors Affecting Students' Achievements in Primary Schools of Nomadic/Denotified Tribal Settlement Schools in Andhra Pradesh*, ERIC, Project Report, NCERT, 2006.

——, *Denotified Tribes: Retrospect and Prospect*, Manak Publishers, Delhi, 2014.

George, Kent, 'ICDS Steering an Ungainly Ship', *Economic and Political Weekly*, Vol. XLVII, No. 37, 2012, pp. 32–35.

Ghatage, B.S., *Nomadic Tribes and Social Work in India*, Shruti Publications, Jaipur, 2006.

Gnanasundaram, V., 'Use of Tribal Languages in Education' (Seminar Paper), Indian Social Science Congress, Baroda, 12–16 November 1994.

Kingdon, Geetha Gandhi and Vandana Sipahimalini Rao, 'Para Teachers in India: Status and Impact', *Economic and Political Weekly*, Vol. XLV, No. 12, 20 March 2010, pp. 59–67.

Krishnan, P.S., 'Contradiction between India's National Aspirations and Neglect of Constitutionally Mandated Rights of Scheduled Castes, Scheduled Tribes and Backward Classes: Can Indian Society and Teachers Take the Challenge to Bridge the Gap?', Gijubhai Badeka Fourth Memorial Lecture, Asian College of Journalism, Chennai, 2011.

Kundu, M., *Tribal Education: New Perspectives*, Gyan Publishing House, New Delhi, 1994.

Lakshmaiah, T., 'Education and Social Change: A Case Study of Tribal Students', *Man in India*, Vol. 71, No. 4, 1991, pp. 587–99.

Lotz, Barbara, 'Promoting Tribal Languages in Education: A Case Study of Santali in Orissa', *Journal of Social Science*, Vol. 8, No. 2, 2004, pp. 129–42.

Malhotra, O.P., *Tribal Education: Impact of Education on Tribal Life and Adjustment*, Cosmo Publications, New Delhi, 1998.

Mandal, Pushpa, *Ashram Schools in Action*, Rajat Publications, New Delhi, 2000.

Mathur, N.N.G., *Problems of Tribal Education: Past, Present and Future*, Shiva Publications, Udaipur, 1994.

Mishra, B.C. and Alhadim Dhar, *Ashram Schools in India: Problems and Prospects*, Discovery Publishing House, New Delhi, 2005.

Nambissan, B. Geetha, 'Language and Schooling of Tribal Children', *Economic and Political Weekly*, 15 October 1994, pp. 2747–54.

Patel, Srisha, *Tribal Education in India*, Mittal Publications, New Delhi, 1991.

Purnima, S. Tripathi, 'Sacrificial Lambs', *Frontline*, Vol. 28, No. 12, 4–17 June 2011, pp. 126–32.

Rani, Midatala, *Tribal Education*, Kanishka Publishers and Distributors, New Delhi, 2010.

——, *Tribal Education: A Status Study of Functioning of Ashram Schools in Karnataka*, Serials Publishers, New Delhi, 2014.

Rath, R.N., 'Impact of Education in Modernising the Tribals', *New Frontiers in Education*, Vol. 33, No. 1, 2003, pp. 58–62.

Sharma, Raj Khem, 'Educational Lifestyles of Tribal Students', *The Indian Journal of Social Work*, Vol. LI, No. 3, July 1990, pp. 457–72.

Sujatha, K., 'Education in Ashram Schools: A Case of Andhra Pradesh' (Occasional Paper), NIEPA, New Delhi, 1990.

——, *Educational Development among Tribes*, South Asian Publishers, Delhi, 1994.

——, *Gramina Vidhya Vikas Kendras: A Study of Single Teacher Schools in Tribal Areas in Andhra Pradesh*, Vikas Publishing House, New Delhi, 1993.

UNESCO, *First Language First: Community Based Literacy Programmes for Minority Language Contexts in Asia*, United Nations Educational, Scientific and Cultural Organisation, UNESCO, Bangkok, 2005.

UNESCO, UNICEF, CIIL, NCERT, *India Workshop on Multilingual Education with Special Focus on Tribal Education*, CIIL, Mysore, 25–27 October 2005.

Venkata Rao, P., 'New Education Policy: Implications for Scheduled Tribes and Scheduled Castes', in M.K. Rao and P.P. Sharma (eds), *Human Resource Development for Rural Development*, Himalaya Publishing House, Bombay, 1989.

13

Human Rights of Scheduled Tribes

Issues and Challenges

When we speak of the human rights of SCs, STs and BCs or of Dalit human rights, we must be clear about what their human rights are which need to be protected, supported, promoted and enhanced. Their human rights arise from what they have been illegitimately denied all through history. Their human rights have two sources of legitimacy. One is the philosophical concept of the rights that inhere in every individual by virtue of his being born as a human being. The other source of legitimacy relevant directly to India is the Constitution of India, which is unique among the world, for the emphasis it has placed on the rights of SCs, STs, BCs, women, children, labourers and other weaker sections. Its very Preamble which is recognized as the key to the Constitution, spells out four basic principles that underlie this Constitution and commits the people of India and the State established by them to secure for its citizens: Justice, Liberty, Equality and Fraternity. First and foremost of these four foundational principles is Justice. Another is Equality, followed by Fraternity. These are not left as empty words free to be interpreted by each. Each of them has been spelt out clearly. Justice is social, economic and political. Of these, Social Justice is of special significance for the SCs, STs and BCs, as explained below. Equality is spelt out as Equality of status and Equality of opportunity. Equality of status harks back to the past and the correction is required therein. Equality of Opportunity refers to the future. The SCs, STs and BCs have suffered inequality of status in different ways and in different degrees. Therefore, equality of status, correcting the historical asymmetry is significant for them. But equality of status will only correct the past. The future depends on equality of opportunity, which has been denied to these three categories in different ways and in different degrees, by various means like denial of land/equal share of land and other resources and denial of access to education. Therefore, equality of opportunity is of practical significance for them. Fraternity places emphasis on the dignity of the individual. The caste system, which was and continues to be a mechanism to facilitate the monopolization of resources and advantages by limited sections of the society and imposition of labour and inferior services on different sections of the majority of the population, also negated the dignity of individuals belonging to the latter. The extreme manifestation of this denial of dignity is 'untouchability' suffered by SCs. There are different degrees and forms of denial of dignity short of 'Untouchability' which the masses of the other two categories have suffered through the operation of the Caste System. Therefore, social justice, social equality and social dignity are important aspects of human rights in India as laid down by the Constitution and these are of greatest significance for the victims of the traditional social order.

I

The term 'Social Justice', which is highly evocative and comprehensive, needs to be clearly understood. It is often taken by educated people of metropolitan India to pertain to matters like prevention of premature marriage, abolition of evil customs like dowry, sati, promotion of widow remarriage, etc. While these have their own significance, in the Indian context and in the context of SCs, STs and BCs, social justice is a much more comprehensive concept embracing economic liberation (being agricultural wage-labourers in rural India and casual wage labourers in urban India, as the largest proportion of SC workers are, is not economic freedom), educational parity with advanced castes at all stages and levels of education, social dignity and real equality of opportunity in all fields at all levels for SCs, STs and BCs including Minorities belonging to these three categories (SCRM, STRM, BCRM). Social justice involves justice for those categories of people who have been denied justice by the inherited social system of India. The denial of justice to them permeates all aspects of life, economic, educational, cultural and even socio-linguistic. Similarly, social equality which is related to equality of status requires equalization of the deprived classes, in units of castes, tribes, communities and other social groups, with the advanced classes in all parameters of life and existence, economic, educational, cultural and in terms of living conditions and real opportunities of life. Only when social justice and social equality are ensured in this comprehensive form covering all aspects of life can we establish a regime of equality in the nation as mandated by the Constitution in a rich profusion of Articles which expand and specify the concept of social justice and social equality. These Articles constitute an integrated whole; they constitute a noble moral edifice, carefully designed and crafted by Dr Babasaheb Ambedkar, within the grand mansion of our Constitution, and this edifice in particular owes its origin to Dr Ambedkar and the principles he espoused and relentlessly struggled for. What are the human and constitutional rights of the SCs, STs and BCs? These and the road-map of comprehensive social justice action required to fulfil these rights have been systematically listed out in a number of documents, which provide a clear road-map for comprehensive Social Justice action (not Affirmative Action, a pale American concept not relevant to Indian in the context of its full-blooded Constitution). This journey of detailed exploration and mapping of the road started with the Report of the Planning Commission's Working Group on the Development of Scheduled Castes in the Sixth Plan 1980–85, the first such Working Group for SCs. Its report of September 1980, is a landmark in the history of Indian planning. There was a similar Working Group report for STs, also in 1980. These were followed by reports of subsequent Working Groups for SCs and STs before each Plan which have broadly traversed the same path as the first two Working Group reports of 1980. This task in respect of BCs has been performed by the Report of the Working Group on Empowerment of BCs in the X Plan (2001), the first such Working Group for BCs. The first document in the public domain in the post-Ambedkar period, which lays the road-map of comprehensive action of Social Justice for SC, ST and BC was the Dalit Manifesto (DM) incorporating the 'Rights and Entitlements of Scheduled Castes, Scheduled Tribes & Backward Classes', formulated under the auspices of the National Action Forum for Social Justice (NAFFSJ) and released on 7 March 1996. This was followed by the following documents: (a) the Memorandum of the Parliamentary Form of SC and ST MPs to Prime Minister dated 17 December, 1996 (and presented subsequently to two successive Prime Ministers), which was based on the DM; (b) recommendations of the Drafting Committee of the All Party SC and ST leaders prepared at the end of the Government-sponsored Convention on 5–7 December 1999; (c) White Paper of the First National Convention of the SC and ST Forum of the Indian National Congress (20 January 2000) which followed the DM; (d) the Expanded White Paper (30 January 2000), based on discussions at the National Convention, the preparation of which was entrusted to P.S. Krishnan by that Convention; (e) Chapter 10 of the Report of the National Commission for Review of the Working of the Constitution (2002) read with its Background Note, the preparation of which was entrusted to P.S. Krishnan by that Commission; (f) the Reports of the Planning Commission's Working Groups on the Empowerment of BCs in the Twelfth Plan (1997) and in the Tenth Plan (2001), both under the chairmanship of P.S. Krishnan, which were the first Working Groups for the BCs; (g) the Himalaya Proclamation of Rights and Entitlements of SCs, STs and BCs including BCRM dated 17 April 2005, issued from Dehradun, which was formulated, under the aegis of the NAFSJ; (h) the Draft Common Minimum Programme, 2009 in Respect of SCs, STs and BCs (DCMP), formulated by P.S. Krishnan on behalf of and in consultation with a number of Dalit, BC, women and human rights organizations including the NAFSJ; (i) the Report (2011) of the Planning Commission's and Ministry of Social Justice & Empowerment's Sub-Group-I on Perspective Planning for Empowerment of SCs during the Twelfth Five-Year Plan. These documents, broadly traversing the same path, provide a clear road-map to a sincere government which wants to find a permanent solution to the Indian socio-economic structural and systemic deadlock, rooted in the Indian caste system and to a wise civil society which seeks to actively work for the upliftment of poorer sections of Indian society.

II

Basic Human Rights of Scheduled Tribes

Economic liberation, educational parity at all levels and stages of education, equality with the Socially Advanced Castes (SACs), i.e. non-SC, non-ST, non-BC castes (NSCTBC) in all parameters, i.e. economic, occupational, educational, residential, health and nutrition related, social dignity are the basic human rights of STs as it is for SCs. In addition, preservation of tribal identity, tribal autonomy and tribal culture including preservation and promotion of tribal languages also are part of the basic human rights of STs. But in order to achieve this basic human rights, a number of specific measures need to be taken. These are also the human rights of STs.

Economic Liberation

A comprehensive National Programme of Minor Irrigation, i.e. irrigation for all irrigable but unirrigated lands held by STs, through wells, community wells, bore wells, community bore wells, tubewells and community tubewells, bandheras, check dams, lift irrigation and other such minor irrigation sources for exploitation of surface or ground water or both conjointly according to the choice of the individuals or groups concerned, based on the ground reality and local situation, should be launched with full financial provisions and organizational arrangements at Central Government, State Government and at local levels. The farming of the lands of STs will become more viable. They will also have other benefits like improved nutrition, health, school enrolment and retention. This will also reduce their compulsion to move to other places for agricultural wage-labour and other labour, disrupting family life and dislocating children's education. Historically, tribals are not a landless class like the SCs. They have been individually or collectively, owners/possessors of lands in tribal areas. But, there has been a continuing erosion of their lands. In view of this, the following measures are necessary: lands in tribal areas which are in the illegal ownership/*benami* ownership/occupation/possession of non-tribals, whether through purchase/benami purchase/lease/ mortgage/ without any formal process, should be fully restored to STs and further loss of tribal lands prevented. Scheduled Tribes Land Transfer regulations/ legislations prohibiting such ownership/occupation/possession of tribal lands by non-tirbals should be fully implemented. Such regulations/legislations existing in different States should be strengthened to plug all loopholes which are exploited by persons belonging to powerful and dominant communities who buy/occupy/possess tribal lands. In States where no such regulations/legislations exist, such Regulations/ legislations should be enacted. The Task Force Approach should be adopted for restoration of tribal lands. An empowered Task Force consisting of a Tehsildar/Mamladar, a surveyor and, where necessary, a police officer, should go village by village and thoroughly implement the restoration of tribal lands of tribals. Though STs are historically not a landless class, by the process of the gradual erosion of their lands, many STs have been reduced to landless agricultural labourers. Many ST families in non-tribal areas are also agricultural labourers. Therefore, every such landless rural family of ST should be endowed with adequate agricultural land through proper implementation of land ceiling and redistribution legislations; with equal focus on women by means such issue of *pattas/*grant deeds jointly in the names of the male and female heads of the family, in the name of the women in the case of woman-headed family, etc. full and sincere implementation of unimplemented Supreme Court judgments; distribution of assessed and unassessed waste lands/*gair mazaruva* lands, allotment of *bhoodan* lands; ensuring actual occupation and peaceful and undisturbed possession, by the ST allottees, of lands allotted to them; with full financial provisions with special preference for women and organizational arrangements at all levels for development of such lands through irrigation under the national programme of minor irrigation mentioned above. In the non-tribal areas the Task Force recommended for SCs can attend to the work of STs also. In the tribal areas the Task Force for STs can be entrusted with the work of providing lands for landless SC agricultural labour families. These three programmes are crucial to the economic liberation of STs and will contribute to their capacity to take advantage of various other developmental programmes in various fields to effectively close the gap between them and the advanced sections of society. Without these two programmes, the bulk of the ST population and families cannot be reached and their state of deprivation and vulnerability will continue, as in the centuries of our history and in the decades of Independence till now. The first of these programmes is an unfulfilled commitment of the CMP, 2004 of the UPA Government. The third is a largely unfulfilled commitment of the national movement. The completion of these three programmes and fulfilment of their goals without further delay is an important human right of the rural masses of STs. Proper implementation of education and health measures should preclude the need for STs to sell their lands. However, despite this, there may be situations in which some STs may have to sell their lands. To meet this contingency without reducing the total ST land ownership, a Land Bank should be created for buying such lands from them at the market rate and making such lands available to other STs. It is now well-recognized that deprivation of STs of their lands by a macabre type of public-private partnership over the last many decades is a major underlying cause of Naxalite/Maoist insurgency in the tribal areas. This is a continuation of tribal revolts that used to take place in many tribal areas in the 18th and 19th centuries on account of deprivation of tribal lands by moneylenders, forest contractors, etc. who could secure the illegitimate support of the colonial government. This pre-colonial and post-colonial deprivation of tribal lands has to stop if India has to progress and be able to successfully face multiple threats. The STs who have migrated to ubran areas are mainly casual labourers in the urban unorganized sector in occupations like rickshaw-pullers and drivers, autorickshaw drivers, etc. It is their human right to be transformed into owners of the instruments of their labour through legislative/executive and financial measures.

Educational Parity at all Levels

The next important area of the needs and rights of STs is educational parity at all levels. There are two specific programmes of significance pertaining to this right:

High Quality Residential Schools for ST Children

Residential schools of high quality from Class–VI to XII, including ITI-type institutions, should be established in every district, one each for ST girls and ST boys – 75 per cent of the seats should be for children of the ST category and the remaining 25 per cent will be for children of other deprived categories and poor children of non-deprived social categories, and subsequently such residential schools should be established at different sub-district levels until all ST children in the country are covered with high-quality school education. This programme will widen the educational base of STs from school level upwards, laying the foundation for the enhancement of their capacity to fill all reserved seats and to secure some merit seats.

Educational Equalization at all Levels, especially Higher and Professional Education with Focus on Women

Every ST hamlet should be provided with an Anganwadi Centre (AWC) with a qualified teacher, trained in Montessori and other such methods. For this purpose, training institutions will have to be opened in large numbers for preparing a few lakhs of pre-school education trained teachers. They should be paid remuneration at rates prevalent in good pre-school institutions so that competent teachers are attracted to the Anganwadi-based institutions. Early childhood education or pre-school education should thus be made available to all ST children, as is available for children of well-to-do families and in essentially the same quality. Reservation/reservation-equivalent share should be made available for ST students in all good educational institutions of all types, including professional institutions, at all levels, Indian and foreign, at government cost. As part of the above measure, a Bill to be known as 'The Private Educational Institutions (Reservation in Admissions) Bill, 2009' providing reservation for SC, ST and BC in private educational institutions, in continuation of the Central Educational Institutions (Reservation in Admissions) Act, 2006, Act No. 5, 2007 which provided reservation for SCs, STs and BCs in Government institutions, should be introduced in the Parliament at the earliest, thus fulfilling the purpose for which the 93rd Constitution Amendment Act inserting new clause (5) in Article 15 of the Constitution was enacted in 2005.

The Right of Children to Free and Compulsory Education

Free and Compulsory Education Act, 2009 (RTE Act) inter alia provides for 25 per cent quota for children of 'Disadvantaged Groups' and 'Weaker Sections' by Section 12(e) of the Act, but because of the loose definition of 'child belonging to disadvantaged group' and 'child belonging to weaker section' in Section 2 of the Act, it has been made possible for unaided schools to fulfil the 25 per cent quota stipulation without admitting a single SC, ST or BC student. Proposals to amend this Act with specific quotas of 8 per cent, 4 per cent and 10 per cent respectively for SC, ST and BC students within the 25 per cent quota for the weaker sections and disadvantaged groups have been made to the government by the Sub-Group–I on Perspective Planning for Empowerment of SCs during XII Plan and the Ministry of HRD's Task Force on Educational Developmental of SCs. The government should act on this proposal at the earliest. An Anti-Discrimination Act should be enacted in order to comprehensively and effectively address and deal with all forms discrimination, specific to educational institutions, harmonizing it with the Protection of Civil Rights Act, 1955 and the Scheduled Castes and Scheduled Tribes (Prevention of Atrocities) Act, 1989. The measures will help in bringing about educational equalization at all levels and will help in bringing about educational equalization in higher and professional education and will be a logical continuation of the earlier Act which provided reservation for SCs, STs and BCs in Government institutions and was upheld by the Supreme Court on 10 April 2008. The Sarva Shiksha Abhiyan and the Right to Education Act are welcome measures, but they are not by themselves adequate to remove the gap between the STs and the SACs/NSCTBCs. For removing the gap, the above measures are essential, along with the Sarva Shiksha Abhiyan and the Right to Education Act.

The Human Rights of STs to Social Dignity and Security

In tribal areas or scheduled areas, the contradiction is between the tribals trying to retain their lands and community rights to lands and other resources and non-tribals or non-tribal bodies of various types trying to dispossess the tribals. But, on account of their numerical majority in such areas, atrocities are not directly inflicted on them by powerful members of non-tribal society. Instead, they take recourse to misusing forest, police and other departmental personnel against tribes. Vachati in Dharmapuri district of Tamil Nadu is an illustration of this. In non-tribal areas, however, the vulnerability of STs to atrocities is similar to that of SCs. Protection against atrocities is a basic human right of STs, just as it is a basic human right of SCs. It is, therefore, essential to strengthen the SC and ST Prevention of Atrocities Act (POA Act), 1989 and its implementation by enactment of the comprehensive amendments to this Act and certain other Acts and implementation of measures recommended by a National Coalition of Dalit and Human Rights Organizations under the guidance of P.S. Krishnan as its Chief Advisor. This has been communicated to the leaders of the government of the past and present. Meanwhile, atrocities are continuing with impunity/virtual impunity/limited impunity. The government formulated its Bill in 2013 incorporating some of the provisions in the draft Bill communicated to it but diluting some others. This somewhat diluted Bill was, after a lot of avoidable delay, placed in the Lok Sabha in December 2013, but not moved for debate and voting. After tremendous efforts by P.S. Krishnan and Dalit activists an Ordinance, namely, the Scheduled Castes and the Scheduled Tribes Prevention of Atrocities, Amendment Ordinance was issued on 4 March 2014. A Bill to replace the

Ordinance was introduced in the Lok Sabha on 17 July 2014 but this was referred to a Standing Committee. The process should be completed urgently and this Bill enacted at the very next session. Among the provisions introduced in the Ordinance and the Bill under consideration is protection of victims, survivors and witnesses, so that the Kambalapalli debacle of Karnataka – typical example of numerous such instances – does not occur in future.

Developmental Autonomy, Relevant Planning Through Proper Formulation and Implementation of Tribal Sub-Plan (TSP) and Territorial Autonomy in Tribal Areas

For the revitalization of the Tribal Sub-Plan (TSP), the population-equivalent proportion of total plan outlay (5 year, Annual) of Centre and States should be set apart, as the corpus of TSP, before the Plan is allocated sector-wise and Ministry-wise, and planning and allocations for programmes and schemes relevant to STs primarily benefiting at micro economy level should be undertaken within this corpus, in accordance with the needs and priorities of STs in keeping with the overarching goals of their economic liberation, educational parity at all levels and social dignity. A network of new Institutions of Relevant Planning for ST should be established, consisting of National Development Council (NDC) for Development of ST; National ST Development Authority (NSTDA); State ST Development Authorities (SSTDAs); District ST Development Authorities (DSTDAs); the NSTDA and SSTDAs should be entrusted with the task of undertaking relevant planning for ST and formulation of TSPs of Centre and States, against the corpus of TSP, based on the needs and priorities of STs and with special attention to the needs and priorities of their women and their children, issue of sanctions to respective Ministries/Departments, concurrent monitoring, timely corrections, rectifications, evaluation, etc. The DSTDAs should be in charge of implementation and feedback reporting. Smooth and easy flow of adequate and timely credit for STs should be ensured as part of their development plans. TSP should be built into the credit system by earmarking STs a due share of advances by banks and co-operatives and loans from the IBRD (World Bank), ADB and other international agencies. This is an important aspect of developmental planning. TSP should be built into and provided in programmes and schemes of Panchayat and other local bodies. Funds released to them by Central and State Governments should earmark the share of STs as TSP. This will help close the gap in developmental planning for STs. Failure to institute this transparent system and methodology for the TSP has resulted in trivialization of this developmental Plan instrument and its reduction into superficial arithmetical-statistical gymnastics and sleights of hand, making no difference to the conditions of STs – of the type which has come into the open with a bang in Delhi, thanks to the large-scale diversion and misapplication of SCP to the Commonwealth Games-related projects with the Government trying to give untenable explanations showing ignorance of and indifference to the SCP and TSP and their purpose. In order to strengthen territorial autonomy of Scheduled Tribes, all areas under Fifth Schedule, which is too weak, should be converted into Sixth Schedule Areas, and all tribal areas which are at present neither included in the Fifth Schedule nor in the Sixth Schedule should be straightway brought under the purview of the Sixth Schedule, and Article 244(1) and 244(2) should be amended for this purpose. The Committee appointed to make recommendations on Extending Provisions of the Constitution 73rd Amendment Act, 1992 to Scheduled Areas (Bhuria Committee) has also made this recommendation in its Report of 2004.

Skill Development and Promotion of Entrepreneurship

In all beneficiary programmes like National Skill Development Mission and Promotion of Entrepreneurship, the principle of TSP should be introduced by earmarking the share of STs and unnecessary and unrealistic formal qualifications which result in keeping out the deserving will be avoided. For the aspiring youth of the STs, integrated measures on a single window basis to promote and sustain entrepreneurship among them is important. An opportunity has been thrown open by the reservation of 4 per cent of all Government purchases for SC and ST entrepreneurs by the Ministry of Micro, Small and Medium Enterprises. This is important for transferring large numbers of ST youth to dignified and productive sectors of employment and self-employment which will also strengthen the national economy and, therefore, has to be undertaken on a massive scale. Human right of STs for effective machinery for expeditious completion of the undiluted implementation of the Panchayats (Extension to Scheduled Areas) Act, 1996 and the Scheduled Tribes and Other Traditional Forest Dwellers (Recognition of Forest Rights) Act (FRA), 2006.

Strengthening and Implementation of Reservation of Posts and Services under the State

A leakage-proof 'Scheduled Castes and Scheduled Tribes (Reservation in Posts and Services) Bill' should be introduced in the Parliament providing reservation for SCs and STs at the existing rate of 7.5 per cent and 15 per cent in direct recruitments and population-equivalent proportion in promotions up to the highest levels, without any exemptions, exceptions and exclusions, as happened in the Bill of 2008, which will also contain provisions for *Arakshan Nyay Adalats* (Tribunals for Justice in Reservation) and their composition, penal provisions and machinery and mechanism for effective implementation, etc. This is necessary for removing loopholes and inadequacies in the present dispensation of reservation and fulfilment of the purpose of providing due share to STs and SCs in governance and administration. The pre-1997 Roster, distorted in 1997 by misinterpretation of the Supreme Court's Sabharwal Judgment, thereby reducing SC from point no. 1 down to 7 and ST from point no. 3 down to no.13 should be restored immediately through an executive order.

Clearance of Backlogs in Reservation for STs

A conclusive special drive should be launched and implemented to fill up backlog vacancies in reservation for STs, with the understanding that 'backlog' means the difference between the number of STs required in terms of the prescribed percentage of reservation in each cadre and the actual number of genuine STs present in each cadre. The drive should be undertaken with sincerity, clarity and determined meticulous planned operations and should be completed in three to five years for STs, so that at the end of the drive the percentage of STs in each cadre is equal to the prescribed percentages. Reservation for STs should be continued in disinvested PSUs and inclusion of this stipulation should be made in future as well as past MoUs. This is among the unfulfilled commitment of the CMP, 2004 of the UPA Government.

Human Right of STs for Due Presence in Judiciary

An All India Judicial Service should be created in accordance with Article 312 of the Constitution which will automatically contain in-built provision for reservation as in all other All India Services in accordance with the national policy. The Constitutional amendment and Bill for establishment of the National Judicial Appointments Commission passed by the Parliament on the 13th and 14th August 2014 contain a provision that one of the two eminent Members to be appointed to the Commission will be nominated from among the SCs, STs, BCs, Minorities or women. Qualified ST persons possessing deep knowledge of India's society and economy especially in the rural areas should be identified for appointment to the higher judiciary so that the present insignificant proportion of presence of these social categories is reasonably increased and thereby the benefit of wider and deeper knowledge of social realities becomes available in the dispensation of justice.

III

Human Right of Particularly Vulnerable Groups among STs for Development, Keeping in View their Special Situation and Greater Vulnerability

Human Right of STs for the total liberation and complete rehabilitation of *Safai* Karmacharis is another important aspect. There is a small percentage of STs pulled into manual-scavenging. Total Liberation and Complete Rehabilitation is a human right of this category of STs, however numerically small, as for SCs. Human Right of STs for Total Liberation and Complete Rehabilitation of Bonded Labourers. Next to SCs, the STs constitute the larger proportion of bonded labourers. In some states, STs are the major victims of bonded labour. Examples are Jharkhand, Odisha, Chattisgarh, West Bengal, Tamil Nadu. The Bonded Labour System (Abolition) Act should be thoroughly implemented and strengthened by including a provision to confiscate the property on which the bonded labourers are put to work and transfer such properties to the ownership of released bonded labourers. Human Rights of STs in employment, health security, children and girl child health, food security, comprehensive social security, etc. These should be secured by providing priority for the residents of ST hamlets in programmes for child survival and child health, girl child survival and health, location (example, Anganwadis) in or close to ST hamlets; priority in health and medical services to STs and various other measures. There has been a continuing tendency to include in the ST schedules, communities which do not fulfil the criteria to be recognized as STs and in some cases who are not even tribes. This is done for extraneous considerations like electoral considerations. By this the posts in the services, seats in educational institutions and other supporting measures which should be available for genuine STs are taken away by such communities wrongly included. This also contributes to tribal discontent with all its consequences. The prevention of this erroneous and unconstitutional practice and to reverse the wrong done in the past is a human right of genuine STs. The human rights movement in India should move forward focusing on the specific human rights of STs, along with those of SCs and BCs.

References

Government of India, *Interim Report of the Task Force on Educational Development of Scheduled Castes*, New Delhi, 2012.

Krishnan, P.S., 'Contradiction between India's National Aspirations and Neglect of Constitutionally-mandated Rights of Scheduled Castes, Scheduled Tribes and Backward Classes: Can Indian Society and Teachers Take the Challenge to Bridge the Gap?', Gijubhai Badekha Fourth Memorial Lecture, Asian College of Journalism, Chennai, 2010.

——, 'Pace of Socio-economic Change and Development', *The Report of the National Commission for Review of the Working of the Constitution*, 2002.

——, *Dalit Manifesto, Incorporating the Rights and Entitlements of Scheduled Castes, Scheduled Tribes and Backward Classes*, National Action Forum for Social Justice (NAFFSJ), 1996.

——, *Draft Common Minimum Programme, 2009 in Respect of SCs, STs and BCs*, New Delhi, 2009.

——, *Empowering Dalits for Empowering India: A Road Map*, Manak Publications, Delhi, 2009.

——, *Himalaya Proclamation of Rights and Entitlements of SCs, STs and BCs Including BCs of Religious Minorities*, National Action Forum for Social Justice and Empowerment (NAFFSJ), 2005.

——, *Report of Sub-Group-I on Perspective Planning for Empowerment of SCs during the XII Five Year Plan of the Working Group on Empowerment of Scheduled Castes during the XII Five Year Plan 2012–17*, Planning Commission, New Delhi, 2011.

——, *Report of the Working Group on Empowerment of Socially and Educationally Backward Classes in the Xth Plan*, Planning Commission, New Delhi, 2001.

——, *Report of the Working Group on the Development of Scheduled Castes in the VIth Plan 1980–85*, Planning Commission, New Delhi 1980.

——, *Report of the Working Group on the Empowerment of Socially and Educationally Backward Classes in the IXth Plan*, Planning Commission, New Delhi, 1997.

Appendices

Appendix I

Scheduled Tribes of Andhra Pradesh and Telangana

1	Andh, Sadhu Andh
2	Bagata
3	Bhil
4	Chenchu, Chenchwar
5	Gadaba, Bodo Gadaba, Gutob Gadaba, Kallayi Gadaba, Parangi Gadaba, Kathera Gadaba, Kapu Gadaba.
6	Gond, Naikpod, Raj Gond, Koitur.
7	Goudu (in the agency tracts)
8	Hill Reddy
9	Jatapus
10	Kammara
11	Kattunayakan
12	Kolam, Kolawar, Mannervarlu.
13	Konda Dora, Kubi.
14	Konda Kapu
15	Konda Reddi
16	Kondhs, Kodi, Kodhu, Desaya Kondhs, Dongria Kondhs, Kuttiy Kondhs, Tikiria Kondhs, Yenity Kondhs, Kuvinga.
17	Kotia, Bentho Oriya, Bartika, Dulia, Holva, Sanrona, Sidhopaiko.
18	Koya, Doli Koya, Guttu Koya, Kammara Koya, Oddi Koya, Pattidi Koya, Rajah, Rasha Koya, Lingadhari Koya (ordinary), Kottu Koya, Bhine Koya, Rajkoya
19	Kulia
20	Mali (excluding Adilabad, Hyderabad, Karimnagar, Khammam, Mahbubnagar, Medak, Nalgonda, Nizamabad and Warangal districts)
21	Manne Dhora
22	Mukha Dhora, Nooka Dhora
23	Nayak (in the agency tracts)
24	Pardhan
25	Porja, Parangiporja
26	Reddi Dhora
27	Rona, Rena
28	Savara, Kapu Savara, Maliya Savara, Khutto Savara
29	Sugali, Lambada, Banjara
30	Thoti (in the agency tracts – Adilabad, Hyderabad, Karimnagar, Khammam, Mahbubnagar, Medak, Nalgonda, Nizamabad, and Warangal districts)
31	Valmiki (in the agency tracts – Scheduled Areas of Visakhapatnam, Srikakulam, Vizianagaram, East Godavari and West Godavari districts)
32	Yanadi, Chella Yanadi, Kappala Yanadi, Manchi Yanadi, Reddi Yanadi
33	Yerukula, Koracha, Dabba Yerukala, Kunchapuri Yerukala, Uppu Yerukala, Nakkala, Kurvikaran
34	Dhulia, Paiko, Putiya (in the districts of Visakhapatnam and Vizianagaram)

Appendix II

Government of India/Bharat Sarkar Ministry of Home Affairs/Grih Mantralaya
North Block New Delhi/CS Division
New Delhi, the 1st April, 2010

OFFICE MEMORANDUM

Subject: Advisory on Crime against Scheduled Castes/Scheduled Tribes – Measures needed to curb – regarding

1. 'Police' and 'Public Order' are State subjects under the Seventh Schedule (List–II) to the Constitution of India and, therefore, the State Governments and UT Administrations are primarily responsible for prevention, detection, detection, registration, investigation and prosecution of all crimes within their jurisdiction including crimes against Scheduled Castes/Scheduled Tribes. The Union Government, however, attaches the highest importance to matters relating to the prevention of crime; and therefore, the Union Government has been advising the State Governments/UT Administrations from time to time to give more focused attention to the administration of the criminal justice system with emphasis on prevention and control of crime including crimes against Scheduled Castes/Scheduled Tribes.
2. The Government of India has been advising the State Governments from time to time regarding the steps that need to be taken to afford a greater measure of protection to the Scheduled Castes and Scheduled Tribes. The advisories issued earlier with particular reference to crimes against SCs/STs vide D.O letters No. 24013/86/97-GPA VI, dtd. 8.10.1997, No. 24013/47/98-GPA VI, dtd. 12.11.1998, No. 24013/74/2001-GPA VI, dtd. 19.9.2001, No. 24013/74/2001-GPA-VI dtd. 11.6.2002, No. 15011/50/2004-SC/ST Cell, dtd. 24.6.2004, letter No. 24024/9/2004-SC/ST Cell, dtd. 3.2.2005, No. 24013/30/2002-GPA VI, dtd 4.4.2006, No. 15018/20/2006-SC/ST Cell, dtd. 18.10.2006, No. 15011/36/2006-SC/ST-W, dated 1.02.2007 (HS's letter to 9 highest crime States), and Letter No. 24024/04/2005-SC/ST-W, dated 23.4.2007. (HS's letter on SC/ST Matters) may be referred to in this regards.
3. These advisories, inter-alia, include sensitization and training of the police personnel/law enforcement agencies; minimizing delays in investigation of cases of atrocities against SCs/STs and improving the quality of investigation; recruitment of sufficient number of persons belonging to SCs/STs/minorities as police personnel; programmes for creating awareness among vulnerable sections of the society and legal recourse open to them; adopting appropriate measures for swift and salutary punishment to public servants found guilty of neglect of duty and violence against SCs/STs; setting up of special courts; and improving the effectiveness of schemes developed for the welfare and rehabilitation of SCs/STs who are victims of crime.
4. Through the aforesaid advisories, the State Governments were also requested to undertake a comprehensive review of the effectiveness of the machinery in tackling the issues of SCs/STs and to take appropriate measures aimed at the increasing the responsiveness of the law enforcement/law and order machinery. No doubt, State Governments have taken some measures in this regard; however, the inputs regarding crimes against SCs/STs available with Governments have taken some measures in this regard; however, the inputs regarding crimes against SCs/STs available with Government of India indicate that these measures need to be strengthened further, so that scheduled Cases/Scheduled Tribes feel secure, enjoy their human rights and live their lives with dignity and respect that every citizen of India deserves. Despite several steps being taken by the State

Governments, the picture is still very grim and needs to be improved. Complaints are still being received regarding non-registration of FIRs and unsympathetic/insensitive attitude of some police personnel towards crimes against Scheduled Castes/Scheduled Tribes.

5. The National Commission for Scheduled Castes/Scheduled Tribes has undertaken visits to various States and UT Administrations to review the cases of atrocities against SCs/STs and has also conducted its own investigations in certain cases of serious incidents of crime against them. The Commission has made available the findings of the inquiries to the State Governments/Central Ministries concerned as well as to this Ministry. The reports of the inquiries conducted by the Commission in these specific incidents indicate that the sensitiveness and care with which crimes against SCs/STs should be handled is not up to the desired level. The Commission has pointed out laxity and insensitiveness on the part of certain police officials in some specific cases. The Commission has observed that non-filing of FIRs even in heinous cases continues to be a problem area. In its Fifth Report, titled 'Public Order' the Second Administrative Reforms Commission has also emphasized the need to combat crimes against vulnerable section of the society, particularly SCs/STs and has made a number of important recommendations.
6. The Government of India is deeply concerned with the trends in crimes against the weaker sections of society, particularly Scheduled Casts/Scheduled Tribes and would therefore, re-emphasize that urgent action should be taken by the State Governments and UN Administrations on the following:
   i Vigorous and conscientious enforcement of the statutory provision and the existing legislations relating to crimes against Scheduled Casts and Scheduled Tribes including the Protection of Civil Rights (PCR) Act, 1955 and the Scheduled Castes and Scheduled Tribes (Prevention of Atrocities) Act, 1989.
   ii Government must ensure proper enforcement of law and convictions in crimes committed against SCs/STs. Enforcement agencies should be instructed in unambiguous terms that enforcement of the rights of the weaker and vulnerable sections should not be downplayed for fear of further disturbances or retribution and adequate preparation should be made to face any such eventuality.
   iii The administration and police should play a more proactive role in detection and investigation of crimes against SCs/STs and ensure that there is no under reporting.
   iv Sensitizing the law enforcement machinery towards crimes against SCs/STs by way of well structured training programmes, meetings, conferences, workshops, seminars, etc. for police personnel and other law enforcement agencies at all levels as well as other functionaries of the criminal justice system. Such programmes should be incorporated in the syllabi of various Police Training Centres/Academies at all levels. Special training to police personnel in effective implementation of Scheduled Castes and Scheduled Tribes (POA) Act, 1989 and Protection of Civil Rights Act, 1955 should be imparted.
   v The Police officials should be directed to apply the appropriate sections of law as per the statements of the victims under the above mentioned Acts and no dilution should be tolerated to help the perpetrators of crimes against SCs/STs.
   vi Government must take concrete steps to increase the awareness in the administration in general and amongst the police personnel in particular,

regarding crimes against SCs/STs and take steps not only to tackle such crimes but also deal with them with sensitivity.

vii For improving general awareness about legislations on crimes against SCs/STs the department concerned of the State Government must, inter-alia, take the following steps:
Create awareness through print and electronic media;
Develop a community monitoring system to check cases of violence, abuse and exploitation and take necessary steps to curb the same;
Involve the Community at large in creating and spreading such awareness; and
Organize legal literacy and legal awareness camps.

viii Proper mechanisms must be put in place for safety and protection of SCs/STs.

ix Explore the possibility of associating NGOs working in the area of combating crimes against SCs/STs. Citizens groups and NGOs should be encouraged to raise awareness about these issues in society and help bring to light the cases of atrocities against SCs/STs and also assist the police in the investigation of crimes against them.

x There should be no delay in the registration of FIR in cases of crimes against SCs/STs.

xi Ensure proper supervisions at appropriate level of cases of crimes against SCs/STs from the recording of FIR to the disposal of the case by the competent court.

xii A separate review involving criminal cases filed by SCs/STs under investigation be conducted by the District Magistrate and District SP in the monthly meeting with I.Os to expedite investigation and guide timely collection of evidence.

xiii The authorities concerned in the State Governments must ensure proper follow up of reports of cases of atrocities against SCs/STs received from various sources, including the National Commission for SCs/STs.

xiv Atrocity-prone areas may be identified for taking preventive measures to save life and property of the members of the SC/ST communities Adequate number police personnel fully equipped with policing infrastructure should be posted in the Police Stations in such vulnerable areas.

xv In police stations located in areas with substantial population of SCs/STs proper representation must be given to SC/ST police personnel in postings to such police stations to gain the confidence of the SC/ST community.

xvi Delay in trial of cases of crimes against SCs/STs may be discussed on regular basis in the Monitoring Committee/monthly meetings Chaired by the District and Sessions Judge attended by District Magistrate, Superintendent of Police and Public Prosecutor of the district.

xvii The District SPs must ensure timely attendance and protection of all prosecution witnesses including Police officers and official witnesses for speedy trial of such cases in the trial courts.

xviii The State Government must ensure adequate measures for the economic and social rehabilitation of the victims of atrocities. The scale of relief to the family of a SC/ST person killed in cases of atrocity needs to be revised, particularly in cases where the deceased was an earning member of the family or physically fit to earn. The States which have not prescribed any scale of monetary relief and rehabilitation facilities to SC/ST victims of atrocities may do so without further delay.

xix For ensuring proper implementation of the Protection of Civil Rights (PCR) Act, 1955 and the Scheduled Castes and Scheduled Tribes (Prevention of Atrocities) Act, 1989 the State Governments and UT Administrations may conduct sample surveys/studies to evaluate the working of the PCRA and PAA with reference to the problems being faced by the police and the judiciary in prompt disposal of cases and take appropriate measures to resolve such problems.

xx In case of extreme violation of human dignity such as stripping of SC/ST women, forcing SC/ST persons to drink urine or eat human excreta, blackening their faces, shaving their heads and parading them in village streets, etc. the police must take prompt preventive action at the initial stage itself. In such incidents of extreme violation of human rights, exemplary punishment should be awarded to the accused after summary trial.

7. You are requested to kindly issue suitable directions to all concerned under intimation to this Ministry. It is further requested that action taken in this regard may be reviewed by the State Governments and UT administrations and a report indicating the present status of crimes against SCs/STs sent to this Ministry within a month.

The receipt of this letter may kindly be acknowledged immediately.

Yours faithfully, (Nirmaljeet Singh Kalsi) Joint Secretary to the Government of India Ministry of Home Affairs, North Block New Delhi 110 001 Tel. No. 23092630

To

1. The Chief Secretaries of all State Governments and UT Administrations
2. The Principal Secretary/Secretary (Home) of all State Governments and UT Administrations
3. Copy also for information and necessary action to:
   a. The DGs/IGs (In-charge of Prisons) – All Governments/UTs for information and necessary action
   b. Ministry of Social Justice and Empowerment, Shastri Bhawan, New Delhi
   c. Ministry of Women and Child Development, Shastri Bhawan, New Delhi
   d. Secretary, National Commission for SCs, 4, Deen Dayal Upadhyaya Marg, New Delhi 110 002
   e. JS (Judicial), JS(PM), JS(P-1), JS(P-11), JS(UT), JS(NM), JS(HR) in Ministry of Home Affairs, Government of India
   f. Director General, NCRB, RK Puram, New Delhi. (Nirmaljeet Singh Kalsi)

Joint Secretary to the Government of India.

Appendix III

Schemes and Programmes Required for Scheduled Castes (SCs) and Scheduled Tribes (STs) to Enable Them to Develop

***P.S. Krishnan**

I. Schemes for Economic Development and Empowerment of SCs and STs

1. (a) Land for All Rural Landless SC Families – and along with them, also for all rural landless agricultural labour ST families and all other rural landless and poor agricultural labour families

All rural SC families should be made owners of viable extents of agricultural land, by various means which have been made known to Government from time to time during the past decades, the latest being the Report of the Sub-Group–I on Perspective Planning (of which I was the Chairman) of the Planning Commission and Ministry of Social Justice & Empowerment's Working Group on Empowerment of SCs in the Twelfth Plan (hereafter referred to as Sub-Group–I Report). This will

- fulfil the promise of 'Land to the Tiller' of the pre-Independence nationalist movement for Independence,
- fulfil the undertaking in the Common Minimum Programme of the UPA, 2004 and
- fulfil the President of India's solemn commitment made in his first Address to Parliament on 7th June, 2004 after the Lok Sabha Election of 2004, wherein he had stated as follows: *'The Government will launch a comprehensive national programme for minor irrigation of lands owned by people belonging to the Scheduled Castes and Scheduled Tribes. Landless families will be endowed with land through implementation of land ceiling and redistribution legislation…'*
- Initiate and complete action on the decade-old Governors' Committee Report which has been put on the backburner.
- Initiate and complete action on the Report of the Group of Ministers on Dalit Affairs (2008) set up in 2005 under the Chairmanship of the then Finance Minister Shri Pranab Mukherjee, which is also consigned to the backburner.

To complete this long neglected and long-delayed task, essential for striking at the helplessness of SC families, the Task Force method suggested and detailed in the Sub-Group–1 Report referred to above should be adopted.

Briefly the Task Force method involves creation in each Block of a small group of empowered officers like a Tehsildar, a Surveyor and where necessary a police officer, with all functional facilities like a jeep, who will go to each village and provide land for every landless SC family by

(i) Giving *patta* to those landless SC families which are in occupation of Government land for cultivation;
(ii) Evicting ineligible occupants of Government land and giving patta with possession to landless SC families
(iii) Taking stock of all Government lands which can be straightaway assigned/allotted to landless SC families (locally called by names like Assessed Wastes, Gair-mazaruva-Aam), Bhoodan lands, etc.
(iv) Where publicly owned lands are not enough, by purchase of private land and land acquisition (for latter, a small amendment in the definition of public purpose in Land Acquisition, Rehabilitation and Resettlement Act, 2013 will be

required about which I am separately writing to Minister for Rural Development with copy and intimation to you)

Extremely important for SCs as they have historically emerged as a collectivity of castes prohibited from owning land and, therefore, even now the largest component of rural landless labour families.

Along with SCs, all rural ST agricultural labour families should also be provided.

Along with SCs and STs, all other landless poor agricultural labour families (who are mostly from the Socially and Educationally Backward Classes or BCs) should also be provided.

(b) *Irrigation for all Unirrigated but Irrigable Lands of SCs, and along with them also of STs*

This is also one of the undertakings in the UPA's CMP 2004 and one of the solemn commitments made by the President in his first Address to the Joint Session of Parliament on 7th June, 2004, but it is still unfulfilled. In fulfilment of this commitment, irrigation should be provided through common bore-wells, tube-wells, etc. for all unirrigated but irrigable lands of the SCs – the limited extent they have and the much more that needs to be made available to them as at 1(a) – and also lands of STs.

These two measures along with legislative and other measures for prevention of grabbing of SC lands by others will, at one stroke, enable rural SC families to

- become economically self-sufficient;
- liberate themselves from humiliating wage-labour,
- prevent exposure of their women to labour in others' fields and compulsion to fall back on child labour to supplement the meagre family income;
- improve nutrition, especially that of pregnant and lactating mothers and children, reduce birth underweight and child malnutrition, sharply reduce neonatal, infant and child mortality and release all their children to go to schools where they should be.

This will also

- enable them to resist 'Untouchability' without fear for the next meal (at present if they cross the line of 'Untouchability' or complain against illegal discrimination, they have to face social and economic boycott and sometimes even atrocities including massacres as in Kilvenmani, Tamil Nadu, Bathani Tola and Laxmanpur Bathe, both in Bihar, in all of which all the accused were acquitted, and numerous other instances in different States) and
- the additional production from their lands will remove all doubts and anxieties about adequacy of supplies of subsidized food under the recently enacted National Food Security Act, 2013.

There is sufficient number of successful examples of this transformation in parts of the country, but what is required is a nation-wide comprehensive programme which can be completed in a short period if the political and administrative heads of the Central and State Governments are determined and goal-oriented.

2. *Provision of Viable Assets for SCs in Urban Areas*

Most SCs in urban areas being casual labourers and in the unorganised sector, they should all be made owners of viable assets (in many cases, they are hired operators of other people's assets like rickshaws, auto-rickshaws, etc.)

E.g.: All hired pullers/drivers of rickshaws/autorickshaws can at one stroke be made their owners. There are many other instances of such possibilities.

Along with SCs, this can and should be done also for STs, BCs and BC Muslims who are causal labourers in the unorganised sector in the urban areas though not the same extent as SCs.

3. *Massive skill development programme along with all necessary resource-related, finance-related, management-related and market-related linkages*

By this programme, large numbers of SCs can move into modern market-oriented occupations for which there is large demand and need, like plumbing, electrical repairs, etc. This should be undertaken to cover all SCs who cannot be provided viable irrigated land or other independent viable assets despite all efforts as at 1 and 2 above.

The National Skill Development Mission established recently for coordination of all existing skill development programmes will reach large numbers of SCs only if special efforts are made.

Along with SCs, STs, BCs and BC Minorities also can and should be provided for by this programme.

4. A massive programme of housing for all SC families and provision of all essential facilities for all SC localities/habitations, rural as well as urban, like safe drinking water supply, electricity, sanitary toilets which does not require to be serviced by manual scavengers, drains, sanitation, all-weather internal roads, and all-weather link roads to all places they have to go to, including schools, market places, funeral places (in many villages they do not even have funeral ground where they can bury/create their dead in peace, etc. should be undertaken and completed (SCs are confined to humanly uninhabitable separate localities, devoid of many essential facilities and amenities, which are often in fact available in the rest of the village).

5. *Food Security for All SCs and STs*

All SC and ST families, both urban as well as rural, should be included in the category of 'Antyodaya Anna Yojana'/'Priority Households' in the National Food Security Act, 2013, except those who are clearly to be excluded, e.g. families of government officers of higher levels, judges, etc.

6. *Special Programmes for Specially Vulnerable Groups (SVGs) among SCs and Particularly Vulnerable Tribal Groups (PTGs) among STs*

The conditions of SVGs among SCs and PTGs among STs are even worse. It is one of the lacunae of Indian statistics including Census that adequate disaggregated information is not available for them like neo-natal, infant and child mortality though some data are available from the census which bring out certain facts about them like their appalling level of literacy within the extremely low SC and ST levels. Special programmes have to be designed for them to remove their special vulnerabilities in addition to the programmes that they need along with all other SCs/STs. SVGs among SCs include manual scavengers and other sanitation workers and their children (there is a lot of child labour, especially girl child labour, in scavenging); Nomadic, Semi-Nomadic and Denotified communities (which had been notified as 'Criminal Castes/Tribes' by the pre-independence colonial legislation); communities whose women are customarily subjected to sexual-exploitation, i.e. prostitution (like Devadasis, a euphemistic name meaning maid-servant of God; Jogins, which is another euphemistic name, which means a female saint; Basavis, and communities like

Banchdas – most such women belong to the SCs and a smaller proportion belong to Most/Extremely Backward castes of BCs); and women and children in general.

PTGs among STS are pre-agricultural/non-agricultural, some are Nomadic/ Semi-Nomadic and some others are Denotified Tribes.

The Report of the Ranke Commission on Nomadic and Denotified Tribes is yet to see the light of day.

7. *Rehabilitation and Resettlement of Manual Scavengers*

A comprehensive scheme has to be devised to rehabilitate and resettle manual scavengers and their communities in occupations unconnected with 'scavenging' and sweeping. The passing of the Prohibition of Employment as Manual Scavengers and their Rehabilitation, 2013 is not enough and the Act, though an improvement over the 1993 Act, is still having many serious gaps and deficits.

Under such a scheme liberated manual scavengers and other members of their communities need to be given training for non-sanitary works like dignified works in plumbing, electrical repair, driving vehicles, etc. by Municipalities and others who employ manual scavengers. Railways have to set a side a certain proportion of contracts for catering to liberated manual scavengers/members of their communities and/or their associations, allocate vending outlets in railway stations. In towns and cities, a good proportion of milk-booths should be entrusted to them.

8. *Strengthening the Working of National Scheduled Castes Finance and Development Corporation (NSCFDC) and National Scheduled Tribes Finance Development Corporation (NSTFDC) and Promotion of Modern Entrepreneurship among SCs and STs, taking full advantage of the 4 per cent Reservation provided by Ministry of MSME*

The programme of assistance and portfolio of NSFDC/NSTFDC should be expanded – one new part to look after SC and ST entrepreneurs of small and medium industries and business unhampered by family income ceiling limit and the other part to continue to remain geared towards very small entrepreneurs as at present. The quantum of assistance for small and medium entrepreneurs should not be less than that provided under the dispensation of the Ministry of Micro, Small and Enterprises (MSME). This Corporation and other Corporations for SCs and STs at the Central and State levels should gear themselves to be able to support SC and ST entrepreneurs to fully avail themselves of the recently introduced 4 per cent reservation provided for them by the Ministry of MSME in procurements without giving scope for benami enterprises.

For the effective working of the NSCFDC and NSTFDC, and the State Channelising Agencies/State SC Development Corporations, it is necessary to bring together the NSCFDC, NSTFDC and successful SC and ST entrepreneurs, the State Channelising Agencies/the Ministry of Finance, representatives of Banks, RBI, expert institutions like the NIRD and the IIPA, experts and successful and unsuccessful SCs entrepreneurs assisted in different States in order to clearly identity their practical difficulties and find effective remedial measures. The NIRD conducted a study on 'Viability and Sustainability of the Scheduled Castes Development Corporations' This should be utilised.

9. *National Safai Karmachari Finance and Development Corporation (NSKFDC)*

This Corporation too require changes in its methodology in order to provide substantive and sustainable support for economic activities by Safai Karmacharis and members of their families in areas unconnected with their caste-bound occupations.

The statutory status of this Corporation, which was allowed to lapse in 2004, should be restored.

II. Schemes for Educational Development and Empowerment of SCs and STs

The educational schemes for SCs and STs should cover the entire educational chain at all levels. At present support is available above post-Matric, i.e. Plus-Two level onwards. Below that there is a vacuum except for children of those engaged in unclean occupations. There is no support for SC children for pre-school education from Class I to X. Whatever support is provided for one section of SCs does not secure for them high quality education. The Ministry of Tribal Affairs has taken the laudable initiative to start from 1.7.2012 an open-ended Pre-Matric Scholarship Scheme for ST children from Class I to X at rates equivalent to the minimum of the Post-Matric scholarship, i.e. ₹ 230 per month for day-scholars and ₹ 380 per month for hostellers. To fill the gaps, the following measures are necessary:

1. Provide an Anganwadi Centre (AWC) in every habitation of SCs and STs and provide every such AWC with a qualified teacher, trained in Montessori and other such methods. For this purpose, training institutions will have to be opened in large numbers for preparing a few lakhs of pre-school education trained teachers. They should be paid remuneration at rates prevalent in good pre-school institutions so that competent teachers are attracted to the Anganwadi-based institutions.

   This can and should be provided also for isolated/distant habitations of BCs also like fishermen's hamlets and Banjara tandas (wherever they are classified as BCs).
2. An open-ended pre-Matric Scholarship Scheme for the SC Children from Class I to X as done by the Ministry of Tribal Affairs for ST children should be initiated immediately.
3. For the level of education from Class VI to XII, High Quality Residential Schools, one each for SC girls and SC boys and one each for ST girls and ST boys should be stared in each of the Blocks of the country – 75 per cent of the seats should be for SC students in SC residential schools and 75 per cent of the seats for ST children in ST residential schools, and the remaining 25 per cent for children of other groups. The number of residential schools should be such as to cover all SC and ST children at this stage of education. This is the recommendation of the Group of Ministers on Dalit Affairs set up in 2005 under the Chairmanship of Shri Pranab Mukherjee in its Report of 2008 and the Sub-Group–I Report and of the Ministry of HRD's Task Forces for Educational Development of SCs and STs in their Reports. Earlier this was recommended by the Dalit Manifesto, 1996 and other documents which I formulated or I was closely associated with.

   A successful model exists since about 3½ decades in Andhra Pradesh. There are 288 residential schools for SCs and a similar number for ST children in the State. Their results at Class XII are considerably higher than the State average.

   The goal should be to have as many high-quality residential schools as are necessary to cover all SC and ST children of school-going age and to make a good beginning now. A good beginning is possible by earmarking a due share (say 1/3rd) of the 6,000 budgeted model schools under Ministry of HRD for SCs and another due proportion for STs, as recommended by the Reports of the Ministry of HRD's Task Force on Educational Development of SCs and the Task Force on Educational Development of STs.

This scheme requires increased intake in existing teachers training institutions with due proportion of SC and ST teachers and setting up of new teachers training institutions to train SC and ST teachers. The total numbers should be adequate to serve all the residential schools. The syllabus and the training content have to be upgraded. In the AP model, the teachers are Post-Graduates. This should be the pattern in all residential schools. Therefore, Post-Graduate intake of SCs and STs should also be commensurately stepped up.

Similar measures are also required for BCs including BCs of Muslims and Christians. Some of the high-quality residential schools for BCs should be located in places with large populations of BCs of Muslims and full intake of their children ensured. This will be an important step in satisfactorily meeting the lament of Prof. Mushirul Hassan, former VC of Jamila Millia Islamia and Syed Maulana Mahmood Madani of Jamiat Ulema Hind who have both complained recently that Muslims are treated only as vote-banks. This measure will also be a step in meaningfully implementing the Sachar Committee's Report.

4. Reservation for SCs, STs and BCs in Professional, Technological and other Higher Educational institutions in the private sector, as recommended by the Sub-Group–I Report, the Ministry of HRD's Task Forces on Educational Development of SCs and of STs, along with other related supporting measures and facilities
5. **Strengthening and Removing Road-Blocks in the Post-Matric Scholarship Scheme for SCs and STs**

One of the road-blocks in the way of this scheme securing better results is the family income-ceiling for eligibility for non-charging of fees and for scholarship. The ceiling was recently raised to ₹ 2 lakh per annum. Before that it was ₹ 1 lakh per annum.

It has to be remembered that Indian standards of enrolment in higher education are well below international standards and it is the stated policy of the Government of India to step this up to international levels. The percentage of enrolment of SCs and STs is much less than the Indian standard and the standard of Socially Advanced Castes (SACs), ie., non-SC, non-ST, non-BC castes (NSCTBCs). Quickly and sharply stepping up the percentage of enrolment of SCs and STs in higher education is absolutely essential to achieve the national goal. This is not only necessary from the point of view of the SCs and STs, but also from the point of view of the nation as a whole. India has got a demographic advantage over other countries except sub-Saharan African countries. The proportion of young people of productive age is higher in India than in western and other advanced countries and even China. This demographic advantage can give us a demographic dividend provided we can step up the quantity and quality of education and skills and the status of health from pre-natal stage onwards of the deprived social classes who are the lowest in these respects and bring them to the level of SACs/NSCTBCs and after such equalisation of SCs and STs and also BCs with the SACs take them all forward together and bring all of them to the level of the most advanced countries. If this is done, India's economy will zoom. But the short-sighted elite of India, in their caste-based anxiety to keep the SCs, STs and BCs down, are depriving India of this potential, demographic dividend. What I have said here is true in respect of all educational and skill development schemes. This is relevant also to economic development schemes and schemes directly connected with neo-natal, infant, child and maternal mortality, malnutrition, stunting, etc. because it is a package of all these that can secure optimal demographic dividend for India's economy and for the optimal and sustained growth of our economy.

Therefore, as recommended by the Sub-Group–I Report,
(1) No fees of any type should be charged from SC and ST students, irrespective of family income, from primary to post graduate level, by any

(a) Government and aided schools
(b) Unaided private schools
(c) Colleges/Universities/other Institutions of higher and professional education (both Government and aided as well as private unaided)

(2) The fee charged by private institutions should be paid by the Government directly to the Schools/Institutions in time, thus eliminating the need for payment of fee by the student and its reimbursement subsequently and to avoid giving a handle to those institutions to avoid this social responsibility of theirs to SC and ST students.
(3) The maximum fee so fixed may not be uniform for all private institutions as the facilities/infrastructure may vary from Institution to Institution and therefore there may be different reasonable maxima for different qualitative categories/types of institutions. Such fees should be fully reimbursed by Government to such private institutions; and private institutions should not collect any fees from the SC and ST students. Any additional fees or charges, by whatever name called, that is imposed by any private management, should be prevented in the case of SC and ST students and penalised.
(4) All SC and ST students of the following categories should be eligible for scholarships at all levels, irrespective of their annual family income.

(a) SC and ST girl students
(b) SC and ST disabled students *[disability as defined in the Persons with Disabilities (Equal Opportunities, Protection of Rights and Full Participation) Act, 1995]*
(c) SC and ST students who are victims or dependent children of SC and ST victim of heinous atrocities like (a) murder (b) rape (c) arson (d) grievous hurt causing loss/impairment of limb/organ
(d) Students who are dependents of SCs and STs deceased in natural disasters/accidents
(e) SC and ST students who are children of SC and ST widows or of SC and ST single mothers (example, divorcees)

(5) In the case of other SC and ST students, the annual family income ceiling for eligibility for scholarships should be raised to ₹ 6 lakh and thereafter periodically and automatically stepped-up by linking it with inflation.
(6) The scholarships should be revised periodically (at least every two years) by linking it with inflation, as is done with regard to DA of Government employees. This revision should be automatic and should not require approval by Finance Ministry.
(7) Scholarships should be disbursed at the beginning of each month/quarter/year by payment into a bank account in the joint name of each student and the educational institution. To facilitate this, the Central Government should release funds in advance. The State Governments should also similarly release funds for the non-Plan part of scholarships in advance of each month/quarter/year.
These recommendations have also been made by the Ministry of HRD's Task Force on Educational Development of SCs in September, 2012 (of which I was a Member) and by the Task Force on Educational Development of STs.

6. **Overseas Scholarship Scheme**

Higher education in universities in advanced countries enables students to secure better careers. Indian students are among the most numerous among students from all developing countries to resort to higher education in foreign universities. But, SCs and ST students are too few among them.

The main reason for this is the exorbitant expenditure involved in such education and the weak financial condition of SCs and STs. As the weak financial conditions of the SCs and STs are owing to reasons beyond their control and caused by the working of the centuries-old Caste System-with-'Untouchability', which has not been fully or even substantially reversed after Independence, it is the duty of the State to step in and enable the SCs and STs to acquire education in foreign institutions in commensurate numbers compared with the number of general category candidates who are able to go to foreign institutions. This is essential because of the obvious career advantage that candidates passing out from foreign institutions have in this country. Making this advantage available to the SCs and STs in due measure is an important aspect of empowerment of SCs and STs of the educated category in the present and future contexts.

As usual this catalytic scheme is hamstrung by various restrictions. At present the number of scholarships is struck at a meagre 30 for SCs and 15 for STs every year. In order remove road-blocks, the following measures are necessary as recommended by the Sub-Group–I Report and keeping in view the recommendations of the Working Group on Empowerment of Scheduled Tribes.

(a) There should be no restriction with regard to the field of study for which the scholarship is given.
(b) There should be no condition of annual family income ceiling – at present there is a very low and unrealistic ceiling of ₹ 3,00,000.
(c) The minimum marks of eligibility should be reduced from the present 60 per cent to 50 per cent.
(d) The amount of scholarships should be revised to cover the entire cost including all fees, costs and expenses.
(e) The number of scholarships should be increased initially to 500 for SCs and 250 for STs and subsequently raised to the level commensurate with the total number of Indian students getting education from abroad as recommended by the Dalit Manifesto.

7. **Hostels for SC and ST Girls and Boys**

The Central scheme for hostels renamed in 2008 as Babu Jagjivan Ram Chhatravas Yojana (i.e. Babu Jagjivan Ram Hostel scheme) provides financial assistance from the Centre to the States for construction of hostels. Earlier, it was only for girls hostels. Later boys hostels were also provided for. Central funding is 100 per cent for girls hostels and 50 per cent for boys hostels. Central assistance is only for construction and there is no contribution from the Centre for post-Construction efficient management and supervision.

I have recommended long back that a small proportion of Central grants should be provided for supervision, security and administrative support. The Planning Commission could not agree to this. The Sub-Group–I has recommended 1 per cent of the total Central grants for this purpose. The condition of hostels is very deplorable. They need to be upgraded to satisfactory and acceptable levels. There is need to provide funds for upgradation of hostels to the required standards, supervision, security and administrative support for all hostels, but to a greater extent for girls hostels, in the formula for sharing of non-Plan resources and earmark this so that it cannot be diverted. The share of SCs and STs in the non-Plan budget is next to nil at present. Making provision for such schemes which cannot come from the Plan is a constructive measure to build up the non-Plan budget share of the SCs and STs and at the same time to meet their essential needs which cannot be provided from Plan resources – this should also be taken up with the current Finance Commission.

On the Plan side the outlay provided for hostels has to be stepped up so that a net-work of hostels with wide coverage can be started. The hostels should be designed in such a manner that they may in future become the nucleus for the High Quality Residential Schools for SCs and STs from Class VI to Class XI mentioned earlier. Roadblocks that exist in this scheme also should be removed such as restrictions on distance, and rural and urban, etc.

8. **Coaching & Allied Scheme**

Under the Central scheme of Assistance for Coaching for SCs and STs, coaching is provided for them through State Governments, universities, NGOs, private bodies for competitive examinations of the Central and State Governments, the PSUs, Banks, etc. and soft skill development programmes for employment in private sector.

This good scheme is also bedevilled by restrictions like a family income eligibility ceiling of ₹ 2 lakh per annum and unrealistically low remuneration for teachers which keep off the best teachers. As a result, this scheme is not able to produce the results that private coaching institutions are able to secure. There is no goal-orientation in the Government scheme and it proceeds in a casual manner.

The institutions run now, the remuneration for the teachers and other facilities should be brought to the level of the best and most successful private coaching institutions. Simultaneously coaching should also be provided through reputed and successful private coaching institutions.

Coaching for SCs and STs should start from Class XI onwards or even earlier. The goal of coaching provided should be provided both to equip them to become capable of filling up all reserved seats and qualify in increasing numbers for general seats both in professional and other higher educational institutions and in employment in the public sector and also secure employment in the private sector.

There is a tendency in Government to restrict coaching schemes only for competitive examinations and selections for higher level posts. There is no reason why coaching cannot be provided for selection to 'humbler' posts. Everyone does not have the minimum educational qualifications required for higher posts. We should find solutions for people with lesser education too.

When I was Joint-Secretary in the Ministry of Home Affairs, Government of India I communicated this suggestion to State Governments. In 1980–81, Tamil Nadu Government undertook with my concurrence and support, a coaching scheme for SC candidates to equip them for recruitment as jawans in the army. The then Secretary, Social Welfare, Government of Tamil Nadu who had also been my class-mate at the post-Graduate level, showed commendable initiative in designing and implementing this scheme. The scheme consisted of a one-month residential training for 100 selected candidates which included marching, PT and other aspects of army life including discipline. Nutritious food was provided so that they could measure up to the standard of army recruitment. Hindi was also taught as it is essential in the army which is composed of people from different language groups. The defence personnel located in Tamil Nadu were closely associated with the training programme. The first camp was conducted in Ramanathapuram. There is no reservation in recruitment to the army. In the open selection, based only on fulfilling the prescribed physical and other conditions, 96 out of the 100 in the batch were selected by the Army Recruitment Unit. The rest were absorbed by other uniformed services of the State. I recall two other such training programmes undertaken in Tamil Nadu in this period. I communicated this experiment to other States. Karnataka also undertook such a programme. In subsequent years, after my term as Joint Secretary in the Centre was over, for want of continuing interest, this programme under Coaching & Allied Schemes ceased to exist. When I came back to the Centre as Special Commissioner for SCs and STs in the Constitutional set-up under Article 338, I made enquiries about why this scheme was discontinued sometime after I left. I shall reserve for another occasion what I came to know on this. It is useful to send large numbers of SCs and STs in the armed forces. Apart from meeting the country's defence, every soldier who returns home comes with a wider vision, experience of a wider world with less discrimination than exists in general society, with greater self-confidence, and is a factor helping social change locally. The scope under this scheme can be expanded widely, taking advantage of the National Skill Development Mission that has been set up to produce candidates with different levels of education for different fields.

9. **Upgradation of Merit**
   Under this scheme funds are provided to educational institutions for conducting remedial and special coaching for SC students from Class IX to XII to upgrade their merit.
   This was started as part of Coaching & Allied Scheme. The lacunae mentioned for Coaching & Allied scheme are also applicable here mutatis mutandis and these lacunae need to be removed.

10. **Rajiv Gandhi National Fellowship (RGNF)**
    This scheme provides assistance to SC and ST scholars for pursing MPhil and PhD courses and is implemented through the UGC. The number of fellowships is 2,000 per year, but this good scheme is also hampered by the condition of family income-ceiling which at present is ₹ 3 lakh per annum. This condition sharply reduces the number of eligible candidates. There should be no family income ceiling for this scheme. The number of fellowships should be increased to 5,000 per year and subsequently to such numbers as are necessary to fill all unfilled reserved posts for which M.Phil, Ph.D qualifications are prescribed.

11. **Top Class Education**
    Under this scheme assistance is provided to meritorious SC and ST students for pursuing professional and specialised courses in 185 identified institutions of excellence. The number of scholarships per year is 1,250 but this scheme is also hampered by the eligibility condition of family income ceiling of ₹ 2 lakh per annum. The income ceiling needs to be removed and the limit of number of scholarships should also be removed.

12. **Educational Loans for SC and ST students for full time professional and technical courses provided by the National Scheduled Castes Finance and Development Corporation**
    Family income-ceiling eligibility for these loans is fixed at a ridiculous low level of ₹ 40,000 in rural areas and ₹ 55,000 in urban areas.
    At this level of education, the family income-ceiling condition should be removed. Such measures as family income ceiling – but not at the present

ridiculously low level – can be considered only after the proportion of SC and ST students in relevant age groups rises to the same level as that of the SAC/NSCTBC students.

III. Banishing 'Untouchability' from Schools

1. The Government should take pro-active steps to ensure that SC and ST children are intermixed with other children in class-room seating and mid-day meal seating. In the mid-day meal scheme either the cook or the server should be an SC woman as an effective measure against 'untouchability'. Resistance should be firmly repelled.
2. Human rights education with emphasis on anti-human, anti-national and anti-Constitutional nature of the caste system, caste loyalties, caste biases and caste antagonisms, and particularly of 'Untouchability' and 'Untouchability'-based discriminations, and with emphasis on equality as enshrined in the Constitution should be introduced in every educational institution, at all levels.
3. Such human rights education also needs to be introduced in teacher-training institutions, IAS, IPS and other Central as well as State service training institutions.
4. The experience of Institute of Human Rights Education should be utilized and the efforts of such institutions strengthened by active government participation, in financial and other terms.
5. The panchayats which show anti-discrimination-cum-gender sensitivity and good performance in enrolment and retention rates, especially of SC girls and total elimination of discrimination against SCs in their areas, should be recognised and rewarded.
6. There should be a comprehensive campaign to sensitise the entire community of teachers so that they become a bulwark against 'Untouchability'-based discriminations in all its forms in educational institutions.
7. The Union Minister and State Ministers in charge of pre-school education, school education and higher education should take pro-active initiatives in making such human rights education a reality and convey to the entire educational machinery the seriousness of the Central and State Governments about this task.

IV. Measures Required to Improve the Health Status of SCs and STs

1. Health and medical personnel and mobile units should be required to cover all inhabitants of SC, ST (and isolated BC habitations) in situ first before moving to the rest of the village and similarly slums and other habitations of SC and ST, BC and BC minorities before moving to the rest of the town.
2. Mandatorily provide safe drinking water source within the SC habitations/localities and ST habitations/localities and isolated BC habitations/localities.
3. Wherever health centres or units are established locally, they should be located in or adjacent to SC bastis, ST hamlets and isolated BC habitations.
4. In view of higher infant mortality (IMR) and under-5 mortality rate (U5MR), severe malnutrition, and greater vulnerability of SC and ST children in all parameters, and reality of their being left out on account of persistent attitudes based on 'untouchability' on the part of a number of health-providers, priority should be given to SC and ST children in schemes for children, particularly girl-children.

V. Specific Measures Required for Scheduled Tribes (STs)

Many of the schemes mentioned for SCs are also applicable, mutatis mutandis, to STs as indicated above.

In addition, STs have characteristic cultural traits and identities including, in many cases, their own languages. These need to be protected.

The Ministry of Tribal Affairs prepared a draft policy to address disparities and discrimination against STs. It is strange that a draft policy is being prepared six decades after the Constitution. There is already a tribal policy. Indications are that the new draft policy may make changes which may go against the interests of genuine tribes by changing the criteria for inclusion in the list of STs.

The Government of India has not tabled in the Parliament the Report of the Second (Bhuria) Commission on Scheduled Areas and the Welfare of the Scheduled Tribes set up in 2002 under Article 339 (1) of the Constitution which submitted its Report in 2004. Action has to be taken on its recommendations. This Commission itself was set up after a long delay and decades after the First (Dhebar) Commission. Without taking action on the Constitutional Commission's Report the Government has set up a new Committee to give a Report on STs similar to the Sachar Committee's Report on Muslims. Sachar Committee was a Committee set up under Executive Order. It was necessary because there was no Constitutional provision for setting a Committee or Commission for examining the conditions of Muslims. The Committee was therefore a good step but action on some of its important recommendations are yet to be taken. Example, recommendation regarding the 'Arzal' category of Muslims. In the case of STs, when the Constitution provides for a Commission, i.e. a Constitutional Commission, there is really no need for a Committee under an Executive Order. What is required is to place the Report of the Second Commission before Parliament and in the public domain, take action on all matters recommended by the Commission and if there is still gap on which the Government want further information, set up another Constitutional Commission. An Executive Committee after an unimplemented Constitutional Commission is not a forward step.

VI. Implementation of Revitalised Special Component Plan for Scheduled Castes (SCP) and Tribal Sub-Plan (TSP) and SC and ST Development Authorities

SCP and TSP are important Plan instruments which can facilitate holistic planning for the development and empowerment of SCs and STs if they are revitalised, along the lines which I have been proposing since 1983 within the government domain and through the Dalit Manifesto 1996 and subsequent documents in the public domain, by introducing relevant systems, relevant formulation (by including in the Central and State SCPs and TSPs the schemes of the type listed above), effective implementation, concurrent monitoring and evaluation, timely corrections, establishment of appropriate institutions with full functional, financial and administrative autonomy, and choosing of the right individuals for these institutions with mechanisms to facilitate people's participation from the stage of formulation to implementation, monitoring and social audit.

I have included in my suggested list of legislations for SCs and STs in Enclosure–I, the legislation for Special Component Plan for Scheduled Castes (SCP) and Tribal Sub-Plan (TSP) and SC and ST Development Authorities. But, while the legislation should be completed as urgently as possible, the process and procedure of the SCP and TSP should be put into operation immediately, without waiting for the enactment of the legislation.

VII. Schemes not only for SCs and STs but which are/can be of substantive benefit to SCs and STs

There are a number of Central and Centrally Sponsored Schemes which are not specifically for SCs and STs, but which can be useful for them, through application of the principle of SCP and TSP and certain other principles. I shall here only give two examples.

(1) Bharat Nirman

The are six specific Bharat Nirman goals, such as, additional area to be brought under assured irrigation; villages to be provided drinking water and other facilities and connectivities; households to be given electric connection, etc. There are targets for each of these goals. In each of these a due share for SCs and STs needs to be earmarked. The share of SCs and STs should be considerably more than their population proportion, taking into account their greater deprivation. In other words, the principle of the SCP and TSP should encompass Bharat Nirman also.

(2) MGNREGA

This is the culmination of the programmes of the past known as the Food for Work Programme, Integrated Rural Development Project (IRDP), Employment Guarantee/ Assurance Scheme (of Maharashtra). Since the scheme provides manual labour, naturally the proportion of SCs and STs and also BCs among labourers is high. The Government calculates benefits for the SCs and STs by computing the share of the wages that go to SCs and STs and displays it as expenditure under the SCP and TSP. I have been pointing out form 1978 onwards (in connection with the precursors of the MGNREGA and later in connection MGNREGA itself) that calculation of SCP and TSP on the basis of wages paid to SCs and STs is conceptually wrong. Giving manual wage employment to SCs is not development. Manual labour has been their fate all through. Providing them such labour for a guaranteed number of days at an assured rate of wages is welcome relief, but not development and empowerment of SCs and STs and cannot be counted as part of SCP and TSP.

What can legitimately be counted in the MGNREGA as part of SCP and TSP is the value of assets, directly and exclusively beneficial respectively to SCs and STs, created through their labour under the MGNREGA. Such works can be group irrigation through bore-wells and channels; improvement of the conditions of their habitations with all facilities and connectivities; construction of houses of SCs and STs; reclamation of usar/choudu/uppu/saline/alkaline lands and other waste lands for distribution to landless rural SC and ST families, etc. It is ethical that SC and ST labourers are engaged in the construction of assets of direct and exclusive benefit to themselves. It is not ethical to make them undertake labour for the creation of assets which benefit others – it is totally improper to treat the wages paid to the SC and ST labourers for creation of assets and benefits to others as part of SCP or TSP.

VIII. Prevention of Transfer of or Tampering with Central and Centrally Sponsored Schemes (CSSs) for SCs and STs

Periodically the Planning Commission undertakes a move to transfer some of the Centrally sponsored schemes to the States and provide the corresponding outlays untied to the States. It is then left to the States to continue the transferred schemes with or without modification or discontinue them and use the resources for any other Plan purpose. This is in response to the feeling of States that there are too many CSSs and too much of Plan outlay is tied up with them reducing the discretion of State

Governments in planning. There is a case for transferring CSSs and the corresponding amounts untied to the States. But this should not be done for the CSSs pertaining to SCs and STs and also CSSs pertaining to BCs, minorities, women, children, artisans and the poor. These classes, particularly SCs and STs, will not receive the required attention in all States. Further, there are other strong claimants in States competing for resources of State Governments. Schemes for SCs and STs and also for other deprived classes and categories, if transferred to the States, will suffer from this competition.

IX. Potential Think Tanks – Dr Ambedkar Foundation and Babu Jagjivan Ram National Foundation

As recommended by the Sub-Group–I Report, the Dr Ambedkar Foundation and Babu Jagjivan Ram National Foundation should be reconstituted into autonomous research organisations of eminence, along lines similar to the Nehru Memorial Museum and Library and Rajiv Gandhi Foundation.

X. An Important Aspiration of BCs

BCs are at different levels of backwardness, namely,

(a) Extremely Backward Castes of BCs

They have no assets, no skills and often no address. Nomadic, Semi-Nomadic and Vimukta Jati communities are of this category.

Also in this category are Muslim castes and Christian castes which too are victims of 'Untouchability' ('Untouchability' is the prime marker for inclusion in list of SCs), but are not included in the lists of SCs only because of Clause (3) of the Presidential Orders. Among Muslim castes of this type, are castes subjected manual scavenging like Halalkhor, Muslim Mehtar, Muslim Lalbegi (Hindu Mehtar and Hindu Lalbegi are included in the SC List).

(b) Most Backward Castes of BCs

These are castes without assets but which have skills, though the skills have become outdated. These include artisan castes, artisanal castes, pastoral castes, fishing castes, service-providing castes, etc. Their sudden and unprepared exposure to global competition has deepened their economic distress, damaged their traditional occupations, without opening to new opportunities, and reduced large numbers of them to wage-labourers.

This is the largest category of BCs and includes most of the Muslim backward castes other than those which are in (a).

(c) Tenant Peasants and other Very Weak Peasants like those on Batai tenure in Bihar, Palu tenure in Andhra Pradesh.

(d) Peasant castes with landed assets

The castes in the category of (a) to (c) are not able to compete with the castes in (d). Recognising this, the States of Kerala, Karnataka and Andhra Pradesh have instituted *ab initio* schemes of categorisation of BCs with sub-quotas for each. Tamil Nadu, Bihar and Maharashtra also have categorisation though not as thorough as the first three States. The Centre, as in all matters pertaining to BCs, is the slowest laggard with some North and East Indian States for company.

There is a strong movement for categorisation of BCs all over India. But, this should be done on a purely objective basis without allowing short-term electoral considerations to intrude. If an expert body with members of impeccable credentials and without political affiliation (no salaries, but only functional facilities and high status) is immediately constituted for this purpose, it will have a good impact on the vast majority of BC castes and will meet a genuine need. The existing schemes of categorisation in some States also need to be fine-tuned. A properly constituted expert body can and should be required to give its report in six months at the most and if possible in three months and the Government should take its decision within three months thereafter and break from its past practice of giving endless extensions to Committees and Commissions and consigning the reports to oblivion as in the case of the Governors' Committee Report, the Group of Ministers on Dalit Affairs Report, the Bhuria Commission Report, the Ranke Commission Report, etc.

Recommendations for categorisation have been made by a dissenting Member of the Mandal Commission, repeatedly by the NCBC, by me personally ab initio on a number of occasions and as Member-Secretary of the NCBC, by the Planning Commission's XII Plan Working Group on BCs and again by me at the Planning Commission's XII Plan Steering Committee meeting and subsequently in writing.

Muslim BCs who are getting much less than their due share can find their due place in this pattern, Government of India announced a sub-quota for already identified BCs of Minorities (the bulk of whom are BCs of Muslims) in the Central List of BCs – a justifiable decision, vitiated by wrong timing as it was promulgated just before the announcement of UP State Assembly elections and left without serious defence in the High Court when it was challenged and was therefore struck down. Government appeal pending in the Supreme Court. No serious and purpose follow-up effort.

XI. Important Aspiration of BCs of Muslims

BCs of Muslims want educational development and fair access to employment opportunities. The measures at II and X above will go a considerable way towards meeting these aspirations.

BC communities of Muslims have been included in the State Lists of most States except some States of East and North East India and in the Central List for those States, covering about 75–80 per cent of the Muslim population. But they are not able to get their due share of Reservation in education and employment because they are not able to compete with less backward castes of BCs. The categorisation of BCs referred to at (X) above will help them to get their due share.

Their aspirations have been met in Andhra Pradesh by the Ordinance followed by legislation of the Government of Andhra Pradesh within one month of my Report on Identification of Socially and Educationally Backward Classes in the Muslim Community of Andhra Pradesh which I have furnished to the State Government in June, 2007 and in which I have comprehensively surveyed Muslim society in India, its social structure, its social stratification and its social hierarchies as existing in each region of India with a peep into neighbouring countries and medieval Iran and Spain. Fourteen Socially and Educationally Backward Classes of Muslims identified by me were given a separate 4 per cent sub-quota of reservation as recommended by me. This is the seventh year of its implementation. The access the Muslim BC boys and girls have got in these seven years to higher education, especially professional and technological education, and jobs especially Class–I jobs (4 BC Muslim girls have been recruited to Class I, civil and police services by the States PSC) has produced a sea-change, given hope for the future to BC Muslim boys and girls and their parents, and poor children of these communities are found deeply engrossed in acquisition of education. This is a heart-warming experience.

BCs of Christians (namely, SC Converts to Christianity) were provided reservation and a sub-quota within BCs from 1970 and so there was need for further exercise for them. But, Muslim BCs had been mostly left out, which has been rectified in 2007.

XII. Women of SC and ST

They need to be given greater focus by

(a) Setting apart 50 per cent of the outlays under SCP and TSP for schemes of development and advancement and empowerment of SC and ST women.
(b) Reservation in Lok Sabha and State Vidhan Sabhas by providing them a sub-quota under the Women's Reservation Bill.
(c) Special Protection for SC and ST women through some of the schemes (mentioned above) and legislations (mentioned in Enclosure–I).

XIII. Women of BCs including BCs of Minorities

They need to be given greater focus by

(a) Undertaking specific schemes for BC women and girls.
(b) Reservation in Lok Sabha and State Vidhan Sabhas by providing them a sub-quota under the Women's Reservation Bill. This sub-quota may be for women of those castes and communities of BCs including BCs of religious minorities which have not been able to get any seats or have got only disproportionately low number of seats hitherto in the Lok Sabha and Vidhan Sabhas. Restricting the BC women's sub-quota to women of such castes and communities will have the double benefit of helping the BC women and also helping the unrepresented and poorly represented castes and communities of BCs.

* *Source:* (unpublished report procured from the author). P.S. Krishnan, IAS (Rtd.) was former Secretary, Minister of Social Welfare, Government of India, New Delhi.

Appendix IV

Photos Depicting the Social Life of Gonds, Yerukulas, Sugalis (Lambadis), Naikapods, Mannevars, Pardans and Thotis in Andhra Pradesh and Telangana

Gonds

Yerukulas

Kolams

Koyas

Lambadas (Sugalis)

Mannevars

Naikpods

Pardhans

Thotis

Tribal Culture in Andhra and Telangana

Bibliography

Abbasayulu, Y.B., 'Tribal Social Change with Special Reference to Community Development Projects', *Tribe*, Vol. 10, No. 4, 1978.

Agarwal, Anil and Sumita Narayan, 'Women and Natural Resources', *Social Action*, Vol. 35, No. 4, 1985.

Agarwal, Binod C., P.C. Gurivi Reddy and N. Sudhakar Rao, 'Determinants of Cultural Adaptation in the Process of Change: A Case of Yanadi', *Man in India*, Vol. 64, No. 2, 1984, pp. 133–42.

——, *Yanadi Response to Change: An Attempt in Action Anthropology*, Concept, New Delhi, 1985.

Aggarwal, D.P., *Tribal Development Planning in India*, Mahaveer & Sons, New Delhi, 2007.

Ailaih, K., 'The Lambadas: Their Identity', *Man in India*, Vol. 75, No. 1, 1995, pp. 97–100.

Aiyappan, A., *The Socio-economic Conditions of the Aboriginal Tribes of the Province of Madras*, Government Press, Madras, 1948.

Aiyer, K.B., 'Tribal Welfare in Andhra Pradesh', *Kurukshetra*, Vol. 19, No. 4, 1970, p. 12.

Ali, Arif, *Study of Health Culture of Lambadas of Ambodh Tanda* (unpublished Ph.D. Thesis), University of Hyderabad, Telangana, 1996.

Amir, Hasan, *Tribal Administration in India*, B.R. Publishing Corporation, Delhi, 1988.

Arora, Dolly, 'From State Regulation to People's Participation: Case of Forest Management in India', *Economic and Political Weekly*, 19 March 1994.

Ashirvad, N., 'Glimpses of Tribal Culture in Andhra Pradesh', *Man and Life*, Vol. 18, No. 3–4, 1992, pp. 175–82.

Avadhani, P.S.R. et al., *A Monograph on Chenchu*, Census of India A.P. Part 5B(4) Ethnographic Notes, Manager of Publications, New Delhi, 1961a.

——, *A Monograph on Gonds*, Census of India A.P. Part 5B(4) Ethnographic Notes, Manager of Publications, New Delhi, 1961b.

Azeez Sahed, S.A. and S. Ghousia Begum, 'Struggle against Starvation: A Study of the Yanadi Food Getting Techniques', *Man in India*, Vol. 70, No. 2, 1990, pp. 169–84.

Babu, B.V., Y.S. Kusuma and J.M. Naidu, 'Ethnography of Jatapu Tribe of Andhra Pradesh', *Man and Life*, Vo1. 26, No. 344, 2000.

——, 'Jatapu Tribe of Andhra Pradesh: An Ethnographic Profile', in D.K. Behera and George Pfeffer (eds), *Contemporary Society: Tribal Studies*, Vol. 6, Concept, New Delhi, 1999.

Bailey, F.G., *Caste and Economic Frontier*, Manchester University Press, Manchester, 1957.

Banarjee, Sumantha, 'Scheduled Tribes: Failure of Placatory Measures', *Economic and Political Weekly*, Vol. 10, 1975.

Bapuji, M. and J.V.K.Y. Pandit, 'Transforming the Tribals in Srikakulam', *Kurukshetra*, Vol. 16, May 1977, pp. 18–19.

Bapuji, M., *Tribal Development Administration*, Kaniskha Publishing House, Delhi, 1993.

Bernard, S. Cohn, *An Anthropologist among the Historians and Other Essays*, OUP, New York, 1987.

Bhanage, N.P., *Tribal Commissions and Committees in India*, Himalaya Publishing House, Bombay, 1993.

Bhowmick, P.K., *Chenchus of the Forests and Plateau*, ISRAA, Calcutta, 1992.

——, *Dynamics of Tribal Development*, Inter-India Publications, New Delhi, 1993.

Bose, N.K., 'Integration of Tribes of Andhra Pradesh', *Man in India*, Vol. 44, 1964, pp. 97–104.

Carmichael, D.E., *Manual of the District Vizagapatnam in the Madras Presidency*, Reprinted in 1995 by the State Editor of District Gazetteers, A.P., Hyderabad, 1869.

Chandra, Mowli, 'Socio-economic Change in the Tribals of Andhra', in M.K. Chaudhuri (ed.), *Trends of Socio-economic Change in India, 1871–1961*, IIAS, Simla, 1969.

Chandrayya, M. and J. Rama Rao, 'Socio-economic Aspects of Tribals: A Case Study in Srikakulam District', *Man and Life*, Vol. 25, No. 1–2, 1999, pp. 41–50.

Chaudhuri, Buddhadeb (ed.), *Tribal Development in India: Problems and Prospects*, Inter-India Publications, New Delhi, 1982.

Chaudhuri, Buddhadeb, *Health, Forest and Development: The Tribal Situation*, Inter-India Publications, New Delhi, 2003.

Chaudhuri, Sarit Kumar and Sucheta Sen Chaudhuri, 'Economic Development of the Konda Reddis: A Primitive Tribe of Andhra Pradesh', *Man and Life*, Vol. 20, No. 1–2, 1994, pp. 77–86.

Danam, B., 'Andhra Pradesh', in S.N. Dubey and Ratna Murdia (eds), *Land Alienation and Restoration in Tribal Communities in India*, Himalaya Publishing House, Bombay, 1977.

Deogaonkar, S.G., *Problem of Development of Tribal Areas*, Leela Devi Publications, New Delhi, 1979.

——, *Tribal Development Plans: Implementation and Evaluation*, Concept, New Delhi, 1992.

——, *Tribal Exploitation: A Study of Victims of Crime and Bondedness*, Inter-India Publications, New Delhi, 1990.

——, *Tribal Administration and Development*, Concept, New Delhi, 1994.

Desai, B.M., 'Formal and Informal Credit Sources', in Ranjit Gupta (ed.), *Planning for Tribal Development*, Indian Institute of Management, Ahmedabad, 1977.

Dube, S.C., 'Inter Tribal Relations: A Case Study', *Man in India*, Vol. 30, No. 1, 1950, pp. 73–80.

Dubey, S.N. and Ratna Murdia (eds), *Land Alienation and Restoration in Tribal Communities in India*, Himalaya Publishing House, Bombay, 1977.

Eight Five Year Plan (1990–95) Tribal Areas Sub Plan, Tribal Welfare Department, Government of A.P.

Elwin, Verrier, *Leaves from the Jungle: Life in a Gond Village*, OUP, Delhi, 1992.

Eswaraiah, G., 'Animal Husbandry Potentiality in the Tribal Sub-Plan Areas of Andhra Pradesh State', *Vanyajati*, Vol. XLVIII, No. 4, 2000, pp. 15–17.

Eswaraiah, G., 'Family Welfare Activities among Some Tribals of Andhra Pradesh', *Vanyajati*, Vol. XLVI, No. 4, 1998, pp. 13–28.

Forscher, 'Fair Deal for Tribes of Andhra Pradesh', *Industrial Economist*, 15 November 1971, pp. 27–29.

Francis, W., 'Bagata', *Census of India*, Vol. XV, Part I, Madras, 1901, pp. 143–44.

Furer-Haimendorf, C. Von with Elizabeth Von Furer-Haimendorf, *The Reddis of Bison Hills: A Study in Acculturation, Vol. 1: Aboriginal Tribes of Hyderabad*, Macmillan and Co., London, 1945.

Furer-Haimendorf, C. Von, 'Aboriginal Education in Hyderabad', *Indian Journal of Social Work*, Vol. 5, No. 2, 1944a, pp. 97–106.

——, 'Beliefs Concerning Human Sacrifice among Hill Reddis', *Man in India*, Vol. 24, 1944b, pp. 11–28.

——, 'Changing Economic and Social Conditions among Gonds of Andhra Pradesh', in K.S. Singh (ed.), *Economies of Tribes and their Transformation*, Concept, New Delhi, 1982a, pp. 409–16.

——, 'Fundamental Research in Indian Anthropology', in Behari L. Abbi and Satish Saberwal (eds), *Urgent Research in Anthropology*, IIAS, Simla, 1968.

——, 'Primitive Aboriginal Cultures of the Deccan', *Man in India*, Vol. 24, 1944b.

——, 'Seasonal Nomadism and Economics of Chenchu of Hyderabad', *Journal of Royal Asiatic Society of Bengal*, Vol. 7, 1941a, pp. 175–96.

——, 'The Decline of Rehabilitation of Tribal Population in Adilabad District upto 1948', *Tribal Cultural Research and Training Institute Bulletin*, Hyderabad, 1963.

——, 'The Fortunes of the Primitive Tribes', *Indian Journal of Social Work*, Vol. 3, 1942–43, pp. 339–406.

——, 'The Position of Tribal Population in India', in H.M. Mathur and C.V. Furer-Haimendorf (eds), *Anthropology in the Development Process*, Vikas, New Delhi, 1977.

——, 'Tribal Population of Hyderabad: Yesterday and Today', *Census of India*, Vol. XXI, Government Printing Press, Hyderabad, 1941b.

——, *Life among Indian Tribes*, OUP, Delhi, 1991.

——, *The Chenchus: Jungle Folk of Deccan, Vol. 1: Aboriginal Tribes of Hyderabad*, Macmillan and Co., London, 1943.

——, *The Gonds of Andhra Pradesh: Tradition and Change in an Indian Tribe*, Vikas, New Delhi, 1979.

——, *The Progress and the Problems of Aboriginal Rehabilitation in Adilabad District*, Government Printing Press, Hyderabad, 1945.

——, *The Rajgonds of Adilabad: A Peasant Culture of the Deccan, Vol. 3: Aboriginal Tribes of Hyderabad*, Macmillan and Co., London, 1948.

——, *Tribes of India: Struggle for Survival*, OUP, Delhi, 1982b.

Gandhi, Malli, *Historical Survey of Ex-Criminal Tribes Settlements in Andhra: A Case Study of Siddhapurm and Stuartpuram Settlements, 1913–1990* (unpublished Ph.D. Thesis), University of Hyderabad, Telangana, 1996.

Gangadharam, V. and M. Raghuram Reddy, 'Human Resource Development among the Tribes: A Study of the Chenchus of Andhra Pradesh', *Vanyajati*, Vol. XXX, No. 3, 1982, pp. 12–15.

Gibbon, Peter, 'The Structural Adjustment of Structural Adjustment: Sub Saharan Africa, 1980–93', *IDS Bulletin*, Vol. 25, No. 3, 1994.

Gopala Rao, N., 'Bairluty Land Colonization Scheme: A Study in Socio-economic Implications', *Vanyajati*, Vol. XIX, 1975, pp. 26–33.

——, 'Land Alienation: A Menace to Tribal Economy', *Tribe*, Vol. 1, 1982, pp. 27–39.

——, 'Primary Education among the Scheduled Tribes of Andhra Pradesh: Problems and Perspectives', *Vanyajati*, Vol. XXXV, No. 1, 1987, pp. 22–26.

Government of Andhra Pradesh, *A Note on Vocational Training Centres for Scheduled Tribes in Andhra Pradesh*, Department of Tribal Welfare, Hyderabad, 2004.

——, *Annual Reports 2006–07 and 2007–08*, Department of Tribal Welfare, Tribal Cultural Research and Training Institute, Hyderabad, 2008a.

——, *Basic Statistics on Scheduled Tribes of Andhra Pradesh*, Department of Tribal Welfare, Tribal Cultural Research and Training Institute, Hyderabad, 2008b.

——, *Departmental Manual*, Department of Tribal Welfare, Tribal Cultural Research and Training Institute, Hyderabad, 2008c.

——, *Tribal Areas Sub-Plan, Draft Plan 1984–85*, Department of Tribal Welfare, Hyderabad, 1983.

Government of India, *Scheme for Providing Credit Facilities in Tribal Areas in the State of Andhra Pradesh*, Report of the Team for the Study of Community Projects and National Extension Service, Vol. 3, Planning Commission, Committee on Plan Projects, New Delhi, 1957, pp. 203–05.

——, *Community Development Programme: Third Year Plan*, Ministry of Community Development and Cooperation, New Delhi, 1961.

——, *Report of Group on Administrative Arrangements and Personnel Policies in Tribal Areas*, Ministry of Home Affairs, New Delhi, 1978a.

——, *Report of the Advisory Committee on the Revision of the Lists of Scheduled Castes and Scheduled Tribes*, Lokur Committee, New Delhi, 25 August 1965.

——, *Report of the Commission for Scheduled Castes and Scheduled Tribes*, Ministry of Home Affairs, New Delhi, April 1982 to March 1983.

——, *Report of the Committee on Forest and Tribals in India*, Ministry of Home Affairs, Tribal Development Division, New Delhi, 1982a.

——, *Report of the National Commission for Scheduled Castes and Scheduled Tribes*, First Report, New Delhi, 12 March 1992 to 31 March 1993.

——, *Report of the Working Group on Tribal Development during Medium Term Plan 1978–83*, Ministry of Home Affairs, New Delhi, July 1978b.

——, *Report of the Working Group on Tribal Development during Sixth Plan 1980–85*, Ministry of Home Affairs, New Delhi, October 1980.

——, *Tribal Development in the Fifth Plan: Some Basic Policy Papers*, Vol. I, Ministry of Home Affairs, New Delhi, 1982b.

Grigson, W.V., *The Challenge of Backwardness: Some Notes and Papers on Tribal Depressed Classes*, Government Printing Press, Hyderabad, 1947.

——, *The Maria Gonds of Bastar* (Reprinted in 1991), OUP, Delhi, 1939.

Hassan, S.S., *The Castes and Tribes of H.E.H. The Nizam's Dominions, Hyderabad State*, Government Central Press, Bombay, 1920, pp. 8–11.

Hooja, Meenakshi, *Policies and Strategies for Tribal Development*, Rawat Publications, Jaipur, 2004.

Hussain, S.K.M., 'Descriptive Account of Koyas', *Man in India*, Vol. 31, No. 1, 1951a, pp. 33–39.

——, 'Medicines among Gond, Kolam and Chenchu', *Man in India*, Vol. 30, 1950, pp. 23–31.

——, 'The Rural Uplift of Tribes and Backward Classes in Hyderabad (Deccan)', *Man in India*, Vol. 29, No. 3–4, 1949, pp. 185–98.

——, 'Tribal Inheritance', *Man in India*, Vol. 31, No. 2 1951b, p. 84.

Jagannadha Rao, V., *Forest Laws in Andhra Pradesh*, Asia Law House, Hyderabad, 1981.

Jain, S.P., 'Panchayat Raj in Tribal Areas: Some Issues', *Tribal Development and its Administration*, National Institute of Community Development, Hyderabad, 1975.

Janardhan Rao, B., *Land Alienation in Tribal Areas*, Kakatiya University, Warangal, 1987.

Jaswanth Rao, P., 'Andhra Pradesh Tribals: Struggle against Land Alienation', *Economic and Political Weekly*, Vol. XXXIII, No. 3, 1998, pp. 81–83.

Jesurathnam, Devarapalli and R. Yathiraj Kumar, 'Biodiversity and Survival Behavior of Chenchus: The Question of Sustainability', *Man in India*, Vol. 79, No. 3–4, 1999, pp. 359–69.

Jesurathnam, Devarapalli, 'Subsistence Systems and Limitations of Ethno-ecology: A Case Study of Chenchus', *Girijana Samskriti*, Vol. 2, No. 2, 1994.

Jeyantyh, K. Newport and G.P. Jowahar Godfrey, 'Yanadi Tribals: The Neglected Segments of the Society', *Vanyajati*, Vol. XLVII, No. 1, 1999, pp. 23–26.

Joseph, A., 'An Appraisal on the Emerging Patterns of Leadership in Tribal Areas of Andhra Pradesh', *Man and Life*, Vol. 5, No. 3–4, 1979, pp. 175–78.

——, 'Banjaras and their Festivals', *Tribal*, Vol. VI, No. 1, 1968.

——, 'Yerukala Traditional Justice', *Tribal World*, Vol. 4, No. 1, 1967.

Joshi, Ram Sharan, 'Impact of Industrialization on Tribals: A Case Study of Balla Dila (Bastar)', in K.S. Singh (ed.), *Economies of Tribes and their Transformation*, Concept, New Delhi, 1982, pp. 369–80.

Kamala Manohar Rao, P. and D.L. Prasada Rao, 'Tribal Movements in Andhra Pradesh', in K.S. Singh (ed.), *Tribal Movements in India*, Vol. II, Manohar Publishers, New Delhi, 1982.

Kamala Manohar Rao, P., *A Report on the Working of Tribal Development Blocks in Andhra Pradesh*, Tribal Welfare Department, Hyderabad, 1968a.

——, *Assessment of Tribal Development Blocks in Andhra Pradesh*, Tribal Welfare Department, Hyderabad, 1968b.

Karve, Iravati and Hemalatha Acharya, *The Role of Markets in the Tribal, Rural and Urban Settings*, Deccan College, Pune, 1970.

Kazgi, Mangal Chandra Jain, *The Constitution of India*, Metropolitan Book Co. Pvt. Ltd., New Delhi, 1985.

Keesing, Rogar M., *Cultural Anthropology: A Contemporary Perspective*, Holt, Rinehart and Winston, New York, 1976.

Khader, Shaik Abdul, *The Impact of Nizam's Forest Policy on Select Tribes of Telangana* (unpublished M.Phil. Dissertation), University of Hyderabad, Telangana, 1984.

Khan, G.A., 'The Chenchus', in J.P. Mills et al. (eds), *Essays in Anthropology Presented to Roy Bahadur S.C. Roy*, Maxwell and Company, Lucknow, 1942, pp. 261–64.

Khasim Adivi, M., 'Hill Tribes in Visakhapatnam District', *Tribal*, Vol. 1, 1965.

Kirpal, Viney, 'Higher Education among SC and ST', *Economic and Political Weekly*, Vol. XV, No. 38, 1980.

Kishwar, Madhu, 'Toilling Without Rights: Ho Women of Singhbum', *Economic and Political Weekly*, Vol. XXII, No. 3, 1987.

Koteswara Raju, P., *Tribal Development: A Case Study of Polavaram Tribal Development Block in Andhra Pradesh* (unpublished Ph.D. Thesis), Andhra University, Waltair, 1990.

Kovai, Vilas, *Dimensions of Tribal Development: Kolavar Experience in Adilabad District* (unpublished M.Phil. Dissertation), University of Hyderabad, Telangana, 1995.

Krishna Murthy, B.H., *Konda or Kubi: A Dravidian Language*, Tribal Cultural Research and Training Institute, Hyderabad, 1969.

Krishna Rao, M.V., 'Konda Reddis of Andhra Pradesh', *Girijana Samskriti*, Vol. l, No. 1, 1993.

——, 'Savaras of Andhra Pradesh', *Man and Life*, Vol. 20, No. 1–2, 1994, pp. 109–29.

——, 'The Structure and Functioning of an Elementary School in the Tribal Areas of Andhra Pradesh', *Tribal*, Vol. VI, No. 1, 1968.

Krishna Rao, M.V. and O.S.V.D. Prasad, 'Ethno-medicines of Tribes of Andhra Pradesh', *Man and Life*, Vol. 21, No. 1–2, 1995, pp. 1–18.

Krishna Reddy, B. and M. Ramchandra Reddy, 'An Ethnographic Account of the Banjaras', *Vanyajati*, Vol. XXXV, No. 2, 1987, pp. 19–23.

Krishna Reddy, B., 'A Note on the Worship of Hindu Deities in a Tribal Community of Andhra Pradesh: The Case of Banjaras', *Man and Life*, Vol. 18, No. 1–2, 1992, pp. 45–53.

——, 'Forests and Sugalis in Andhra Pradesh: Historical and Anthropological Perspectives', *Man in India*, Vol. 71, No. 4, 1991, pp. 611–20.

——, *A Tribe in Transition: The Sugalis of Rayalaseema Region in Andhra Pradesh* (unpublished Ph.D. Thesis), S.V. University, Tirupati, 1984.

Krishna Reddy, S., 'Disease and Curing Patterns among Yerukalas: A Study of Indian Village', *Vanyajati*, Vol. XXXVIII, No. 3, 1990, pp. 6–9.

——, 'Glimpses of Tribal Culture in Andhra Pradesh', *Man and Life*, Vol. 18, No. 3–4, 1992, pp. 175–82.

——, 'Indigenous Methods for Child Disease Treatment among Yanadis: An Anthropological Survey with Special Reference to Cultural Factors', *Vanyajati*, Vol. XXXIV, No. 1, 1998, pp. 1–5.

Kumar, A., *Tribal Development in India*, Sarup & Sons, New Delhi, 2002.

Kumar, Arvind (ed.), *Tribal Development and Planning*, Vol. I-II, Anmol Publications, New Delhi, 2004.

Kumar, G.S.J., *Tribals from Tradition to Transition: A Study of Yanadi Tribe of Andhra Pradesh*, M.D. Publications, New Delhi, 1995.

Kumar, P.M., 'Status of Women in Tribal Society with Special Reference to the Tribes in Andhra Pradesh', *Tribe*, Vol. 9, No. 3, 1975, pp. 34–42.

Kumar, R.Y., *School System and Tribal Community: A Study of Scheduled Tribes of Bhadagiri Block* (unpublished Ph.D. Thesis), Andhra University, Waltair, 1981.

Kumar, Vijay, *Tribal Welfare and Development in India*, Vol. 1–2, Anmol Publications Pvt. Ltd., New Delhi, 2006.

Kumari, Surya, *Tribal Development and Financial Institutions in India*, Chug Publishers, Allahabad, 1990.

Kuper, Adam, *The Invention of Primitive Society*, Routledge, London, 1988.

Kurien, C.T., *Poverty and Development*, CCL Publications, Madras, 1967.

Kurup, A.M. and B.K. Roy Burman, *Lambada: A Scheduled Tribe of Andhra Pradesh* (monograph), Census of India, 1961.

Lakhmaih, T. and Aravind Yadappanwar, 'A Study of Educational Facilities for Tribal Students: Problems and Prospects in Paderu Samithi', *Man in India*, Vol. 68, No. 4, 1988, pp. 380–400.

Lakhmaih, T., 'Education and Social Change: A Study of Tribal Students', *Man in India*, Vol. 71, No. 4, 1991, pp. 587–600.

Lakshminarayana, P. Ch., *A Study of Adult Education among Tribals of Visakhapatnam District, Andhra Pradesh* (unpublished Ph.D. Thesis), Andhra University, Waltair, 1982.

——, 'Educational Programmes for Tribals of Andhra Pradesh', *Girijana Samskriti*, Vol. 1, No. 2, 1993.

Lalita, V., *The Making of Criminal Tribes: Patterns and Transition*, New Era Publishers, Madras, 1995.

Madagada: A Multi-ethnic Village in Araku Valley, Tribal Cultural Research and Training Institute Visakhapatnam, Tribal Welfare Department, Government of Andhra Pradesh, Hyderabad.

Madan, T.N. and D.N. Majumdar, *An Introduction to Social Anthropology*, Asia Publishing House, Bombay, 1956.

Madhusudhana Rao, G., 'Occupational Classification of Scheduled Tribes of Andhra Pradesh 1981', *Girijana Samacharam*, Vol. 1, No. 3, 1983.

Mahale, Prabha, 'Towards an Anthropology of Women', in B.G. Halbar and Hussain Khan (eds), *Relevance of Anthropology Today*, Rawat Publications, Jaipur, 1991.

Mahapatra, L.K., 'Cultural Anthropology', in *Survey of Research in Sociology and Social Anthropology*, Vol. III, Popular Prakashan, Bombay, 1972.

——, *Tribal Development in India: Myth and Reality*, Vikas Publishing House Pvt. Ltd., New Delhi, 1994.

Mair, Lucy, *Anthropology and Development*, Macmillan, London, 1984.

Malayappan, R.S., *Report of the Special Agency Development Officer*, Government Printing Press, Madras, 1952.

Malhotra, K.C. and M. Poffenberger, *Forest Regeneration through Community Participation: The West Bengal Experience*, West Bengal Forest Department, Calcutta, 1989.

Mathur, L.P., *Movements of Tribals during the Colonial Rule: Role of Ideologies*, Inter-India Publications, New Delhi, 1995.

Meena, Ram Singh, *Tribal Development Programmes: A Critical Appraisal*, Ritu Publications, Jaipur, 2006.

Mehta, B.H., 'Forestry and Tensions in Tribal Areas', in L.P. Vidhyarthi (ed.), *Applied Anthropology in India*, Kitab Mahal, Allahabad, 1968.

Mishra, K.K., 'Trees in the Religion and Folklore of the Konda Reddi of South India', *Journal of Human Ecology*, Vol. IX, No. 3, 1999, pp. 257–62.

Mishra, P.K., 'From Bride Price to Dowry', in K.S. Singh (ed.), *Economies of the Tribes and their Transformation*, Concept, New Delhi, 1982.

Mohammad, P.H., 'Child Rearing and Socialization among the Savaras', *Man and Life*, Vol. 23, No. 3–4, 1997, pp. 173–82.

Mohan Rao, K. and K. Chandra Raju, 'Koyas of Andhra Pradesh', *Girijana Samskriti*, Vol. 1, No. 1, 1994.

Mohan Rao, K., 'Banjaras of Andhra Pradesh', *Girijana Samskriti*, Vol. 2, No. 1, 1994a.

——, 'Dimsa Dance of Tribes of Visakhapatnam District of Andhra Pradesh', *Girijana Samskriti*, Vol. 2, No. 2, 1994b.

——, 'Marriage Patterns in Tribal Communities of Araku Valley', *Tribal*, Vol. VI, No. 1, 1968.

——, 'Socio-cultural Factors in Development of Tribal Areas', *Man and Life*, Vol. 9, No. 3–4, 1983a, pp. 157–68.

——, 'Socio-economic and Demographic Profile of Poroja: A Primitive Tribe of Visakhapatnam District', *Man in India*, Vol. 71, No. 4, 1991, pp. 647–64.

——, 'The Ceremonial Friendship among Tribal People of Andhra Pradesh', *Man in India*, Vol. 68, No. 1, 1988, pp. 93–104.

——, 'The Chenchus of Nallamalai Hills and their Development', *Girijana Samacharam*, Vol. 1, 1983b.

——, 'The Gadaba', *Girijana Samskriti*, Vol. l, No. 2, 1993a.

——, 'Towards Understanding the Culture of Tribal Communities in India', *Girijana Samskriti*, Vol. 3, No. 1, 1995.

——, 'Tribal Development in Andhra Pradesh: Problems, Performance and Prospects', *Economic and Political Weekly*, 4 November 2000.

——, 'Tribal Folklore and Integration', *Girijana Samskriti*, Vol. l, No. 1, 1993b.

——, *Kolams: A Primitive Tribe in Transition*, Book Links Corporation, Hyderabad, 1990.

——, *Tribal Development in Andhra Pradesh: Problems, Performance and Prospects*, Book Links Corporation, Hyderabad, 1999.

——, *Tribal Profile of Andhra Pradesh*, Tribal Cultural Research and Training Institute, Hyderabad, 1969.

——, 'Basic Dimensions of Displacement and Rehabilitation as a Mode of and Adjustment and Loss of Command Over Resources', paper presented at the Seminar on *Displacement and Rehabilitation of Tribals*, Tribal Cultural Research and Training Institute, Hyderabad, 1990.

——, *Socio-cultural Profile of Tribes of Andhra Pradesh*, Tribal Cultural Research and Training Institute, Tribal Welfare Department, Government of A.P., Hyderabad, 1993.

Mohan Rao, K. et al. (eds), *Displacement and Rehabilitation of Tribals in India with Special Reference to Andhra Pradesh*, TCR & TI, Tribal Welfare Department, Hyderabad, 1993.

Mohanan, T.S., 'Declining Importance of Ecology in the Tribal Areas: A Case Study of Andhra Pradesh', *Vanyajati*, Vol. XLIV, No. 3, 1996, pp. 2–10.

Mohanty, P.K., *Development of Primitive Tribal Groups in India*, Kalpaz Publications, New Delhi, 2002.

Moorthy, O.K., 'The Tribal Situation in South India', in K. Suresh Singh (ed.), *Tribal Situation in India*, IIAS, Simla, 1972.

Mujrali Manohar, K. and B. Janardhana Rao, 'Tribal Women in India: A Study in Political Economy of Social Change', in J.P. Singh, N.N. Vyas and R.S. Mann (eds), *Tribal Women and Development*, Rawat Publications, Jaipur, 1988, pp. 109–35.

Mukherjee, A.B., *A Study of the Scheduled Castes and Scheduled Tribes Population in Andhra Pradesh*, Indian Publications, Calcutta, 1971.

Mukherjee, S.D., 'Tribal and Forest', Seminar on *Forest Policy and Tribal Development*, Administrative Staff College, Hyderabad, 1987.

Mukhopadhyay, Rajatsubhra, 'Dilemma of Tribal Transformation: The Case of Chenchus', *Vanyajati*, Vol. XXXII, No. 2, 1984, pp. 19–24.

Muni Ratnam Reddy, A., 'A Study of Personal Care of the Bagathas of Visakhapatnam Agency (Andhra Pradesh)', *Folklore*, Vo1. 20, No. 8, 1979, pp. 133–40.

——, 'Developmental Properties of Domestic Group among the Bagatha of Visakhapatnam Agency', *Journal of Social Research*, Vol. 19, 1976, p. 22 and pp. 127–50.

——, 'On the Role of Ritual Friendship in the Mobility of Wealth in the Visakhapatnam Agency', *Man in India*, Vol. 53, 1973, pp. 243–55.

——, 'The Hierarchy of Tribes in the Visakhapatnam Agency', *Journal of Social Research*, Vol. 15, 1972, pp. 23–27.

——, *The Bagatha and the Related Tribes: A Study of Inter-Tribal and Intra-Tribal Pattern of Life in the Visakhapatnam Agency* (unpublished Ph.D. Thesis), Andhra University, Waltair, 1971.

——, 'On the Dynamics of Tribes and Sub-Tribes in Visakhapatnam Agency', *Man and Life*, Vol. 7, No. 1–2, 1979, pp. 33–50.

Murali Krishna Rao, I., *Marketing in Tribal Economy: Study with Special Reference to Shandies*, Inter-India Publications, New Delhi, 1986.

Murali Manohar, K. and B. Janardhana Rao, 'Tribal Women in India: A Study in Political Economy of Social Change', in J.P. Singh, N.N. Vyas and R.S. Mann (eds), *Tribal Women and Development*, Rawat Publications, Jaipur, 1988, pp. 109–35.

Murali Manohar, K., P. Ramaiah and C.S. Krishna Rao (eds), *Political Economy of Tribal Development*, IIPA Local Branch, Warangal, 1985, pp. 137–40.

Murthy, A. Radhakrishna, *A Study of Tribal Economy in the Andhra Agency* (unpublished Ph.D. Thesis), Osmania University, Hyderabad, 1968.

Murthy, A.S.N. et al., 'Social Welfare of Tribals in the Agency Region of Andhra Pradesh', *Vanyajati*, Vol. 24, No. 4, 1976, pp. 1–4.

Murthy, A.S.N., *Religion and Society of Koyas in the Agency Areas, Andhra Pradesh* (unpublished Ph.D. Thesis), Andhra University, Waltair, 1972.

——, *Religion and Society: A Study of Koyas*, Discovery Publishing House, New Delhi, 1981.

Murthy, Satyanarayan A., 'Family, Property Inheritance and Patrimony among Koyas', *Folklore*, Vol. XVII, No. 5, 1975, pp. 179–81.

——, 'Koya Dora Society of Andhra Pradesh', *Folklore*, Vol. 22, No. 10, 1981, pp. 213–15.

Nag, Amit Kumar, 'The Scheduled Tribes in Andhra Pradesh', *Indian Review*, Vol. 59, No. 4, 1958, p. 176.

Nagalakshmi, T., *Tribal Women in a Changing Society with Special Reference to Sugalis in Ananthapur District, A.F.* (unpublished M.Phil. Thesis), University of Hyderabad, Telangana, 1997.

Naidu, N.Y., 'Scheduled Tribes Exploited by Cooperatives', *Economic and Political Weekly*, Vol. X, No. 18, 1975.

——, 'Tribal Revolt in Parvatipuram Agency', *Economic and Political Weekly*, Vol. 7, No. 48, 25 November 1972, pp. 2337–44.

Naik, Sarveswara B., 'Status and Role of Women in the Changing Banjara', *The Indian Anthropologist*, Vol. XIII, No. 1, 1983, pp. 17–26.

Nair, V.M., 'Girijan Revolt: Marxist Organize Armed Action by Andhra Tribes; Police Action Alone Cannot Cure Chronic Unrest', *Statesman* (11 April), 7; (22 April) 7, 1968.

Narahari, S., 'An Ethnographic Account of the Mali Tribe: Andhra Pradesh', *Vanyajati*, Vol. XLI, No. 4, 1993, pp. 24–27.

——, 'The Challa: An Ethnographic Account', *Vanyajati*, Vol. XXXVIII, No. 1, 1990, pp. 20–23.

Narayan, P.L., 'Tradition and Change among Jatapu of Srikakulam District', *Folklore*, October 1973.

Narayana Reddi, V., 'Tribes of Andhra Pradesh', *Man and Life*, Vol. 19, No. 3–4, 1993, pp. 213–17.

Narayana, P.L., 'Saora Kinship Terminology', *Folklore*, Vol. XIII, 1972, pp. 391–96.

Narwani, G.S., *Tribal Law in India*, Rawat Publications, Jaipur, 2004.

NCERT, *A Study of Methods, Processes and Practices of Non-Formal Education Programme for Tribal Students*, SC and ST Education Unit, 1984.

Pachauri, S.K., *Dynamics of Rural Development in Tribal Areas: A Study of Srikakulam District*, Concept, New Delhi, 1984.

Padala, Rama Reddi, *Agency Laws in Andhra Pradesh*, Asia Law House, Hyderabad, 1985.

Padmavati, A. and J. Sridhar, 'The Ollek Cult', *Man in India*, Vol. 94, No. 4, 1994, pp. 349–57.

Panda, Nishakar, *Policies, Programmes and Strategies for Tribal Development*, Kalpaz Publications, New Delhi, 2006.

Pareek, R.N., *Tribal Culture in Flux: The Jatapu of Eastern Ghats*, B.R. Publishing Corporation, Delhi, 1977.

Patanaik, Nityananda, 'Importance of Ethnographic Data in Administration: A Study of Savara Community in the Scheduled Areas of Andhra Pradesh and Orissa', *Community Development and Panchayat Raj Digest*, Vol. 2, No. 2, 1970, pp. 197–203.

——, 'Social Conflict and Development in Tribal Areas: A Study in Andhra Pradesh and Orissa', *Community Development and Panchayati Raj Digest*, Vol. 2, No. 3, 1971, pp. 294–305.

——, *Tribes and their Development*, National Institute of Community Development, Hyderabad, 1972.

Paul, Kakali, *Development Programmes and Tribals: Some Emerging Issues*, Kalpaz Publications, New Delhi, 2004.

Pingle, Urmila and C. Von Furer-Haimendorf, *Gonds and their Neighbours: A Study in Genetic Diversity*, Ethnographic and Folk Culture Society, Lucknow, 1989.

Pingle, Urmila, *Tribal Cohesion in the Godavari Valley*, Book Links Corporation, Hyderabad, 1998.

Prasad Reddy, B.R., *Tribals in Revolt: A Study of the Rampa Uprising of 1879–80* (unpublished M.Phil. Thesis), University of Hyderabad, Telangana, 1987.

Prasad, O.S.V.D., *Change in Forest Policy and its Impact on Chenchu of Nallamalai Forest* (unpublished seminar paper).

Prasad, Ramachandra, 'Koya Mythology', *The Eastern Anthropologist*, Vol. 4, No. 3–4, 1951, 160–165.

Prasad, S.D.J.M., *Forests, Indigenous People and Institutions: A Study of Rampa Country* (unpublished Ph.D. Thesis), University of Hyderabad, Telangana, 1999.

Prasad, Sushma Sahay, *Tribal Women Labourers*, Gyan Publishing House, New Delhi, 1988.

Prasada Rao, D.L. and P. Venkata Rao, 'Cooperatives in Tribal Areas', *Tamil Nadu Journal of Cooperation*, Vol. 75, No. 3, 1983a.

——, 'Problems of Teachers Working in Tribal Areas', *The Educational Review*, Vol. LXXXIX, No. 8, 1983b.

——, 'Tribal Development: An Appraisal', *Man and Life*, Vol. 6, No. 3–4, 1980, pp. 130–42.

Prasada Rao, D.L., 'Exploitation in Tribal Areas with Special Reference to Land Alienation', in D.K. Behera and George Pfeffer (eds), *Contemporary Society: Tribal Studies*, Vol. III, Concept, New Delhi, 1999, pp. 152–57.

——, 'Shahukar and Tribal Society', *Tribe*, Vol. 8, No. 3–4, 1971–72.

——, 'Who are Jatapu Doras?', *Vanyajati*, Vol. XXXI, 1975.

——, 'Women in Jatapu Society', *Tribe*, Vol. 9, No. 4, 1976, pp. 9–17.

——, *An Analysis of Kinship, Economy, and Religion of Jatapu Doras* (unpublished Ph.D. Thesis), Andhra University, Waltair, 1971.

Pratap, D.R. and S. Bose, 'Integrated Area Development Plan for the Tribal Areas of Visakhapatnam District', in *Perspectives on Tribal Development and Administration*, NIRD, Hyderabad, 1975.

Pratap, D.R., 'Growth Centre Approach in Visakhapatnam Tribal Areas: An Exercise', *Kurukshetra*, 16 October 1974, pp. 8–9.

——, 'Planning for Tribal Development', *Occasional Papers on Tribal Development, X ICEAS*, Government of India, Ministry of Home Affairs, New Delhi, 1978.

——, 'Tribal Situation in Andhra Pradesh', in K.S. Singh (ed.), *Tribal Situation in India*, Indian Institute of Advanced Study, Simla, 1972.

——, *Andhra Pradesh Adimajathulu* (in Telugu), Tribal Cultural Research and Training Institute, Government of Andhra Pradesh, Hyderabad (n.d.).

——, *The D.B.K. Railway Project and the Tribals of Araku Valley*, Tribal Cultural Research and Training Institute, Department of Tribal Welfare, Government of Andhra Pradesh, Hyderabad, 1979.

——, *The Naikapods and their Language*, ISRA, Bidisa, 1980.

Prathasarathy, Jakka, *The Yerukala: An Ethnographic Study*, Anthropological Survey of India, Calcutta, 1988.

Purendra Prasad, N., 'Some Issues in Development Process: A Case Study of Lambada Thanda', *Girijana Samskriti*, Vol. 2, No. 2, 1994.

Quinn, Naomi, 'Anthropological Studies on Women's Status', *Annual Review of Anthropology*, Vol. 6, 1977, pp. 181–226.

Radhakrishna, Meena, 'The Criminal Tribes Act in Madras Presidency: Implications for Itinerant Trading Communities', *The Indian Economic and Social History Review*, Vol. 26, No. 3, 1989.

Raghava Rao, D.V., 'Child Birth and Child Rearing Practices among Konda Doras of Araku Valley', *Tribal Bulletin*, Hyderabad, Vol. VI, No. I, 1968a.

——, 'Ritual Activity in the Kubi Society', *Folklore*, Vol. IX, No. 4, 1968b.

——, 'The Domb Kinship Terms', *Man in India*, Vol. 48, No. 2, 1968c.

——, 'Significance of Nandi Festival among Konda Doras of Araku Valley', *Folklore*, Vol. XI, No. 3, 1970a.

——, *Chinnalabudu: Socio-economic Survey of a Multi-Tribal Village in Araku Valley*, AER Centre, Andhra University (Microfilmed by IDS, Sussex, U.K.), 1970b.

——, *Marketing of Produce and Indebtedness among Tribals* (mimeographed), Agro-Economic Research Centre, Waltair, 1973.

——, 'Institutional Framework for Agriculture Development in Tribal Areas', in Guy Hunter and Anthony F. Bottrall (eds), *Serving the Small Farmers*, Croom Helm, London, 1974.

——, *Jatapu Kotapadu Colony: Evaluation Study of an Agricultural Colony for Shifting Cultivators in Srikakulam District*, Agro-Economic Research Centre, Waltair, 1975a.

——, *Konda Doras: A Study in Socio-cultural Change* (unpublished Ph.D. Thesis), Andhra University, Waltair, 1975b.

——, 'Indebtedness in a Tribal Society', *Journal of Social Research*, Vol. XIV, No. 1, 1979.

Raghava Rao, Koka, *The Law Relating to Scheduled Areas in Andhra Pradesh*, Andhra Pradesh Law Publishers, Hyderabad, 1972.

Raghavaiah, V., 'The Enadi', *Man in India*, Vol. 24, 1944, p. 170.

——, *The Yanadi: A Tribe of Andhra Pradesh*, Bharatiya Adimjati Sevak Sangh, New Delhi, 1962.

——, *Tribal Revolts*, Andhra Rashtra Adimjati Sevak Sangh, Nellore, 1971.

Raja Reddi, K., *Family and Kinship among Yerukalas of Rayalaseema* (unpublished Ph.D. Thesis), S.V. University, Tirupati, 1995.

Rajagoplan, T., 'Marriage Customs among Some Andhra Tribes', *Vivekananda Kendra Patrika*, Vol. 1, No. 2, 1972, pp. 298–99.

Rajanikanth, G. and K. Suman Chandra, 'Education of Tribals: The Role of Political Organization', *Man in India*, Vol. 68, No. 4, 1988, pp. 454–58.

Rajendra Prasad, N., *Tribal Revolts: A Study of the Revolt of Adilabad Gonds in 1940* (unpublished M.Phil. Dissertation), University of Hyderabad, Telangana, 1987.

Rajpramukh, K.E., 'A Note on Shaman among Jatapu of Andhra Pradesh', *Folklore*, December 1976.

——, 'Ethological Factors in the Etiology of Disease: A Case Study', *Man in India*, Vol. 73, No. 4, 1993, pp. 371–77.

Raju, M.V.T., 'A Study of Tribal Rehabilitation Programme in Jatapu, Kotapadu Colony, Srikakulam, Andhra Pradesh', *Journal of the Indian Anthropological Society*, Vol. VI, No. 1, 1971.

Raju, P.S.S., 'Religious Beliefs of Koyas as Described in Koya Folktales', *The Eastern Anthropologist*, Vol. 41, No. 1, 1988, pp. 99–102.

Raju, Ramachandra, 'Naikpods: Their Society and Culture (Telugu)', *Tribal*, Vol. VI, No. 1, 1968.

Rajyalakshmi, P. and P. Geervani, 'Studies on Tribal Foods in South India: Food Consumption, Morbidity, Traditions, Customs and Attitudes Related to Food and Diet', Seminar paper, 1981.

——, 'Traditional Food and Agricultural Practices of Tribals of Vizianagaram District, Andhra Pradesh', *Girijana Samskriti*, Vol. 3, No. 1, 1995.

Rajyalakshmi, P., *Tribal Food Habits*, Gyan Publishing House, New Delhi, 1991.

Ram, Nandu, 'Socio-structural Variants and Higher Education among SC and ST', *Social Action*, Vo1. 36, No. 2, 1986.

Rama Rao, V., *Schooling among Scheduled Tribes of Andhra Pradesh: A Study of Factors Affecting Teacher Functioning* (unpublished Ph.D. Thesis), Andhra University, Waltair, 1991.

Ramachandra Reddy, M., *Population Structure and Family Planning among the Sugalis of Chittoor District (A.P.)* (unpublished M.Phil. Thesis), S.V. University, Tirupati, 1984.

Ramachandra Reddy, M., V. Narayana Reddy and P. Chengal Reddy, 'Ethnographic Study of the Sugalis of Andhra Pradesh', *Man in Asia*, Vol. 1, No. 1, 1998, pp. 78–82.

Ramaiah, P., *Issues in Tribal Development*, Chugh Publications, Allahabad, 1988.

——, *Tribal Economy of India: A Case Study of Koyas of Andhra Pradesh*, Light and Life Publishers, New Delhi, 1981.

Ramaiah, P., K. Murali Manohar and C.S. Krishna Rao (eds), *Political Economy of Tribal Development*, Indian Institute of Public Administration, Warangal, 1985.

Ramakrishna Rao, P., 'Buttayagudem Tribal Block Marching Ahead', *Andhra Pradesh*, Vol. 12, No. 10, 1968, pp. 52–53.

Ramakrishna, K., 'A Note on the Samantha of Andhra Pradesh', *Folklore*, October 1972.

Ramamani, V.S., *Tribal Economy: Problems and Prospects*, Chug Publishers, Allahabad, 1988.

Ramana Rao, D.V.V., *Tribal Development: New Approaches*, Discovery Publishing House, New Delhi, 1992.

Ramarao, V., 'Tribal Education and the Role of the Teacher', *Man and Life*, Vol. 14, No. 1–2, 1988, pp. 77–84.

Rangaswami, Amrita, 'And Then There were None: A Report from Srikakulam', *Economic and Political Weekly*, 17 November 1973, pp. 2041–42.

Rao, Jayaprakasha, 'Konda Reddis in Transition: The Case Studies', in C.V. Furer-Haimendorf (ed.), *Tribes of India: Struggle for Survival*, OUP, New Delhi, 1982.

Rao, K.S., 'Megalithic Religion among Savara of Srikakulam District, South India', *The Eastern Anthropologist*, Vo1. 42, No. 3, 1989, pp. 289–93.

Rao, Murali Krishna, *Marketing in Tribal Economy*, Inter-India Publications, New Delhi, 1988.

Rao, N.V.K., 'Customary Law and Politics: A Case Study of Bagata and Related Tribes of Andhra Pradesh', in K.S. Singh (ed.), *Tribal Ethnography Customary Law and Change*, Concept, New Delhi, 1993.

——, *An Ethnographic Study of Kondadora* (unpublished), Anthropological Survey of India, Calcutta, 1980.

——, *Tribal Education: A Case Study of Visakhapatnam District in Andhra Pradesh* (unpublished), Anthropological Survey of India, Mysore, 1979.

——, *An Ethnographic Study of Kanda Kapu* (unpublished report), Anthropological Survey of India, Mysore, 1976.

——, *Bagathas of Andhra Pradesh* (unpublished report), Anthropological Survey of India, Mysore, 1977.

Rao, P.D. Prasad, 'Tribal People of Araku Valley: Visakhapatnam District, Andhra Pradesh', *Vanyajati*, Vol. 7, 1971, pp. 103–05.

Rao, P.V., *Institutional Framework for Tribal Development*, Inter-India Publications, New Delhi, 1988.

Rao, R.S., V. Hanumantha Rao and N. Venugopal (eds), *Fifty Years of Andhra Pradesh 1956–2006*, Centre for Documentation Research and Communication, Hyderabad, 2007.

Rao, Vasudeva, *Tribal Development Studies*, Associated Publishers, Ambala Cantt, 2005.

Rath, Alok, 'Structural Analysis of a Jatapu Myth', *The Eastern Anthropologist*, Vol. 48, No. 2, 1995, pp. 165–76.

Ratnaiah, E.V., *Structural Constraints in Tribal Education: A Regional Study*, Sterling Publications, New Delhi, 1977.

Ratnakar, R., I. Srinivasarao and M. Anjanppa, 'The Koyas: Their Personal, Socio-psychological, Situational, Cultural, and Agro-economic Characters', *Man in India*, Vol. 71, No. 4, 1991, pp. 621–28.

Ray, Amp, 'Cashew Nut Plantation Scheme and the Savara of Andhra Pradesh', *Vanyajati*, Vol. XLI, No. 3, 1993, pp. 16–18.

Reddy, A.P., 'Ethnographic Note about the Yanadi Tribe of Andhra Pradesh', *Vanyajati*, Vol. XXXII, No. 2, 1984, pp. 14–18.

Reddy, G.P., 'Cause of Wastage in Tribal Education of Andhra Pradesh', *Vanyajati*, Vol. 18, No. 3, 1970, pp. 109–20.

——, 'Festivals Connected with Agriculture in Tribal Village in Andhra Pradesh', *Folklore*, Vol. 9, No. 12, 1968, pp. 451–57.

——, 'Introducing Agriculture in a Tribal Community: The Case of Chenchus', *Man and Life*, Vol. 5, No. 1–2, 1979, pp. 81–92.

——, 'Role of Liquor in the Culture of the Tribes of Andhra Pradesh and its Economic Implications', *Vanyajati*, Vol. 17, No. 2, 1969, pp. 37–45.

——, 'Structural and Functional Change in the Traditional Rituals of a Tribal Village in Andhra Pradesh', *Vanyajati*, Vol. 19, No. 1, 1971, pp. 8–21.

——, *Politics of Tribal Exploitation: A Study of Tribal Unrest in Adilabad*, Mittal Publishers, Delhi, 1987.

——, *The Lambadas* (A Scheduled Tribe of Andhra Pradesh), Census of India, Vol. 1, Monograph Series, Part V-B (IV), 1961.

Reddy, K.T. and S.K. Rao, 'Savara Art: A Model for an Interpretation of Prehistoric Rock Art', *The Eastern Anthropologist*, Vol. 45, No. 4, 1992, pp. 385–94.

Reddy, Narayana and Suma Narayana Reddy, *Women and Child Development: Some Contemporary Issues*, Chug Publishers, Allahabad, 1987.

Reddy, P.C., 'The Yanadis of the Madras Presidency', *Man in India*, Vol. 20, 1940, pp. 44–55.

Renuka, D., *Tribal Women in Urban Setting Banjaras of Hyderabad* (unpublished M.Phil. Thesis), University of Hyderabad, Telangana, 1990.

Report of the Commission for Scheduled Castes and Scheduled Tribes, First Report, Ministry of Home Affairs, New Delhi, 1978–79, p. 36.

Report of the Commissioner for Scheduled Castes and Scheduled Tribes, Ministry of Home Affairs, New Delhi, 1983.

Report of the Committee of the House to Enquire into Matters Related to Deficits and Misappropriations in the Girijan Cooperative Corporation, A.P. Legislative Assembly, Hyderabad, 1976, p. 26.

Report of the Committee on Forests and Tribals in India, Government of India, Ministry of Home Affairs, New Delhi, 1982.

Report of the Committee on Panchayati Raj Institutions (Ashok Mehata Report), Government of India, Ministry of Rural Development, 1978.

Report of the Committee on Special Multipurpose Tribal Blocks (Elwin Committee Report), Ministry of Home Affairs, New Delhi, 1960.

Report of the Study Team for the Study of Community Projects and National Extension Service (Balwant Roy Mehta Report), Planning Commission, Committee on Plan Projects, 1959.

Report of the Study Team on Credit, Marketing and Cooperation in Tribal Areas during Medium Term Plan (1978–83), Ministry of Home Affairs, New Delhi, 1978, pp. 32–37.

Report of the Study Team on Social Welfare and Welfare of Backward Classes (Renuka Ray Committee Report), 1959.

Report of the Study Team on Tribal Development Programmes (Shilu AO Report), Planning Commission, Committee on Plan Projects, 1969.

Report of the Working Group on Development and Welfare of Scheduled Tribes during VII Five Year Plan Period, Ministry of Welfare, Government of India, 1985.

Report of the Working Group on Development and Welfare of Scheduled Tribes during VIII Five Year Plan Period, Ministry of Welfare, Government of India, 1990.

Report on the A.P. Scheduled Tribes Finance and Development Corporation (memeo), TCR and TI, 1968.

Report on the Socio-economic Conditions of the Aboriginal Tribes of the Province of Madras, Government Printing Press, Madras, 1948.

Robertson, A.F., *People and State Anthropology of Planned Development*, Cambridge University Press, Cambridge, 1983.

Roy Burman, B.K., 'Challenges of Development and Tribal Women of India', in J.P. Singh, N.N. Vyas and R.S. Mann (eds), *Tribal Women and Development*, Rawat Publications, Jaipur, 1988, pp. 11–21.

Sachchidananda, 'Tribal Women in the Theories of Development', in J.P. Singh, N.N. Vyas and R.S. Mann (eds), *Tribal Women and Development*, Rawat Publications, Jaipur, 1988, pp. 79–90.

Sah, D.C. and Yatindra Singh Sisodia (eds), *Tribal Issues in India*, Rawat Publications, Jaipur, 2004.

Samantha, R.K. and R.L. Shyamsundar, 'The Lambadis: Their Socio-psychological and Agro-economic Characteristics', *Man in India*, Vol. 65, No. 3, 1985, pp. 269–77.

Sankara Reddy, T., 'Development Efforts for Tribal Women in Kodur, Andhra Pradesh', *Vanyajati*, Vol. XLIV, No. 4, 1996, pp. 22–24.

Sarkar, R.M. (ed.), *Land and Forest Rights of the Tribals Today*, Serials Publications, New Delhi, 2006.

Sastry, V.N.V.K. and K.V. Subba Reddy, 'Dandari Festival of Gonds of Adilabad District', *Girijana Samskriti*, Vol. 1, No. 2, 1993.

Sastry, V.N.V.K. and K.V.S. Sastry, *Process Evaluation of Andhra Pradesh Tribal Development Project*, Tribal Cultural Research and Training Institute, Hyderabad, 1993.

Sastry, V.N.V.K., 'Chenchu Mallanna: Then and Now', in K. Thimma Reddy (ed.), *Saivism*, Telugu University, Hyderabad, 1994a.

——, 'Differential Development among Villages of A.P.: A Case Study', in K. Murali Manohar, P. Ramaiah and C.S. Krishna Rao (eds), *Political Economy of Tribal Development*, IIP, Warangal, 1995.

——, 'Participatory Tribal Development in Andhra Pradesh', *Journal of Rural Development*, Vol. 20, No. 1, 2001.

——, 'Saivism in Gond Mythology and Religion', in K. Thimma Reddy (ed.), *Saivism*, Telugu University, Hyderabad, 1994b.

——, 'Sammakka Saaralamma Jatara (Telugu)', *Girijana Samskriti*, Vol. l, No. 1, 1993.

——, 'Toddy in Tribal Life', *Vanyajati*, April 1970.

——, 'Two Hundred Years of Tensions in Tribal Areas of Andhra Pradesh', in K.P. Kumaran (ed.), *Rural Tensions in India*, Illustrated Book Publishers, Jaipur, 1992.

——, 'Two Rajgond Uprisings in Forty Years: A Conflict Analysis', *Man and Life*, Vol. 10, No. 1–2, 1984, pp. 62–76.

——, *Between Gond Rebellions*, Anupama Printers, Hyderabad, 1989.

Satyanarayan Murthy, A. and B.Y. Subba Reddy, 'Hindu Elements in Koya Religion', *Vanyajati*, Vol. XXVIII, No. 3, 1990, pp. 26–28.

Satyanarayana Rao, S.V.V. and C.R. Prasad Rao, 'Drinking in the Tribal World: A Cross-cultural Study in "Culture Theme" Approach', *Man in India*, Vol. 57, 1997, p. 97.

Satyanarayana, M., *Tribal Development in India: A Trend Report*, Inter-India Publications, New Delhi, 1990.

Satyanarayana, P., 'Tribal Welfare in Andhra Pradesh', *Yojana*, Vol. 17, No. 8, 15 May 1973.

Saxena, N.C., 'Sustainable Development of Forest Lands and Forest Management in India', *Indian Journal of Public Administration*, Vol. XXXIX, No. 3, 1993.

Second Five Year Plan, Government of India, Planning Commission, 1956.

Sen, Jyoti, N. Saha and S.K. Mukherjee, 'Role of Women in Tribal Economy', in K.S. Singh (ed.), *Economies of Tribes and their Transformation*, Concept, New Delhi, 1982.

Sethu Madhava Rao, P., *Among Gonds of Adilabad*, Popular Book Depot, Bombay, 1941.

Seventh Five Year Plan and Tribal Areas Sub Plan (1985–90), Government of Andhra Pradesh, Tribal Welfare Department, Hyderabad, 1985.

Shantudu, *Institutional Finance and Tribal Development*, Manak Publishers, New Delhi, 1993.

Sharma, B.D., 'Administration for Tribal Development', *Journal of Social and Economic Studies*, Vol. 2, No. 4, October–December 1985.

——, 'Environmental Context and the Personnel System and its Implications for Tribal Areas', Occasional Papers, Ministry of Home Affairs, New Delhi, 1976.

——, 'Growth Centres in Tribal Areas', in *Integrated Tribal Development Planning*, NIRD, Hyderabad, 1975.

——, *Tribal Development: The Concept and the Frame*, Prachi Prakashan, New Delhi, 1978.

Sharma, B.V., 'Shifting Cultivation among the Savara Tribe', *Vanyajati*, Vol. XLII, No. 4, 1984, pp. 24–30.

Sharma, S.R., *Process of Social Change among the Tribes*, Manak Publications Pvt. Ltd., New Delhi, 2000.

Shashi, S.S., *Nehru and the Tribals*, Concept, New Delhi, 1990.

Sherring, M.A., *Tribes and Castes of Madras Presidency*, Cosmo Publishers, Delhi, 1975.

Shifting Cultivation in Andhra Pradesh (memeo), Tribal Cultural Research and Training Institute, Hyderabad, 1969.

Shrikant, L.M., 'Evaluation of Tribal Welfare Work in Nellore District (Andhra Pradesh)', *Vanyajati*, Vol. 7, 1959, pp. 124–26.

Simhadri, Y.C., 'Institutional Factors and Tribal Criminality: An Analysis of Yerukula Tribe in Andhra Village', *The Eastern Anthropologist*, Vol. 27, No. 1, 1974, pp. 45–60.

——, *The Ex-Criminal Tribes of India*, National Publishing House, Delhi, 1979.

Singh, A.K., *Tribals under the Jawahar Rojgar Yojana*, Classical Publishing, New Delhi, 1999.

Singh, Bhupender and Neeti Mahanti (eds), *Tribal Policy in India*, Inter-India Publications, New Delhi, 1997.

Singh, I.P., 'Tribes of Andhra Pradesh', *Kurukshetra*, 16 August 1977, pp. 37–38.

Singh, K.S. (ed.), *Jawaharlal Nehru, Tribes and Tribal Policy*, Anthropological Survey of India, Calcutta, 1980.

Sinha, B.B., *Society in Tribal India*, B.R. Publishing, Delhi, 1982.

Sinha, Subrata and Arun Ghosh, 'Literacy Campaign, Land Literacy and Watershed Development', *Economic and Political Weekly*, 8 February 1997.

Sirasalkar, P.R., *Marriage and Family Life among the Raj Gond of Adilabad* (Ph.D. Thesis), Osmania University, Hyderabad, 1955.

Sitapathi, Gidugu, 'The Saoras and their Country', *Journal of the Andhra Historical Research Society*, 1943.

Siva Rama Krishna Rao, C. and A. Bobbili, 'Tribal Movements in Andhra Pradesh: A Short History', in K. Murali Manohar, P. Ramaiah and C.S. Krishna Rao (eds), *Political Economy of Tribal Development*, Indian Institute of Public Administration, Warangal, 1985.

Siva Ramakrishna, P., *A Note on the Forest-Tribal Relationship in East Godavari District of Andhra Pradesh* (unpublished Seminar Paper), n.d.

Sobha, I. and M.S.N. Reddy, 'Socio-economic Conditions of Yanadi Tribal Women in an Urban Centre: A Study in Tirupati', *Vanyajati*, Vol. XLI, No. 2, 1993, pp. 19–24.

Somasekhar, A. and M.Y. Krishna Rao, 'Shandies in Scheduled Areas of A.P.', *Tribal*, July–December 1967.

Somasekhar, A., 'Cooperative Movement among Tribals of Khammam District', *Girijan Samacharam*, 1983.

——, 'Development Programmes in a Tribal Village: A Case Study', *Tribal*, Vol. VI, No. 1, 1968.

——, 'Tribal Development in Andhra Pradesh: Certain Issues', *Man and Life*, Vol. 13, No. 2, 1987, pp. 67–76.

——, *Development Programmes and Social Change among the Tribals*, Serials Publications, New Delhi, 2008.

Srikanth Prabhakar, K. and B.D.J. Narendra, 'Symbolism in the Marriage Rituals of Chenchus and Savaras', *Girijana Samskriti*, Vol. 2, No. 2, 1994.

Srinivas, M.N., *Some Reflection Dowry*, OUP, New Delhi, 1984.

Stanely Jaya Kumar, G., *Tribals from Tradition to Transition: A Study of Yanadi Tribe of Andhra Pradesh*, M.D. Publications, New Delhi, 1995.

——, 'Criteria for the Preservation of Yanadi Folklore through Mass Media', *Man and Life*, Vol. 24, No. 3–4, 1998, pp. 149–52.

Subba Rao, A.V., 'Role of Festivals among Gadaba of Andhra Pradesh', *Folklore*, October 1970.

——, *Culture and Society of the Gadaba of Andhra Pradesh* (unpublished Ph.D. Thesis), Calcutta University, 1975.

Subba Reddy, N., 'Caste in a Tribal Society: The Formative Process', *Contributions to Indian Sociology*, Vol. 7, 1973, pp. 159–67.

——, 'Crisis of Confidence among Tribal People and Naxalite Movement in Srikakulam District', *Human Organization*, Vol. 36, No. 2, 1977, pp. 142–49.

——, 'Damocles' Sword Over Andhra Tribals', *Economic and Political Weekly*, 1 July 1989.

——, 'Depriving Tribals of Land: Andhra Move to Amend Land Transfer Law', *Economic and Political Weekly*, 16 July 1988.

Subbarau, C., 'Srikakulam: Bullet Beats the Bow', *Times Weekly*, 21 March 1971, pp. 1–3.

Subha Reddy, B.Y., *Tradition and Transition: A Study of Socio-culture Change among the Yanadi of Andhra Pradesh* (unpublished Ph.D. Thesis), S.V. University, Tirupati, 1982.

Sudersanam, B., 'Tribal Development in Warangal', *Kurukshetra*, Vol. 24, No. 6, 1975, p. 15.

Sudhakar Rao, N., 'A Structural Perspective of Yanadi's Two Forms of Entertainment: Melam and Keelugurralu', *The Eastern Anthropologist*, Vo1. 50, No. 1, 1997, pp. 46.

Sudhakar Rao, N., 'Nutritional Ecosystem among Tribes: A Case of Yanadi of Sriharikota', *Girijana Samskriti*, Vol. 2, No. 1, 1994.

Sudhakar Reddy, P. and Muniratnama Reddy, 'Fission and Fusion among Yanadi of Sriharikota Island', *The Eastern Anthropologist*, Vol. 39, No. 2, 1986, pp. 131–38.

Sudhakara Rao, N., 'Rangam of Yanadi of Sriharikota', *The Eastern Anthropologist*, Vol. , No. 3, 1983, pp. 223–26.

Sudhakara Reddy, P., *The Displaced Yanadis of Sriharikota Island: A Study in Socio-cultural Continuity and Change* (unpublished Ph.D. Thesis), S.V. University, Tirupati, 1981.

Suguna and P. Prabhavathi, 'New Policy Initiations for Tribal Welfare in Andhra Pradesh', *Vanyajati*, Vol. XLVII, No. 3, 1999, pp. 3–7.

Suguna, A.V., A. Khan and K.E. Rajpramukh, 'The Role of Decent Group among Mannedoras', *Man in India*, Vol. 68, No. 4, 1988, pp. 459–64.

Suguna, B. and G. Sandhya Rani, 'An Appraisal of Tribal Welfare Programmes in Andhra Pradesh', *Vanyajati*, Vol. XLVI, No. 2, 1998, pp. 26–28.

Sujata, K., 'Inter and Intra-Tribal Inequalities in Education: A Case of Andhra Pradesh', *Man and Life*, Vol. 16, No. 1–2, 1990, pp. 19–30.

Sujatha Rao, K., 'Health Care Services in Tribal Areas of Andhra Pradesh: A Tribal Policy Perspective', *Economic and Political Weekly*, Vol. XXXIII, No. 9, 1998, pp. 481–86.

Sundara Rao, M. and Majji Sankara Reddy (eds), *Human Resource Development in Tribal Areas*, The Associated Publishers, Ambala Cantt, 2006.

Surendra, Lawrence, 'Srikakulam Tribal Uprising', *Religion and Society*, Vol. 22, No. 2, 1975.

Suresh Kumar, I. Gindi, 'Ethno-medicine among the Yanadi, a Hunter-Gatherer of South India', *Girijana Samskriti*, Vo1. 2, No. 2, 1994.

Suryanarayana Raju, M., 'Further Contribution towards the Ethnobotany of East Godavari District, Andhra Pradesh: Plants Used in Veterinary Medicine', *Vanyajati*, Vol. XLIV, 1996, pp. 3–6.

——, 'Unreported Medical Uses of Some Plants in the East Godavari District of Andhra Pradesh', *Vanyajati*, Vol. XLIII, No. 3, 1995, pp. 14–17.

Suryanarayana, M. and V. Gangadharam, 'Chenchus and Development Programmes', in Buddhadeb Chaudhuri (ed.), *Tribal Development in India: Problems and Prospects*, Inter-India Publications, New Delhi, 1982.

Suryanarayana, M., 'Impact of Dravidian Marriage Practices on a Mundari Speaking Saora Kinship Terminology', in D.K. Behera and George Pfeffer (eds), *Contemporary Society: Tribal Studies*, Vol. 4, Concept, New Delhi, 1999.

——, 'The Significance of Games in the Savara Culture', *Folklore*, Vol. 5, 1969, pp. 187–92.

——, *Marriage, Family and Kinship of the Saoras of Andhra Pradesh* (unpublished Ph.D. Thesis), Andhra University, Waltair, 1977.

Suryanarayana, M.H., 'Economic Reforms, Nature and Poverty', *Economic and Political Weekly*, Vol. XXXI, No. 10, 1996.

Swaroopa Rani, C.H., *Tribe-Peasant-Elite: A Study of Acculturation in Medieval Andhra* (unpublished M.Phil. Thesis), University of Hyderabad, Telangana, 1995.

Taradatt, Dr., *Tribal Development in India with Special Reference to Orissa*, Gyan Publishing House, New Delhi, 2001.

Thorner, Daniel, 'The Village Panchayat as a Vehicle of Change', *Economic Development and Cultural Change*, Vol. 2, 1953.

Thurston, E., *Castes and Tribes of South India*, Vol. I to VIII, Cosmo Publications, New Delhi, 1909 (Reprinted in 1975).

Tribal Industrialization in Andhra Pradesh: A Status Report (memeo), Commissioner of Industries, A.P.

Tribal Sub Plan, Draft IX Five Year Plan 1997–2002 and Annual Plan 1997–98, Government of Andhra Pradesh, Tribal Welfare Department, Hyderabad, 1997.

Trivedi, G.M., *Linguistic Study of the Chenchus of Andhra Pradesh*, Anthropological Survey of India, Calcutta, 1978.

Trivedi, Harshid R., *Tribal Land Systems: Land Reform Measures and Development of Tribals*, Concept, New Delhi, 1993.

Tyler, Stephen A., 'Koya Social Organization: Change and Persistence in Andhra Pradesh', in K. Iswaran (ed.), *Change and Continuity in Indian Villages*, Columbia University Press, New York, 1970.

Vaid, N.K., *Who Cares for Tribal Development*, Mittal Publications, New Delhi, 2004.

Venkata Rao, P., 'Aging in the Tribal Context: A Study of the Chenchu', in D.K. Behera and George Pfeffer (eds), *Contemporary Society: Tribal Studies*, Concept, New Delhi, 1999a, pp. 247–55.

——, 'Common Property Resources in Tribal Areas of Andhra Pradesh', in B.C. Barik (ed.), *Resource Management and Contours of Development*, Rawat Publications, Jaipur, 2000a.

——, 'Girijabivrudhi Karya Kramala Parisilana', *Telugu*, Vol. 6, No. 8, 1978.

——, 'Liberalization and Scheduled Tribes: Emerging Challenges', *Indian Journal of Public Administration*, Vol. XLII, No. 3, 1996a, pp. 490–97.

——, 'Mahimadharma: A Hindu Reform Movement in Visakhapatnam Agency', *The Eastern Anthropologist*, Vol. 52, No. 1, 1999b, pp. 45–56.

——, 'New Education Policy: Implications for Scheduled Tribes and Castes', in N.K. Rao and P.P. Sharma (eds), *Human Resource Development for Rural Development*, Himalaya Publishing House, Bombay, 1989.

——, 'Reflections on Tribal Development', *Journal of Rural Development*, Vol. 20, No. 1, January–March 2001, pp. 87–98.

——, 'Some Aspects of Development Infrastructure in a Tribal Area', *Adivasi*, Vol. XXXIV, No. 1–2, 1994, pp. 34–41.

——, 'Structural and Organizational Factors in Tribal Development', in Vasudeva Rao (ed.), *Development with Human Touch*, Atlantic Publishers, New Delhi, 2000b, pp. 39–48.

——, 'The Paradox of Harmony: Forest, Tribal, and Development Nexus in Andhra Pradesh', in K.K. Mishra and M.L.K. Muthy (eds), *Peoples and Environment in India*, Discovery Publishing House, New Delhi, 2001a

——, 'Tribal Development: An Appraisal', *Man and Life*, Vol. 6, No. 4, 1980.

——, 'Tribal Development: Some Observations', *Vanyajati*, Vol. XXX, No. 4, 1982.

——, 'Tribal Welfare in Hyderabad State: The Contribution of C.V. Furer-Haimendorf', *The Eastern Anthropologist*, Vol. 49, No. 2, 1996, pp. 203–12.

——, 'Tribal Women and Development Programmes: A Perspective', in C. Chakrapani and S. Vijaya Kumar (eds), *Changing Status and Role of Women in Indian Society*, M.D. Publications Pvt. Ltd., New Delhi, 1994.

——, *Tribal Development: Policy and Practice*, Sarup & Sons, New Delhi, 2001b.

Venkata Ratnam, T., *Tribal Peasant Struggle of Srikakulam 1950–75* (unpublished Ph.D. Thesis), Visakhapatnam, Waltair, 1988.

Venkatesh, K., P. Sivaram and D.S. Bhaskar, 'Socio-economic Conditions of Sugalis in an Andhra Tanda', *Vanyajati*, Vol. XXXVIII, No. 4, 1990, pp. 6–16.

Venkati, B., *Land Transfers and Alienation in Tribal Economy* (unpublished Ph.D. Thesis), University of Hyderabad, Telangana, 1994.

Venkatramulu, K., *Tribal Development Policy: A Case Study of the Chenchus of Mahaboobnagar District* (unpublished M.Phil. Thesis), University of Hyderabad, Telangana, 1983.

Verma, Y.M., *Problems of Tribal India*, Classical Publishing Company, New Delhi, 1986.

Vidya Sagar, A., *Bhadrachalam-Mannem Kathalu* (Telugu), Goutami Publications, Hyderabad, 1993.

Vidyarthi, L.P. (ed.), *Tribal Development and its Administration*, Concept, New Delhi, 1981.

Vidyarthi, L.P. and B.K. Rai, *Tribal Culture of India*, Concept, New Delhi, 1977.

Vidyarthi, L.P. and K.N. Sahay (eds), *The Dynamics of Tribal Leadership in Bihar*, Kitab Mahal, Allahabad, 1978.

Vidyarthi, L.P. and R.N. Sahay (eds), *Applied Anthropology and Development in India*, National Book House, New Delhi, 1980.

Vijay Kumar, S. and V. Narayana Reddy, 'Indebtedness among the Gadaba: A Symptom of Underdevelopment', *Man and Life*, Vol. 16, No. 3–4, 1990, pp. 183–86.

——, 'Towards Tribal Development: A Case Study of the Chenchus in Andhra Pradesh', *Man and Life*, Vol. 14, No. 3–4, 1988, pp. 179–85.

——, 'Utilization of Public Health Services by the Gadaba Tribe of Andhra Pradesh', *Man and Life*, Vo1. 19, No. 3–4, 1993, pp. 213–18.

Vijaya Prakash, P., 'Cultural-Historical Process in Northern Ghats of Andhra Pradesh: A Predictive Model', *Man in India*, Vol. 80, No. 1–2, 2000, pp. 57–73.

Vithal, C.P., 'Socio-economic Transformation of a Primitive Tribal Group: A Study of Chenchus in Andhra Pradesh', *Man in India*, Vol. 72, No. 2, 1992, pp. 189–206.

Vyas, N.N. (ed.), *Indian Tribes in Transition*, Rawat Publications, Jaipur, 1980.

Yorke, Michael, 'Kinship, Marriage and Ideology among the Raj Gonds: A Tribal System in the Context of South India', *Contributions to Indian Sociology*, Vol. 13, 1979, pp. 85–166.

Index